KV-351-482

Table of Contents

Preface to First Edition by Phya Anuman Rajadhon   *v*

Preface by Professor Patya Saihoo   *vi*

Foreword   *viii*

Introduction   *1*

Chapter 1   The Environment and Population   *12*

Chapter 2   The Village Economy   *29*

Chapter 3   The Family   *51*

Chapter 4   Education   *60*

Chapter 5   Age and Sex Roles   *80*

Chapter 6   Government   *88*

Chapter 7   The Basic Elements of Buddhism in Ku Daeng   *108*

Chapter 8   The Buddhist Monkhood in Ku Dæng   *137*

Chapter 9   Buddhist Views Towards Life and Death in Ku Dæng   *153*

Chapter 10   "Non-Buddhist" Religious Expression in Ku Dæng   *183*

Chapter 11   The Religious Calendar of Ku Dæng   *209*

Chapter 12   Acculturation and Development   *234*

Conclusion   *249*

Map 1   Thailand and Neighboring Countries   *251*

Map 2   Saraphi District   *252*

Map 3   Ku Daeng Village   *253*

Appendix A   The Twelve Communes of Saraphi   254

Appendix B   Age and Sex Statistics   255

Appendix C   Weights and Measures   259

Appendix D   Kinship Terminology   260

Appendix E   Age and Sex Roles in Ku Daeng   263

Appendix F   Prestige Rating   266

Appendix G   Brief Biographies of the
              Ten Ku Daeng Novices   270

Appendix H   Autobiography of a 73-Year-Old Woman   277

Appendix I   Biographical Sketch
              of Kamnan Mong's Widow   282

Glossary   286

Bibliography   297

Index   303

PREFACE TO FIRST EDITION

The mass of the people of Thailand live in villages, and their way of life is mainly that of rice culture. Viewed in such a perspective, one may understand the culture of Thailand in its broadest outline. What is true of Thailand is, in my view, also true of the people of other countries in this part of the world. Here generalization goes no further. Each race and society, whether large or small, has its own individual peculiarities due to various forces—economic, social, and political—from which develop a particular pattern in each community.

Of the books written in English depicting the life of the Thai people, I have come across only a few that present the facts free from the possibilities of distorted interpretations by the readers. This book seems to me to be relatively free of such distortions.

Someone has rightly said that the culture of a country or a village has to be studied in an international spirit to broaden sympathies and understanding, for "diversity is the essence of human culture."

I write this in appreciation of this book. The author has given a picture of various aspects of village culture in one of the districts of Northern Thailand. I have never been to this particular district, but what the author has written may be generalized relatively well to other parts of the North, of which Chiang Mai is the chief city.

I wish to stress the point that in the not too distant future there will inevitably be a change in the villages of that district in conformity with the large changes that are taking place in urban life. There is a saying, "Every metal has its reverse side." Unless the villagers know how to preserve what is good and discard what is bad in their own traditional culture, and to adapt their culture gradually to their needs and surroundings, there will be undesirable effects on their culture, which for centuries has given them an integrated village life with relative peace and happiness.

Considerable social changes will occur along with technological changes. Thus, "old times are changed, old manners gone," to quote Sir Walter Scott from memory. And deep in the villagers' inner life, with their village economy and their old ways of thinking, feeling, and believing, there will also be changes in their attitudes to their new life and to their new problems.

Mr. Kingshill's book will be a valuable record of some of these changes in progress in village life. It is also a valuable record of cooperation in the international effort towards mutual appreciation and sympathetic understanding.

Phya Anuman Rajadhon
The Royal Institute, Bangkok
August 1959

v

PREFACE

Towards the end of the decade of the 1980s, a claim—and counter-claim—is beginning to be heard that Thailand may soon be joining the family of the Newly Industrialized Countries (NIC). Though this could be merely wishful thinking on the part of some economic planners or manufacturing investors, the final conformation of the claim—and counter-claim—must come from the economic experts. The trend seems obvious, even to the untutored observer, that the industrial-urban life-style can only be spreading in the immediate future with or without the corresponding mode of production (just as the country has been described by some as having had "modernization" without "development"). And so, why a village study now or in the future?

Anything can happen between now and the year 2000 in Thailand. One might observe that from the late 1950s (when the first edition of this book appeared in 1959) to the early 1990s (when this edition appears), the population classification of Thailand as being 85% rural has not changed appreciably. The latest official population statistics of 1985 shows an urban-rural ratio of 9,230,773 : 42,564,878, or roughly 18 : 82. If such statistics could serve as a guideline for study and research about the country, without hasty conclusions being made, one could plan with some degree of confidence that the nation's villages and rural communities must be looked at if one wishes to properly understand the nature of this country and its people.

No doubt, one village study such as this—when there are according to the latest official count 57,415 villages around—cannot tell us anything about the whole situation of rural Thailand, especially when the bulk of the description is based on the more complete picture of village life as it was in the 1950s. Even if no re-look had ever been made at regular intervals (as indeed it has been profitably done for this particular village), and even though no one village could ever be truly representative of all other villages (just as no one village is ever completely unique), a well-conducted ethnographic study—with as little distortion and bias as is humanly possible on the part of a reliably trained ethnographer—stands as a valuable historical record of a people and their culture. It is a contribution to our understanding of that particular segment of humankind as well as of all humanity at large.

But apart from this standard professional claim of the discipline of ethnography/anthropology, which should be neither exaggerated nor minimized, it should be plain by now to all students of a complex and changing society such as Thailand, that no one discipline alone can provide a complete understanding of that society. Anthropology, of the kind that I understand, has long ceased to generalize from one single cultural "survival," "trait," or "theme" from one single study of a "village," "community," or "tribe" to the whole of that society, let alone the entire humankind. The anthropologist is now content to make a modest contribution to supplement or complement the findings of other specialists in the same area studies. In this professional spirit, we could all recognize the worth of this pioneering and now-classic study of Thai village life alongside the few other studies of the same period that represent the first serious attempts at professional documentation of village life in Thailand. The author has provided us, "the natives," a service for which I shall ever remain grateful.

To the student of change and development at the grass roots level in a developing country, what is usually missing is baseline information of the overall social and cultural conditions that could serve as the backdrop for a specific project or program. In the early days of "sectorial" development, this extensive background information was not considered necessary by technical experts, but with the later concept of "integrated" or "participatory" development, a good description of the community system has become useful. A good village study may not answer all the questions and meet all the needs of rural development planners, but it can offer some constructive ideas in the right direction.

The village of Ku Dæng has been studied and re-studied over the years (and not by just this author alone), so that we now have a sustained longitudinal case study that finds no parallel in other village studies that have come out of Thailand. The present edition should ensure that a significant piece of information in Thai studies is available to those who seek to understand the process of change and continuity in a major sector of Thai society, which may or not be completely transformed by the year 2000 or beyond.

Patya Saihoo
Sociology and Anthropology
Chulalongkorn University
October 1987

FOREWORD

The material for the present book was originally collected during the author's research study of the village of Ku Daeng from April 1953 until April 1954. Assisted by Northern Thai friends, I was able to maintain year-round residence in Ku Daeng and could thus observe the calendrical cycle of social, economic, and religious events that are the mainstays of the life of the average cultivator in Northern Thailand. Results of this study were published at The Prince Royal's College in Chiang Mai in 1960 as *Ku Daeng—The Red Tomb: A Village Study in Northern Thailand.*

The chief purpose of this study was to provide a source of ethnographic data comparable to that gathered by other anthropological field investigators in villages elsewhere in Thailand. To this end, particular attention was paid to the problem of culture change, the village status hierarchy, and the role of the Buddhist religious institutions.

Ethnographic and anthropological studies of village life in Northern Thailand have over the years been weighted consistently in favor of diverse ethnic groups, usually referred to as "hill tribes." The writer's original study in 1953-54 was one of the first village studies of lowland agricultural people of Northern Thailand.

It was possible for me to maintain contact with the village in the years following my residence there up to the present time, inasmuch as I continued living in Thailand, where I was working in the field of secondary and higher education mostly in Chiang Mai, but also in Bangkok and other parts of the country. I was able to evaluate my original study, while, at the same time, observing evident changes at ten-year intervals. In 1965, a second revised edition of *Ku Daeng* was published at Bangkok Christian College, and a third edition by Suriyaban Publishers in Bangkok in 1976.

The population of Ku Daeng reflects the general demographic pattern found in Northern Thailand. While the number of households increased steadily at an annual rate of approximately 1.5% over the thirty-year period covered by the study, the change in total population of the village showed quite a different pattern. During the first ten years there was a 50% increase in the number of people living in Ku Daeng, a 12% decline the following ten years, and a further 16% decrease during the decade ending in 1984. The population of Ku Daeng today is only 6% larger than it was in 1954. The emigration pattern seems to have remained much the same over the thirty-year period, while the success in family planning must be credited for the stability in size of Ku Daeng.

Basically, the present book contains the material of the actual field study in 1953-1954 supplemented by observations and data collected subsequently at ten-year intervals. In 1974 the writer joined the administrative staff of the newly-founded Payap College in Chiang Mai as Vice President for Planning and Development. With rapid increase in enrollment and stress on academic achievement, the college received accreditation in 1984 as the first private university in Thailand. At this time the Ministry of University Affairs of Thailand made available a number of grants to encourage academic research in private institutions. The writer was thus enabled to assemble a team of instructors and students in the departments of history, sociology and anthropology, and Thai language to participate in collecting new field data for Ku Daeng. I received valuable assistance and support in this task from Professor Prasert Bhandhachat, then dean of the Faculty of Social Science, and Ronald D. Renard, then director of the Payap University Research Center.

Special appreciation and thanks are due Professor Patya Saihoo of Chulalongkorn University, Bangkok, for taking the time to write a preface. Dr. James Wray of Washington, D.C., prepared the original maps from sketches produced by me; he graciously supplied me with new copies and transparencies for inclusion in this book. My special gratitude is respectfully conferred on the abbot of Ku Daeng temple. Together with the villagers, he has been a willing and cheerful source of data throughout the thirty years covered here.

The governor of Chiang Mai province kindly gave official permission to collect ethnographic data in Ku Daeng at each stage of the study. Invaluable help was received from officials at all levels of administration related to the various aspects of village government: the Chief District Officer, the *kamnan* of Nong Fæk commune, and the headmen of Hamlets 6 and 7.

Over the years many friends and colleagues have provided source material as well as critical advice, which were much appreciated. Special thanks to Vachara Sindhuprama of Payap University, who was always ready to assist with problems in language or interpretation. Acharn Thanit Kunkhajonphan of the University Computer Center and Dr. Lamar Robert of the Center for Research and Development provided endless hours of help wrestling with computer glitches, thus helping to produce the manuscript according to schedule. Waragarn Pootajak provided skill for the art work in the appendix. Kriangsak Chaipradit, grandson of Farmer Tun, who was our landlord during the original period of field study, is now working at Payap University and has provided invaluable assistance in maintaining liason with the current village leadership. The secretarial staff of the President's Office of Payap University helped with preparation of the manuscript. Their generous help was greatly appreciated. Space, unfortunately, does not permit a complete listing of names.

Konrad Kingshill
Payap University 1987

Note: This manuscript uses a slightly modified Library of Congress system of romanization that does not indicate tones or vowel length.

ix

INTRODUCTION

As part of a study of the effects of modern technology and sociological changes introduced into many of the then so-called "underdeveloped" areas of the world, Cornell University established a research center in Bangkok, Thailand, in 1948. Bang Chan, a rural community north of Bangkok, was chosen for study by a team of scholars under the direction of Lauriston Sharp, then professor of anthropology and head of the department of anthropology at Cornell. In 1953 it was decided to widen the geographic scope of the investigation by including a rural community in the northern part of the country. A field study of the village of Ku Dæng near Chiang Mai was the result and provided the major portion of the data used for writing the present monograph.

The purpose of the study was to obtain a comprehensive picture of conditions in a relatively representative rural community in the Chiang Mai plain. The results, it was hoped, would provide a basis for further comparative studies of other villages in the same region where certain aspects of Western culture had been introduced in more concentrated form than was the case for Ku Dæng. Special emphasis was to be placed on the role of the Buddhist temple and the monkhood in the community, since village life in Northern Thailand was then and still is today influenced to a considerable degree by the religious activities of the population.

Two prerequisites are necessary before a study of this nature can be carried out within a period of twelve months of actual observation in the field: (a) The field worker must be thoroughly familiar with the general pattern of life of the people to be studied, among whom he or she will be living; (b) The field worker must be familiar with the language to be able to know what is taking place, to be aware of the general subject of conversation, and to act as informant for the villagers, who, invariably, wish to learn something from the foreigner in their midst. My own period of preparation for this study can be said to have commenced in 1947, when I was engaged as a teacher at The Prince Royal's College in Chiang Mai. For three years, from 1947 to 1950, I acquired sufficient knowledge of the Thai language to pass the government examination for foreign teachers in Thai schools. I became acquainted with the Northern language, Lanna Thai, through contact with students and extensive travels in rural areas. During these visits, which included trips to seven Northern Thai provinces, I also became acquainted with some of the more general expressions of the culture of the people. More than with any other area, I became familiar with the immediate vicinity of the Chiang Mai plain. These factors enabled me, upon my return to Thailand in 1953, to initiate the study reported in these pages without delay.

In 1951 and 1952 I pursued graduate study at Cornell University in cultural anthropology with a major emphasis in Southeast Asia. This education provided me with the necessary theoretical framework for the basically ethnographic study of the village of Ku Dæng. There remained two additional tasks essential to a field study of this type. I had to find a capable Thai associate and a suitable village.

My previous experience in Chiang Mai proved invaluable. The Thai teacher-student relationship, which continues for the lifetime of both parties, is ideally suited for the recruitment of the necessary assistant. The teacher or professor in Thailand continues as advisor and confidant to former students long after the actual classroom relationship has been severed. I had not made my need for an assistant known for very long before several former students appeared on my doorstep to inquire about the possibility of working with me. I was able to choose Withun Leraman, who proved to be of such value that I was able to fulfill my task within the time parameters set at the beginning. The use of an indigenous assistant was imperative, since the variation of the northern language from that of the central area of Thailand is such that not even an ethnic Thai from Bangkok would likely have been able to record conversations in Northern Thai with any degree of accuracy. Furthermore, a local person was completely acceptable to the villagers as one of themselves, whereas one from some other region of the country would have been considered an outsider.

The second task was to find a suitable village. The selection of the site was conditioned by several criteria. The first was location within reasonable distance from the city of Chiang Mai. I was dependent for financial support on part-time teaching at The Prince Royal's College in Chiang Mai. In order to be able to commute from the city to the village and vice versa, the distance between them could not be too great nor too difficult to transverse. At the same time, it was considered undesirable to have the village too close to the city, since a community was desired in which there had been a minimal amount of urban or Western cultural influence.

The second criterion in choosing the village was that it should be of workable size. A village with a population of about one thousand persons, distributed in some two hundred households, was considered an optimum size for a field study to be undertaken by one person with the help of a full-time assistant to be completed within a period of one year.

A third consideration, less specifically definable, was the degree to which the village should be representative of the Northern Thai rural culture, or, at least, of community life in the rural areas in the Chiang Mai-Lamphun plain. We recognized that various factors made it impossible to consider one community to be representative of the rest to any considerable degree: there are fertile and poor soils, irrigated and dry land, communities accessible only by hours or days on foot or by oxcart, and there are others that can be reached by automobile. It was, therefore, decided to choose a community that was 1) essentially agricultural, since 85% of the population of Thailand were at that time considered rural, 2) reasonably isolated from daily contact with the city and the influence of various government or United Nations agencies, and 3) relatively free from special problems in recent years, such as extensive floods, epidemics among the people or domesticated animals, or mass employment of large sections of the population outside the village for essentially non-agricultural pursuits.

A fourth criterion for choice of a village was the religion of the people. In the Chiang Mai-Lamphun plain there are a number of Christian communities that usually draw members from several hamlets within the vicinity of the church. It was considered desirable, for an initial study, to choose a village that was predominantly, or preferably entirely, Buddhist, that is, where there was no Christian church within easy reach that might claim as members some of the people of the village under study.

We traveled for four weeks through several districts within a thirty-five mile radius of the city of Chiang Mai. We were assisted by a number of teachers from The Prince Royal's College who were natives of or had relatives living in particular communities under consideration. In each village we tried to have lengthy interviews with the head monk of the temple, the village headman, and other leaders of the community. Invariably, we were welcomed hospitably by these men who were anxious to learn the reason for our visit, since foreigners in those days seldom ventured into the countryside. In no case did we encounter negative responses. All those whom we interviewed would have acceded to our request to study their villages. Nevertheless, we found differences in the degree of reception accorded us. In some places the leaders of the village seemed to be very cooperative and understanding, doing everything in their power to make us feel at home. In other communities, though still well received, we sensed a certain amount of indifference on the part of either the headman or the head monk. These first impressions inevitably influenced our final choice.

We considered one village that had been studied a few years earlier by a student of anthropology from the University of Chicago.[1] When we arrived, reception by the village elders was friendly but not enthusiastic. The village was accessible on a road in very poor condition, and the village lay within hailing distance of the highway. All these were factors weighing against restudying this particular community.

Another village under consideration was located east of the city of Chiang Mai in a dry and arid region. This village, as well as several neighboring communities, specialized in the manufacture of umbrellas during the dry season. Such a community would have been of interest to a study emphasizing the development of cottage industries in Northern Thailand. For our purpose, we preferred a predominantly agricultural village without major, seasonal variations in occupation.

---

[1] See John E. deYoung, *Village Life in Modern Thailand* (Berkeley: University of California Press, 1955).

Ku Dæng, the village of our choice, is located in a large district some ten kilometers south of Chiang Mai city (see map 2). The road from Chiang Mai leading to this district was, at the time of our study, the best in the province. The district official had been known to us for a number of years. In the dry season the village could be reached from the district seat in half an hour by bicycle. When the rains made this impossible, the distance could be covered on foot in little more than an hour. Our initial impression of the leadership of the village, when we visited Ku Dæng for the first time, was most favorable. In addition to the village headman, the head of the next higher administrative unit of local government, the *kamnan*, was resident in this village and welcomed us with open arms beginning with our very first introduction. Indeed, Kamnan Mong Namwong assisted us throughout our stay in the village and was one of the main contributing factors to uninterrupted good rapport with the entire village population. A considerable number of monks of different age and personality were resident in neighboring temples within easy reach of Ku Dæng; they proved to be a valuable source of information on many customs and ceremonies.

Having decided upon a location, the next problem, that of housing, was immediately tackled with the help of the *kamnan*. He devoted two afternoons to negotiations with different villagers. First, there was the possibility of renting a small, bamboo house. The owners wanted to sell rather than rent it and demanded an unreasonably high price. At two or three other places various other difficulties were encountered. Our needs were not great. I was planning to spend four days and nights each week in the village, while Withun was to stay there the entire week, with occasional days off in the city. We needed only a place to sleep and a place to work. Finally, we were fortunate in finding a house that had been built only five months earlier. The landlord, Tun Phobun, agreed to rent two rooms to us. This arrangement suited us well and proved to be invaluable to the pursuit of our studies in the village. Our host's daughter was engaged to do our laundry, and one of the local storekeepers, an ex-soldier, volunteered to prepare our meals. All these arrangements were simplified by the introduction we had through Khru Charœn Somanat, a teacher at The Prince Royal's College, who also happened to be a former student of mine. Since he was related to the *kamnan*, we were received as members of the family.

Partly through luck we had made an arrangement that proved to become a fount of information. By living with a farmer and his family in their house and actually making our abode there for most or all of each week, we found that many people came to visit us and talk informally, when it would have been difficult for us to reach them in their respective homes. In the beginning, villagers used visits to our landlord as pretexts to see us and find out what we were like close up. These informal conversations with friendly villagers provided us with volumes of information that otherwise could have been collected only with difficulty. We were able to witness the intimate home life of one particular family in this way, even though, admit-

4

tedly, it was no longer entirely representative due to our presence in their house. More than fifty different persons came to visit us on a total of over three hundred occasions.

The village turned out to be ideally suited as a base for additional studies. Many of the villagers expressed their desire to have us live with them in their homes the "next time" we came to Ku Dæng. Many aspects of village life remained outside our study in our relatively short period of inquiry and could well have been studied by specialists in a number of fields. Indeed about twenty years after our study, Jack and Sulamith Potter established residence in Ku Dæng to investigate social structure and family life in the village.

In 1985 two additional studies centered on Ku Dæng: Werasit Sittitrai of the University of Hawaii wrote on culture change in two Northern Thai villages, one of which was Ku Dæng.[2] Malee Viriya made a study of recreational activities of Northern Thai children with data collected in Ku Dæng.[3]

Life in Ku Dæng in 1954 and the following decade was still one of simple subsistence farming. The villagers grew the main crop of rice for their own use. This was followed by a second cash crop of either rice or such vegetables as cabbage or garlic. In addition, the villagers went fishing and hunting, both for their own use and for sale in nearby markets. Domesticated animals were raised for the same purpose. Cottage industry was practiced by villagers too old or otherwise not inclined to go fishing or hunting. Cloth, reed utensils or furniture, candles, and woodwork were produced for home use and for sale. During World War II an enterprising villager invented and produced a simple cigarette lighter, made entirely of discarded rifle and grenade shells and other, locally available materials. Today, this industry has become a tourist attraction.

This period was one of self-reliance. It was rarely necessary to deal with outsiders or methods not indigenous to the village. It was a quiet and peaceful existence, guided mainly by the principles of Buddhism, transmitted through the monks, both present and former. The head monk was highly esteemed perhaps mainly because of his long period of service to the village, giving him seniority among the monks of neighboring temples. Moreover, the villagers relied on spirit propitiation and shamanism to ward off those influences that could not be explained in other ways. Health problems that did not respond to medicines available were assigned to faith healers, who used herbs and traditional medicines as well as incantations to alleviate the situation. Life and health ceremonies were also conducted by these traditional practitioners.

---

[2] Werasit Sittitrai, "Rural Transformation in Two Northern Thai Villages" (Ph.D. dissertation, University of Hawaii, 1985).

[3] Malee Viriya, *Kanplian-plæng khong kanlalen khong dek Thai phak nüa* [A case study of recreational activities of children in Northern Thailand (Ku Dæng)] (Bangkok: Sri Nakharinwirot University Press, 1985).

There was intimate communion and close fellowship among the villagers. While many were related through marriage, a number of diverse groups were living peacefully side by side. In 1976, Potter described social differentiation in Ku Dæng as due to differences in economic status.[4] Villagers who owned much property also had considerably higher social status and position than those villagers without land or who were poor. The wealthier villagers determined the policy of the village. The poor had to hire themselves out for labor in order to purchase the rice necessary for livelihood; they did not have the time or inclination to act as leaders in village affairs.

Potter maintains that Ku Dæng does not fit into the pattern of a loosely structured society, as conceived by Embree.[5] The divisions due to economic status mentioned above form a more or less rigid system of social control. Potter also disagrees with the Sharp-Hanks observations at Bang Chan, which tended to support the loosely structured theory.[6] Potter maintains that this type of observation is inaccurate and that a more thorough study would indicate that there are very definite and rigid social structures in such communities as Ku Dæng and Bang Chan.[7] There are, in addition, voluntary social structures not necessarily dependent on economic status, according to Potter. Such groupings would vary from community to community; however, an overall pattern could be discerned, and some generalization contradicting the Embree theory would be valid.

Furthermore, in a study on family structure in Northern Thailand, Sulamith Heins Potter describes characteristics of family life in Ku Dæng as not being particularly loosely structured.[8] There is an especially important role played by the women of a household, who are the purveyors of the bloodline as well as the main authority in the family.

Before we took up residence in Ku Dæng, we had some knowledge of Thai customs and traditions from different parts of the country. My assistant was thoroughly acquainted with city life in the North and had traveled with a teak company through parts of the jungle areas of Northern Thailand. We were able to make use of some of the findings of the Cornell research group in Bang Chan. In addition, we had contacts with students at The Prince

---

4 Jack M. Potter, *Thai Peasant Social Structure* (Chicago: The University of Chicago Press, 1976).

5 John F. Embree, "Thailand—A Loosely Structured Social System," *American Anthropologist* 52, pp. 181-193.

6 Lauriston Sharp and Lucien Hanks, *Bang Chan: Social History of a Rural Community in Thailand* (Ithaca: Cornell University Press, 1978).

7 Potter's fieldwork was carried out in Ku Dæng where he was able to build on earlier anthropological and ethnographic studies carried out by others. In his dissertation, Potter does not mention these earlier investigations, nor does he refer to Ku Dæng village by name. Instead he chooses to call it "Chiang Mai Village," a rather confusing terminology, to say the least.

8 Sulamith Heins Potter, *Family Life in a Northern Thai Village* (Berkeley: University of California Press, 1977).

Royal's College who came from many provinces throughout the country. We were, therefore, able to anticipate some of the findings of our study and draw up a number of tentative hypotheses with regard to village life in particular as well as cultural aspects found in the rural areas of the North in general.

An underlying pattern of culture, in Ruth Benedict's sense, is difficult to determine for the Ku Dæng population as a whole. There seems to be nothing that dominates all phases of the life of the villagers. We were able to observe a number of characteristic themes that appear again and again in the various manifestations of village life. A theme, according to Opler, is a postulate or proposition, declared or applied, and usually controlling behavior or stimulus activity, which is tacitly approved or openly promoted in a society.[9] Themes are dynamic affirmations that control behavior or stimulus activity. A thorough thematic analysis of a culture would relate one theme to another, determine counter-themes, and describe the interrelation and balance of the various themes. No attempt was made in the Ku Dæng study to give a complete thematic analysis. A few themes are mentioned as a possible starting point for further study or analysis. I have encountered nothing in the thirty years that have elapsed since our stay in the village that negates the hypotheses on which the introduction of themes described below is based.

The foremost of these themes is one of expediency or utility, a theme somewhat more abstract then what would be implied by the word "usefulness." Regardless of prescription or tradition, the villagers seem to govern their actions by what is expedient for them at any given moment. They will readily adopt a new method or procedure, if it gives promise of producing valuable results. Thus, for many years, we were told, a man from a not-too-distant village came to Ku Dæng after the harvest of the main crop of rice to offer the service of his tractor to plow the land for the villagers' use for their second crop. The year of our study there was no plowing by any tractor. The man had failed to appear, and no one had troubled to go and seek him out; that would have been a nuisance. In the years since then, tractors have become quite common in many parts of Thailand, and many farmers in the Ku Dæng area rely on tractor plowing instead of keeping water buffaloes or oxen for this purpose. It is now quite convenient to make use of this type of equipment, and, therefore, it is accepted.

Closely related to the utility theme is the theme of profit. If something will bring profit, it will be done, and, conversely, if the villager sees no immediate return on his investment of time, labor, or money, he will be reluctant to undertake a particular task. A new crop, such as tobacco, is easily introduced, because it can be demonstrated that profit can be made in a brief period of time.

---

[9] See M. E. Opler, "Themes as Dynamic Forces in Culture," *American Journal of Sociology* 51:3, pp. 198-206.

Agricultural extension workers have attempted, with the aid of American experts and advice, to instruct farmers throughout Thailand in the use of fertilizers. This program had not produced impressive results by the time of our study, because, as the extension workers readily admitted, application of some of the easily available fertilizers did not seem immediately effective. In fact, one American adviser told us that the plowing under of stubble in the field, which, the agronomists say enriches the soil more than applying the ashes of burned straw, would actually decrease yields slightly for the first year or two before a permanent increase could be recorded. Few farmers would be willing to continue a practice for a long time that would, in the short run, reduce their profits.

A farmer will sell almost anything he possesses if it can be shown that he can make a profit in the transaction. Many of the women of the village keep pigs. It is not a question of "raising" pigs in the majority of cases. Traveling salesmen come through the village with small piglets for sale in baskets strapped on bicycles or, more recently, motorcycles. A farm wife may buy one or two pigs and feed them for a period of time. They will not be sold when they are fat or when they are considered ready for slaughter. Rather, they will be sold whenever someone comes along and offers a price reasonably higher than the one she paid in the first place. Women may sell a half-grown pig one day and buy one almost the same size the next, in a transaction by which they may have made 100 baht profit.[10]

Similarly, the sale of buffaloes or oxen is governed by the profit motive. A farmer bought a buffalo just before the plowing season. He used the animal for three months, then sold it for 30 baht more than he had paid for it. He was satisfied that he had made a satisfactory deal. He had not only obtained the buffalo's labor for an entire season but also made a small financial gain in the end.

In the field of education, the profit motive is also evident. A man will send his children to school above the minimum requirement because he thinks they may be able to earn more money in the future and succor him in his old age.

The profit motive is also present in relation to one of the main aspects of religious expression of the villagers. Almost every action related to performance of religious duties is governed by the amount of merit involved. If something brings merit, it is deemed good. If something brings demerit, it is deemed bad. Conversely, it is constantly stressed that good actions bring merit and bad ones demerit. One member of the family usually takes food to the temple on the appointed day with the rest of the family sharing in the merit. It is not a question of providing food for the

---

[10] The baht is the unit of Thai currency, divided into 100 satang. Foreigners used to call this unit of currency "tical." In 1953 the baht was roughly equivalent to five U.S. cents. Thirty years later the value of the baht had decreased only slightly in relation to the U.S. dollar (1 U.S.$ = 25 baht).

monks but one of making merit. An old woman told us that she was devoting the remaining days of her life to making further merit so as to store up riches for her next life.

The theme of making merit is tempered by the utility theme. Taking food to the temple instead of letting the monks and novices walk through rain or sunshine each morning may seem to be designed to benefit those in the temple. More likely, it has come about because it is more convenient for the villagers to take turns in taking the food to the temple than to have to wait each morning for the procession of monks and novices to arrive at their doorsteps. Although taking food to the temple may bring profit in the form of merit, it may be far more expedient at the moment to go to town or to the market or to work in the fields. Let someone else receive the merit for taking food to the monks.

The third theme is identified as "fun." We observed frequently that villagers did something simply because they enjoyed doing it. A temple festival in a neighboring community may bring out the profit motive, because devout pilgrims make merit by attending the ceremonies. It may be expedient and not much trouble to go since it is not far from our own village. But above all, the villagers only go if they anticipate the excursion to be enjoyable.

No temple festival is complete without some sort of entertainment, whether it be the local comic theater, a motion picture, a boxing match, or a combination of these. At harvest time the labor involved in cutting rice is not considered a chore, nor do the villagers take any particular pride in reaping the harvest of their labors. Rather it is a communal experience of being in the fields in large groups, of helping one another, of joking and laughing; in other words, this is an event of great enjoyment; everybody has a very good time, "fun," even though the labor is heavy.

The next two themes seemingly contradict each other. They both are present in many village activities. One is a strong individuality and the other a strong sense of communal responsibility. Individuality manifests itself in the absence of coercion. Small children may be scolded from time to time, but coercion is the exception. Children up to school age are permitted to be everywhere. Occasionally, a child may be told to do something, but there is generally not much coercion related to the order. Older children participate in the agricultural tasks on the farm. We questioned a number of boys as to why they did certain tasks. Very seldom did we get the answer that they had been told to do so. In general, the answer was that the job needed doing, and they just "knew" that they should do it.

Individuality is reinforced by the Buddhist emphasis on self-reliance. According to the teachings of the Lord Buddha, a person's fate depends on his or her own actions and only upon them. Reliance on an outside force or a "savior" is completely alien to Buddhist thinking. The Buddhist monk is supposed to teach others the way to salvation. Every action by an individual causes a reaction in his future life; every cause has its effect; hence, the future is determined solely by our present, individual conduct.

Communal responsibility arises out of the utility and profit motives. When a villager wants to do something he usually does it. This manifests his individuality. Of course, he will do it only if it will show a profit or if it promises to be enjoyable. Furthermore, if it is not convenient, he will probably not do it. If something seems to be profitable, it will usually be done, regardless whether it is part of the community life or not. When a man feels that he can make a better living in some other part of the province, he packs up and leaves. Younger men may go to the city to find jobs during the slack seasons of the year.

When a need is seen for something that may benefit the whole community, a person may demonstrate his or her individuality by convincing neighbors to take joint action. A young man saw the need for a bridge across one of the irrigation ditches near his home. He went to all his neighbors who would be profiting from a new bridge, asking them for contributions of money. Even though he collected very little, he went ahead with the work, spending his own money building the bridge. When the time came for actual construction, others participated in the labor.

Such a sense of communal responsibility shows itself at many occasions. All public works, such as roads, bridges, or irrigation canals, are built by cooperative labor. The village headman is usually in charge, but there is very little coercion involved in bringing out the labor. When a villager prepares for a house-blessing ceremony, a wedding, or a funeral, others will stream to his house for days before the event to help with preparing food, decorations, and gifts for the monks. When a man is sick, others come to his house every night, to help with whatever is needed while he is incapacitated.

An American Mutual Security Administration (MSA) official came to visit Ku Dæng one night. He told his driver to take his jeep home, while the official spent the night in the village. The driver, being in a hurry, missed a turn and drove the jeep into an irrigation ditch. Within ten minutes some forty villagers, including the *kamnan*, were in and around the ditch, heaving and pulling the jeep until it was back on the road. No one had called these villagers. Word had spread that a jeep was in the ditch, and the response was a manifestation of the ever-present sense of community responsibility.

Another theme is less a characteristic of the people themselves than one of verbal expression of many of their activities. It is found in most of the religious teachings and reasoning: *"tham di, dai di—tham chua, dai chua,"* which means, "Do good, receive good—Do evil, receive evil." Here the villagers are constantly reminded that whatever they do will have its consequences. From earliest childhood one is told that all good deeds will bring reward, while all evil deeds are punished. More than anything else, behavior is based on this axiom. This provides a certain amount of reassurance for persons to know that if they do something evil, they can always extricate themselves by doing a greater amount of good. At the same time, it provides an effective means of group control by promising inevitable punishment in a person's own life, whether present or future, for any infringement of good behavior-that might be committed.

A final characteristic, perhaps closely related to the previous one, is that "it is better to play it safe." It is always better to make a lot of merit in order to counteract anything that one may have done in a previous existence. "Playing it safe" is an important factor in medical care. A person who is sick will go to any length to consult a variety of healers. One may not believe in the explicit powers of a doctor, whether it be an herbalist, one who communicates with spirits, an "injection doctor," or a physician in the city. It is always safe, however, to consult as many of them as possible. This attitude may be responsible for the relative ease with which modern medicine has entered rural areas of Thailand and has been accepted by the villagers. The belief in spirits, according to our informants, is disappearing from the area. Most villagers, however, when confronted by a spirit propitiation ceremony or a healing, will play it safe by appeasing whatever supernatural beings may possibly exist.

The following seven themes have stood out among our many observations as being characteristic of village life on the whole:

The seven themes will be referred to as follows:

Theme 1: Utility
Theme 2: Profit
Theme 3: Fun
Theme 4: Individuality
Theme 5: Communal responsibility
Theme 6: "Do good, receive good—Do evil, receive evil"
Theme 7: Playing it safe

The following pages will illustrate them again and again. No attempt has been made to organize the material under these themes, but rather they are allowed to speak for themselves as they become evident in the material presented.

These themes were postulated at the end of our study in 1954. Data collected subsequently, including that from the 1984 follow-up study, do not indicate in any way that these themes are less valid today than they were thirty years ago.

11

1

THE ENVIRONMENT AND POPULATION

In 1953, Chiang Mai was generally considered the second city of Thailand.[1] Even though considerably smaller than Bangkok, Chiang Mai's size outranked other cities in the kingdom. The province of Chiang Mai today stretches from just south of the city of Chiang Mai for about 120 miles north up to the Burmese border (see map 2). A narrow "peninsula" extends 150 miles southwest, and the greatest width of the province is about 100 miles on an east-west line passing through the capital.

Until 1873 A.D., Chiang Mai was the capital of the Kingdom of Lanna Thai, one of the largest independent principalities within the general boundaries of what is present-day Thailand.[2] It extended south as far as Phitsanulok and north to Müang Fang, then called the Kingdom of Chai Prakan. During the reign of the Thai King Rama IV (1851-1868 A.D.), generally known in the West as King Mongkut, Chiang Mai was involved in a war with Burma, while at the same time it was attacked from the south by Thai forces. The campaign against Burma was turning into defeat for Chiang Mai, while the Thai troops advanced through Phræ to Lampang. The King of Chiang Mai then turned for assistance to the commander of the Thai army, Cao Phaya Kalahom, who agreed to help Chiang Mai and subsequently defeated the Burmese. As a result, Chiang Mai came more and more within the Thai sphere of influence and was placed under Thai suzerainty in 1873, during the reign of King Chulalongkorn, Rama V (1868-1910). A governor was appointed from Bangkok, and the Kingdom of Lanna Thai gradually lost whatever independence it had retained. With the advent of constitutional monarchy in 1932, the entire territory was divided into six provinces *(cangwat)* and totally absorbed into the administrative pattern of Thailand.

The province of Chiang Mai lies in one of the river valleys characteristic of the northern part of mainland Southeast Asia and along

---

[1] The city of Chiang Mai maintained its rank as second city in the kingdom until the early 1980s. In 1979, its population was 97,839, outranking Hat Yai, the third largest city, by 5,353 and fifth-ranked Nakhon Ratchasima by 8,738. By 1986, registration data of the Ministry of the Interior listed Nakhon Ratchasima as the second largest city in the country with a population of 200,051. In total urban population for the province, Chiang Mai ranked by this time only fifth. See Santhat Sermsri, *Impacts of Rapid Urbanization on Health Status in Thailand,* Technical Paper no. 1 (Tokyo: Second Asian Conference on Health and Medical Sociology, 1986).

[2] The term "Lanna Thai"—variously spelled as "Lannathai" or "Lan Na Thai"— seems to be acceptable to the northern people, who commonly call themselves "country people" *(khon müang)* but not "Lao." For this study the term "Lanna Thai" is used to denote both the people and the language of Northern Thailand.

which various people groups of Southeast Asia are said to have migrated from north to south (see map 1). The Mæ Ping River valley widens into a plain in the general vicinity of the city of Chiang Mai, which gives the impression of a large plateau surrounded by mountain chains. This plain is one of the most fertile rice-growing areas in Thailand. In many parts of the valley multiple cropping is possible annually.

Ku Dæng is a village in the district of Saraphi, which is located along the eastern bank of the Mæ Ping River between the city of Chiang Mai and the province of Lamphun (see map 2). The approximate latitude of Saraphi is 18 degrees 47 minutes North, and the longitude is 98 degrees 58 minutes East.[3] The elevation of the Chiang Mai plain is about 1,000 feet, with Doi Pui towering 4,500 feet above the plain just to the west of the city.

The road from Chiang Mai to Lamphun passes through the district seat (amphœ) of Saraphi about ten kilometers (six miles) south of the city of Chiang Mai. The boundaries of the district are the Mæ Ping River to the west and the Mæ Kuang, a tributary of the Mæ Ping, to the east. The road from Chiang Mai to Saraphi rises gradually, so that the district seat is at a considerably higher elevation than the river, which is seven kilometers to the west.

About halfway between the amphœ and the river lies the village of Ku Dæng in the commune (tambon) of Nong Fæk.[4] In 1953, Ku Dæng was accessible by car, bicycle, or oxcart during the dry season along two or three dirt roads. The main dirt road, the one connecting the district seat with an irrigation dam at the river, was built in 1937 at the same time that the dam was completed. The hard-surface highway between Chiang Mai and Lamphun was built twenty years earlier, in 1917, four years before the northern branch of the State Railway of Thailand was completed to Chiang Mai. During the rainy season, the dirt roads from the district seat to Ku Dæng and neighboring villages were passable only by bicycle or on foot.

Ku Dæng was established as a community in the reign of King Mengrai the Great (1239 A.D.). Ku Dæng lies on the boundary between the provinces of Chiang Mai and Lamphun. An early name of the village is given as Ku Dæn, meaning "tomb on the border." There was a curved brick wall delineating the border between the two provinces, then kingdoms or principalities. Ku Dæng, therefore, was the last outpost of Chiang Mai before one entered the Kingdom of Lamphun.[5]

---

[3] Food and Agricultural Organization (FAO) of the United Nations, *Agricultural Economic Survey of Sarapee District, Chiangmai Province, Thailand* (New York: United Nations Food and Agriculture Organization, 1951), p. 2.

[4] For terminology and administrative division of populated areas in rural Thailand, see chapter 6, pp. 88-107.

[5] King Mengrai lived from 1239 to 1317 or 1323 A.D. He ruled from 1259 or 1261 until he died. See Hans Penth, *Prawat khwampenma khong Lan Na Thai* (Chiang Mai: Social Research Center, Chiang Mai University, 1983), p. 62.

We were told that the kings ("Lords of the Realm") of Chiang Mai and Lamphun arbitrated the boundaries between their two kingdoms by means of an elephant, which was set free at the city gate of Chiang Mai. The animal proceeded as far as the present site of Ku Dæng, where it stopped to rest. This, then, became the official and generally accepted boundary between the two kingdoms.

Another account relates the story of a hunter, named Pu Mon, who encountered a tiger on one of his forays into the jungle. He shot the tiger but failed to kill him. The wounded animal fled until it came to Ku Dæng. The villagers later found large quantities of tiger blood on the ground and erected a stupa or *cedi* made of brick on the spot where the tiger had shed his blood.[6] The tiger continued in his flight and later died in the general vicinity of Saraphi District, where the village and temple of Ku Süa ("Tiger Tomb") are located today. The *cedi* built over the spot where the tiger's blood had seeped into the ground became known as *ku dæng* ("the red tomb"). To this day villagers believe that there are valuable artifacts hidden in the ground under the site of the *cedi*. However, due to fear of the evil consequences, nobody has had sufficient courage to dig for these treasures. Today, only the base of the *cedi* is left, which is overgrown by trees and grass. Still no one is willing to dig in this area, for it would be disrespectful; furthermore, it might even be dangerous and harmful not only to the digger's own life and well-being, but also to that of his family and the entire village community.

In 1975, Sommai Premchit published a list of old temples in the vicinity of Chiang Mai and Lamphun.[7] The author surmises that the list was issued by the Ecclesiastical Organization in Bangkok during the reign of King Rama V (ruled 1868-1910 A.D.). At that time the independent administrations of the northern states were formally dissolved and incorporated into the central government. The Ku Dæng temple is listed as one of fourteen temples southeast of the city of Chiang Mai, with two monks, eighteen novices, and an abbot named Cao Athikan Thuthananüacarya.[8]

The village of Ku Dæng consists of two hamlets *(muban)*, numbers 6 and 7, one of the seven hamlets making up the commune Nong Fæk, which, in turn, lies at the center of twelve communes making up the district of

---

[6] The word *"ku"* means stupa or *cedi*, a structure made of brick and used for the storing of bones of the deceased.

[7] Sommai Premchit, *A List of Old Temples and Religious Sects in Chiengmai* (Chiang Mai: Chiang Mai University, 1975), p. 29.

[8] Over the years four spellings have been in general use for the city and the province of Chiang Mai: Chiang Mai (The Royal Institute spelling), Chieng Mai, Chiangmai, and Chiengmai. When the first state university outside Bangkok was established in the city, the name in English was spelled Chiengmai University. Some ten years later, the Royal Institute system of transliteration into English was adopted by the Ministry of the Interior for geographic terms, and the name of the city became Chiang Mai. However, it was a number of years before the incorporated name of the university could be similarly changed. Hence, the above reference (7) as indicated.

Saraphi (see map 3). Some of the farms of one of the two hamlets lie along the largest irrigation canal in the vicinity across a large rice field from the main part of Ku Dæng. This area, though structurally a part of Hamlet 7, is not considered functionally belonging to Ku Dæng, since the villagers living in that section patronize a temple and a school lying across the irrigation canal in another commune. For the purpose of the present study, the village is defined as that community of households that patronizes the village temple and sends its children to the village school.

The village of Ku Dæng itself is unusual in one specific respect. It is formed in a circle around a central rice field with a road circumscribing the field and part of the village. Other villages usually are stretched out along roads or rivers. The circumference of Ku Dæng is approximately two miles. Administratively, the village is divided into two hamlets, 6 and 7, each governed by a headman.

Northeast of Ku Dæng, about one kilometer distant, lies Nong Fæk the largest village of the commune of the same name. This village consists of three hamlets, stretching out along three branches of the road. Directly east of Ku Dæng, beyond Nong Fæk, is the smallest village, San Pa Sak (see map 2), which was founded only some twenty years before our study by emigrants from Nong Fæk, who built a new temple and a new school under the leadership of an energetic monk. Southeast of Ku Dæng, less than a mile away across a rice field, lies Hamlet 1, Nong Si Cæng. All these villages combined make up the commune Nong Fæk, which, in terms of total population, is the median unit among the twelve communes making up the district of Saraphi (see appendix A).

The climate of Ku Dæng and of the district is that generally found in the Chiang Mai plain: a tropical climate tempered by the elevation of the valley. The annual mean temperature reported over a five-year period (1937-1941) was 78.1 degrees F., with the highest mean temperature recorded for April as 83.8 degrees and the lowest for January as 69.6. The southwest monsoon, though considerably tamed when it reaches Chiang Mai, governs the rainfall in the area. Correlation is high between storm warnings heard from radio stations in Manila and actual rainstorms in Chiang Mai and vicinity. Rains generally start in mid-April (in 1953 they started April 20th) and continue through mid-November. The last rainfall of the 1953 rainy season was on November 28th. However, we were told by a 51-year-old woman that this was only the second time in her life that it rained after the second month full moon, which falls in early November. Subsequent observations over the next thirty years support this dating for the end of the monsoon. The annual rainfall is 46.3 inches.[9]

Though rainfall is heavy during the monsoon season, it is not the main direct water supply for the area. The main source of water for crops is the Mæ Ping River, which is dammed at several places to divert water into

---

[9] FAO (1951), p. 3.

irrigation canals dating back to at least the reign of King Mengrai (see p. 13). One of the most ambitious projects in irrigation up to 1953 was the big irrigation dam at Don Kæw, two miles from Ku Dæng, which, however, for the most part irrigated the land south of Saraphi in Lamphun province. During the thirty years following our study, the entire watershed area north and west of Chiang Mai was developed through encouragement of the King, and today there are innumerable smaller dams along many of the waterways north of the city. There are three large irrigation canals with numerous subsidiaries that irrigate the Ku Dæng area. Most of the fields were irrigated by gravitational flow, although there were a few manually operated watershovels to add to the water in some of the fields. Today, most of such additional irrigation is taken care of with gasoline engine-driven pumps. All of the land cultivated within the Ku Dæng boundaries was then and still is irrigated.

The soil of the Ku Dæng area, as that found in most parts of the district, is rich in alluvium, suitable for rice growing. The soil is constantly enriched by silting from the Mæ Ping River at the annual rate of about 5.9 inches, which alleviates the danger of soil impoverishment through continuous use year in and year out.[10] One of the MSA officials associated with the FAO survey in Chiang Mai made the statement that the use of fertilizer would probably have only a slight, long-range effect on the productivity of the land in this area, with none, or even a negative effect discernible within the first few years. Most of the land is under cultivation with the exception of a few areas of swamp. Even there, however, a dry season crop can be grown. Today, there is very little unused land that could be converted into crop-producing fields. The trend in the past has been for the fields to expand at the expense of the village area and the bamboo jungle. According to one informant, eighty years prior to our original study, the village covered nearly twice the area of today with only about one-third the present population.

The main source of wealth for the area is the rice crop. On land associated with Ku Dæng, rice is the only crop grown during the rainy season and is the main crop of the year. Nearby, on higher, drier ground, some peanuts and vegetables have been observed during this same time. After the harvest of the principal crop, a second crop of rice is grown on much of the same land during the dry season. During this time, however, a considerable acreage is devoted to such cash crops as peanuts, tobacco, soybeans, cabbage, and other vegetables.

Fish abound in the canals and ditches during the rainy season and are caught in large quantities and in all sizes, principally to augment the diet of the villagers. Pigs, ducks, and chickens are raised by the women of the village to obtain cash for home use and for making merit.

---

[10] FAO (1951), p. 3.

There are a number of ways in which villagers can earn cash. The most general of these activities is by daily labor, for which one could earn from 40 to 100 baht per day in 1984. This type of labor may be in the form of working on garden plots, plowing and harrowing the fields, rice harvest, carpentry, basketmaking, or engaging in other handicrafts. Income is also generated by taking produce to the market, such as rice, vegetables, fruit, or meat products. Longan (lamyai) trees are especially valued for the income they can produce. Almost every household has some longan trees. In some instances the character of the farm has been changed from a rice-producing farm to one producing mainly fruit. A household may take in from 5 to 20,000 baht per year from longan. This income will vary, of course, from year to year, depending on the yield. The most recent year for which we have figures, 1984, happened to be a very good year for longan. However, because of the fruit being plentiful, the price was accordingly low, and the villagers found it difficult to sell at a price they considered satisfactory.

Ku Dæng is a representative village of the district as far as population is concerned. The population of the entire district did not change much from before World War II until 1953 in sharp contrast to the population increase for the entire country. From 1953 to 1964, there was a slow increase in population comparable to the increase in number of households from 168 to 194. By 1974, this number had again increased to 223, while the average size of family decreased from 6.3 in 1964 to 4.8 in 1974, well below the 5.03 figure determined in 1953.

According to the 1949 FAO survey of the district, the average size of a household of those reporting was 4.78 persons. In our complete census of Ku Dæng taken in 1953, the average household was found to be 5.03. From 1953 to 1964 the average household size for the commune increased from 5.3 to 6.4. This would indicate an average household size for Ku Dæng of 5.7. By 1974 the figures supplied by the kamnan indicated a somewhat smaller average household size of 4.8.

Population statistics obtained in 1984 from the official population register kept by the kamnan and by spot checking in the village showed that the Ku Dæng population consisted of 487 men and 469 women for a total of 956. There were 272 households with 302 families registered. The population was almost equally divided between the two hamlets, 475 in Hamlet 6 and 481 in Hamlet 7. These figures give an average household size for Ku Dæng in 1984 of 3.5.

The ups and downs in household size parallel advances in public health procedures introduced in Ku Dæng over the years following World War II up to the early 1970s. By then family planning had taken firm root in the area with a subsequent drop in family size (see appendix B).

The district of Saraphi was one of the first districts in the Chiang Mai area to be surveyed and sprayed by the WHO-UNICEF Malaria Control Group, beginning in 1949. The FAO survey, undertaken at the request of the Malaria Control Group, was completed before the first spraying. The village

17

of Ku Dæng was sprayed twice during this program, once in 1950 and again in 1951. In a breakdown of population according to age groups, the percentages for Ku Dæng as found by us in 1953 and for the entire Saraphi district as found by the FAO survey correlated closely, except for the age group 0-3 years of age. In Ku Dæng those individuals between the ages of 0 and 3 in 1953 were 12.3% of the population; in Saraphi the corresponding figure for 1949 was 6.6%. If the 1953 census for Ku Dæng is, therefore, corrected so as to show a percentage of 6.6% for this age group, the average household would come out to 4.74 persons, which differs from the district average by less than 1%. The only plausible reason for this increase in the 0-3 age group for Ku Dæng over this particular period of time is the malaria control program.[11] A Chiang Mai malaria control official, who visited Ku Dæng in October to check the children of the village for evidence of malaria, found a spleen count of only 6%.[12] In a similar check prior to the first spraying in 1950, the incidence of malaria among school children as per spleen count had been 95%. We were not able to find any other evidence that could account for the doubling of the potential 0-3 age group in a period of less than five years.

The same conclusion can be drawn from the study of the Ku Dæng census itself. There was a more than a 50% decrease from the first age group to the second. When the first age group is broken up further into individual years, a definite drop from 3.0% of the population for age 3-4 years to 1.9% for the next higher year can be seen. In other areas of Asia it has been observed that the infant mortality rate is greatest for those under four years of age. If this were the case here, the drop in percentage should come two years earlier than it does. Statistically, the numbers for each year are not large enough to make a significant comparison possible. The whole age group allows us to make a more meaningful observation.

A histogram of the size of each age group tells graphically the same story (see appendix B). However, it also shows another reason for the sudden decline in population for the age group from 5-9 years: there is a population low for ages 35-44, which shows a reduction in number of adults of child-bearing age, which in turn affects the numbers in the 5-10 age group.

The two most likely causes for the small number of people in the age groups from 35-45 years were emigration and epidemics. We interviewed a number of villagers who were 59 years of age or older, asking them to recall any particular time in their lives when a large number of people had died, or

---

[11] By 1957, the work of this group had been taken over by the Thai government with U.S. assistance. While the program almost succeeded in eradicating malaria wherever it was applied, the worldwide scare of DDT environmental pollution ten years later put a stop to complete control of the disease. By the early 1980s, malaria was again beginning to spread throughout the rural areas of Northern Thailand.

[12] A figure confirmed by a team of Thai and American doctors and nurses from the McCormick Hospital in Chiang Mai, who made a medical check of school children in Ku Daeng in early 1954.

when an unusual number of families had moved away from Ku Dæng. One man remembered a "mass migration." In 1941, according to this informant, thirteen families moved from Ku Dæng north to Müang Fang. From other informants and from observation, we knew that emigration to Müang Fang had been and was still taking place, and that a "New Ku Dæng" had been established in this particular northern district. However, no one else mentioned such a large simultaneous exodus. Since most of the emigrants about whom we had information were under 40 years of age, this event should have decreased all age groups below that age by approximately the same amount, which it did not, and, therefore, could not have been a cause for the shape of the histogram.

All but one informant remembered a time when a large number of villagers died. Recollection was generally vague; most informants referred to the time when they were novices or when they had just been married or some other specific event in their lives. There seemed to have been two general periods of epidemics: one fell in the decade between 1910 and 1920 and the other about 1930.

The first epidemic probably was one of malaria. At that time, from 1917 to 1918, according to some informants a large number of young men from Ku Dæng went to Khun Tan, a mountain between Lamphun and Lampang, where a tunnel was being constructed for the northern branch of the State Railway of Thailand. Many of these seasonal workers contracted malaria (or "jungle fever") while living at Khun Tan. The sick people returned home to their village, where mosquitoes spread the disease to others. Estimates of the number of deaths for that period ranged from twenty to seventy.[13] Since those who labored at Khun Tan were mostly in their early twenties, this could have been a cause for reducing the birthrate for the following ten or twenty years. Furthermore, those infected by the returning workers would most likely have been small children who had not yet built up any appreciable resistance to malaria.

An alternate possibility, fitting into this same period of time, is that the world epidemic of influenza reached Thailand about two or three years after it had been at its height in Europe. This would have caused a considerable toll in lives in or about the year 1920, especially among children, which would in turn have reduced the number of 35-39-year-olds surviving in 1953.

The second epidemic seems to have occurred about 1930 and was probably caused by influenza or pneumonia. Estimates of the number of deaths were as high as one hundred for this period. We failed to obtain any further details. Evidence concerning the drop in numbers of the 5-10 age group is, therefore, inconclusive. The earlier epidemic, ending apparently in 1923, could well have been a contributing factor to the lack of children born in the mid- or late 1940s. However, the low in 1908 should, by similar

---

[13] Also see appendices H and I.

reasoning, have caused a low during 1928 to 1933, which it did not. Further detailed analysis of our census data and further questioning of older villagers would undoubtedly have revealed more precise causes for the shape of the age-group histogram. Such investigations and considerations did not seem germane to the purpose of our study at the time.

The Ku Dæng population of 842 persons in 1953 was evenly divided between the sexes, 50.2% female and 49.8% male, which differed slightly from the district as a whole that showed a reverse of 49.8% female and 50.2% male. By 1984 the corresponding figures for Ku Dæng were 50.9% male and 49.1% female.

More than half of the population in 1953 (59.8%) were adults (15-54 years of age), 31% children (under 15), and 9.2% over 54—on the whole, a rather young population. By 1984, the percentage of children was reduced to 19.6%, a direct result of successful family planning. The percentage of adults was also reduced (to 9.2%), in part because this age group includes the lows already discussed. Consequently, the middle age group in 1984 was even more predominant (65.1%) than it had been in 1953. Though old age is generally respected, the leadership and the main activities of the villagers were and continue to be in the hands of the middle age group of adults, those between the ages of 35-50.

Most of the adult population of 20 years of age or older is married. Of this adult group, 8.5% were widowed without having remarried as of 1953, and 6.8% were separated, not living then with their spouses. There were only two persons under 20 who were married, both women. Among the adults (20 years or over), 18.7% were still single (never having married) and under 30. Another 5.1% were over 30 and never married.

The general health of the population seemed excellent in 1953, in part, at least, due to the malaria control program. According to a number of informants, including the resident doctor of the commune (who lived in Ku Dæng) and the kamnan (who also lived in Ku Dæng), nobody had died in the village during the three years preceding our study. During the year we lived in the village, ten people died. One child of 6 years died as a result of constipation accompanied by muscular spasm, possibly tetanus or strychnine poisoning. A 3-month-old baby died, probably of diarrhea, and a 32-year-old woman died of high fever after two days' sickness. A 42-year-old man died of an infection in his neck, and a 57-year-old man died after three weeks of illness with a tumor in his kidney, diagnosed by x-ray in a Chiang Mai hospital, and, according to the doctor in charge, not fatal if it had been operated upon. A 44-year-old man died of a swelling of the stomach, a so-called "unlucky" disease, and a woman died of a virus infection after two days of illness.

There was little sickness in the village while we were there. Four or five people came to us for medicine for malaria (provided by the Malaria Control Group in Chiang Mai). One young woman had dengue fever or something with similar symptoms. The usual colds with fever laid people low for a few days. Judging from the household in which we lived, and the neighbors whom we observed daily, little time was lost in the course of a year through sickness. The FAO survey reported the average loss of work days due to malaria and other fevers as seventeen days per year per person working.[14] Nothing of this magnitude was observed in Ku Dæng. One of the storekeepers in the village kept at our request a record of his daily consumption of food and the incidence of sickness in his family of four throughout the year of our study. There were no entries in the second part of the record, since, he told us, nobody in his family had been sick. Similarly, other records that were kept for us by the head teacher and by one of the novices in the temple were void of references to disease.

Immigration is almost entirely through marriage. According to villagers' statements during census interviews, 62 out of 88 persons not born in Ku Dæng had moved there to live with their spouses. Two families and two individuals, making a total of twelve persons, had moved to Ku Dæng as regular immigrants without having had family connections before. Ten persons were born at their mother's parents' home in other villages, where the mother had gone for delivery. Two women had moved to Ku Dæng to live with their in-laws after their husbands, who had emigrated from Ku Dæng, had died. One man first lived with his parents-in-law elsewhere, then moved back to Ku Dæng with his family. One child was born in a hospital in Chiang Mai.

Emigration by marriage, for which no records exist, but judging from the reciprocal courtship between villagers from neighboring communities, may be assumed to be similar in scope to the immigration pattern due to marriage discussed above. In addition there seemed to be a trend toward emigration in search of economically more profitable lands. The exact reasons for the desire of some people to leave Ku Dæng was not clear. Undoubtedly the profit theme played an important role.[15]

A 52-year-old farmer, who had moved to Ku Dæng to live with his wife, sold the two *rai* of land he owned in Ku Dæng for 4,050 baht as well as his buffalo and two oxen.[16] He was a respected citizen of the village, but better profits and greater opportunities beckoned in Müang Fang, 150 kilometers north of the city of Chiang Mai. He had realized enough money from the sale of his property in Ku Dæng to buy seven *rai* of land in Müang Fang, leaving him enough to pay for a *tham bun* ceremony for his deceased father and his two sons, all three of whom had died some five years earlier.[17] Before the transactions in relation to his departure from Ku Dæng, he had not had sufficient funds to undertake this obligation on behalf of the dead.

---

[14] FAO (1951), p. 7.
[15] Theme 2: Profit.
[16] 2.5 *rai* = 1 acre; 6.25 *rai* = 1 hectare.
[17] *Tham bun* is a religious ceremony for making merit; see chapter 7 and pp. 177-182.

Another villager, one of the elders of the temple, told us that he was moving to Müang Fang because land there was so much cheaper. In Ku Dæng a *rai* of land sold for from 2,000 to 3,000 baht in 1954. In Müang Fang at that time one could buy thirty-three *rai* for 10,000 baht. The land in Fang is not quite as good as that in Ku Dæng, and there was no irrigation at that time, so that farmers could plant only one crop per year. The yield per *rai* of that one crop was also somewhat less than that in Ku Dæng. However, even after everything was considered, a person moving to Fang would gain at a two to one ratio.

The elder of the temple said he would like to move to Müang Fang himself, provided he could get a good price for his land in Ku Dæng, since he was quite well-to-do with fourteen *rai* of his own. He also mentioned an added attraction for moving: in Müang Fang all the farmers who came from the Saraphi area seemed to be living together in a new village called, "New Ku Dæng." According to our records, this elder never did make the move to "greener pastures."

The *kamnan* once went to a village thirty miles north of Chiang Mai to attend the wedding of one of his sons. He liked the village so much that he wanted to move there. He could buy land there for half the price in Ku Dæng. Even though there was only one crop per year in the other village, the yield was reputed to be twice that obtainable at Ku Dæng. However, the *kamnan*'s mother-in-law, who had also attended the wedding, told us she preferred to live in Ku Dæng. In the other village, "the people are dirty, the roads are muddy, and they don't even have toilets or bathrooms but simply use the jungle."

Much of the talk of the wealthier villagers about moving elsewhere seemed only to be so much talk about sour grapes. Coming down to earth, facing the facts of prestige and status, none of these people would actually contemplate selling their land and moving to a new community. For younger people and those of smaller means the story was different. They were actually moving away and making a good bargain of it. Those who moved to Müang Fang were not only making a good deal immediately, but they were gambling on the future. Oil in modest quantity was discovered near Müang Fang in the late 1940s, and the Thai government later built an experimental oil refinery there. Speculation over the possible development of oil production was sufficient cause to see a rise in the price of land in the foreseeable future. There was, however, no overt expression of this possibility on the part of our contacts in Ku Dæng.

This emigration from the Ku Dæng area has had a long-range influence on the rate of change toward mechanization of the farms. The poorer farmers and their families largely made up the labor force necessary for those who owned more land than they could handle alone. This labor could have been in the form of actual work for wages, or renting the land from the landowners, or simply a cooperative labor effort along the usual pattern then in practice in the village. Whatever the case may have been, as the labor force moved away, the landowners, who at the same time increased their holdings by the land that the emigrants sold, were finding it more and more difficult to secure manpower to work their fields. Mechanization, which had already made some inroads into the area in the form of tractor plowing and rice milling, was then the inevitable answer.

Partially as a result of the effects of emigration of available labor, agricultural methods have changed considerably from the traditional style of manual and animal labor. Modern technology has introduced the use of tractors for cultivating the fields. Pesticides and fertilizers are employed to ensure good crops. This has changed the entire system of cooperative labor. Productivity per farmer have increased, as has the yield per *rai* of land. Where hired labor continues to be employed, the going rate is 40 to 50 baht per day or payment in kind, as compared to 8 baht per day thirty years ago. As a matter of fact, at that time there was very little hired labor involved in growing rice. Then, it was mostly a matter of give and take between relatives and neighbors.

As a result of using up-to-date agricultural methods, the yield and quality of the crops have increased substantially. The villagers have, therefore, increased their economic status, enabling them to send their children into town for schooling. It also has resulted in more members of the community going outside the village for remunerative work, adding to the available cash in the village.

Some of the villagers emigrate temporarily during their younger years to find employment in the towns. The son of one of the village midwives, an "injection doctor," moved to a village in the hills behind Amphœ Mæ Rim, ten miles north of the city of Chiang Mai, to live with his wife, whom he had met on a medical call early in 1953.[18] He was the only doctor in the entire commune, which gave him more business than he could handle. During his first ten days there he made 1000 baht from medical calls, each of which brought in 20 baht or less. Some years previous this doctor had had a profitable business in the general vicinity of Ku Dæng, mostly from calls by people with fever. With the success of the malaria control program, however, the demand for his services decreased sharply, and he had to go elsewhere to find patients. This development due to mass public health methods did not seem to have bothered this doctor in particular, especially, since it provided him with more income.[19]

One of the younger sons of a well-to-do villager went to work in Chiang Mai during the rainy season of 1953. He worked in a friend's store selling hardware for a salary of 180 baht per month. After ten days he was back home recuperating from a cold and fever he had contracted in the city. Two months later he informed us that he had saved almost enough to buy a

---

[18] An "injection doctor" is a person with some pharmaceutical training who has obtained a government license to dispense some medicines and give injections.

[19] Theme 2: Profit.

23

bicycle. But shortly thereafter he was back in the village, ostensibly to help his father with the harvest, which was, however, not to begin for another month. He quite frankly admitted that he did not like city life.[20]

One of the daughters of a village leader was working in the Department of Roads at Lamphun. During the dry season she commuted daily the fifteen miles by bicycle. When the rains started, she moved to Lamphun to live in the house of relatives of another Ku Dæng villager and returned to Ku Dæng only on weekends. Toward the end of 1953, she was sent by her employers to Bangkok to participate in the Miss Thailand beauty contest. Her father accompanied her on the plane trip to the capital.

Apart from these cases of emigration for better land or remunerative occupation elsewhere, only one family moved away from Ku Dæng during the period of our study. This was the family of the midwife, who originally had come from further south, Nakhon Pathom, and, therefore, was always regarded as an immigrant—a Thai—by the other villagers. Together with her family of five, she moved to Mæ Rim north of the city of Chiang Mai, to live with another son. The Ku Dæng villagers were not particularly upset about her leaving. One comment was that, had she lived in a neighboring village rather than Ku Dæng, the people would have thrown stones to drive her out a long time ago. This actually happened to another Thai immigrant—according to our informant—who then moved to Ku Dæng, where the villagers, by their own estimate, are more tolerant of outsiders.

Land tenure does not seem to present a problem in Ku Dæng, according to our census data and general observation. The total land under cultivation or lying fallow in 1953 was 952 *rai* (380.8 acres) as reported by the villagers. This figure was, undoubtedly, not very accurate. We completed our census during the time of the second or third crop. If we had gathered our data during the main rice cultivation season, we would have received more nearly accurate answers as to ownership of the land. During the time between the harvest of the principal crop of rice and the planting of the same the following year, the farmers used various parcels of land for soybeans, garlic, peanuts, tobacco, cucumbers, tomatoes, or other cash crops. The land that is left over, as well as some of the land from which soybeans and some vegetables had already been harvested, was then planted with the second crop of rice. Some farmers rent small plots of land for certain crops. A young man may rent a fraction of a *rai* to plant some tobacco. Such land is rented for only two or three months, the time it takes to grow the crop. Frequently, the owner lets the person use the land free of charge. Thus, at the time of our census, people were unsure how to answer our questions concerning ownership or the renting of land.

There are two systems in use for renting land. In one system, the land owner is responsible for the irrigation system leading to the land and must supply labor for the common construction of the irrigation canals. The

---

[20] Theme 3: Fun.

renter works the land with his own labor and his own buffalo or bullock. After the harvest, the land owner gets 50% of the crop. The second system is that usually followed by the absentee landlords. Here, the renter takes care of everything, and the owner simply supplies the land. In return, the latter gets a fixed price of ten or twelve *thang* of rice out of every crop.[21] Sometimes the landlord returns two *thang* after the harvest, to show his generosity and his pleasure at the good work of his tenant. Since all the land in the Ku Dæng area was owned locally at the time of our study, the first system was the customary in use there.

One informant told us that the rate of renting land (in 1953) was fifteen *thang* per *rai*. When questioned whether he thought this was an excessive rate, he answered that it was not. He explained his reasoning as follows: If you rent ten *rai* of land, you have, in effect, borrowed 30,000 baht-worth of property at the then-prevailing rate of selling land. On this you pay 150 *thang* of rice, which was worth about 900 baht in 1953; that is, about 3% of the value of the property. If you borrowed the same amount of money, 30,000 baht, from the Farmers' Cooperative in Saraphi, you would have had to pay 9% interest per year, or 2,700 baht. In other words, if you borrow money, you have to pay three times the rate of interest that you pay for borrowed land. Furthermore, if the harvest is poor, the landlord usually takes only a nominal fee. If the money cannot be borrowed from the cooperative, then the farmer will have to borrow it locally from other farmers. In such transactions the rate of interest in 1953 was 5 baht per 100 baht borrowed per month, or 60% per year, even though, according to Thai law, interest on borrowed money was limited to 15% per year. These figures, as given by the villager, seemed to indicate that there was no serious land problem in Ku Dæng.

The 952 *rai* reported under cultivation in 1953 were worked by 144 households, 80.3% of the total. The twenty-three remaining households neither worked their own land nor rented land for work. The heads of these households had the following occupations: ten were farm laborers, working for others in return for rice or money; five were old people who were supported, in part, by their children or other relatives; three were old women who helped with various kinds of work in the village; one gave as his occupation "trader," the only one who could be considered a landlord in the usual sense of the word; four others were storekeepers, teachers, or house builders, professions that provided them with the major part of their income; but even this group of people worked in the fields during the harvest season.

In 1953, Ku Dæng villagers owned 768 *rai* of land, an average of 6.4 *rai* per land owner. This was somewhat less than the 8.1 *rai* per land owner for the entire district of Saraphi as reported by FAO.[22] There were some

---

[21] 1 *thang* = 20 liters; also see appendix C.
[22] FAO (1951), p. 6.

landlords living in Chiang Mai who owned considerable tracts of land in other parts of the district, which would have accounted for the higher figure. The average land worked per household in Ku Dæng was 6.6 *rai*, practically the same amount as that owned per land owner. This supports the observation that there was no large-scale absentee ownership problem in the village.

In 1972 Potter observed that 206 households in Ku Dæng owned 739 *rai* of land, or 3.6 *rai* per land owner.[23] Thus, in a period of twenty years considerable fragmentation of land had taken place.

Further data on land ownership in 1953 were obtained through an official census ordered by the government for taxation purposes. The *kamnan* and his assistants had a special form for every person who owned land in the official Ku Dæng village area. This area was somewhat larger than that covered by our study, since it covered the seventeen families living near the main irrigation canal that were not included in our definition of the Ku Dæng community.[24] Hence, the area covered by the *kamnan's* census may be considered roughly 10% larger than that of our study.

The *kamnan's* data is in no way comparable to the data of our investigation. The purpose of the government census was to assess every parcel of land in a given area. The *kamnan*, therefore, had to contact every person who owned land in Ku Dæng, regardless of where he or she lived. In our census we were interested in what every Ku Dæng villager owned regardless of where the land was located. Nevertheless, the *kamnan's* census was of considerable interest. Reliability of the official census is undoubtedly not very high. When we copied the data from the blanks used by the *kamnan*, we found several discrepancies: there were wrong additions; some land that was used only for house and garden was added to the taxable land erroneously in some cases; some land was assessed twice. On the whole, though, the data gave a fair indication of the distribution of the land in the Ku Dæng area.

The total taxable land in Hamlets 6 and 7 (which is the Ku Dæng area plus the area along the irrigation canal) was 1,107 *rai* in 1953 (442.8 acres), which was owned by 202 persons. In addition there were another twenty-seven parcels of land used only for houses and yards, which are not taxable. Thus, there were a total of 229 land owners for the two hamlets. Most of the ownership was in the name of men (72.5%), who usually were listed as heads of households, although in some cases a son-in-law may have owned some land separately from that of his wife's parents. Women were registered as owners of 16.6% of the holdings. A small number of plots (10.5%) were registered jointly by two or more persons, usually husband and wife or siblings. One holding was registered in the name of an 8-year-old girl. Three others were listed in names of people who were no longer living.

---

[23] Potter (1976), p. 56.
[24] See pp. 14-15.

We were told that they had to be listed in that fashion until another official personal census would be taken, probably in 1954.

Lamphun borders on Chiang Mai province near Ku Dæng (see map 2). The small plot of land owned by a resident of Nakhon Ratchasima, a province in Northeast Thailand, is a house plot within the residential sector of the village and consists of only one-half *rai* of land. In 1953 it was neither used by the owner nor rented out. The table of distribution of ownership according to residence below illustrates the earlier observation that there was very little absentee ownership of land in Ku Dæng in 1953.

Residence of Landowner (1953)	# of Landowners Holding Land in Ku Dæng Area	% of Total # of Holdings in Ku Dæng
Hamlet 6 (Ku Dæng)	83	36.2%
Hamlet 7 (Ku Dæng)	77	34.0%
Hua Fai (part of Hamlet 7 along irrigation canal)	15	6.6%
Other hamlets of Nong Fæk commune	10	4.4%
Neighboring commune in Saraphi district		
Don Kæw	12	5.2%
Khua Mung	12	5.2%
Tha Kwang	11	4.8%
Lamphun (neighboring province)	8	3.5%
Nakhon Ratchasima (province NE of Bangkok)	1	0.4%
TOTAL	229	100.2%

The nine holdings by owners who lived outside the district comprised a total of a little over forty-two *rai* (16.8 acres) or less than 4% of the land of the Ku Dæng area. Furthermore, over one-third of this land (fifteen *rai*) was actually cultivated by the owners themselves.

These data, imprecise though they are, justify our conclusion that we were dealing here with a village that consisted almost entirely of small land holders who worked their own land and rented additional areas from each other if someone required more land.

On the whole the farmsteads in Ku Dæng were of modest size. The 167 households consisted of a total of 430 buildings in 1953. This included barns, shelters for pigs, and chicken houses, for an average of 2.5 structures per farm. Cattle, including ninety-seven buffaloes and 114 oxen were owned by 68.3% of the households. Frequently, men who had no land owned a buffalo with which they then worked other people's land.

Major equipment was noteworthy by its absence. In the whole village there were only ten oxcarts, sufficient for the demand of the village. In addition there were forty-two bicycles, owned mostly by the richer villagers; also two pressure lanterns, two record players, three sewing machines, a clock, and a radio. Nearly every farmer had tools that included plows to be pulled by oxen or buffaloes, one or more hoes, and a large assortment of knives and axes.

By 1964 a considerable increase in mechanization had taken place. There were now five buses where there had been none. The village also boasted one motor scooter and 122 bicycles, and there were twenty-nine pressure lanterns, five sewing machines, forty-two clocks, and eighty-one radios.

Ten years later, in 1974, electric power had reached the village, and electric lights were installed in most houses. Within two years of the advent of electricity, television sets made their appearance. Motorcycles continued to multiply until in 1984 there was more than one per household. At this time, the villagers also owned more than twenty pickup trucks for hauling people and agricultural products. While in 1954 excess cash was almost entirely invested in land or livestock, by 1984 the situation had changed to the acquisition of mechanized agricultural implements, personal vehicles, and household appliances.

The village gives the impression of being well-kept and relatively prosperous. In 1953, over 40% of the houses were permanent wooden structures, their roofs usually covered with clay tiles. One of the last houses finished in 1954 during our stay in Ku Dæng was built with corrugated zinc roofing, the first of its kind in the village. The other 57% of houses were built of bamboo, all except one, with straw roofs. The first investment of the farmer in those days was in land; when he had acquired a sufficient number of rai, he usually put his next profit into a house, which, most likely, cost as much as the value of all the land he owned.

By 1984, prestigious housing had changed to brick-and-mortar construction. Some of the larger homes could almost be classified as "town houses." Upper stories still tended to be constructed of wood, although a few three-story concrete structures could already be seen. Bamboo housing had almost completely disappeared.

2

THE VILLAGE ECONOMY

The Ku Dæng economy is based on agriculture, which is, as elsewhere in Thailand, based on rice. Although only a few villagers listed occupations other than farming for our 1953 census, even these people helped harvest the rice. Other crops are sown between or in addition to the rice crops, primarily for the purpose of additional cash income. Fruit trees, which were planted during our original study, had become a major source of cash by 1984. In a few instances, farmers have switched predominantly to longan trees (lamyai). A household may take in from 5 to 20,000 baht per year from this fruit alone.

Beginning with the preparation of the fields for the main crop of rice, the agricultural year is divided as follows:

Middle of May–Beginning of August:

When sufficient rain has fallen to flood the fields with the help of water from the irrigation canals, the main rice growing cycle begins. Two ceremonies are performed to inaugurate the season:

1) Field Preparation Ceremony (hæk na)

This ceremony is performed in order to insure a plentiful harvest. It is carried out each year beginning in the sixth month (approximately May). An even-numbered day is more likely to be chosen for this ceremony than an odd-numbered one. Hæk na is expected to prevent insects or other natural disasters from damaging the crops. A miniature paddy field is prepared by building small dykes to contain the water. The various tools for cultivating the land are made ready, including hoes, rakes, spades, plows, and harrows. A small platform is made out of woven bamboo and affixed to six bamboo poles at approximately eye level. A railing is built around the platform to accommodate the offerings. If no bamboo is available, other wood will do. Food offerings may consist of anything edible according to custom, but the usual ingredients are shrimp paste, fish, and some kernels of grain taken from the top of a pot full of rice. The food is placed into small containers made of "banana leaves" (bai tong) or placed on small squares of the same material. Other dishes may not be used, because bai tong is considered purer and cleaner than ordinary vessels.

When the ceremony of offering food and saying the appropriate incantations is completed, the miniature field is plowed for about one hour. Nothing further needs to be done: everything is left in place until the rains begin to fall, and preparation of the fields may commence. When everything is ready for the rice seedlings to be transplanted to the regular fields, another offering of food is made to the spirits to implore them to prevent damage to the crop from animals or insects. A cooked chicken is included to insure good fortune. Four three-cornered flags of any or no particular color are stuck into the ground at the northern corner of the field.

2) Rice-Sprouting Ceremony and Plowing

In order to prepare the paddy rice for seeding, it is first placed into a pan and covered with water for three days. The lighter grains of rice will float to the top and are discarded. The good rice is then drained and put into another container and covered with dry rice straw or hay. The rice is kept moist for two more days until it has begun to sprout and thus is ready for sowing. Rice seedling beds will have been prepared in rows with spaces left for walking between the rows and for drainage of water. Before the rice is actually sown, the spirit of rice planting, Mæ Phosop, is called by name to be informed of what is going to happen and to be implored to assure that the rice will sprout into healthy seedlings, which in turn will insure a plentiful rice crop.

As early as the end of June, some of the sprouting rice may be sown broadcast in the small, rectangular seedbeds. This is usually done when the moon is full, or nearly so. One villager told us she likes to plant her seed on a full moon night, because she hopes that her seed will grow up to be as beautiful as the moon.

When the rice has been sown in the seedbeds, it must be watched carefully until the seedlings have reached a height of about one cubit. If there is too much water the sprouting rice could be drowned; if there is not enough, it could wither. While the rice seedlings are still growing, the farmer must rise early in the morning and take plow, hoe, harrow, and other utensils to the field for plowing. If he does not wish to carry these items himself, he may use his buffalo or bullock to carry them for him. He must begin plowing in the ceremonial field where the Rice-Sprouting Ceremony was held. It is customary to plow only in the early morning or the late afternoon, between four and six o'clock, which is referred to by the farmers as "buffalo afternoon." The rest of the day the buffalo is allowed to rest so that work can be resumed early the following morning.

After the plowing, the field is gone over a couple of times with a wooden harrow, also pulled by a single buffalo or bullock. A layer of mud is thus formed, about one foot deep, on top of which there may be as much as six inches of water.

After a minimum of thirty days in the seedbeds, the young rice seedlings are transplanted into the regular fields. All the rice grown in the Ku Dæng vicinity is transplanted in this way; none is sown broadcast. Rice is sown and transplanted over a long period of time, so as to stagger the time when it will be ready for harvest. Village labor is cooperative, the farmers and their families helping each other in the fields with the various tasks.[1] If all the rice had to be planted or harvested at the same time, not enough labor would be available to complete the work.

All the tasks of rice planting and harvesting, with the exception of plowing and harrowing, are performed by women as well as by men. Children help according to their ability. Usually, a 14-year-old son participates in all tasks like an adult, although physically he usually still is a child.

When the main part of a farmer's land is to be transplanted, he usually invites friends and neighbors to help. Somehow they seem to know when another person is going to need help. One farmer told us that during this time young fellows come by his house almost every day to ask when he will be ready for transplanting. Some of the rice seedlings are usually pulled the day before transplanting, so that twenty or thirty people are kept busy in the fields once they are there. The rice is usually taken out of the seedbeds by the farmer and his family. One or two persons pull the rice, others tie it into bundles, and someone else carries it to the house for safekeeping until the next day, or to the field, where the young people of the village transplant it immediately. They stand in rows about five feet apart and stick bundles of seven or eight plants about three or four inches into the mud, leaving a space of ten inches to one foot. Another bunch of rice seedlings is planted in the same manner. Talking and joking, accompanied by laughter, can be heard throughout the time the group is working in the field.[2]

When all the rice has been planted, which seldom takes more than half a day, the workers return to the house of the owner, where his wife and perhaps two or three neighbors have prepared lunch. No record is kept who came to help, but we were assured that the people remember and that every villager had to return services rendered.[3]

July:

During July, the main profit-bringing fruit of the Chiang Mai area, the longan, or *lamyai*, ripens and is harvested. The villagers, themselves, did not have very much to do with this harvest in 1953, for the longan trees were then usually sold at the time they bloomed. Only in rare instances did the villagers collect the longan themselves to sell directly in the market. It was too much trouble, even if the profit could have been a little higher.[4] One villager tried to handle this by herself during our stay in the village. She traveled halfway to Bangkok to sell the fruit, where she expected to make a

---

[1] Theme 5: Communal responsibility.
[2] Theme 3: Fun.
[3] Potter describes this process of cooperative labor exchange in considerable detail as he observed it in his study centered on Ku Dæng in 1972. See Potter (1976), pp. 42-44.
[4] Theme 1: Utility.

greater profit. She would have succeeded, she told us, had not someone stolen two bushel baskets full of fruit from her.

Lamyai is a fruit similar to the Chinese lychee *(linci)*. In Southeast Asia longan is seldom found other than in Northern Thailand. If planted from a seed, the tree takes from five to ten years to begin to bear fruit. However, if a branch is circled, bound with coconut husks, and transplanted after it has sprouted new roots, it will develop into a bearing tree within three years.

The value of a tree varies according to the size of the fruit and the quantity. In 1953 some trees brought as much as 500 baht, others as little as ten. The owner of the largest number of *lamyai* trees in Ku Dæng sold his crop in 1953 for 3,700 baht. The previous year, we were told, the fruit harvest was much bigger, but brought correspondingly lower prices. When the crop is much smaller than expected, the farmers reduce the agreed-upon price, so that the merchant who bought the longans will not lose too much money.

By 1984 the value of this fruit had risen to ten or twenty times what it had been thirty years earlier. By this time also many of the farmers had added lychee trees to their fruit orchards, thereby diversifying production. Since *lamyai* trees bear only every other year, the lychee trees can be relied upon to provide income during the lean years.

In 1953 we took an opportunity sample of approximately two-thirds of the Ku Dæng area, covering some twenty households in a brief questioning period lasting three hours. These twenty households had a total of eighty-nine *lamyai* trees. Sixty-eight trees were sold for 6,680 baht, or an average of 98 baht for the fruit of one tree. The previous year, forty-six trees had been sold for 2,440 baht, or approximately 53 baht per tree. The number of trees sold the previous year was probably larger than or at least as large as that in 1953. The smaller number of reported sales was undoubtedly due to lack of memory. The twenty farms that we covered had an average landholding of 7.65 *rai*, indicating that our opportunity sample was somewhat weighted on the land-owning side of the village. However, the average landholding of the eleven houses that indicated they had sold their longan trees was 10.1 *rai*. This would indicate that the wealthier farmers engage in the fruit trade to a greater extent than the poorer ones. It seemed strange at the time that more villagers did not plant *lamyai* trees, since they require little attention once they are grown. In many cases, of course, the poorer villagers plant banana trees on the little land they own or rent, since bananas provide them with an immediate source of food, both for themselves and for their pigs.

Most of the *lamyai* are bought by Chinese in the district seat of Saraphi or in Chiang Mai. None of the farmers whom we interviewed seemed to have sold to the same *lamyai* merchants two years in succession. A merchant who wishes to buy fruit in Ku Dæng must be introduced to the villagers by some other villager.[5] A total stranger would not be permitted to buy fruit in the village, or rather, he would be boycotted by the farmers.

Much improvement was possible in the *lamyai* growing enterprise. With some selective breeding, large *lamyai*, which are in great demand, could be grown at great profit for the villagers. Some of this seems to have taken place during the intervening years, although, in 1953, there seemed to be no great interest in trying to improve the variety. In most cases the farmers seemed to regard the fruit as a free gift.

August:

Shortly after the rice has been transplanted, the farmer and his family return to the fields to "tread the mud." For most of August, the farmers can be seen standing in their fields at all hours of the day, often holding on to a hoe for support, smoothing the mud under the water with their bare feet. Grass and other weeds that have begun to grow are thereby eliminated, and the soil is made smooth to improve rice growth. With the conclusion of this work there is nothing further to do in the fields until the end of the rainy season, when the harvest begins.

A few plots of land, too high to be flooded by irrigation water, are planted with peanuts after all the rice planting has been completed. We observed this practice in a nearby village; no peanuts were grown during this season in Ku Dæng.

September-October:

There is no work in the fields at this time. The rice grows by itself without any special attention. Since all the land has been planted with rice, there is no space left on which to work other crops. Heavy daily rain makes it almost impossible to work very much outdoors. We observed one villager in late October digging up part of his garden in preparation for growing tobacco. He was able to do this at such an early time because of moderate but sufficient rainfall in 1953.

Most of the villagers stay at home during this time, repairing various farm implements, making rope for tethering buffaloes, or working on new structures on their farmstead, such as a new house, a new barn, or a new pig sty. In October, much of the time of the people is taken up by large-scale religious festivals.

Throughout this period, the villagers go fishing almost daily. Wearing big hats, made out of old paper umbrellas, for protection against the rain, men, women, and children go out in any kind of weather to fish. At this time of the year, when water is plentiful in irrigation canals as well as in the fields, fish abound and are caught in great quantities.

---

[5] Theme 5: Communal responsibility.

The men usually fish with big throw-nets, weighted at the edges with metal rings. Small platforms, ten feet apart, are built on the banks of irrigation canals, as many as eight or ten in a row. Downstream from the platforms a bamboo dam is built across the canal, which will let the water pass but is a hindrance to the free movement of fish. With the nets slung over their arms, the men squat patiently on the platforms, watching the dam intently. When a fish reaches the dam, it stops and turns back to swim back upriver. This turning motion brings the fish near the surface, where it is quickly spotted by an alert fisherman. As soon as a sighting has been made, a general cry of "Take it!" is the signal for the men to rise from their squatting positions and throw the net across the water, usually covering the entire area between the banks and perhaps as much as thirty yards upstream. The theory is that the fish usually come in groups; hence, if one fish has been sighted, there should be many more in the neighborhood. One man may catch as many as eight or ten fairly large fish at one throw.

Some of the men go out every day and frequently spend many hours at this pastime. Much talk is carried on between catches while the nets are being cleaned and while everyone is waiting for the others to get ready for the next throw. Once the nets are ready, though, and the fishermen are prepared for another strike, everybody quiets down so as not to frighten away the fish. There is as much recreation involved in this pursuit as there is work. As in the planting of the crops, it is done in groups, which provide fellowship for the participants.[6] Occasionally, we observed a lone man with his net. He may have been motivated by a desire to make a big catch. In general, however, the social factor seemed to outweigh the economic one in fishing as a pastime.

The women have their own specialization in fishing. They use big nets attached to bamboo cross sticks at the end of a long bamboo pole. The largest of these nets is as much as eight feet in diameter. The size is determined by the size of the stream or ditch in which the women wish to make their catch. Fishing of this type is usually done in several feet of water. The net is lowered into the water and allowed to rest there for several minutes. The water flows undisturbed over the net. After some time the net is suddenly pulled up. The natural spring in the bamboo enables the net to be lifted with a sudden jerk; any fish that may have been swimming just above the net is inevitably caught in this upward motion. Usually smaller fish, one to three inches in length, are caught in this manner.

Some of the women go out alone, others can be seen in groups of three or four. Little girls, 10 or 12 years old, sometimes carry nets of this type for fishing in small ditches, although this is mainly done for play. It is an indication of early transmission of skills related to sex roles.

Sometimes women come back with more than a thousand little fish in their baskets. The fish are then spread on bamboo racks and placed in the

---

[6] Theme 3: Fun.

sun to die and dry. Here the securing of food seems to be the prime motivation, less so than recreation. The dried fish are used for making a delectible fish paste, a hot, peppery mixture, which is eaten with glutinous rice.

Innumerable other ways and means of catching fish can be observed. Traps of various kinds and varieties are set up in the rice fields and along the banks of the canals to catch the larger fish and eels. Young people and women are charged with the preparation and the setting of the fish traps. The catch that each person makes is generally considered "his" or "hers." Some may be used for family consumption, some sold on the market. Any profit that a person makes out of this belongs to him or her. It does not go into the family coffers.[7]

Sometimes a section of one of the canals is dammed off by a group of villagers and drained, so as to get at the fish at the bottom of the canal. Permission from the *kamnan* or the irrigation headman must be obtained for this, since the water in the irrigation canals is common property. Later in the season, when the rice is nearly ripe, the water level in the irrigation canals is lowered in order to keep the fields dry and prevent damage to low-lying rice. At this time, the villagers are prohibited from damming the ditches for fishing purposes. Some, nevertheless, continue with this activity regardless of the damage it might cause. To avoid detection, they do it at night. When one such case was reported to the *kamnan*, he went out with two assistants and arrested three men whom he found fishing. They were sent to the district police office the following morning, where they were fined 20 baht each.

Fishing with hook and line is less common; it is mainly practiced by women but also occasionaly by men and children. Bait consists of the meat of a live crab seasoned with a little lime—"to hold the meat together"—or ants eggs. Catfish, and similar large fish, are caught in this manner. Occasionally fish are speared on long bamboo poles with six or eight sharpened metal prongs at the end.

One day in late October, around two hundred villagers, mostly in their twenties, staged a communal fishing event in one of the big irrigation canals in the east field. Men, women, and children had come to help from all the surrounding villages. Some men stood in the water with nets and traps, stirring up mud and driving the fish downstream. Others stood on the banks well ahead of the main crowd to catch the advance guard of fish with their throw nets. Women with dip nets were lined up along the banks as well as in the water. Others walked in the water with a variety of traps, which they submerged from time to time to catch individual fish. Some men and a few boys carried spears, watching for fish near the surface, and spearing them when sighted. The average catch per person was nearly one hundred, mostly small, fish. In this type of concerted campaign the chances

---

[7] Theme 4: Individuality.

for the fish to survive are practically nil. There did not seem to have been much advance planning. Apparently some of the young men had been fishing the previous day and decided to call for large-scale fishing the following day. Word-of-mouth spread from village to village, and at the appointed time the villagers were all there. The atmosphere seemed to be more like a picnic; the actual catching of fish played a secondary role to the general "fun."[8]

November-Middle of December:

The first harvest in the general area of Nong Fæk commune was observed on the 9th of November 1953 and in the Ku Dæng fields on the 12th. This harvest was of the so-called "three-month rice," which had been sown in June and transplanted in early July. This main crop consists almost entirely of glutinous rice, which is the staple diet of the people in Northern Thailand. A small acreage is planted to non-glutinous rice, and each farmer has, perhaps, one-fourth of a *rai* in "black" rice, a dark purple, glutinous variety. Both of these kinds are used by the villagers for making condiments and desserts.

The rice is cut in the fields by communal efforts, ten to forty people working in one field at a time. As in the case of transplanting, the villagers seem to "know" when or where to work. Each farmer knows to whom he owes work. Sometimes people without land help with the harvest. They are given rice or, occasionally, money for their labors, at the rate of one *thang* of rice per day, worth in 1953 about 6 baht.[9] Generally a farmer does not like to have too many people help him, for that would require him to return labor too often. If a labor debt is not repaid during the current harvesting season, it may be "owed" until the second crop is ready. Occasionally, we were told, the names of those who helped and who had not yet been repaid would be written on the wooden walls of the house.[10]

We observed about thirty people working in a particular field one day. Each person had a curved knife about six inches long, with which he or she cut the rice at about knee height. Whenever six or seven bundles of rice had been cut, they were put on the ground behind the person cutting to dry in the sun. After some time other workers gathered up the rice in piles around a dry area about twenty feet in diameter, which would later be used for threshing.

---

[8] Theme 3: Fun.

[9] As stated earlier, one *thang* of rice is a large basketful, standardized by government action to contain twenty liters of paddy and weighing approximately 10.2 kg. The old, local measure of rice, the *thang*, is about 20% larger. See FAO, (1951), p. 10.

[10] See Potter (1976), pp. 42-47.

Here again was an opportunity for social contact between young men and women. Much talking and laughter was in evidence.[11] One incidental result of this general noise was that snakes and rats, which abound in the fields, were driven away. We heard of no snake bites during our stay in the village. In fact, we were told that only one man had ever died of snakebite in Ku Dæng, and that had occurred ten years prior to our study. To protect their legs from scratches from the rice stubble, the women wear long skirts and the men long pants. Often both men and women roll leggings up to their knees. The women always wear bandannas around their heads and long-sleeved blouses for protection against the sun. Most men wear hats for the same reason.

At noon, when the group had cut about two *rai* of land (nearly one acre), they returned to the farm house in the village, where the farmer's wife fed everybody a big meal. If the work was not yet finished, the workers would return to the fields after one or two hours' rest, and then would return for another meal in the evening. Usually, this type of communal work lasts only half a day, with one meal provided at the end of the work.

On one occasion in 1953, we obtained the expenses involved in feeding twenty persons:

1	chicken	8.00
2	banana trunks	1.00
20	cucumbers	.70
33	peppers	.25
10	salted fish for fish paste	.25
15	liters of glutinous rice	15.00
23	leaves of tobacco	1.00
25	leaves of fermented tea	1.00
	TOTAL (baht)	**27.20**

The cost of food listed above was the market value in 1953. Most of the food was home grown on the farm. Some items, such as the cucumbers, the tobacco, and the tea, were actually bought in the market. There was, of course, considerable work involved in the preparation of the food. But here, just as with the work in the fields, neighbors were expected to help.

When the rice is cut and gathered into large heaps in the fields, and when it is sufficiently dry, it is threshed in huge threshing baskets. Three methods of threshing are employed in the Chiang Mai plain. One is to prepare a hard threshing ground out of mud and buffalo dung on which the rice stalks are then beaten. Another is to use large woven baskets, which can be set anywhere in the field. The third, not very common in this area, is to build a wooden or bamboo railing about fifteen feet long, across which the

---

[11] Theme 3: Fun.

rice stalks are beaten. The basket method is the only one employed in the general vicinity of Ku Dæng.

For several weeks before the rice harvest, the villagers prepare their baskets, which measure eight to ten feet in diameter and are about four feet deep. This work is done during the slack season in September and October. Cooperative labor is usually required. Three or four men help each other to make new baskets. A hole is dug into the ground, which corresponds in size to that required for the basket. Then the basket is woven out of a particular type of bamboo, which is cut into long strips. The strips are hammered into place with wooden mallets. The wealthier villagers use a particular basket for only two or three seasons and then sell it to someone else for 150 or 200 baht (in 1953) and buy or make a new one for their own use.

Every morning the baskets are carried to the fields and in the evening back home if the work is finished. At this time of the year the nights are rather cold, and villagers would just as soon work in the fields as sit shivering at home. Some of the straw is burned so that the workers can warm themselves from time to time. Some young men, rather than carry the heavy baskets home each night, sleep out in the middle of the fields, using the up-turned baskets as shelters from the heavy dew that falls every night. This work is done individually by each farmer's family. There is little or no mutual help among neighbors, since this work can be done by one or two persons. There is generally enough wind to winnow the grain as it is threshed by beating bundles of rice against the side of the basket. Occasionally, a member of the family waves one or two large bamboo fans to create additional wind. Usually the rice is winnowed once more near the house before it is taken to be milled.

When the rice is threshed, it is placed on bamboo mats in the field near the threshing basket. The women of the house, with occasional help from neighbors, carry the rice back to the rice barn. Nobody in the family, men, women, or children, returns empty-handed from the fields. Each person carries one *hap* of rice back to the barn.[12] A few families perform a ceremony of calling the rice *khwan*, an animistic association, before they take the first rice back to the barn.[13] For most people there is no special ceremony related to carrying the rice home or dumping it into the rice barn.

Often the rice is carried back to the house at night, when the moon lights the way. While the young men thresh, groups of young women carry the rice home. Each time they return to the fields, the men stop working, stand by the straw fire, and chat and joke with the girls. At home the mother and some helpers prepare black rice dessert or other condiments to be taken out to the fields by the girls. Once more we have a social input

---

[12] A *hap* consists of two baskets supported from the ends of a bamboo stick that is carried over the shoulder.
[13] See chapter 9, pp. 161-163; for more information on animism, see chapter 10.

accompanying a purely economic event of threshing and bringing in the rice.[14]

The rice harvest in 1953 was better than it had been for six or seven years. One reason given by the villagers was that even though floods had occurred that year elsewhere in the province, none had damaged the crops in Ku Dæng. Another reason voiced occasionally by villagers was that the village had good luck in 1953, because a "foreigner" was staying in their midst. In general the area produces good results in rice. The average yield is thirty to fifty *thang* per *rai* of land, although, according to MSA officials, the yield elsewhere in the Chiang Mai region is higher. Villagers told us that the yield in 1953 was at least eighty *thang* of rice per *rai*.

According to old-timers, the yield in Ku Dæng has been steadily decreasing over the years. One old woman told us that the people worked harder when she was young. They pulled out all the weeds found in their fields, using both hands, whereas nowadays, she continued, the workers use only one hand. In "her time" the yield was nearly twice what it is today.

Another villager said that the farmers watched more carefully for insects when he was young, thus reducing crop damage. He added that people today are too lazy to take proper care of their crops. Furthermore, cooperation and leadership are lacking with regard to regulation of the water supply. A few people, nowadays, attend to the work of building the irrigation system, but when it is finished, everybody wants to use the water to his own advantage without consideration for his neighbors, the man concluded.[15]

The decrease in productivity is undoubtedly due to over-cultivation of the soil. This seems to be true for the country as a whole.[16] According to one informant, fertilizer had been distributed by the government in 1952. Favorable results failed to materialize, a situation blamed on inadequate instructions received with the fertilizer.

When the harvest is in, every farmer must pay tax in kind at the *kamnan's* house. With help from his assistants, he keeps careful record of all the rice delivered. Each farmer must pay three *thang* of rice for every *rai* of land that he has planted with rice. This amounts to a tax of approximately 8% of a normal crop. We were told that this tax is for irrigation. Whether the money obtained from the sale of this tax was actually used for the stated purpose, or whether it disappeared into the government coffers, we were unable to ascertain. The villagers are required to provide labor for irrigation

---

[14] Theme 3: Fun.

[15] Theme 1: Utility and Theme 4: Individuality.

[16] See Division of Central Services, Thailand, *Statistical Yearbook, Thailand 1945-55*, no. 30 (Bangkok: Central Statistical Office [and] Office of the National Economic Development Board); Lauriston Sharp, H. Hauck, K. Janlekha, and R. Textor, *Siamese Rice Village: A Preliminary Study of Bang Chan, 1948-1949* (Bangkok: Cornell Research Center, 1953), p. 130.

purposes. After the rice is harvested, each household that is planning to use irrigation water for the second crop must supply labor for digging of ditches.

December:

As soon as some fields have been cleared of rice, soybeans are planted. The soil is still wet enough at this time to permit cultivation without further irrigation. The soybean seeds are simply stuck into the ground alongside the rice stubble. In a short while, green sprouts can be seen all over. The farmers stick a bamboo post into the ground at a corner of the field and tie a few strands of straw to the top. This is a marker to indicate that something has been sown in the field, warning others to keep their ducks and buffaloes away.

December-January:

Following the harvest of the main crop of rice, some fields close to the village are planted with cash crops. Preparation of these fields begins almost as soon as they are cleared of rice. We were told that at this time of the year in 1952 a man from Pak Kong, a village near the Lamphun-Chiang Mai highway, had come to Ku Dæng with a tractor to plow the fields for a fee. However, during our stay in the village in 1953-54, no one appeared. The villagers seemed not very much interested in determining why he had not come. They said the results of tractor plowing had not been satisfactory. The plow had cut too deeply and plowed all the good topsoil under.[17] The traditional method of preparation of the fields was to work them with a simple steel hoe. The soil at this time of the year was too dry, and there was not sufficent water available for plowing with a buffalo or bullock. By 1974, tractors had reappeared and seemed to have been accepted as an alternative tool for soil cultivation.

Tobacco is planted mostly by young people. A young man may rent a small section of land from a relative for 10 baht (in 1953). He hoes the soil, perhaps with the help of brothers or sisters. When the land has been prepared, he goes to one of the tobacco curing barns, where the tobacco seedlings are raised. The plants are given free to the villagers, who are, in return, obligated to sell the grown tobacco leaves to this same barn. Often the curing barn owner conducts a contest by offering a cash reward of several hundred baht to encourage careful planting of the seedlings.

One young man in Ku Dæng was planning to plant one *rai* of land with one thousand tobacco plants, for which he hoped to get at least 1 baht per plant when the tobacco was ready for harvest. There is much money in

---

[17] Theme 2: Profit.

tobacco, but it also takes heavy work to get a good harvest.[18] Perhaps this is one of the deterrents for more extensive tobacco cultivation.

After the soil has been prepared, the seedlings are planted a foot or two apart. Water must be carried from specially built wells to water the small plants every morning and evening. At first the plants must be covered with large leaves or with straw to protect them from the burning sun. Finally, they must be protected from insects, since only a perfect leaf brings full value when sold.

People who do not plant tobacco will invest their time and effort in vegetable patches, where they grow cabbage, cucumbers, peppers, tomatoes, and other vegetables, which are readily salable in the markets. Some people grow entire fields of one kind of vegetable, while others cultivate many varieties in small quantities.

Another significant secondary crop is garlic, grown extensively in this region, although primarily in areas outside Ku Dæng. The fields are prepared as for soybeans except that the raised strips of field are somewhat wider (80-100 cm.) and higher, so that irrigation water can drain into the small ditches between the seedbeds. Sprouting garlic bulbs are then planted in the beds and covered with rice straw to maintain an even moisture and protect the small sprouts from the rays of the sun. The harvested garlic is tied up in bunches and either sold immediately or dried for later sale. In 1984 the price of garlic was very low. One kilogram brought only 17 baht, as compared to 35 baht per kilo the previous year.

February:

The last of the "in-between" crops to be planted is peanuts. Fields used for this purpose are either prepared with a hoe or, in a few cases, with plow and buffalo. Beds one to two feet wide are prepared along the entire length of the field. Irrigation water is permitted to run between these beds, from where it can easily be "shoveled" on to the growing plants.

Both peanut and soybean seeds have to be bought in the market. They cannot be kept from the time of the harvest for the following year's planting. Some people in other parts of the country, we were told, plant peanuts and soybeans on a year-round basis, thereby being able to use their own crop as seeds. Part of such a crop is then sold as seed for use elsewhere in the country.

A few days before the seeds are planted, the peanuts have to be shelled. This task is usually assigned to the daughters of the house. In the evenings, the girls shell the peanuts in a comfortable place in or under the house. Usually, one or several young men appear on the scene to visit and

---

[18] Theme 2: Profit.

help with the peanut shelling. This provides a ready means for courtship under acceptable conditions.[19]

The profit from peanuts and from soybeans seems to be about the same. Soybeans are sold "on the bush." The merchants take the soybeans and boil them before selling them in the markets.

Peanuts have to be processed by the villager before the crop is sold. Often they are used as a speculative crop. For example, a villager may buy several bushels of peanuts in the shell. He then shells them and resells them, hoping thereby to make a profit.[20] One young villager spent 100 baht in 1954 to buy eight baskets of peanuts. Together with a friend he spent three days grinding off the shells. When he sold the peanuts in the market, he netted 9 baht profit. He said he would never try it again.

There seems to be no special reason why the farmers in Ku Dæng prefer growing peanuts to soybeans. There is more labor involved in growing peanuts, but, on the other hand, there is more of the peanuts that is useful than in the case of soybeans: the shells and the greens can be used for growing mushrooms or as feed for the cattle.

March:

In March, those fields that were not planted with peanuts or tobacco are prepared again for rice planting. The procedure is much the same as that for the main crop. This time more than half of the rice sown is of the non-glutinous type, which is more profitable, while the first crop was mainly for home consumption.

During this month most of the soybeans and vegetables are harvested, as well as the tobacco that goes to the curing barns. Younger leaves or other varieties are cut later for the villagers' own use.

End of April-May:

The peanut harvest begins the last week of April. First, the main part of the foliage is cut off with a sharp knife. Then the stalks with the peanuts on the roots are pulled out of the soil and washed in water between the rows, "so that the soil stays in the fields and is not carried home to the house." Then someone, usually one of the women, carries the bundles of peanuts back to the farm. In one case, a young man was helping another to harvest peanuts. Since the fields were near the helper's farm, he kept the foliage to feed to his cattle. Occasionally, it is plowed under. There is some recognition of the nutritious value of the foliage for the soil. One farmer told us that he grows peanuts or soybeans every year; otherwise, the rice crop would not be very good. It would grow tall with very little grain.

---

[19] Theme 3: Fun.
[20] Theme 2: Profit.

42

At the farm, the peanut bushes are beaten over the side of a basket, so that the peanuts drop into the basket. An alternate method, frequently observed, is to pluck the peanuts off individually. The remaining stalks, and usually the foliage as well, are piled up in the farmyard for mushrooms to grow on when there is sufficient rainfall.

The peanuts in the shell are then spread out on bamboo mats to dry in the sun. Several of the villagers owned homemade shelling machines, which they rented out to others as needed. These shelling machines consist of heavy wooden or concrete disks, which rotate over a heavy wire screen. The disk is turned either by a simple handle or by an elaborate system of ropes and levers, providing considerable mechanical advantage. One section of the disk is cut away where the peanuts are poured in. The shelled peanuts drop out at the bottom together with the smashed pieces of shell. This machine is usually operated by a man. Women pick up the mixture of peanuts and shells on a woven tray and throw them up into the air in such a manner that the shells fall on to the ground, while the peanuts remain on the tray. Occasionally, this work is carried on at night, presumably to save time, but also because it is cooler than in daytime. We were never able to determine the exact reason for any kind of night work. There did not seem to be a pressing need to finish certain types of work by a given deadline. The recreational value usually seemed paramount, especially when young people of both sexes were involved.[21]

June:

The harvest of the second crop takes place very quickly. Within four weeks all the rice was cut, threshed, and, in most cases, sold. Most of the second rice crop had been planted within a short period of time and, hence, could also be harvested quickly. There is not much time to extend harvesting of this crop, since the ground must be prepared for the next crop.

The procedure of this harvest is nearly identical to that for the main crop. Most of the rice is harvested while the fields are still under water. The workers stand in several inches of water when they are cutting the grain. Occasionally the farmers are caught by heavy rains with their rice cut but not yet threshed. When this happens, they have to pick up the rice immediately, even in the middle of a storm, and carry it to a dry place, often alongside the road. Such work, though unpleasant, is usually carried out with much frolic by the young people, with whiskey flowing freely to keep the workers warm.

When the rice is brought in, it is often held for several days or even weeks until the price is good.[22] Some farmers, in need of immediate cash, will sell as soon as the harvest is finished.

---

[21] Theme 3: Fun.
[22] Theme 2: Profit.

As soon as the rice is harvested, the fields are prepared for the main crop. Almost everybody burns his straw in the fields. It would be too cumbersome to carry it home, where they still have plenty from the previous harvest. The ashes from the straw are useful as immediate fertilizer. Long-range effects of plowing in the straw are not realized by the farmers. Indirectly, this is achieved, to some extent, by the plowing in of the remaining stubble, which is usually knee-high. Some farmers plow as soon as they have sufficient water in their fields. Others will first cut the stubble with special knives on long wooden sticks, which they swing over their heads to cut the straw near the base. Some villagers cut the stubble only near the edges of their fields. One farmer told us that it took him six hours to slash one *rai* of land in this fashion.

The agricultural cycle is thus completed. The work does not seem excessive at any time. The farmers are content to obtain the results they do with the amount of labor expended.[23] There seems to be no particular desire to increase productivity by an increase in labor.

Domesticated Animals

Animals play a relatively minor role in the village economy. The buffalo and the bullock once were important animals. Approximately 68% of the households in 1953 owned at least one buffalo or one bullock. Some farmers had as many as eight head of cattle. The average, however, was two cattle per farm among those who possessed any at all. Both oxen and buffaloes were used for work in the fields. Buffaloes were preferred for their greater strength, but bullocks seemed to respond better to the work. Most buffaloes and some bullocks have names given to them, usually referring to their color. We were told that there was no other significance to the names than that it made the task of calling them home from the fields easier. Some of the cattle did not bear any names at all.

Because of the widespread use of tractors, water buffaloes are rapidly dying out in Ku Dæng with less than twenty head in the village today. Even though the initial cost of tractors is higher, the villagers prefer using them, because they are faster and do not need attention after work. The number of bullocks has remained constant at ten over the thirty-year period of our study. They are occasionally still used as draft animals for oxcarts. But even this utilization has been replaced almost completely by the use of pickup trucks.

Cattle were bought and sold quite freely. They did not form an integral part of the family, with sentimental attachment, as was the case in other parts of the country. If someone offered a good price for a buffalo, it was sold.[24] One could always buy a new one. Occasionally, an animal was

---

[23] Theme 1: Utility.
[24] Theme 2: Profit.

being raised by a child and thereby received recognition as a pet, being kept on the farmstead indefinitely without being sold. This, however, was the exception.

When a buffalo or a bullock died, the meat was sold. The death of an animal had to be reported to the *kamnan* immediately. In some cases, he sent to the district office for an official to inspect the animal, to see whether the meat could be sold. At other times, the *kamnan* simply told the owner to bury the carcass. In every case that we witnessed, whether the *kamnan* had given permission or not, the meat was butchered and sold. The villagers will not buy the meat of an animal that has died in their own village, for they are afraid of disease. The meat was usually sold in some distant village, where the facts were not known. In like manner, villagers from elsewhere would sell their animal meat in Ku Dæng. The skin of the dead animal was cut up and sold as food. The skin as a whole was very valuable for the production of leather, but the government prohibited selling or possessing hides. During and after World War II, slaughtering was restricted and strictly controlled by the government because of a shortage of cattle throughout the country caused by the Japanese occupation of Thailand. In 1953 only one buffalo or one ox could be slaughtered on any one day by a licensed butcher. If hides had been allowed to be sold freely, much abuse could have resulted, since a person having a hide could easily have said that his buffalo had just died. A farmer at that time could get about 200 or 300 baht for the meat of a dead buffalo, which alive would have been worth a thousand. Thus, it would not have been very profitable to kill an animal clandestinely.

Most households raise two to four pigs, the work being done mostly by women. Piglets are bought from roving tradesmen or in special "pig markets" in Saraphi or Chiang Mai. Here, again, it is more a case of speculation in the price of the pigs than one of raising them until they are fully grown for sale.[25] Feed for pigs continues to be made up of traditional materials: rice bran, papaya, and banana stalks, all boiled together and then laced with scientifically produced feed or vitamins available in the market. There is considerable labor connected with preparing this feed, almost all of which is done by women with an occasional helping hand from the men. A woman may buy a pig of any size, if she believes the price is right. After she has fed it for a while, perhaps for as little as four weeks, someone may pass by and offer her a good price. In that case, she will sell the pig immediately. The next day she may buy another one the same size as the one she just sold, but for a lower price. Pig raising is a type of savings investment for the villagers, which includes relatively high risk. Disease or a falling market for pigs may reduce the villager's realization to less than her investment. The profit belongs to the woman who raised the pig. She usually puts her

---

[25] Theme 2: Profit.

savings into an earthenware jar, a method considered safer than the use of bank accounts, which have not yet become popular among the rural people. The women also raise ducks, keeping them primarily for the production of eggs, which may be sold in the market. Chickens are also raised, but less for the eggs, which they lay occasionally, than for the supply of meat for unforeseen guests or special occasions, such as after-harvest dinners. Chickens are permitted to roam freely about the farmyard, picking up food as they find it, not infrequently from the stored grain in the rice bin.

Nearly every household has one or more dogs, which are kept as watchdogs to warn of approaching strangers. Few dogs in Ku Dæng are known to bite; they usually are only good barkers. The dogs are generally well kept and cared for. Most of the dogs in the village are male. We were told that the Ku Dæng villagers do not like female dogs. Occasionally, when one of the few remaining bitches has a litter, the female puppies are taken and set free in a distant village so that they will never find their way back. One can only speculate that other villages pay the same courtesy in return to Ku Dæng. The male dogs in the village frequently are castrated. Such dogs grow larger and are better watch dogs, according to our informants.

A few houses keep cats. Even though cats are supposed to be held in high esteem, because of the service they are said to have rendered the Lord Buddha when he was bothered by rats, there does not seem to be a general love for these animals. When a cat dies, it frequently is buried under a longan tree. This is supposed to bring better and larger fruit.

Investment of Money

The wealth of the villagers rested almost entirely in real estate until there was a gradual shift in the mid-1970s. In the 1950s, whenever a villager had some extra money, he would invest it in land. If he needed money for building purposes or special occasions such as funerals, he might sell some of his land, or more likely, he would borrow, using his land as collateral. In 1953 the richest man in the village owned thirty-two *rai* of land with a value then of approximately 100,000 baht. Toward the end of the year, he built a new house worth, perhaps, 50,000 baht. Including movable property he had, this man, if he had sold everything, would have had less than 200,000 baht, which certainly did not amount to being rich by any standards. In their younger years, the farmers usually concentrated on buying land. When they had ten or more *rai* of land, they began thinking about building a new house, unless they had inherited a large one from their parents.

Today, the economic life of the village is still rooted in agriculture and supplemented by cash earnings from labor or entrepreneurial activities. However, reliance on traditional methods of rice cultivation has gradually been supplemented by an increased awareness of the importance of cash crops like *lamyai* and by utilization of modern technologies in rice planting, new strains of seed rice, crop rotation, use of tractors and of fertilizers. All of these have contributed to a higher level of income for the farmers. This has resulted in a higher standard of living, manifested in material possessions such as radios, television sets, motorcycles, and cars.

Money was never kept in large quantities. It was better to have a barn full of rice than to have much money lying about in the house. In 1953 only the teacher and one other villager had accounts in the government savings bank, a branch of which was located in Saraphi, the only bank outside the cities of Chiang Mai and Lamphun in those days. Today, there are branches of many of the commercial banks in such district seats as Saraphi.

The teachers, of course, had a relatively large cash income, with which they could buy land if they did not deposit it in a savings account. The head teacher had taken out two life insurance policies, one with the government, and one with a private company. He paid a premium equivalent to nearly three months salary for both policies, each of which had a face value of 10,000 baht. He told us that all of his money would go to his children in case he should die. They were at that time living with his wife, from whom he was separated.

Most villagers would like to have much money, if they could get it in an easy way. As a result, the national lottery is very popular. People often put their meager resources together to buy a single ticket. Small amounts are won quite frequently. In most cases the individual share in the prize is small, since so many people have joined in buying the ticket. Illegal lotteries of property, such as bicycles, or, in more recent years, motorcycles, also find subscribers in the village. In 1954 one of the novices in the temple won an almost new bicycle in this manner. He sold it for 750 baht. Another villager won a bicycle on a 2.50 baht ticket. The owner of the bicycle was not willing to let him have it, even though his number had won. When the matter was taken to the *kamnan* for arbitration, the lottery seller was told to pay the winner 250 baht. Both parties had to agree, otherwise the *kamnan* would have taken them to the district office, where both would have been fined for participating in an illegal lottery.

The publication of the national lottery numbers in the local newspapers is avidly followed by most villagers. Many of them talk about what they would do with the money if they were to win first prize. One of the village leaders said that he would give 10,000 baht for repairing one of the roads leading into the village; then he would buy himself a house in the city; and, finally, he would buy some valuable land north of Chiang Mai. Other villagers said they would like to make a trip to America if they won first prize.

Some money, even in 1953, was spent on modern implements. A few sewing machines were found in the village in those days. There were more than forty bicycles in Ku Dæng. Many gadgets were bought for the bicycles, such as mirrors, bells, flags, or speedometers. Modern furniture was beginning to appear in the richer households. Glass was being used in some of the newer homes for small sections above the main parts of the windows.

As early as 1953 there was already considerable evidence in the village of an increasing demand for consumer goods, which had been absent from the scene only a few years earlier.

With the advent of electricity in the early 1970s, demand for cash increased rapidly. Today almost every home has a television set, and there are more motor vehicles than there are households. The demand for such goods is changing the money habits of the people and has contributed to a drive for greater productivity and innovation, which in turn has made more cash available for investment in property other than land.

Trade, Home Industries, and Other Pursuits

Trade in Ku Dæng has three aspects: the marketing of produce in the daily markets in Saraphi and elsewhere; second, the production of artifacts and goods by the villagers for sale to others; and third, the trade of traveling salesmen or itinerant merchants.

Most of the villagers have small vegetable plots. Produce from these gardens is usually taken to the market in Saraphi, three miles distant, or to one of the other markets about equally far away (see map 2). Some of the women go to the market every morning. In the 1950s, they had to rise well before daybreak to reach the market on foot just when it began to be light. They were back in the village by 8 a.m. Today, nobody walks to the market anymore. The women still go there, but the mode of transportation is either by motorcycle or bicycle.

Various kinds of food, such as meat or fermented tea leaves, must be obtained in the market. It is, therefore, customary for the women to go to the market frequently, even though they may have nothing to sell. Sometimes a woman goes to a small rural market some distance from the highway to buy fairly large quantities of vegetables, such as onions or garlic. Back home, she then divides the vegetables into small bundles for sale in the big market at the highway the following morning. In this way, she can easily realize 100% profit.

Some women are experts in making condiments and different kinds of dessert. Two women in Ku Dæng took such homemade snacks every morning to a small market in the next village, where they sold as much as 10 baht worth per day, a fairly considerable sum of money thirty years ago. Thus, even in those days, there was a significant amount of small trade going on in and out of the village.

There were three stores in the village in 1953. One was only seasonal and opened when work in the fields was slack, or when there was a big festival at the temple. The owner of the biggest store went to the market every day to buy supplies. He made a small profit by buying a dozen of a kind, such as pencils, and then selling them one at a time. None of the shopkeepers made their entire living in this way. They all owned land or worked in other people's fields for their rice. Today, the number of shops has increased to seven, but their characteristics remain much the same as during our original field study.

Some villagers are craftsmen making articles for sale. The temple leader produces high-quality fireworks and drums. The head monk is a carpenter, as is the head teacher. An old man is renowned for the rattan mats he makes. Another makes water dippers out of coconut shells. Some of the women sew clothes for themselves or for others. Some make mattresses for sale. One woman operates a weaving stool and makes Karen-style shoulder bags. Thus, there are a variety of skills that the villagers utilize in their spare time to earn some extra money. Many of the small-scale industrialists work according to demand. Others make large quantities of their articles and take them to the city for sale. In many cases, these skills are more like hobbies than occupations; this was especially true for some of the wealthier villagers, who still produced minor articles, even though this could not possibly have added much to their income.

In 1987 a new home industry was observed in Ku Dæng, which, apparently had been introduced within the previous two years. This was the production of frames for making water jars, *khantok* tables, stands for such tables, and a type of ceremonial drum. The bamboo is bought from elsewhere, perhaps the Fang district or Lampang province. It must be carefully selected, since only long, straight sections can be used for cutting into thin strips, which are left in the sun to dry. The strips are then woven into the body of the item being produced and held together with latex and nails. After two or three days drying in the sun, the product is taken to the city for sale to finishing shops at 200 to 250 baht per item. There it is sanded down, lacquered, and decorated with gold paint according to demand. The finished product brings four to five times what the villager was paid. While this endeavor seems to be quite profitable, it still is only a part-time occupation for villagers otherwise engaged in agriculture.

Many of the things necessary for everyday life are unavailable in the village. If a person needs them, he or she has to go to the market in Saraphi or the city. However, there is another source. Seldom does a day pass without some itinerant merchant passing through the village, hawking his wares at the farms. At the beginning of the rainy season, a merchant comes to sell umbrellas, which he carries in baskets at the end of a carrying pole balanced on his shoulder. Others bring cloth, earthenware pots, cooking utensils, clothing, knives, scissors, teakwood boxes, rice baskets, or medicines. These merchants may be Chinese, Indian, or Thai, although the Chinese seem to predominate. They usually travel in pairs or larger groups, starting from their own village or from towns as distant as Lampang and going from village to village until their stock is exhausted. City pharmacists occasionally come with loudspeakers and cassette players (phonographs in former days) mounted on pickup trucks, vans, or occasionally even on pedicabs—to sell their wares. These, however, are the exception, since most peddlers bring only what they can carry on their shoulders. These merchants form an important source of supply for the villagers. The quality of the goods is usually not very high, but neither are the prices. If the villager goes to the city, he will first have to pay for transportation and then, as likely as not, be cheated by the merchants.

In general, it seems that the Ku Dæng villager can live a rather independent existence. He grows the rice he needs; he has his own vegetable garden; he raises his own meat supply and catches his own fish. Some of the things he needs are brought to him by itinerant merchants, some he buys in the market. His existence seems to be quite independent of the economy of the country as a whole.[26] If the price of rice drops, he may not like it, and he may make a little less profit than usual, but his basic means of existence will not have been materially changed. Not much will cause him to exert himself to earn a little more. If something strikes his fancy as worth having, and if it is only slightly beyond his means, he probably will increase his efforts. If it is, however, completely beyond his means, or too much trouble, he will only dream about it, perhaps buy a lottery ticket, but never make any serious effort to increase his earning power.[27]

In conclusion we may say that the economy of the village remains basically agricultural in nature, even though technological and scientific changes have been introduced. The lifestyle of the villagers is still relatively simple, and income is predominantly generated from agricultural pursuits.

---

[26] Theme 4: Individuality.
[27] Theme 2: Profit.

3

THE FAMILY

The family structure in Ku Dæng tends to reflect the predominant theme of utility. There is no extended family of the usual type found in China or India. The nuclear family is modified, however, in some instances by the joint residence of in-laws. Whether this is matrilocal or patrilocal in nature depends on the situation in each case. If it seems more convenient to live with the husband's family than with the wife's, then the bride and groom will live there. Often it is more expedient to establish a separate household immediately.

Residence

Out of 261 married couples living in Ku Dæng in 1953, only 24.2% lived with their parents-in-law (either husband's parents or wife's parents). This figure cannot be considered an accurate measure of in-law residence, since it includes sixteen cases where a couple was living with a widowed or separated parent-in-law. Under such circumstances, the younger couple ran the household for all practical purposes, even though the parent-in-law was officially listed as "head of the household." If these cases are excluded, the percentage of married couples living in households with both parents-in-law is reduced to 14.3% of the total number of married couples in the village. There was no household where more than one son-in-law or one daughter-in-law lived with the family.

It is clear that the extended family, where it does exist, is thus of a very limited nature. Furthermore, in most cases the joint residence continues only for a few years after marriage of a young couple. Usually the last married child and spouse remain indefinitely in the parental home that they eventually inherit. There are, however, no definite rules laid down for this procedure.

There is a decided tendency toward matrilocal residence, again tempered by utility. According to our census of 1953, fifty-five of the 325 married people in Ku Dæng (or 16.9%) were born outside the village. Forty-one of these were men (74.5%) who had moved to Ku Dæng to live with their wives. It can be assumed that these men lived with their in-laws until they established their own households a few years after marriage. We can project this percentage to the whole population of Ku Dæng and conclude that more than half the newlyweds live initially with their maternal parents-in-law, but later, in more than 80% of these cases, establish their separate residences.

The figures on the married villagers born outside Ku Dæng give an indication of the extent of endogamy practiced in choosing marriage partners. In fifty-five cases, which represent 34.2% of all married couples, the spouse was chosen outside the village. This does not include the single case where both husband and wife were born outside Ku Dæng and, presumably, immigrated at a later time in their lives. Out of these exogamous marriages, forty-one (74.5%) involved native-born girls of Ku Dæng who married men from other villages. Most of the marriage partners were chosen from neighboring villages. We found only one case of a man born in Central Thailand, who was already living in a village near Ku Dæng when he met his future wife and moved in with her family after they were married.

We may conclude, then, that marriage in Ku Dæng is predominantly endogamous, but when it is exogamous, three-fourths of the marriages are matrilocal. There are no rules governing the type of marriage or residence. General practice and circumstances point in the direction outlined above.[1]

In case of separation—which is usually equivalent to divorce in Ku Dæng—children stay with their mother and her family. Most separated marriage partners continue on friendly terms, especially if there are children. If the ex-husband has moved back to his parents' house, the child or children are occasionally brought there for a few days or weeks and taken care of by the paternal grandparents. In one particular case, the separated wife's parents came to visit the former husband's parents to plead for the husband's return. It seems that the husband was a good worker and that his former parents-in-law were in need of help for their fields. The wife's parents succeeded in bringing about a reconciliation, and the estranged husband moved back to his wife's house. Such instances of reconciliation, however, are rare.

In 1953 there were two types of houses in Ku Dæng, each reflecting the owner's economic situation. In an opportunity sample of 113 of the 167 houses in the village, forty-nine houses (43.4%) were found to be of wooden construction with all but one having clay tile roofs. The one exception was a new house covered with corrugated zinc. Some of the wooden houses were as much as forty years old. Mostly, however, the wooden structures were built more recently, reflecting the owner's increasing economic wealth. The remaining 56.6% of houses were of bamboo construction, some made entirely of bamboo, others built on wooden posts with floors and walls of bamboo matting. Sixty-three houses had straw roofs, which are good for two or three years before they must be renewed. One house had a leaf roof.

---

[1] See Howard K. Kaufman, *Bangkhuad: A Community Study in Thailand* (New York: Locust Valley, 1960); Herbert P. Phillips, *Thai Peasant Personality* (Berkeley: University of California Press, 1965); Gehan Wijeyewardene, "Some Aspects of Rural Life in Thailand," in *Thailand: Social and Economic Studies in Development*, edited by T. H. Silcock (Durham: University of North Carolina Press, 1967); and Sulamith Heins Potter (1977).

More than half of the houses checked had relatively good sanitary arrangements. Out of a random sample of twenty-two houses, only six (28%) had no toilet facilities whatsoever. Of the remaining 72%, half had cement toilets with attached septic tanks; 12.5% were locally made wooden structures with a zinc pipe running to a covered hole in the ground behind the toilet; 37.5% consisted simply of wooden footrests above holes in the ground. Actually, the number of people not using toilets at all was probably less than these figures indicate, since some of the households were sharing toilet facilities. Twelve (54.5%) of the houses had enclosed bathrooms in the yard or behind the house. Elsewhere, the people bathed by the well or took a bucket of water into the backyard or behind the stable.

Courtship and Marriage

Marriage is generally brought about by courtship of the young people. There are practically no arranged marriages without the consent of the persons involved. The usual custom is for the young men of the village to visit eligible girls at night in their homes. This custom seems to be long-standing, since it has entered into the Lanna Thai language. When young men go out on moonlit nights, they will say—when questioned—that they are going *æo sao*, to visit the girls. There is no equivalent expression in the Thai language, which may indicate that this particular custom is distinctive of the people of Northern Thailand.

When the couple have fallen in love and agreed to get married, the man asks his parents to go to the girl's parents to ask for her hand in marriage. When agreement has been reached, the wedding is set, provided the families are reasonably well-to-do. Otherwise, the young man simply moves in with his new wife without a wedding ceremony whatsoever. It is the general, but not universal, practice in Ku Dæng for the bridegroom to give a present to his bride before they are married. This may be a *rai* of land or a lump of silver. There is no fixed rule governing these gifts. They do not constitute a "bride price." A poor man can marry a girl from a rich family, if the two agree. Even if the girl's parents do not approve of their prospective son-in-law, they cannot prevent the marriage. The young couple simply runs away from home. After some time, usually as little as ten days, the couple returns and the parents-in-law have to accept the *fait accompli*. There seldom is a wedding festival in such cases.

One elderly villager told us that courting regulations were much stricter in his day than they were now (in 1953). When he was a young man, it took nearly a year of courtship before a couple would come to an agreement. Nowadays, he said, the young people will sleep together after a very short time, either at home or even at work in the fields. If it takes place at home, the parents usually have full knowledge of what is going on. That this practice cannot be too widespread is indicated by the small number of illegitimate births recorded in the village. There had been only four in the years prior to our 1953 study, according to recollections of several villagers including the midwife. The latter informed us that for as long as she could remember, there had been only three or four requests for abortions, which she had consistently refused, even though much money was offered. Nearly all the first-born children whom she helped deliver were born at least one year after marriage, and often later than that. These figures are supported by statistical information regarding the length of time after marriage when a first child is born to a couple, indicating that there is either some form of pre-marital sterility or very little or no pre-marital sexual intercourse. In lieu of · more definite medical data on the first hypothesis, I would support the second.

One villager related a custom with regard to pre-marital intercourse that may have been the rule in former times but seemed to be refuted by the facts mentioned above. A young man comes to visit a girl at night. During his stay, he will *phit phi*, the meaning of which seems to range from a simple embrace to sexual intercourse. The following morning the girl asks a relative to tell her parents about the *phit phi*. Her parents send a message to the parents of the young man, suggesting that he pay some money for the *phit phi*. If the young man wishes to marry the girl, he asks his parents to take 12 baht to the girl's parents, where the wedding will be jointly planned. This is called *sai ao*. If he does not wish to marry the girl, he sends 24 baht together with a message saying that he is not interested in marriage. This is called *sai sia*, and in this case he may not visit the girl's house again.

Occasionally, convenience marriages, or marriages for money, take place in Ku Dæng. A 17-year-old girl from a large family married a 55-year-old man who had never been married and who had once been a patient in a mental hospital in Chiang Mai. The girl came from a poor family where everybody was crowded into a small hut. This was her chance to leave a poor environment. The man owned three *rai* of land and had a house of his own, all of which he gave to his bride in return for her marrying him. This is another example of how expediency coupled to a profit motive outweighs all other considerations.[2]

The Household

The average household size in Ku Dæng was 5.0 in 1953. We did not have definite figures on the average size of a nuclear family. However, in a sample of family statistics of sixty-eight couples, widows, or widowers of over 45 years of age, we found that they had had a total of 344 children, or 5.1 per family, of which 109, or 31.7%, had died, leaving 235 living children, or an average of 3.5 children per family. Two couples who never had children were included in this sample. In those days the number of children

---

[2] Theme 1: Utility and Theme 2: Profit.

born into a family was quite high. Because of the malaria control already mentioned, as well as increased availability of modern medicine, there was a noticeable decline in infant mortality, although the only figures available were those cited in chapter two. There seemed to be no specific premium on large families. The economic condition of a family had much to do with the number of children desired. A farmer with large holdings of land would have wanted many children to serve as his labor force. Poorer villagers were content with fewer children. One young couple, who had just had their third child, asked us whether we had some medicine for avoiding further children. Thus, it is not surprising that, with a declining infant mortality rate, family planning and population control took hold so successfully (see appendix B).

There is no specific seat of authority in a household. According to Thai law, the husband of the property-owning couple is the head of the family. There seems to be no trend toward either patriarchy or matriarchy. Both husband and wife have authority over their respective sections of the household. The husband supervises the field work and tells his sons and sons-in-law, and sometimes also the women, what specific tasks have to be done at a given time. Even here, though, a strong individuality is exhibited by the villagers.[3] Usually the farmer uses his authority sparingly. The members of the family generally know what is required of them at a given time. When young men working in the fields were asked who told them to do a particular task, the inevitable reply was that nobody told them; they just knew what had to be done.

Work related to the first rice crop, which supplies the needs of the household for the entire year, is carried out by everyone for the common good. Later crops are usually the property of the one who grows them. Thus, if a brother and sister join in planting a field of tobacco, they rent the field (or secure it from a relative for nothing), obtain the seedlings from the tobacco curing barns, prepare the field, plant the seedlings, and nurture them to full growth. Any profit is then their own. Similarly, if a woman wishes to raise a pig, she asks no one's permission, but just goes ahead doing it. This does not mean, of course, that a person will do anything regardless of the wishes of other members of the household. The husband may want to raise a cat to control the mice that eat the grain in his barn. He will not get a cat, though, if his wife objects to cats because they eat the dried fish she has labored to prepare.

Generally, relations within a household are good. We noticed very little quarreling among members of the same family. Once in a while we heard of a case of family trouble. One of our neighbors seemed to be in the habit of beating her 17-year-old daughter when she would not do the work she was supposed to do. We heard of a young man in another village hitting

---

[3] Theme 4: Individuality.

his brother over the head with a stick. Most such troubles are not related to family life. They seem to stem from disagreements while people are working or from quarrels while the participants are under the influence of alcohol.

The family may eat together or not, whatever is more convenient at the moment.[4] The Northern style of eating glutinous rice makes it unnecessary for all members of a family to eat at the same time. The rice is cooked early in the morning and then stored in a wooden keg. Members of the family help themselves whenever they are ready to eat. The side dishes are prepared two or three times during the day. Since their "heat" derives from peppers, curries, and chili, rather than from the stove, it does not matter when they are eaten. Male and female members of a family eat together if they happen to be ready at the same time. There seems to be no prohibition against eating together. When there are guests, the women usually eat after the men. At a farewell party for us, the *kamnan* had invited a few villagers to dinner, including the one woman teacher in Ku Dæng. She was the only woman to eat with the rest of us.

A person may live with relatives for some time, if circumstances warrant it. He or she will be treated like any other member of the household. After he had separated from his wife, the head teacher lived with his uncle for some time. Even though he ate all his meals there, he did not have to pay anything to his uncle. During harvest time, he was expected to help in the fields, provided he could spare the time from his duties at school. Orphaned children are taken in by relatives as a matter of course, without any thought of compensation.

Visitors are always welcome. Woven mats are brought out to sit on, unless there are Western-style chairs available. If the visitors are older people, betel-chewing paraphernalia is offered to the guests. If they happen to arrive around meal time, they are, as a matter of course, encouraged to eat with the family. If a visitor should come while the family is eating, the food will be put aside while the guest is in the house, unless he or she joins the family in the meal. Guests from other villages may come and stay overnight. Most families have some extra mattresses, which are spread out for guests, even at the expense of sleeping space for members of the family. Hospitality is regarded as a virtue. Whenever food is served to guests, it must always be more than can possibly be eaten. It would be embarrassing to have one dish cleaned up entirely. Friends and neighbors often brought us fruit or special sweet dishes. Even though there were only two of us, there was invariably enough for ten.

In the evening, the whole family usually sits around whatever light is available. In 1953 this was, at best, the light from two or three kerosene lanterns. More likely, it would have been small oil lamps or, perhaps, even

---

[4] Theme 1: Utility.

just candles. With the advent of electricity in the 1970s, every house had at least one light bulb in one or two rooms. Perhaps the 19-year-old son will have gone *æo sao*, but his absence may be compensated for by some other young men who have come to visit one of the daughters of the house. The younger children will most likely be practicing their school lessons, chanting like the novices in the temple.

One evening we came to the *kamnan's* house to find the entire family of eight sitting in the main room. The youngest son was playing songs on the wind-up gramophone; two daughters were embroidering; and father and mother were just talking and chewing betel. A generally harmonious atmosphere pervaded the room.

Someone may tell stories in the evenings or read aloud parts of sermons or passages from books. There are some tasks, such as the shelling of peanuts or preparing garlic bulbs for planting, that can be done at leisure in the evening hours. Casual visitors come to help with these small tasks, chatting the while with the person they are particularly interested in, or with some other member of the household, if their prime object of attention seems to be otherwise occupied or not at home. During the cold season, people go to bed early, but throughout the major part of the year, family members sit up until midnight or later.

General friendship and hospitality is made evident through the extension of kinship terminology to persons outside the family (also see appendix D). The extended use of the terms for father, mother, and grandparent is referred to below.[5] Likewise the term for uncle—*lung*—is used for men generally older than the speaker, who have come into a special friendly relationship. Persons ouside the family are pointed out to little children as "uncle so-and-so" or "auntie." Although in some cases we served as threats to little children, with subsequent dire results, we usually were called by the affectionate term for "uncle." We were not able to determine any specific reason why one person was consistently called "father," while another of the same age was always referred to as "uncle." In many cases, the term of address "father" or "uncle" had actually become part of the name of the person, so that some of them never were called anything other than "Uncle Red."

Property

Property rights within the family are similar to those recognized in Western society. Each member of the family has his or her own property. After the first crop, one can strike out on one's own to try to increase

---

[5] See chapter 5, "Age and Sex Roles."

personal wealth.[6] If a man makes a fish trap, it is his; if a woman catches fish, it is her's; but she, most likely, will give it to the family for supper.

If a couple who live with the wife's parents decide to separate, the husband will be able to take only very little with him. He can take back any personal property that he brought along when he married the girl. However, he has no share in the fields, unless he bought some personally and established a clear title. If a wife leaves her husband, she, too, can take along only her personal property. In most cases the movable articles stay in the house where the couple lived, whether this is the paternal or maternal residence or neither.

When a man dies, his property is usually divided among his wife and children. We were not able to determine who received what proportion. Generally, a man makes a will before he dies, if he has time to do so. Such a will must be notarized by the district office. A man told us that his father had left all his property to his new wife, whom he had married just before he died. His children got nothing. Usually, though, we were told, the children of the first marriage inherit everything. If one of the children of a deceased man already has a fair amount of property, he or she may refuse to take any inheritance, prefering to have it go to one of the less fortunate of his father's children. Usually a bigger-than-average share goes to the youngest or whoever stays at home. This person is considered to have sacrificed time and individual freedom to stay on the parents' farm and help with the work. It seems, therefore, only fair to the villagers that such a person should inherit more of the property than the rest. We have here, in other words, a modified ultimogeniture system.

An inheritance tax must be paid on the land one inherits but not on the house or movable property. When Mr. Khieo died, his heirs were supposed to pay 7 baht per *rai* for all twelve *rai* of land he owned.[7] His children went to the district office and pleaded with the officials to reduce the amount, which finally was done by setting the tax at one-half the usual rate.

Childhood

From early childhood, the Ku Dæng villager is trained toward or accustomed to individuality and self-reliance. A child is coddled during his first few years, while he is the only one in the family. He is breast-fed until the next sibling arrives. In the case of the last-born child, this may continue for several years. We observed a 3-year-old boy, able to walk and talk, sucking at his mother's breast. A villager told us that some children

---

[6] Theme 4: Individuality.

[7] See chapter 9, "Buddhist Views Towards Life and Death in Ku Dæng."

continue in this fashion until they are 10 years old. This, however, was not observed.

Children acquire independence and a sense of responsibility from an early age.[8] They usually have to take care of one or more younger siblings—unless, of course, they are the youngest. A child assigned to a slightly older one for safekeeping is taken along wherever the older sibling goes. The baby is usually carried on the other person's hip, even if the older child is not much bigger than the one being carried. As children grow older, they follow their big brothers or sisters to work. Back home they may fashion simple toys to imitate the older people at work. They will make small threshing baskets or fishing nets, with which they pretend to work like the grown-ups.

When children are 7 years old, they have to attend school. According to the law, compulsory school attendance is required from 7 to 14 years of age, or until the child has successfully passed the fourth grade, whichever is earlier. Although the law has been changed twice since our first study of the village, once to require seven years of education, and the second time reducing it to six, the government has not been able to enforce this level in all parts of the country. The effect of compulsory education at least to fourth grade is quite evident in Ku Dæng, where almost all of the villagers by now are literate, whereas in 1953 only those under 38 years of age could read and write, unless they had been monks or novices.

---

[8] Theme 4: Individuality and Theme 5: Communal responsibility.

4

EDUCATION

Traditional education in Thailand was from its inception in 1257 A.D. that of the temple, with monks acting as teachers.[1] In 1283, King Ramkhamhæng, the third king of the Sukhothai period, introduced the Thai alphabet, which has been used with minor changes to the present day. For six centuries the curriculum consisted of the reading and writing of Buddhist scriptures in Pali as well as in the vernacular. An informal system of education was kept alive through the temple. Some of the monks who entered the temple as novices remained to make a lifetime career as learned and devoted teachers. Mostly, though, the level of achievement was not very high. The universal ideal for every male to enter the monkhood soon after the age of twenty for a minimum period of three months was widely practiced. The goal that he should achieve some degree of literacy further strengthened the important role that the temple schools played in providing the Thai nation with the rudiments of a universal and homogeneous education, albeit only for the male members of society.

General Educational Organization

The mid-19th century saw the establishment of so-called modern schools in Thailand, first through the efforts of Protestant missionaries, who had come to Thailand as early as 1828, and who had initiated classes at the King's request inside the palace for daughters of royalty and nobility. Later, actual schools were established separately for boys and girls. In 1837, Rev. Daniel Beach Bradley, a Presbyterian missionary, set up the first printing press, which was instrumental in speeding up the development of education in Thailand.

The Ministry of Education and Ecclesiastical Affairs was established by King Chulalongkorn in 1892 with the objective of making education more consistent and more effective. The system set up at that time has since been changed at least five times. The latest plan, called "Thailand National Educational Scheme 1977," is in effect at the present time (1984).

---

[1] Material in this chapter on the Thai educational system has been compiled from W. J. S. Thompson, "Integration of a Mission School System in Thailand," (1951) typescript; Joint Thai-U.S. Task Force on Human Resource Development in Thailand, *Preliminary Assessment of Education and Human Resources in Thailand* (Bangkok: Agency for International Development, USOM, 1963); *Current and Projected Secondary Education Programs for Thailand* (Bangkok: Educational Planning Office, Ministry of Education, 1966); *Thailand National Educational Scheme 1977* (Bangkok: Ministry of Education, 1977); and various other Ministry of Education publications in the Thai language.

At the beginning of formal education there is an optional period of one to three years of pre-school education. This may be organized as formal or as out-of-school education. It may take the form of a nursery school, a child care center, classes for small children, or kindergarten. Sometimes this form of education is referred to as primary-preparatory school—*triam prathom* or *mun*.

Elementary education formerly consisted of four compulsory grades. In 1960 this was increased to seven grades, hoping, thereby, to increase the minimum level of education. However, this turned out to be mere wishful thinking, since the rural population did not accept the necessity of having their children stay in school this long. In 1977, primary grades were reduced to six, followed by secondary school, also of six years in duration, divided into a three-year lower and a three-year upper level.

At the end of each level of education, the child may leave school and enter a vocational stream. Under the 1977 scheme this type of education is identified as "special or welfare education," an unfortunate use of these terms since it stresses division of class by occupation in condescending terminology.

The upper secondary division is organized on a credit system in contrast to earlier educational schemes that followed a class system of success or failure in all or nothing. A grade point average of 1.0 on a 4-point scale is required for graduation. While this seems low, it stands in contrast to the high selectivity in entrance examinations administered by all institutions of higher education except for the two open universities, Ramkhamhæng and Sukhothai Thammathirat.

According to the 1977 National Educational Scheme, compulsory education continues to a certain, somewhat flexible age. Each district of the country is to determine the minimum and maximum age for a child to receive compulsory education, which will vary according to local circumstances. Nationally, the child is not required to attend school before the age of 6 but must do so not later than age 8. "The State will accelerate compulsory education as stipulated in this scheme to cover each and every district."[2]

In most rural areas only the first four years of elementary education are effectively compulsory. A law passed in 1921-22 requires attendance in school from 7 to 14 years of age, unless the person has passed the fourth grade successfully at an earlier age. According to the 1960 Plan of Education, the government was trying to extend general, compulsory education to the full seven years of primary education. While this plan was more or less successful for the urban areas, it failed to achieve implementation in rural settings. Although considerable advances in education at all levels were observed in Ku Dæng in 1984, the fact that the local school in

---

[2] Ministry of Education (1977), p. 40.

this village still only goes to the fourth grade is an indication that agricultural people continue to consider education necessary only to this level.

The following table illustrates the development of education at the various levels over a period of nearly twenty-five years.

	1961	1974	1984
Lower elementary division (Prathom 1-4) (P1-3)	3,717,000	5,906,600	8,363,250
Upper elementary division (Prathom 5-7) (P4-6)	375,900	4,347,100	6,155,129
Lower secondary division (MS 1-3) (M1-3)	253,100	668,900	1,003,350
Upper secondary division (MS 4-5) (M4-6)	65,320	96,200	453,617
All levels of higher education	37,534	55,370[3]	156,000[4]

A student normally enters the six-year primary school at 7 years of age. Before this, the child may, if the parents wish, attend a "preparatory" class for a year or two to help get a head start on reading. Many of the bigger schools in the cities will not accept students for the first grade unless they already know how to read. As a matter of fact, most of the better schools, which have waiting lists for new students, will base their selection on entrance examinations that test the students' ability to read. These preparatory classes are very widespread. True kindergarten schools are much rarer. In recent years, better ones have been opened, a few on a nonprofit basis; they are generally replacing strictly "preparatory" schools. In the Sixth National Education Plan to be in force from 1987 to 1991, considerable stress is being laid by the government on the development of pre-school education. In rural areas, formal education usually starts with the primary grades. In Ku Dæng, however, there is now (in 1984) a pre-school nursery for which a room in the school building has been set aside. The villagers conduct this enterprise themselves. Daily activities resemble those of a daycare center rather than those of a school.

On completion of the first four years of primary school, the pupil takes a government examination, which in recent years has been administered in rural areas by the district education office. A pupil who passes is eligible to continue with two more years of primary school, possibly in a different locale. This is the case in Ku Dæng, where primary education goes only through fourth grade. Moving to another school may require passing a

---

[3] Not including students in the "open" universities, for which statistics were not available.
[4] There were an additional 1,150,000 students enrolled in the "open" universities.

new entrance examination, since available space in most schools is less than demand requires.

At the end of sixth grade, the pupil must take another uniform government examination. If successful, the student may then enter the lower secondary education stream. As an alternative, the student may enter a vocational school for "special" or "welfare" education. This type of school provides skills for effective living in rural Thailand.

Completion of ninth grade is the terminal point for the majority of high school students. At this point, if the young person chooses not to stop, upper secondary education will provide preparation for university entrance. Alternately, vocational or trade schools of advanced standing are also available. Of the relatively small number of students that do continue beyond lower secondary education, most prefer to enter the pre-university preparatory stream. Vocational schools at this level provide effective technical training of a high caliber.

Those individuals who are among the few students that pass the entrance examination to the upper secondary division must choose whether to pursue the arts, the sciences, or the general curriculum. Successful passage of the three-year course entitles one to take the entrance examinations to the various institutions of higher learning in Bangkok, Chiang Mai, the Northeast, or the South. On the whole, the science course is the most difficult of the three, and students are advised to pursue the arts or the general curriculum if they are not strong in mathematics and physics in the lower secondary division.

An effort is made by this overall program to provide an education suited to the mental capacity of all students in the kingdom. Practical vocational courses are provided at every level of the ladder for those individuals whose ability does not permit them to continue up the road of academic studies to its summit at the university. The final steps are purposely made difficult to insure that only the more competent finally secure a university education. An idle educated class has traditionally been undesirable.

One of the consequences of this program, however, is its subordination of the vocational program to the academic. Consequently, a student in a vocational school is automatically one who could not make the grade in the regular academic program. This stigma is probably at least as important as the traditional Thai dislike for physical labor in the relatively unsuccessful vocational program. This factor is also recognized in the recommendations of the UNESCO mission that studied the Thai educational system in 1949.[5]

In 1951, a pilot comprehensive secondary school was set up in Chachœngsao province with the help of UNESCO. In 1960, the first permanent comprehensive secondary school was established in Korat, and a

---

[5] United Nations Educational, Scientific, and Cultural Organization, *Report of the Mission to Thailand* (Paris: United Nations, 1950).

Committee for Comprehensive Schools was established in the Ministry of Education. By 1966, comprehensive high schools were expanded with the help of a team from Canada to include twenty model schools offering industrial arts courses alongside regular college preparatory courses in the same school. This system was later expanded to include schools in almost all provincial capitals, while the same scheme was being tried in *amphœ* schools at the lower secondary level to include agricultural and home economics courses. This support of and stress on vocational education in the regular stream courses has further tended to downgrade the already lowly-esteemed, vocational school stream, while within the comprehensive schools themselves the prestige continues to reside in the college preparatory sections.

By 1977, the concept of vocational education in parallel with an academic stream was incorporated into the general school system of the country in the National Educational Scheme of that year: "The State shall promote extensively vocational education in harmony with the economic and social conditions of the country. On the one hand, it is perceived as part and parcel of every educational level; on the other, it is a discipline in its own right, with the emphasis being laid upon agriculture and agriculturally oriented industry."[6]

There are four governmental bodies that concern themselves with education: 1) the National Education Council was established in 1960 and is directly responsible to the Prime Minister's Office. This council is charged with educational policy-making at all levels; 2) the Ministry of Education is responsible for administering most levels of primary and secondary education, both private and government, developing the curricula used in the schools, and supervising all teacher training institutions;[7] 3) the National Economic Development Board is concerned, among other things, with present and future manpower needs, and, thereby, becomes involved in the training and preparation of students at all levels; and, finally, 4) the Ministry of University Affairs, established in 1972 as the Office of University Affairs, is responsible for supervision of government and private institutions of tertiary education.

The Minister of Education is chosen by the prime minister; and hence, his tenure depends upon that of the prime minister and his government. The Minister of Education in consultation with the entire cabinet determines the educational policies, a situation comparable to that of a State Board of Education in the United States. The Ministry of Education is divided into eight departments: 1) Elementary and Adult Education, 2) Secondary Education, 3) Vocational Education, 4) Teacher Education, 5) Physical Education, 6) Educational Techniques, 7) Religious Affairs, and 8) Fine Arts.

---

[6] Ministry of Education (1977), pp. 32-33, item #20.

[7] In 1965 all elementary government schools were placed administratively under the Ministry of the Interior.

Each department is headed by a secretary and subdivided into several functional divisions.

The chief educational officer of the Ministry of Education is the permanent secretary *(palat krasuang)*. He is the top-ranking administrator, and being non-political, he does not change when the minister is removed by the fall of a cabinet or at the whim of the prime minister. He is a civil servant, and thus his office preserves stability and continuity through various changes of political atmosphere. He is the executive who puts into practice the policies formulated by the minister of education in the council of ministers.

Under the permanent secretary are the educational commissioners *(süksathikan)* of the twelve educational regions of the country. These are followed by the provincial commissioners, one for each of the seventy-three provinces of Thailand. Finally, there are the district commissioners for each of the more than six hundred districts in the country. Each of these commissioners is accountable to the one in the next higher order of administration, although there are a few overlapping responsibilities. The educational commissioners have full authority over schools of all types in their respective administrative areas, with the power to settle matters of local concern and make decisions within the framework of the general directives issued by the Ministry, without reference to Bangkok. In some cases, the educational commissioners are titular principals of the government schools under their jurisdiction.

The system of education in Thailand, although attempting to place some initiative and authority into the hands of provincial school officials, is a highly centralized system of education, bearing some resemblance to that of France. It is very efficient in transmitting the directives of the central authorities to the schools throughout the kingdom. An order from Bangkok can reach every school within a matter of two or three days. Conversely, the system is slow in adjusting to variations in local conditions or in rectifying injustices. The 1949 UNESCO mission on education, in their very brief survey of educational conditions in Thailand, recognized this danger of over-centralization in their report:

> We venture the tentative suggestion that local committees might be set up to advise Governors and their educational officers. These committees should consist of people whose integrity as well as their knowledge of and interest in education are beyond question. In the beginning they should be nominated by the Minister of Education in consultation with the provincial Governor. At a later stage, if they prove their value, the elective principle might be introduced and they might be entrusted with some executive as well as advisory functions. Such a plan might prove to be adult education in itself of a most effective kind, since it would touch on community leadership along

very vital lines. Community participation may be extended still further later as the people acquire a greater and more competent interest in their own affairs; it might even extend to the levying of local taxes to supplement the national budget. The formation of Parent Teacher Associations should also be encouraged and given official recognition as a means of educating the common people for democratic living.[8]

Types of Schools

There are four categories of schools in Thailand, classified roughly according to the agency responsible for their support. In 1938 the Ministry of Education published a statement that was reproduced in the *Statistical Yearbook* of the Kingdom, which includes definitions of these four types of schools, which, for all practical purposes, still accurately describes the various types of schools as they exist in 1985:

a. Government Schools
Government schools are established and maintained by the government. They provide both general and vocational education. Only schools of general education have been established, in all provinces, according to the needs of the localities. This is due to the lack of funds, but next year the government will increase the budgetary allowance to the Ministry of Public Instruction, and consequently schools of vocational education will be established in every province.

b. Local Schools
Local schools are established according to the Primary Education Act. They are under the control of local officials and committees, and are organized in accordance with the educational policy of the Ministry. Such schools are called Local Schools Established by (District) Commissioners. Local schools are primary schools supported by the government.
There is another kind of local schools which are called Local Schools established by the Public. Such local schools are supported by the funds collected from the people in the districts. There are, however, very few such schools.
Besides there are Monastery Schools, which are founded by the collaboration of the monks and people in the districts. As local Schools Established by the (District) Commissioners, they are under the control of local

---

[8] UNESCO (1950), p. 25.

authorities. Monks and novices form the teaching staff of such schools, but lately the number of Monastery Schools has decreased, owing to the increase in the number of local schools and the absorption of monastery schools by local schools.

c. Municipal Schools

Municipal Schools are primary schools, which the municipalities have founded or which have been transferred from the care of local authorities to that of the municipalities. They are supported by the municipal funds.

d. Private Schools

Private Schools are established and maintained by private individuals or associations in accordance with the Private Schools Act (1936). Private Schools are divided into four categories:

1. Private schools that entirely conform to the Act;
2. Kindergartens;
3. Religious Schools;
4. Schools by correspondence.

Most private schools provide general education in accordance with the Government syllabus. A few of them are vocational ones.[9]

Education at Various Levels

As previously mentioned, primary education is compulsory through the first four elementary grades. A law passed in 1921-22 specified that compulsory attendance be from 7 to 14 years of age. The specification of a seven-year span for compulsory education undoubtedly anticipated the development of the 1960 scheme of education with the seven-year primary school instead of the previous four. However, it was evident in 1965 that a large number of students did not even complete their first year of primary work in the allotted time of seven years. In 1961, 30.4% of the students who had entered first grade had dropped out before completing the fourth grade. The tardy progress of students in rural schools must be laid to inadequate teaching, irregular attendance, and much repeating of grades on the part of students, especially in the fourth grade, where students must pass the government prescribed examination or its equivalent to graduate from the lower primary school. The figures cited below show that this situation improved dramatically during the succeeding years (to 1984).

---

[9] UNESCO (1950), vol. 20, section 8.

The 1977 Thailand National Educational Scheme modified the compulsory school requirement, taking a more realistic point of view than that mentioned above.[10] Elementary education (formerly referred to as primary school) was changed from the two-stage system to one taking six years to complete the course. Compulsory education was defined as "that which requires every boy and girl to attend school up to a certain age as laid down by law." Moreover, each district would henceforth determine the minimum and maximum age for a child to receive compulsory education, as long as such education does not begin before the age of 6 or not later than age 8. Thus, the total number of years of compulsory education was reduced from a theoretical seven grades to a still theoretical six grades. The number of pupils completing sixth grade, however, is rapidly increasing. A national standard should be attained within a very few years.

Children in the primary grades attend classes from twenty-six to thirty hours per week. Each period theoretically lasts one hour, but frequently teachers permit their students to study or play for a major part of the class period.

Required subjects taught throughout the four years include the following: morality (the life of the Lord Buddha and his teachings, manners, honesty, duty to family, other citizens, the nation, King, and government); Thai language; geography and history; nature study; hygiene; and drawing and manual arts. There are no data available on how much of this primary education "gets across" from teacher to child. The material is presented by the teachers and mostly is transmitted in the form of rote learning. What retention or comprehension takes place is unknown, except for what could be gleaned from the results of common government examinations still required in some schools.

One of the greatest problems faced by the government is the supply of educated teachers for the expanding elementary education system throughout the kingdom. While an oversupply of graduates of teachers' training colleges did exist in 1984, most available teachers try to avoid assignment to rural areas if at all possible. With nearly 70% of Thailand still in an agricultural category, we may conclude that in 1984 teacher supply continues to be a serious problem.

Great strides have been made throughout the kingdom in the years covered by the Ku Dæng study (1954-84). The UNESCO Mission in 1950 estimated that seven out of every eight elementary school teachers in Thailand lack adequate academic preparation for teaching, and a 1962 teacher survey of the Ministry of Education gives the percentages for unqualified teachers—those who have certifications for lower local and municipal schools and 48.6% for private schools in urban areas.[11] In

---

[10] Ministry of Education (1977), article 40.
[11] See UNESCO (1951), p. 21; *Teacher Survey A.D. 1962* (Bangkok: Educational Planning Office, Ministry of Education, 1962).

general, younger teachers tend to be better qualified. For example, in lower local and municipal schools, 46% of teachers with fifteen to twenty-five years of teaching experience are unqualified, while the percentage of those who have taught from five to fifteen years is only 32%.

Between 1957 and 1962, an estimated 42,310 teachers joined the teaching force in the kingdom. In spite of the expansion of the teacher training program during the previous ten years, a large percentage of those new teachers was still unqualified: 28.4% for lower local schools, and almost 60% for private schools. However, improvement continued both in government and private schools. In 1957, of those teachers who joined the teaching force of local schools, only 27% had Lower Teaching Certificates or better, while of those who became teachers in 1960, 84% were similarly qualified. Private schools were still able to accept unqualified personnel in the early 1970s, but the government required such teachers to be certified within a given number of years. Since 1977, unqualified teachers are no longer permitted to teach officially in any primary or secondary school in Thailand.

In the immediate post-World War II period, the Thai government was willing to leave a major share of secondary education in private hands. While in 1948 the enrollment in government secondary schools was 52% of the total, in 1962 it was 49.4%. The government's policy for many years was to set up "example" schools as standards, hoping that private schools would emulate them and thus multiply facilities. However, where low population level and low income make the creation of private schools impractical, and where local resources are inadequate for the job, the central government steps in to provide facilities of at least minimum standards. The objective of having at least one government secondary school in every province offering education through the twelfth grade was fulfilled by 1960, while twenty years later such schools existed in every district (*amphœ*) of the kingdom.

Regardless of efforts to decentralize most of the educational machinery, most of the first-class secondary schools continue to be concentrated in the capital or larger population centers. In 1963, the Bangkok metropolitan area had 186 secondary schools (*mathayom süksa* 1-5) to 811 for the rest of the country, a ratio of a little over 4 to 1, as compared to a population ratio of approximately 10 to 1. Chiang Mai province is generally considered high on the list of educational opportunity in Thailand, second only to Bangkok. In 1960, a medical school was established in Chiang Mai and elevated to full university status within two years. The first private university in Thailand, Payap University, was accredited by the Thai government in 1984. And yet, there were only sixteen secondary schools in the entire province. Furthermore, most of the educational facilities outside Bangkok are concentrated in the provincial capitals, with a few scattered in the larger towns that serve as administrative district headquarters. In the villages outside of these towns, there is very little secondary or even upper primary education available to the rural child.

Many villages are not so far from one of these towns that a student could not make the trip in and back on a bicycle or in a tricycle taxi. But the distance does deter most children, and the proportion that continue with secondary education in the typical rural village is very low. The children of most Thai villages find their formal education beginning and ending at the village or temple schools. There are exceptions, of course. Ku Dæng is one village where considerable progress has been made in the level of education reached by some children.

Secondary education is not yet compulsory in Thailand. As has been said above, the government has been struggling to advance the level of compulsory education even for as little as two years beyond fourth grade. Government policy has been to restrict the educational offerings above the elementary level, so as not to produce more of an intelligentsia than the country can support. Warning has been taken from India's experience of a large and somewhat explosive body of university-trained people without a base of mass education needed for an intelligent and informed public. The government of Thailand has always been resolved to promote primary education as a matter of policy. When that foundation has been laid, secondary education can properly follow. At the present time, any thought of compulsory secondary education would be premature.

Furthermore, the Thai government very realistically appraises its capacity to set up and maintain a large educational system at all levels. Without the financial resources of wealthier nations, Thailand prefers to give training that is believed to be adequate for intelligent citizenship for all children at elementary level. Funds for secondary education, when available, are allocated to selected schools that can provide the necessary quality of education to children who are likely to benefit from such instruction.

The relatively recent adoption and enforcement of compulsory primary education gives the country some years of breathing space before the large body of students so educated will be demanding substantially better education for their own children. Although this trend is already in evidence, demand for more advanced education is still mostly limited to the developing middle class in predominantly urban settings. In 1948, out of a total of 2,700,000 students in grades one through ten, 96.6% were in the four-year primary grades, while the remaining 3.4% were in classes of all types beyond this level. For 1961, the corresponding figures are 85.5% and 14.5%; and for 1974, they are 53.6% and 46.4%.

This reduction in the enrollment of students continuing in school is not due solely to the official policy sketched above. Lack of facilities accounts for part of this reduction in many districts. Although there are provinces where even government secondary schools operate below capacity, most cities and towns find their government schools filled, while the overflow keeps two or three private schools operating comfortably. In some cases, the student demand exceeds the capacity of all facilities available locally, and the students must go to other towns or provinces for secondary schooling.

A further factor is the reluctance of rural parents to have their children continue in school beyond the legally required period. If a boy is going to be a farmer like his father before him, or a girl is to be a farmer's wife, parents see little point in their child continuing to learn arithmetic, English, or other erudite matters beyond the fourth grade. The fact that the education is not required by the government is sufficient proof that it can be dispensed with. Many children who are doing well in the intermediate grades, are withdrawn by their parents, simply because they think that the children have had enough. Demand for education has not been a grass-roots movement in Thailand. It has been a program of the government.

Trends in Education from 1918 to 1948

To adequately understand the expansion of education that took place in Thailand from the end of World War I to the end of World War II requires more than inspection of statistics of that period. Insignificant as some of this data may appear from an American viewpoint with its much longer history and perspective, the figures for Thailand indicate tremendous development in responsible education within the span of a single generation.

Local public schools increased from 2,423 in 1918 to 18,066 in 1948. Student enrollment, similarly, increased from a little over 100,000 in 1918 to nearly two and a half million in 1948, with a corresponding teacher increase from 3,000 to 63,000.

The picture of the "average" elementary school in Thailand in 1948, taken from figures given by the Ministry of Education, was something like this: a local primary school had less than four teachers and enrolled 130 pupils, an average of about thirty-seven pupils per teacher; the municipal school had seven teachers and 247 students, with a class load per teacher of thirty-five students; the private school had just over four teachers, enrolled 145 students, with each teacher responsible for thirty-four pupils.

These averages, however, may be misleading, unless different situations in various parts of the kingdom are taken into account. An informant made a visit to a fine, new municipal school building in Nakhon Si Thammarat, where he was proudly shown an attractive one-story brick structure with a fine assembly room, a teachers' office, four nicely painted classrooms about twenty feet by thirty feet, and 102 children in the first grade in one room. They were sitting five to a bench in a solid phalanx from the narrow corridor on one side of the room all the way to the wall on the other side, and from the back wall to within five feet of the front wall, where the teacher had a portable blackboard on an easel. Though the period of instruction had long since started, the teacher and his class were not yet doing anything when the informant appeared. The children were simply sitting in their places. Possibly, they had been ordered to be on good behavior for the visitor's sake. Perhaps the teacher had not yet plucked up enough courage to begin his formidable task. At any rate, the children did not show any spirit normal for that age. Their passivity, crowdedness, and fearful meekness did not contribute to a healthy educational picture.

On another occasion, the same observer visited a local school in the compound of a northern village temple, consisting of a rectangular thatched roof on posts over a packed dirt floor, with a single blackboard on an easel. A single teacher presided over the school with about forty pupils in the first three grades seated four abreast on narrow benches with wobbly tables attached.

The average is useful and tells a story, but the extremes are often more revealing for an understanding of the conditions under which much Thai education is offered and for an appreciation of the really remarkable strides that have been made in some quarters against a background of such conditions.

Trends in Education in Ku Dæng from 1954-1984

The educational picture at Ku Dæng did not change materially in the ten years following our original study. By 1964 there were 120 pupils; the previous year there had been 128. There were still only four teachers, one with a Lower Teaching Certificate, two with Pre-primary Teaching Certificates, and one with no teaching qualifications. All four were in their second year of teaching at Ku Dæng.

Demand for education beyond fourth grade seems to have increased considerably since 1953. In 1964, eight children of Ku Dæng were studying in higher grades, five in the district and three in secondary schools in Chiang Mai. One of the latter studied nursing (post-tenth grade) at the government nursing school related to Chiang Mai Medical University (now the Faculty of Medicine of Chiang Mai University). The girls (6) outnumbered the boys (2) at this level of education.

In 1974, the demand for education had increased further. According to the principal, 25% of each graduating class (*prathom* 4) were continuing to higher grades in the *amphœ* or in Chiang Mai.

By 1984, population control had reduced the school population to forty-seven pupils, twenty-six boys and twenty-one girls. There are still only four grades, but the number of teachers had increased to five, with the principal being resident in a different village. In addition to the already small school age population, improved road transportation and the short distance to the district seat have contributed to some parents sending their children to the somewhat better schools in Saraphi and, in a few cases, to the city of Chiang Mai.

Educational results, as reflected in the percentage of pupils passing the fourth grade (*prathom* 4) final examination, seemed to reflect a policy of passing all students. The following table indicates no particular trend.

72

Results seem to follow the whims and actions of the local education officials rather than the achievements of the pupils.

Year	# in P4	# Passing	% Passing
1953	16	3	18%
1954	20	20	100%
1955	3	3	100%
1956	7	7	100%
1957	12	5	41%
1958	17	17	100%
1959	23	3	13%
1960	42	35	83%
1961	30	30	100%
1962	33	29	90%
1963	30	30	100%
1964	32	32	100%
1965	33	33	100%
1966	20	20	100%
1967	23	23	100%
1968	29	29	100%
1969	34	34	100%
1970	21	21	100%
1971	29	29	100%
1972	27	22	81%
1973	27	27	100%
1974	22	21	95%
1975	20	20	100%
1976	18	18	100%
1977	12	12	100%
1978	11	11	100%
1979	11	11	100%
1980	10	10	100%
1981	12	12	100%
1982	12	12	100%
1983	12	12	100%
1984	12	12	100%
1985	12	12	100%

The number of students enrolled in fourth grade follows the population trend as found in the 1953 study fairly accurately. A comparison with the histogram in appendix B shows that the 5-10 age group of 1953 would have been in fourth grade between 1953 and 1957; the 0-5 age group would have constituted the fourth grade population in the years from 1958 to 1962.

There is no evidence available from our study to explain the anomaly in student population in fourth grade for the years 1955 and 1956. In 1954 there were twenty pupils in P4 out of a total school enrollment of 103, while the 0-10 age group consisted of 190 children. By 1964 the percentage of children enrolled in school had remained constant at 54% of the 0-10 age group, with thirty pupils in P4. In 1984 the total enrollment had decreased to forty-seven children, which was only 41% of the 0-10 age group, with twelve pupils in fourth grade. While the decline in total number of school children parallels the successful family planning program in Northern Thailand over this period, the additional decline in percentage of children actually enrolled in the Ku Dæng school in 1984 must be attributed to other factors, such as improved roads, availability of transportation, and increasing demands for higher quality of education than that available in the village school.

The Ku Dæng Primary School

The specific case of Ku Dæng illustrates the general picture of the Thai educational system described in the previous pages. There seemed to be nearly 100% school registration for the 1953-54 school year in Ku Dæng. According to the head teacher and to the *kamnan*, practically all those children who were of school age, and who had not yet passed fourth grade, were in school. This was confirmed by our census figures. We found only two or three children who were not in school, or older ones who had never gone. Each of these children was or had been mentally abnormal. If some villagers would not let their child go to school, the *kamnan* would soon hear about it and summon the parents. If they were unwilling to enroll their child in school, even after a discussion with the *kamnan*, he would send them to the district office, where they would be fined. We were told that no villager had ever been dealt with in this fashion.

In former years, younger children could enter first grade as soon as their parents wanted them to. Since 1953, however, the district office has ordered the schools to enforce the Education Act by accepting only children after their seventh birthday. Younger children are still admitted to the Ku Dæng school, but they are no longer carried on the rolls.[12] In 1972, a day-care center for small children was established by the village development committee with full cooperation of the villagers. A room in the school was made available, and a teacher was hired, who was supported by the villagers with children enrolled in the center.

Children are not allowed to cut classes more than seven days out of each month, which consists of twenty-five to twenty-seven school days. If a child is absent in excess of this number, a report is made to the *kamnan*, who, in turn, informs the district office. The parents are then called to the district

---

[12] Theme 1: Utility.

and reprimanded. If there is still no improvement in attendance, the child is told to leave school and try to study elsewhere. Since this seemed to contradict the compulsory school law, we asked what happens to parents who do not let or make their children go to school. The answer was that there are no such parents, and hence the problem has never arisen.

In 1953, there were 103 pupils in the Ku Dæng school taught by four teachers; a fifth was added later in the year. The pupils' attendance was generally good. During the seven months of school, for which we kept records, the average daily attendance was 78.9%, well above the minimum that would be expected if every student had cut his maximum permissible number of days. The monthly averages ranged from a low of 73.5% in July to a high of 82.3% in November. Teachers' attendance also varied. Perfect attendance was rare; often only two were present to teach. When all the teachers were absent, which happened a number of times, school would simply be closed. This usually happened when all the teachers had to attend a teachers' meeting or go to some special function in the city. In 1953, school was held six days a week and closed on Sundays. On Precept Day (Buddhist Holy Day) school is open as usual. This is in accordance with government regulations. The situation seems to differ from that at Bang Chan, a village in Central Thailand studied by a number of scholars from Cornell University; in Bang Chan school closed on Buddhist Holy Day but remains open on Sunday. In 1984, it was observed that the Ku Dæng school was in session only five days a week, conforming to official working days for government offices, which are closed on Saturdays, Sundays, and national holidays.

The curriculum and textbooks used are strictly prescribed by the Ministry of Education in Bangkok. Most of the learning is by rote. The children repeat what the teacher says or what they read in books. At home they practice the various chants that they have learned in school, while their younger siblings listen with rapt attention, occasionally trying to imitate their learned older brothers or sisters.

Until the year before our original study, general supervision from above was rather lax. Many of the pupils in fourth grade passed the exam-ination. The year that had ended just prior to our arrival was more strictly supervised. Examinations were not only set by the district but were graded by students from the Teachers' Training School in Chiang Mai. As a result, only three out of twenty-three students passed. For the district as a whole, the passing rate was 30%. Those students who failed the examination had to repeat fourth grade unless they were already beyond the compulsory school age of 14. A few children go on to fifth grade at a school near the highway, three miles from Ku Dæng. In 1953, this distance could be negotiated by bicycle during the dry season; when the rains came, the children had to walk. At that time only two children, a boy and a girl, were studying in seventh grade in Saraphi. No one in Ku Dæng, not even the head teacher of the local school, had ever gone higher than that. In general, there seemed not much desire on the part of the parents of the children or of the children themselves to pursue education to a very advanced level. The father of the boy enrolled in seventh grade had become successful through his own efforts; he wanted to have his son continue education as long as possible. In 1953 the Ku Dæng teachers, themselves, had reached only the seventh grade. Extension of the nation-wide compulsory educational system to higher grades was impractical at that time mainly because of a lack of qualified teachers. In the Chiang Mai area, the compulsory four-grade system seems to have been fairly successful, well enforced, and adequately staffed during the 1953-54 school year. Efforts to go beyond this level, although officially encouraged, have only begun to become more generally accepted and enforced since 1980.

Village schools in the Ku Dæng area have been co-educational since primary education became compulsory in 1921. Usually boys sit on one side of the classroom and girls on the other. When the children go into the *wihan* for religious instruction, they follow the usual sex differentiation observed in the temple: boys sit in front and girls behind. At play in the yard outside the temple, boys and girls rarely mix. Each group plays its own games in well-defined sex roles. After school, however, when the children are back home, boys and girls mix quite readily in their play around the farmyard.

Religious instruction is included in the school curriculum by order of the government. Every morning, after the flag raising ceremony, the children chant *(suat)* in their rooms. Similarly, each afternoon before the flag is taken down, school is concluded with a chant. Every Saturday afternoon one of the monks is supposed to teach the children the Buddhist Law. In addition, they are supposed to hear preaching in Thai twice each month. Neither form of religious instruction was observed regularly in Ku Dæng. For the half hour of instruction on Saturday afternoon, the monk used the "question and answer" book.[13] We attended one particular lecture for third and fourth grade pupils. The monk read the first ten questions with the corresponding answers directly from the book. This he repeated three times. When he had finished, he asked the first question again, "What is the religion of the Thai people?" Nobody in the class was able (or willing) to answer. Finally, the head teacher lent a hand by asking all the boys, one after another, until he finally came to one who could answer correctly, "The religion of the Thai people is Buddhism." One probable reason for this poor showing was that the monk did not have the children repeat after him, as is usual in rote learning. Had he done so, he might have found someone who could have given the correct answer.

The teaching is supposed to be in the Thai language. Neither Ku Dæng monks, nor pupils or teachers like to use the Central Thai language. They much prefer to talk in Lanna Thai, their native tongue. In earlier years

---

[13] Bhikkhu Panyanantha, *Khamtham-khamtop* [Questions and answers (regarding the Lord Buddha)], (Chiang Mai: Buddhist Association, 1953).

the teachers were permitted to use their own language, even though the books were written in Thai. But since 1953 a government directive has made the Thai language mandatory—at least as long as someone is listening. During the 1953-54 study we observed teachers using Lanna Thai almost exclusively, as long as we were only within earshot without being physically seen.

Once a year there is an official "Respect-the-teacher day" *(wan wai khru)*. Word came from the district to the head teacher on June 3, 1953, to hold this ceremony the following day. The pupils gathered eggplant flowers and Bermuda grass to present to the temple, since these plants grow easily and are thereby symbolic of education, which is to be absorbed easily by the children. The pupils also had collected 5.25 baht to give to the temple. At 10 a.m. the children and their teachers went into the *wihan* where the boys sat in front, the girls behind, and the teachers at the side. The head teacher lit incense before the Buddha image. After three prostrations by everybody, one of the boys led the other children in a chant. One representative of the boys of each of the four classes went to present a tray of flowers to the Buddha image. Then the head teacher stood up and delivered a speech. He explained that this was teachers' day, a very important day for the students. The pupils were supposed to respect the teachers, because they gave them their lessons. The person in the classroom is not the only teacher. Parents, friends, and relatives who teach one the secrets of life and other everyday matters are also teachers. Unless we have teachers, he said, we never will learn anything. That is why it is important to have teachers. At the conclusion of this short speech, the student leader again led a chant, which was written by an official in the Ministry of Education especially for this occasion. After the five-minute-long chant, the head monk entered. The children paid their respects in the usual manner, and the monk gave them the five precepts, which were repeated verse by verse.[14] Then he preached for a while, using material similar to that presented previously by the head teacher. He concluded by saying there were four ways in which to pay respect to a teacher: first, to carry out a ceremony like the present one; second, to follow and obey the teacher's rules and regulations; third, to pay attention to one's lessons; and fourth, to follow the ways and teachings that are presented by the teacher. If we follow these rules, we will have respected our teachers. With these words and a blessing the head monk dismissed the children, who returned to their regular tasks.

Other activities take the school children outside the village and bring them in contact with children of other communities. Each year an athletic contest is held in a school near the highway for the entire district. The Ku Dæng children practice for weeks prior to the event. Elimination races are held outside the temple. A girls' relay team from Ku Dæng won the competition in 1954.

---

[14] See chapter 7, "The Basic Elements of Buddhism in Ku Dæng," p. 114.

In the same year the children went to the biggest school in the commune for two other occasions: the first, to honor the memory of King Chulalongkorn (Rama V), the founder of modern education in Thailand; and the second, to honor King Vajiravudh (Rama VI), the founder of the Thai Boy Scout Movement. In both cases, flowers and wreaths were taken in memory of the two kings. These ceremonies are observed by all schools in the kingdom.

When a child leaves school, a boy will help his father with work on the farm while a girl will help her mother in the kitchen. Formal education has terminated. Informal learning by doing seems to be the general practice at this stage. A boy will go out into the fields with his elders and do what they are doing. Smaller boys learn from older boys in the neighborhood. Thus, the 14-year-old boy of one of our neighbors was the avid assistant of the 19-year-old son in our house who was making and setting bamboo fish traps. If a person wants to learn some specific task, such as carpentry, he will go and watch an expert and learn from him the secrets of his trade. As in the case of the temple leader, such learning may continue into old age.[15]

Education in Ku Dæng did not progress as might have been expected during the span of thirty years from 1954 to 1984 . Most of the villagers have still not progressed beyond a fourth grade education. As for higher levels of education, there are only two persons who have achieved bachelor's degrees, two with vocational certificates, and a rather small number who have finished either lower or upper secondary schooling. The number of children in school at all levels in 1984 was surprisingly small.

Those students who have finished fourth grade in the village school and who want to continue into secondary education must go to a school in the Saraphi district about five kilometers away. Bicycles or commercial minibus service are the means of transportation. Quite a few children are sent to secondary school in the city of Chiang Mai. With improvement of roads during the past ten years, transportation to and from the city has become very convenient, taking only about forty-five minutes one way. Studying in the city carries with it considerable prestige. Thus, even those parents who do not have their own transportation to send their children to school can make use of daily commercial transportation at relatively low cost. The prestige factor outweighs the inconvenience of studying away from home, even though the facilities in the village are quite satisfactory and the teachers are qualified according to standards set by the government.

Literacy and general education in Ku Dæng is mainly dependent on age. Older villagers, those over 55 years of age, generally have not benefited from formal education; some of the men have had education as novices in the temple, while some of the women have been able to glean some educational benefits from their yearly periods of residence in the temple during Buddhist Lent or the rains retreat. The middle age group, namely,

---

[15] See chapter 8, p. 150-152.

those between 31 and 55 years of age, have mostly completed the compulsory four-year primary education in the village school. Many of them are functional illiterates, since they have not made use of their knowledge of reading and writing after leaving school. When they were children, their parents did not greatly value education. They looked upon children as prospective labor in the fields; transportation to more advanced schools was difficult; and financial resources were not sufficient to pay for further education. The youngest age group, those under 31, shows a marked increase in the level of eduation attained. This is due to better communications, an increased awareness of the value of somewhat more advanced education, the government's decision to increase compulsory education to at least the sixth grade, and peer pressure to continue with secondary, vocational, and higher education. Thus, it can be said that in 1984 educational expectations for the children of Ku Dæng was higher than ever before.

5

AGE AND SEX ROLES

A wit once said that half the population of America and half the population of Thailand should be exchanged for half their lives, for in America highest honors are accorded to young people, while in Thailand a person has to wait until old age before acceptance as a leader is possible. This may have been true traditionally for large parts of Thailand. It may still be true for the situation in the extended family, but it hardly is true when one considers status and prestige in a community such as Ku Dæng. It is quite obvious that young men and women are not accorded the external respect that a septuagenarian receives; yet such a person can hardly be called the leader of the village. In general, it was observed that leadership and prestige rested in persons in their 40s or 50s.

On the surface much obeisance is still paid to the older person. This is as much true in 1984 as it was thirty years earlier. Older people sit in front of their sex-differentiated groups in the temple. At special events in the homes, such as house-blessing ceremonies or funerals, the older men are always given the seats of honor at the head of the room, farthest away from the door. An element of expediency can be discerned in this practice: it is ingrained into Thai etiquette to lower one's head below that of a person higher on the scale of age or prestige, even if the lowering is done only symbolically. If the older person sat near the door, every newcomer would have to bend low to pass by. Thus, it is far more convenient to have the elders sit away from the door, which is thereby held free for others to enter unhindered.[1] When several people walk together through the village, the older person always walks at the head, followed by others in descending order. In the homes, the older people usually eat before the youngsters, and although this rule is not universally followed, a father is frequently found eating with his son.

In all of these cases there is a further division according to sex. In the temple, the men sit in front, the women in the back part of the *wihan* or the *sala* or wherever an event takes place. The same is true for special occasions in the home. The main room of the house is always reserved for the men. The women crowd into the bedrooms or the hallway to the kitchen or even into the kitchen itself. The *wihan* is usually so arranged that there is a door that divides the hall into sections for males and females respectively, so that the men do not have to pass through the rows of women or vice versa. When groups of people walk together, the men precede the women, each

---

[1] Theme 1: Utility.

group automatically arranging itself in descending order by age. At home women usually eat after the men, although exceptions are often observed.

This general, overt pattern of age and sex differentiation is broken by the children, who may usually be wherever they please. When a group of people walk together, the children may walk at the head of the procession or run in between the adults or walk behind. At home, children eat before, at the same time, or after the others. At formal occasions, an attempt is made to keep small children in check, but usually there is not much effort expended in this direction. In the temple the children usually are kept with the women. When a child reaches school age, he or she is expected to learn to conform to the generally established age-sex pattern of adults.

These general behavior patterns are not, however, without exception. A person of real or apparent high prestige, of whatever age, is given the seat of honor in place of an older person. Thus, the *kamnan* is always accorded the privilege of sitting in front of the room or near the front of the *wihan*. Visitors, such as American field research workers, were seated with the *kamnan*, or, in his absence, with the older people in the particular gathering. If such a person insisted on sitting in a less exalted position in the room, even after repeated urging on the part of his hosts, the result was that late-comers would sit down behind him, and the space in front would remain empty. At one time we were walking home past the school house just as school let out. Usually the children run and chase each other home with considerable shouting and laughing. This time, however, there formed an unusual procession: the children ran as usual until they came up behind us; then they quieted down and followed us at our normal, casual pace. Very soon all of the hundred school children were stretched out in a long line behind us. This procession was only broken up when we stepped into a farm house entrance, thereby releasing the children to their usual frolic.

The leadership in the village is in general in the hands of the middle-aged people. Shortly after our initial arrival in the village, the *kamnan* called a meeting of the village leaders. Of the fourteen men present, the average age was 51; only four men were less than 50. The *kamnan* himself was 52 years old, and by the time he reached 53 would have been *kamnan* for nineteen years. He felt that he ought to retire, because he was getting too old for the job.

With the help and advice of several community leaders we made out a list of thirty-six villagers to whom we gave a set of prestige rating cards (see appendix F). This list included both men and women. The average age of this group was 47. Here the age factor seemed subordinate to other considerations. The second man on the list, for example, was the junior monk, 24 years of age. The two oldest men were both 66 years old. One of them rated number five and was described in such terms as "kind-hearted," "always helpful," or "active in temple affairs." The other man was rated fifth from the bottom and described as "immoral," "frequently drunk," and "lazy." However, age did have some influence in general. All those younger than the average age, with the exception of the two monks, were in the lower half of the list.

Most of the active leadership in village affairs is carried out by middle-aged men and by a few women of the same age group. Older men are usually too feeble to be very active in enterprises that require physical stamina. They still assist with a large number of tasks. Thus, the position of temple leader can be carried by an old man, since it requires leadership in devotions at the temple, which are more vocal than physical in nature. When cooperative work is done, such as building roads or bridges or repairing irrigation canals, the middle-aged or younger men assume the leadership or are assigned to the particular task by the villagers.

Most of the labor connected with the regular tasks of the agricultural year is carried out by people in the lower, middle-aged group. When a man has reached his 40s, he usually feels he has reached the age at which he can "retire" from the normal chores of tilling the fields, provided he has a fairly large family and sufficient land. He will send his children to do the job, while he himself stays around the farmyard, still doing a full day's work of less heavy physical labor, which can be done at leisure. He will make baskets, prepare food for the pigs or cattle, work in the vegetable garden, or even build a new addition to the number of buildings on his farmstead. The age at which a farmer starts to retire from the fields varies, of course, considerably, depending upon several circumstances. By and large, this situation did not change materially over the thirty years of our observation. The reduction in family size due to family planning is beginning to have an impact on the division of labor, inasmuch as it depends on children working together with their parents. Nowadays hired labor is somewhat more common than it was thirty years ago, in part due to the reduction in family size.

Kinship terminology gives some hints as to the relative importance of age and sex differentiation. Siblings are generally not differentiated by sex but rather by age. In the immediate family one refers to one's older siblings or younger siblings, who are, respectively, older or younger than Ego. The terms "older" and "younger siblings," however, are further extended to children of one's parents' siblings of either sex. In this case the age differentiation is that of the siblings of the parents. Thus, all the children of a parent's older siblings become Ego's older siblings, regardless of whether they actually are of greater age than Ego or not. Similarly, either parent's younger sibling's children become Ego's younger siblings. In the next descending generation, not only the sex differentiation disappears, but also the age differentiation. All children of Ego's siblings, his wife's siblings, and the children of his own children are uniformly referred to as grandchildren (lan). It is thus quite possible to have a "grandchild" who is older than Ego (in Western kinship terminology, this would mean that uncle is younger than nephew). In ascending generations there is some sex differentiation, but only for the parents' older siblings. The parents' younger siblings carry a uniform term.[2]

To this point, sex and age differentiation are identical for Thai and Lanna Thai kinship terminologies. In the third ascending generation, the Thai distinguish grandparents and their siblings by sex and by matrilineal or patrilineal lineage, while the Lanna Thai do not. To a lesser extent, age differentiation occurs by the addition of the words "great" or "small." In ordinary usage these suffixes are dropped. In the Lanna Thai language all sex and lineage differentiations disappear. Every grandparent is uniformly referred to as *ui*. There is some minor age differentiation as in Thai, but it is used only if this type of information is specifically requested.

Extended kinship terminology is a clue to the relative value attached to age. In Ku Dæng and elsewhere in Northern Thailand, according to informants native to the various provinces, old people are generally called *ui*, whereas middle-aged people are called "father" or "mother " *(pho* or *mæ)*. There are quite definite age limits within which these terms are used. A person under 40 years of age is seldom called "father," except by his own children. Similarly, a person has to be in his 60s before he or she will be called *ui*. In general, older people seem not to be too eager to be called *ui*. The prestige accorded old age does not seem to be sufficient to counteract the feeling that one has reached the age where one is considered more or less useless and relegated to the role of playing with the grandchildren. Two neighbors, both in their 60s, differed in age by only two years. One of them was a tall, well-built person, who did not give the appearance of having reached the age of 60. The villagers generally called him "father." The other man was small and frail, with wrinkled face and completely white hair. He was invariably called *ui*. When talking with others, he usually referred to himself as "father" rather than *ui*, indicating that he resented being called by the term denoting older age. Perhaps he compared himself subconsciously to his neighbor. Other old people were also observed to respond with the term for a younger person when addressed as *ui*.

A comparison of the Cornell Field Research study of Bang Chan in Amphœ Minburi and Amphœ Bangkapi near Bangkok with results obtained at Ku Dæng showed that the sex differentiations were not the same for the two communities.[3] Some activities absent in Bang Chan were present in Ku Dæng and vice versa (see appendix B, "Age and Sex Roles"). Some of the more striking examples: Women could plow or harrow the fields in Bang Chan, whereas they never did in Ku Dæng; male midwives, noted in Bang Chan, were absent in Ku Dæng; sewing and making netting was done exclusively by women in Bang Chan, whereas men predominated in this task in Ku Dæng; women of Bang Chan did not ride bicycles, whereas there

---

[2] Also see appendix D, "Kinship Terminology," for complete kinship terminology in both Thai and Lanna Thai.

[3] Sharp, et al., *Siamese Rice Village* (1953), pp. 94-98.

is no sex differentiation for this activity in Ku Dæng. Many of these differences are due, of course, to different environmental circumstances. Ku Dæng lies in an essentially overland transportation system, whereas Bang Chan in the 1940s and 1950s was served almost exclusively by canal and river traffic.

There has been only a slight shift in sex roles during the thirty years of observation. While some activities have become more specifically sex differentiated, on an average there is slightly more equality in the various activities recorded in 1984 than there was in 1954.

It can be said with some certainty that there is less sex differentiation among the people of the North than among the Thai of the central plains. This becomes evident by comparing usage in the Lanna Thai language with that of Thai. In the language used in Northern Thailand, there is practically no differentiation between usage by the sexes, while in Thai there is a decided difference. Personal pronouns are, in general, identical for all the residents of a Northern Thai village. A high language exists for addressing royalty or high personages from outside the village. Since no descendants of nobility make their abode in Ku Dæng, all villagers address each other by the same set of terms. In Lanna Thai there is only one so-called "polite" word added to the end of phrases or sentences and used by old and young alike. In Thai, on the other hand, there are different polite words depending on the age and sex of the speaker. Personal pronouns are either not used at all in Lanna Thai or replaced by personal names or titles. Sex differentiation is introduced through the use of Thai in the Ku Dæng school. Such language usage is generally reserved for contact with outsiders, who are expected to know only Thai. If such a person speaks Lanna Thai, all reserves are dropped, and he or she is accepted as one of "our own."

Sex differentiation is most pronounced in the field of religion. The Lord Buddha established an order of nuns with his foster mother as the first ordained member. He established this order mainly at the urging of his chief disciple, Ananda, but only reluctantly, "because it would soon destroy the unity of the family life of the Indian peoples, and this would cause much trouble and dissension among the monks."[4] These nuns were called *phiksuni* (Pali, *bhikkhuni*). Today there are no *phiksuni* nuns in Thailand.[5] One monk told us that nuns were not able to keep a monk's precepts. Furthermore, there was a rule that a nun could not leave the temple without being accompanied by a monk to protect her from danger. As time went by no monk was willing to undertake this duty. As a result the order of nuns was abolished. Before the nuns left the order, they gave the monks as a token of their esteem one special garment, *pha camlong,* a vest slung over one

---

[4] Bhikkhu Khemo, *Phutthasatsana kü arai: kham-tham kham-top 300 prakan* [What is Buddhism?: 300 questions and answers] (Bangkok: Buddhist Association, 1935), p. 76.

[5] Bhikkhu Panyanantha (1953), p. 37.

shoulder and tied around the waist; from that day on, monks have worn this special garment. There is an order of women devotees in some parts of Thailand today, who wear white robes, shave their heads and eyebrows, and may give the precepts and accept offerings from the faithful. They are required to keep the ten precepts for novices. These women are called *yai chi* or "ordained grandmothers," not *phiksuni*.

Buddhism was introduced into Chiang Mai in 1331 A.D. by Phra Uttarathera and Phra Sobhanathera ten years before Ayutthaya became the capital of Thailand.[6] In the six hundred years since, male emphasis in Buddhism has undoubtedly left its mark on the population in general. There are many indications, however, that at least for Northern Thailand religious leadership even before the introduction of Buddhism was in the hands of men. In the vicinity of Ku Dæng, there were in 1954 and are today no women active in such religious or semi-religious practices as propitiation of spirits or traditional healing processes. Women do take a significant part in one spirit ceremony: they act as mediums through whom the spirits make themselves manifest to the male leaders of the ceremony. This does not seem to indicate any degree of leadership for women in religious affairs but rather their relegation to the inferior role of being possessed by a spirit.

Sharp has defined the monkhood as a "neuter sex" at the apex of the Buddhist system, followed by the male and then the female.[7] Actually, as observed at Ku Dæng, the monk's "maleness" is much less restricted than that of, say, a Catholic priest, who presumably enters his religious order for life, foreswearing sexual activities forever. Not so the Buddhist monk. He promises chastity only for the duration of his stay in the monkhood, which seldom is planned to extend for the remainder of his life. None of the younger monks of Ku Dæng or neighboring temples, who were questioned on this subject, would say how long they were planning to stay in the monkhood, neither would they say that they were staying for life. The uniform answer to our questions was, "I am not sure." Furthermore, a monk or novice, who feels he cannot keep the precepts, especially the one relating to chastity, will leave the temple, but in later years it is possible for him to be reordained and resume life in the yellow robe.

Traditionally, Buddhism has emphasized a "spiritual maleness" rather than neutrality of the sexes. The spiritual man was ahead of both the physical man and the physical woman. This was one of the causes for Buddhist women to desire to be reborn as men, which was within their means of achievement if they had gathered enough merit in their present lives. The Pali texts give an example of a lady, Gopika, who abandoned

---

[6] See *Rüang Yanok* [The story of the Yanok] translated (from Lanna Thai into Thai) by Phya Prachakit Koracak (Bangkok: Buddhist Association, 1907).

[7] Sharp, et al., (1953), pp. 91-92.

woman's thoughts, cultivated the thoughts of man, and was reborn in heaven as a man.[8]

There seems to be no all-pervading desire on the part of women to be reborn as men in the next life. Women whom we questioned usually responded that they did not know how they would be reborn, but that they hoped they would have accumulated sufficient merit to have a "good" next existence, which usually meant being wealthy, regardless of sex. Male and female children are about equally desired. Families that have one or two small boys would like to have a baby girl next. One reason is that girls usually stay at home as they grow older, whereas boys are frequently away and in the end usually marry outside the village. On the other hand, girls bring their husbands home to take care of the farm and the girl's parents in their old age. One old woman had a son who said he wished to be a woman in his next life. When this son died, we were told, he was reborn as the daughter of the old woman's daughter but died before reaching maturity. The telling marks on the baby girl were her dark-colored hips, which looked like the man's tattooed "pants."

Apart from the monkhood, the structural leadership of the village religious life is in the hands of the men. The temple committee is made up entirely of men, although there is no rule to exclude women. Men may enter the *bot* during a ceremony involving the monks, women may not, although at other times they may do so.[9] This prohibition seems to have been adopted through Burmese Buddhist influence in the Chiang Mai area, dating from the various historical periods when Chiang Mai and Lamphun were under Burmese suzerainty. Terwiel reports from Ratchaburi in Central Thailand that ordination ceremonies taking place in the *bot* were attended by both men and women, both actively participating.[10]

Men offer food and gifts to the monks. At one time there were only women at the temple in the early morning to bring food to the monks. When we arrived to witness the morning offering of food, some of the women asked us to present the food to the presiding monk and request the precepts. When we declined the request, one of the temple boys, a lad of 12 or 13, offered the food to the monks, who chanted his acceptance. There were no precepts that morning, since that would have required chanting on the part of a male leader. When a woman wishes to make merit, she usually requests a man to present her gifts to the monks. Women may burn candles on their trays of flowers near the place where they squat or kneel during the

---

[8] Ananda K. Coomaraswamy, *Buddha and the Gospel of Buddhism* (London: G. P. Putnam, 1914), pp. 161-164.

[9] One of the buildings in the temple reserved for special ceremonies of the priests. Also see chapter 7, "The Basic Elements of Buddhism in Ku Dæng."

[10] B. J. Terwiel, *Monks and Magic: An Analysis of Religious Ceremonies in Central Thailand*, Scandinavian Institute of Asian Studies Monograph Series no. 24 (London and Bangkok: Scandinavian Institute of Asian Studies, 1975), pp. 186-217.

devotions in the temple, but only the men may go up and light candles at the base of the Buddha statue.

Aside from these official functions, women and men are about equally active in temple affairs. Food in the morning is generally brought by more women than men, especially at times other than Buddhist Lent.[11] At the longer services during Lent, the women usually outnumbered the men for the presentation of food, but later in the day, when preaching took place, the ratio was often reversed. At big temple fairs, both men and women helped in the preparation of food, with a man frequently acting as chief cook.

Today, sex differentiation is probably on the increase due to Western cultural influence. Formerly, men wore sarongs resembling the long skirts worn by the women. Today, men wear short or long pants, the sarong being worn only around the home when no heavy labor is being carried out.

Women, with the exception of some older ones, always wear upper garments. Various roles have been introduced that have become the exclusive concern of women. Thus, girls from time to time participate in beauty contests at district, provincial, or national fairs. These contests are invariably patterned on the Western style, and participants usually bring new habits of dress and behavior back to the village. The sewing machines in the village are solely operated by women. Some younger women have a considerable wardrobe of both local and Western dress. The invitations to the house-blessing ceremony of one of the leading villagers were issued in the name of his 19-year-old daughter, an unprecedented step in village life. Undoubtedly this acculturation to Western sex differentiation will continue, bringing an ever greater number of specific sex roles to the village.

---

[11] The rainy season retreat, usually beginning the end of July and ending the end of October.

6

GOVERNMENT

Government control over the affairs of the villages in Saraphi District generally conforms to that in other parts of Thailand. Indeed, agriculturally dominant village life observed throughout Southeast Asia exhibits many of the characteristics of political structure found here. There are two distinct types of control: first, that of the national government, usually authoritarian in character, if not in actual design; and second, that of the popularly elected or selected leaders of the local community. In Ku Dæng the two types of governmental control meet in the leadership of the hamlets and the villages. The elected officials are usually also appointed by the national government, from which they receive a nominal salary, and whose orders have to be transmitted to their respective "electorates." During the period of observation of Ku Dæng, little has changed in this general relationship other than relatively minor details in the selection of local leadership.

With the advent of constitutional monarchy in Thailand in 1932, provincial governors, including the one in Chiang Mai, were appointed directly from the national capital. Administrative control from above was complete through the bureaucratic pattern established by the constitution. The provincial governor has the power to appoint the district officer, *nai amphœ*, and all those working directly under him in the district office. These persons are national government employees and may be transferred from one province to another, usually at the recommendation of the provincial governor. It is customary to transfer district officials from time to time, so that they do not form too close an attachment to one particular locality or constituency. The district officer of Saraphi had been transferred from Müang Fang in the northern part of the province just prior to our study of Ku Dæng in 1953. When he began his duties, he had to work with a full staff of assistants and other officials inherited from his predecessor.

The district is the smallest administrative unit of Thailand directly controlled by a trained and appointed group of officials. Four deputies help the *nai amphœ* in his work. These deputies are usually young men or women who have just graduated from one of the universities in the country, where they majored in government. In the early 1950s university training was only available in the nation's capital. By 1964, with the establishment of Chiang Mai University, higher education became available in the North and, eventually, in the Northeast and South as well. These officials are also shifted frequently until, through advancement and special training or further study, they achieve higher and more responsible office.

There is a school commissioner for the district, who is in charge of the private and government schools, supervising the curriculum and overseeing observation of the general regulations governing all schools and students. This person is the direct superior of all teachers employed in the government schools.

The police force, which numbered twenty-five men in 1953, was stationed in the district seat in a building directly next door to the *amphœ* office and was headed by a police lieutenant—the same rank incidentally, as that of the *nai amphœ* at the time. The police detachment is part of the national police force, which, in 1953, had a status equal to, if not above that of the regular military forces. After the 1958 coup d'etat, which brought Marshal Sarit to power, the police force was downgraded and was no longer a competitive threat to the other armed forces of the country. Policemen are usually not detailed to points outside the district seat. Local law-keeping activities rest under the control of the elected village officials.

Other bureaucrats—including three health officers, one forest official, one agricultural extension worker, one excise officer, a conscription registrar, three revenue officers, a postmaster, six education officials (in addition to the school commissioner), three clerks, and one caretaker—all have their offices at or near the district office. All of the officials mentioned here are appointed from Chiang Mai, draw such benefits as pensions and health care, and are entitled to wear the khaki uniforms of the bureaucracy.

The district is divided administratively into twelve communes, *tambon,* which are subdivided again into smaller units, the hamlets, or *mu ban,* of which there are a total of ninety-five in the district. The hamlet is the smallest administrative unit. At one time, each hamlet was, perhaps, a separate community or village. Today, however, in many instances the hamlet seems to be an arbitrary subdivision of a community, sometimes even including small segments from different communities. Thus, the village of Ku Dæng consists of two hamlets, 6 and 7. For all practical purposes, however, some ten households of Hamlet 7 do not form part of the Ku Dæng community, since they patronize a different temple and a different government school from that of Ku Dæng.[1] This small segment of households lies along the irrigation canal, which arbitrarily was designated by the government as the boundary between two districts. Since the villagers in the Saraphi district could not very well belong to a commune in the Hang Dong district, those villagers living along the canal were assigned to the nearest hamlet, which was number 7.

Nong Fæk commune, with a 1953 population of 3,651 according to statistics obtained from the district office, is one of the twelve communes in Saraphi District. This commune is subdivided into seven hamlets. Each of the hamlets is presided over by a headman, who represents the overlapping portion of imposed authority from above and elected or selected leadership

---

[1] Also see pp. 14-15 and map 2.

from below.[2] One of the headmen of the various hamlets is selected as commune headman or *kamnan*. According to our observations in the Nong Fæk commune and in Ku Dæng, the *kamnan* is the most influential person in the daily lives of the villagers. The headmen follow immediately after the *kamnan* in prestige and status and in the responsibilities that they carry on behalf of both the government at the district level and the people of their hamlets.

Election of Village Officials

All village officials are elected in a manner similar to that of the headmen, according to our informants. We were unable to observe many village elections, since most holders of office were elected for unspecified terms. Non-governmental positions, such as those of members of the temple committee, were for two-year terms, none of which happened to terminate during our stay in the village.

Until 1982 the procedure of electing a headman to replace one who had died in office was as follows: The headman of a nearby hamlet calls a meeting of all the residents of the former headman's hamlet. Sometimes the *kamnan* of the commune presides over such an election. If the vacancy occurs because of the headman's resignation, he, himself, will preside over the election of his successor. The villagers are asked to nominate someone out of their midst to be their new headman. If only one person has been nominated, he automatically becomes the new headman, subject to approval of and appointment by the *nai amphœ*, which is usually forthcoming. If more than one man is nominated, the villagers assembled cast their vote by means of colored card-ballots. If the vacancy occurs because the *kamnan* resigns, he appoints three men in his own hamlet as possible successors to him as headman, since he carries both positions. At a meeting of the villagers of the hamlet, each person votes by passing in front of the old *kamnan*, telling him for whom the person is voting. We were told that the three candidates also vote, but that they never cast votes for themselves. When the new headman has thus been chosen, the old *kamnan* calls for all the headmen in the commune to meet with the *nai amphœ*, his deputies, and the heads of the district police force. After some discussion of the qualifications needed for the office of *kamnan*, everyone present writes the name of one of the headmen of the commune on a piece of paper. The headman with the highest number of votes will then be the new *kamnan*, an office which he carries in addition to that of headman of his own hamlet.

In 1971, the Ministry of the Interior promulgated a law providing for an elected council for each hamlet. Shortly thereafter, regulations were issued for the election of *kamnan* and village headmen. In 1982 these posi-

---

[2] The Thai language does not distinguish between the sexes for the term used for this position—*phuyaiban*.

tions were filled for the first time by popular elections with candidates, both men and women, campaigning in the usual parliamentary style. While in the early 1950s there were no women holders of these offices in Thailand, by 1986 sixteen women *kamnan* and 228 women heads of hamlets had been elected in approximately one thousand communes and close to ten thousand hamlets throughout the country. In addition, there are seven elected female mayors in some three hundred municipalities.

The Headman and the *Kamnan*

The office of village headman or of commune *kamnan* was not necessarily one sought after, even though it carried considerable prestige while the person held the position. Although appointments used to be for lifetime, many headmen resigned after they had served five or ten years; they felt the burden too great and the rewards too small. Whether a headman stayed on for a long time or not often depended on the *nai amphœ*. A district official who demanded too much work of his *kamnan* and headmen was frequently confronted by resignations. With the advent of popular elections for these positions the term of office has now been fixed at four years. Frequent resignations are, therefore, no longer a problem. Reelection along lines of usual democratic procedures is, of course, possible.

Remuneration for government service of the headmen is nominal. Additional perquisites include some tax exemption and the rank of government official with the privilege of wearing a uniform.

According to our prestige rating, there seems to be some correlation between wealth and prestige.[3] In all cases that we observed, hamlet headmen were relatively well-to-do men, frequently owning rice mills or shops of one kind or another. They seemed to have sufficient wealth in land to be able to branch out into other activities of entrepreneurial nature. The prestige rating also showed that the positions of *kamnan* and headman carried prestige as long as the person held the particular office. Thus, not counting the monks, the *kamnan* and the headman of Hamlet 6 ranked first and second, respectively as Ku Dæng village leaders. In many cases, when doing the prestige ratings, villagers chose only two or three men who, they said, stood out from the rest. The *kamnan* usually was one of these select few. According to comments of the villagers, the *kamnan* was not always a person beloved by everybody in the village; however, there was almost unanimous agreement regarding the high respect accorded the person who was *kamnan*. This respect indicated that he was the only person considered capable of holding this particular office.

The position of headman or *kamnan* did not seem to bestow on the bearer the kind of lasting prestige that membership in the monkhood did. Former novices or former monks retain titles for the rest of their lives. On

---

[3] See appendix F, "Prestige Rating."

the other hand, a person resigning from the position of headman or *kamnan* would be distinguished in no special way from other villagers as far as form of address is concerned.

For the commune Nong Fæk and for the village of Ku Dæng the *kamnan* was the most important person with regard to practically every phase of village life. In other villages we observed head monks with considerable influence over the villagers, an indication of leadership not found in Ku Dæng. Yet, even in those villages the position of *kamnan* carried prestige alongside that of the head monk. Of the four villages making up Nong Fæk commune, Ku Dæng was unique in that it was the residence of the *kamnan* (see map 2). For that reason, perhaps, Ku Dæng was purportedly a more peaceful, law-abiding, and contented village than the other three. When Ku Dæng villagers wished to show a contrast between their village and others in the same commune, they would point out conditions in the other villages in comparison to the good situation prevailing in Ku Dæng. However, location, type of land, and occupation of the villagers had undoubtedly as much to do with the peacefulness of the village as did the presence and personality of the *kamnan*.

As agent of the central government, the *kamnan* is responsible for transmitting to the people the desires and demands of the government, as handed down the chain of command from the *nai amphœ*, or, occasionally, from the governor of the province.[4] The *nai amphœ* holds regular meetings of all the headmen and *kamnan* in his district, usually twice a month. Some of these meetings are attended only by the twelve *kamnan*. At others, all of the ninety-five headmen are expected to be present. Occasionally, the governor of Chiang Mai calls meetings of all the *nai amphœ* and *kamnan* of the entire province or parts thereof. At all of these meetings, the *kamnan* and the headmen are informed of the wishes and demands of the national government and of special problems relating to their districts. The *kamnan* usually attends these meetings in person. Occasionally, when he is on a trip elsewhere, or otherwise unable to attend, he sends a representative, such as the head teacher of the village school.

In his work as leader of the village, the *kamnan* is assisted by various elected local officials. The *kamnan* has three assistants or deputy *kamnan;* the headman of Hamlet 6 has one assistant. There is a resident doctor for the *tambon,* who, in the case of commune Nong Fæk, resides at Ku Dæng. There is an irrigation headman and a tobacco headman, each of whom is aided by one or two assistants. This group, which is elected in a manner similar to the election of *kamnan* or headman, forms a kind of village council. It is interesting to note that this council serves the village as a whole, rather than the two hamlets separately. For practical local administration, then, the

---

[4] The following discussion of the functions of the office of *kamnan* applies also to those of headman, although to a somewhat lesser degree.

village forms a unit, whereas for administrative purposes directed from above, the village is divided into two hamlets.

Taxation

The *nai amphœ* is responsible for the collection of all taxes; he is the official tax collector who goes out to collect taxes. The *nai amphœ* delegates his responsibility in this matter to the *kamnan* and the headmen, who, in turn, must see to it that the villagers pay the tax collector. Official receipts are issued to the *kamnan*, who then distributes them to the taxpayers. All the money that the district collects is sent to Chiang Mai, from where it goes to the national capital. The district then receives from the national government an annual budget, according to recommendations from the *amphœ*. This money is then reallocated for use in the various communes. Land tax is usually fixed after consultation with the *kamnan*. If a commune requires a large number of public works for the coming year, then the land tax is set high, and vice versa. According to figures received from the district office, the income from land taxes for the entire district in 1953 was 15,892.50 baht. In May, the *kamnan* received 1,800 baht for use in the Nong Fæk commune. Since there are twelve communes in Saraphi district, the average share for each commune in land tax would have been 1,324.40 baht, which seems to check roughly with the amount of money that actually reached Nong Fæk. Corresponding figures for 1986 were 81,598 baht for the commune and 718,699 baht for the entire district, reflecting thirty years of inflation and economic development. It is of interest to note that Commune Nong Fæk's share in 1986 (11.35%) was almost exactly the same as it had been in 1953 (11.33%).

Most of the money received by the *kamnan* for 1953 was to be spent for the building and repairing of roads and bridges; a small amount went into irrigation. In addition to this allocation of tax money, the *kamnan* and the headmen set a tax for irrigation of the fields in the commune. This tax usually differs for the four villages of the commune, depending on the amount of irrigation water required. In 1953 the *kamnan* and the headman of Hamlet 6, together with their assistants, set the irrigation tax at three *thang* of rice for every *rai* of rice planted on irrigated land. This amounted to a tax rate of from 5 to 8% of yield. At the conclusion of the rice harvest, the tax-rice was collected at the *kamnan*'s house. He then sold it and used the proceeds (approximately 10,000 baht in 1953) for irrigation purposes.

Once every two years the government requires that a census of land use, livestock, and the occupation of the villagers be taken. The land use report then becomes a basis for taxation. We were told that these census reports were sent to Chiang Mai, where they were filed. The *nai amphœ* distributed the census forms to the *kamnan* with instructions for their use. The *kamnan* then called meetings of the headmen of their respective communes to transmit the instructions. The *kamnan*, together with his assistants, held office in each of the hamlets of the commune. On these occasions, every villager who held land in that hamlet had to come and report the various parcels of land he owned. We noted that the census contained land under the names of people who were no longer living. We were told that the land had to be reported in the name of the dead person because it had not yet officially been transferred to the heirs. Inheritance tax problems may have played a role in these cases.

The *kamnan* is also the contact agent for the conscription registrar. When a young man in the village reaches his 20th birthday, he must present himself for conscription. The notice to do so is served on him by the *kamnan*. Many villagers have their sons register their age as more than it actually is so that they will be called to report at a younger age. The chances then are that the young man will be rejected because he is physically underdeveloped. This practice is quite generally known and accepted. When we asked a young man's age, we would frequently be told, "He is 20—that is his draft age; but his real age is 19." By 1960 this practice had fallen by the wayside, because every birth since shortly after World War II has had to be registered by the *kamnan* at the *amphœ* office in the same month that it occurred.

Agricultural Extension and Public Works in 1953

The *kamnan* or the headman usually also heads the agricultural extension work for his hamlet or for the commune. When new methods are introduced to the farmers, the district agricultural officer calls a meeting of the *kamnan* and headmen through the *nai amphœ*. At these meetings he explains new seeds, new methods of fertilizing the fields, or other improvements introduced by government or international agencies. The *kamnan* and the headmen then take this information back to their villages. In some cases they may call a meeting of the entire village, at which time they repeat the information acquired at district headquarters.

Once the *kamnan* called a meeting of the Ku Dæng villagers in front of the temple. Here he told the assembled farmers (about eighty men and twenty women) that the government had suggested that the people should raise more animals to supplement their diet—especially, fowl, rabbits, frogs, and fish. He told them that work means money, and he urged every farmer to be as industrious as possible so as to get ahead and become rich.

At the same meeting, the *kamnan* informed the villagers that a veterinarian from Chiang Mai would come in a few days to inject all cattle against Rinderpest. A corral would have to be built in the neighborhood of the temple, so that the cattle could be immunized without trouble. Since this was the season of heavy work in the fields, the *kamnan* suggested that every buffalo or cattle owner pay 25 satang to hire others to build the corral. If the immunization had come at some other time of the year, the farmers would have built the corral themselves at no cost to the individual.

When a pamphlet was distributed to the headmen and the *kamnan* about the newly introduced tilapia fish (locally called "doctor fish"), the *kamnan* made a special trip to Chiang Mai to see the American Mutual Security Administration (MSA) representative to ask for help in securing some of these new fish.[5] The MSA official sent his car with the *kamnan* to the government agricultural experiment station north of Chiang Mai to receive four hundred of the little fish. The *kamnan* put most of these fish into his own pond but also distributed some of them to various headmen in other hamlets. This particular experiment in fish breeding turned out to be a failure in Ku Dæng. Some of the ponds dried up during the dry season, and in others marauding fish were allowed to get in and devour the new, defenseless tilapia fish. The *kamnan*, however, promised to build a bigger and better pond and try again the following year. In actual fact, the introduction of tilapia fish to rural Thailand was very successful. It has become one of the major supplies of fish in many parts of the country.

When roads or bridges have to be built or repaired, the *kamnan* organizes the work parties. In some cases, he sends a messenger to a number of houses to request the farmers to assign one or two representatives to help build the road or the bridge. Usually, the persons mainly concerned with a stretch of road or a bridge have to help maintain it. When peanuts were being harvested in April, the *kamnan* asked the oxcart owners to take more care in using roads and to repair those parts that were giving way under the weight of their loads.

The district usually has a small budget for building roads, which is, however, far from adequate for the needs of the villages. When there is no further money for road building, the *nai amphœ* can no longer ask the villagers to do such work, but he can ask the *kamnan* to assist with the problem. The *nai amphœ* himself told us that he had absolutely no authority to give orders to the villagers. He is permitted to deal only with the *kamnan* and the headmen who are, in turn, the representatives of the people.

On one occasion a big road needed rebuilding. This road did not lead through any particular village but was of benefit to several. All these villages were asked to contribute to the reconstruction. Since at that time field work was rather heavy, the *kamnan* asked the villagers to contribute 50 satang per household, so that laborers could be hired to do the share of Ku Dæng.

On another occasion, a young man in the village felt that there ought to be a new, more substantial bridge over one of the ditches near his house. On his own initiative he collected money and saw to it that the bridge was built.

Sometimes the *kamnan* delegates his power to an assistant to be foreman of a road building or bridge construction gang. In general,

---

[5] This was a U.S. agency, a forerunner of the Agency for International Development (AID).

however, the *kamnan* supervises the work; this is especially true if the project is in or near his own hamlet. When an agricultural extension worker drove his jeep into a ditch, it was the *kamnan* who was immediately on hand to direct the rescue operation.

Occasionally the *kamnan* contracts for work in another village. He was asked to build a dam forty miles north of Chiang Mai. The *kamnan* recruited twenty Ku Dæng villagers with whom he went to carry out the work. They received 40,000 baht for this task.

Law and Order

For all practical purposes, the *kamnan* is in charge of law and order in his commune. In the *kamnan*'s absence, law and order is kept by the hamlet headman. Occasionally, a patrol of district policemen comes to the village to ferret out illegal gambling or liquor establishments. During the year of our study only two such patrols came near Ku Dæng. In each case they stopped first at the *kamnan*'s house. He then accompanied them on their rounds.

At formal functions, the *kamnan* is always present, usually with a stick in his hand, signifying his authority. When trouble breaks out at a temple fair because of too much drinking, the *kamnan*, who is usually within earshot, quickly restores order before serious fighting ensues. If he finds concealed weapons, he confiscates them or, occasionally, sends the owners to the district office for punishment.

Very few serious disorders occurred during our year's study. Just prior to our arrival, someone took a pot shot at the headteacher, allegedly because of jealousy. Although an arrest was made, with guilt established quite conclusively in the minds of the villagers, the judge in Chiang Mai dismissed the case for lack of evidence.

The *kamnan* himself has power to arbitrate differences between villagers. One day the headman of another hamlet brought a young man to the *kamnan*. After quarreling at breakfast time, the youngster had hit his brother over the head with a stick and caused a three-inch-long cut. The *kamnan* called the resident doctor of the commune and ordered the young man to write and sign a confession. The *kamnan* signed as witness. Both the resident doctor and the headman of the hamlet where the beating had taken place also signed the report. The headman then asked the *kamnan* whether or not to send this man to the district office for punishment. If he were sent, he would get a jail sentence of at least three years. The *kamnan* said that this was a quarrel within the family. The father of the two brothers should, therefore, be called in, since a jail sentence would bring him great sorrow. When the father arrived, he pleaded with the *kamnan* not to send his son to jail. The son, in turn, promised to behave better in the future. The *kamnan* kept the confession for fifteen days. At the end of this period, when there was no further report of bad behavior on the part of the young man, the *kamnan* destroyed the document and the matter was forgotten. The *kamnan* told us that it was entirely within his power to decide whether or not to send a delinquent to the district office for punishment or whether to take care of the matter himself.

Early one morning two girls from Ku Dæng were going to the market in Saraphi. When they passed through Nong Fæk village, a married man came rushing out of the gate of one of the houses and grabbed one of the girls' breasts—as reported by the two girls. They screamed, and the man was apprehended by neighbors and taken to the headman's house, who in turn took everybody to see the *kamnan*. The man claimed that he had been in a hurry to go to his fields, and as he ran out of his yard, his elbow accidentally struck the girl's arm. The man had no witness, the girl did. So the *kamnan* ruled that they would have to go to the district office in the morning. If the man was found guilty, he would be fined at least 200 baht. The *kamnan*, however, was willing to let the man settle "out of court" by paying 80 baht to the girl, if he would admit his guilt. The man maintained he was innocent. The next morning, just before they were to leave for the district office, the man said that he had changed his mind, that he would confess to the deed, but that he begged to be let off with a fine of only 60 baht, since that was all he had. The girl consented to this settlement, and the money was deposited at the *kamnan*'s house in the afternoon. Both parties to the dispute signed statements to the effect that the case was closed. Word went out to all men to be careful and to be accompanied by witnesses when they went out. The possibility for making easy money had become a great temptation.

In November and December, when rice is growing in the fields, the height of the dikes in the irrigation ditches has to be strictly controlled, so that the fields will not flood beyond a certain depth. Too much water ruins the rice. However, some type of fishing is best done by building small dams across the canals, lowering the water in some fields and raising it in others. To prevent damage, fishing by this means is prohibited during the rice-growing season. Nevertheless, some young men like to eat forbidden fruit by going out at night to fish. From time to time the *kamnan* assembles a posse of villagers to catch the transgressors. One night the *kamnan* and two other headmen caught three Ku Dæng villagers letting water through the dikes. None of the three needed fish for subsistence. It was simply an adventurous outing. The *kamnan* sent the culprits to police headquarters in Saraphi, where they were fined 20 baht each.

At other times, the *kamnan* and his assistants patrol the hamlets to find illegal gambling dens or liquor stores. One night they caught a man carrying a knife. He was sent immediately to the district seat. The following day graffiti were found on the back wall of the temple at Nong Fæk, challenging the *kamnan* and his assistants to a fight that same night. The *kamnan* and one assistant armed themselves and appeared at the appointed place and time. No one showed up to challenge the authority of the *kamnan*. Undoubtedly, it is this sort of demonstration of personal courage that contributes to the general stability and peacefulness of the commune of Nong Fæk and Ku Dæng village.

Even if trouble occurs in his own family, the *kamnan* does not shirk his duty. His son and a friend were involved in assaulting and beating of a man, or so the accusation went. At that time, four months prior to our study of Ku Dæng, the *kamnan* was seriously sick and could not investigate personally. The judge in Chiang Mai sentenced the two boys to six months imprisonment each. It was reported that prior to the trial the judge had been bribed with 2000 baht. When the time came for the boys' release, the *kamnan* enlisted our aid in securing a car to bring his son home. The *kamnan*, his wife, their youngest son, and the mother of the other boy went to Chiang Mai, where they met the two released prisoners in Wat Dap Phai, a temple near the prison. The two boys sat before an old monk; they were dressed in their old prison clothes. They placed a tray of flowers and candles and a bucket of water in front of the monk. The monk lit a candle and chanted. When he had finished, he stuck the candle to the side of the bucket and put some flower petals into the water, transforming it into lustral water. Then he instructed the boys to bathe in the water and change their clothes to new ones brought by their parents. The old clothes as well as the boys' bad luck were left in the temple. After this ceremony, the whole group of people proceeded to another temple, Wat Loi Kho, where they asked another old monk to perform a similar ceremony. Again they bathed in lustral water, but there was no further change of clothes.[6] Neither of the monks received payment for his services. After the boys' return to the village there was no evidence of any kind of stigma attached to either boy, the *kamnan*, or his family for the prison experience of his son. As far as we know, it was never mentioned again.

The *kamnan* himself told us that there had been only one serious crime in the seven years that he had occupied his office; namely, the shooting of the head teacher. The *kamnan* told us that if the criminal flees from the scene of the crime, strong men in the village organize a posse to catch him. Then he is sent to Saraphi, the district seat. There he is put in jail prior to his transfer to prison in Chiang Mai, where he has to await his trial.

Disobedience seems to be rare. We observed only one case, involving the nephew of the *kamnan*. He had been told by his father to help with work on an irrigation canal some five miles from Ku Dæng. This was the household's contribution to a communal project. The *kamnan*'s nephew had attended an all-night wake at the house of a recently deceased villager and not returned home until early the next morning. He overslept and did not show up for work. Five other villagers likewise overslept. The *kamnan* called them all to his house and berated them for their laziness. He asked his nephew to bring his father; this the boy refused to do. Therefore, the *kamnan* sent his nephew to the district office, where he was fined 25 baht.

---

[6] Theme 7: Playing it safe.

The *kamnan* said that he had to punish his nephew severely, otherwise the villagers would think that he loved his relatives more than his duty.

With the establishment of village councils in 1971, village volunteer corps were organized in order to assist with the orderly control of the village and to help individual villagers with their problems. In particular, there are four separate active volunteer organizations in the village: 1) Thai Volunteers *(Thai asa pongkan chat)*, responsible for assisting with policing the village, preventing crime, and settling quarrels among villagers; 2) Youth Volunteers *(yawachon asasamak)*, who are provided with training in military matters to prevent subversive activities within the village boundaries; 3) National Security Corps *(kongnun phüa khwam mankhong hæng chat)* under the supervision of district officials, to assist with matters of national security; and 4) Village Scouts *(luk süa chaoban)*, responsible to the *kamnan* and the village headman for general help in all matters of community service.

The *Kamnan*'s Role in Agriculture

As leader of the community the *kamnan* is expected to supervise agricultural work in the fields; this seems to have been one of the traditional functions of his office.

A 60-year-old man recalled that in "his time" work on the land was more difficult but yield was greater than today. In those days all the villagers worked very hard and carefully, watching for insects that might harm the crops, and pulling out weeds between the rice plants. Today, the man continued, there is no good leader to make sure that the farmers work properly. Everyone seems to be more concerned with himself than with the welfare of the community as a whole. When a new dam has been built, the farmers use all the water they can possibly get, with no concern for those who are farther away from the water supply and whose crops may suffer from lack of water. Today, the *kamnan* or the headman cannot stop this type of abuse or cannot supervise the work in the fields, because he is too busy with his own work. At the time when our informant was a young man, the *kamnan* always appointed a foreman, who would see to it that the farmers performed their tasks properly. This man functioned with the same authority as that of *kamnan*. The old man seemed to think that supervised field work in those days produced better results than more individual type of agriculture practiced today. Other informants confirmed the statement that agriculture seems to have been more efficient in former days.

For one phase of agriculture, the *kamnan*'s authority, or that vested in the irrigation headman, is still paramount today. This is the work in connection with the irrigation of the fields. All crops grown in the vicinity of Ku Dæng are dependent on an artificial water supply. Even during the rainy season, the water in the fields is regulated through the irrigation dams and canals. The irrigation water comes from two rivers, north and south of Ku Dæng (see map 2). The ditches or canals pass through miles of land before they reach the land that they are intended to irrigate. Along these canals villagers have been appointed to keep an eye on the level of the water and on the depth of the ditches. If work is needed, these men send a message to the irrigation headmen or the *kamnan* of the communes that draw water from that particular canal. The *kamnan* then informs the people who use this water to send representatives of their households on a specified day to work on the irrigation canal. If a man owns only a little land, say two or three *rai*, he may join with another farmer who owns a similarly small parcel of land in supplying one person for the irrigation levy. If a man draws much water for perhaps ten *rai* or more, he must go himself or send someone from his own household to represent him.

Smaller ditches and dikes near the village are built in like manner. The farmers who want to use the water must contribute the physical labor. In 1953, after the main rice crop had been harvested, the *kamnan* called a village meeting on the temple grounds. He asked the villagers what they were going to plant during the dry season, and how many *rai* of land they wanted to plant. Only those planning to use their land for this purpose were required to help dig the necessary local ditches. The *kamnan* asked each farmer to report to him as soon as possible the exact number of *rai* to be used so that the digging of the ditches could begin without delay. The actual manual labor was supervised by the *kamnan* himself.

Another responsibility of the *kamnan* relates to the pursuit of livelihood of the people: he must keep himself informed about animal husbandry. Each year the district office sends someone to the village to prepare registration forms for all the animals a particular farmer owns. It is the *kamnan*'s responsibility to facilitate this work within his commune. He requires all the farmers to bring their larger animals, such as buffaloes, cattle, or pigs, to the temple grounds, where they are checked and registered. Thereafter, whenever a farmer wishes to slaughter or sell such an animal, he must report first to the *kamnan*. As a matter of fact, the farmers are not allowed to slaughter livestock without a special license from the district office. Licensed butchers may slaughter only one buffalo or one ox per day. This restriction dates back to the conditions existing during the Second World War, when the Japanese depleted the supply of cattle and buffalo in the country.

When an animal dies, permission must be obtained from the *kamnan* to dispose of the carcass. Usually, the villagers wish to cut up a dead animal and sell the meat so as to make up for part of the loss of the animal. The meat of a dead buffalo seldom brings more than one-fourth of the value of a live animal. When a buffalo dies, the *kamnan* has to decide whether it should be buried, burned, or sold. Occasionally, he goes to the district office to obtain the advice of the agricultural official, who may come to take a blood sample of the dead animal to determine whether any serious disease was present. If the decision is to bury or burn the animal, the *kamnan* usually informs the owner of this decision and then returns to his house, which he will not leave again until the animal has been disposed of. No inquiry is made as to whether or not the owner has complied with the *kamnan*'s order.

Other Functions of the *Kamnan*

As mentioned earlier, the *kamnan* is the leader of the commune and of the village in which he lives. He must be concerned with every phase of life, even that extending into the realm of religion. In other communities, we observed monks not only being responsible for religious affairs in the village but also carrying a considerable share of secular leadership. The converse was true in Ku Dæng. Here the monks kept aloof from the "ways of the world"; moreover, even their religious leadership was encroached upon by the *kamnan*.

When a young boy was to be ordained as a novice into the monkhood, the *kamnan* was the main spokesman at a village meeting in front of the temple. The monks participated in the actual ceremony, while the *kamnan* led discussions about the various events to take place. He also went to Chiang Mai to invite a famous Buddhist monk to preach to the villagers as part of the ceremony.

On more than one occasion the *kamnan* led discussions in the temple about the rebuilding of the base for the Buddha statue. The head monk was in charge of all the arrangements with the artist who was hired to carry out the work. The *kamnan* talked with the villagers about the terms of the contract.

Official approval had to be obtained for major events in or near the temple, such as fairs or festivities in connection with ordinations. Usually the *kamnan* or the headman had to act on the request before it would be considered by the district office.

When a death occurs, the *kamnan* is responsible for making the decision of what to do with the corpse. When a little boy died, the *kamnan* told the father he would have to bury him immediately, since it was raining and there would not have been sufficient firewood for cremation of the body. The *kamnan*, however, has little to say about the place of burial or cremation, unless such action infringes upon the rights of some other villagers. When one influential villager wished to have his wife cremated in one of her own fields, the *kamnan* expressed his dislike of this action, but he said he was powerless to prevent the man from carrying out his purpose since it was to be done on his own land.

Even in the field of public education the *kamnan* has a certain amount of responsibility. In theory, the head teacher is in complete control over the school children. When, however, certain questions of discipline arise, the *kamnan* is called in. For example, when a woman complained that her daughter had been kicked in front of the school building, the *kamnan* had to settle the dispute to the satisfaction of all parties concerned.

At the annual memorial services held throughout the country in honor of King Chulalongkorn, the founder of modern education in Thailand, the *kamnan* had to preside over the ceremony at the school building in the village of Nong Fæk, where all the children and teachers of the commune gathered to present wreaths in memory of the king. In previous years all the school children of the district had gathered at the district office. In 1953, the *nai amphœ* added observation of this ceremony to the many other duties of the *kamnan*.

In addition to these specific functions, the *kamnan* is the general representative of the commune. He is invited to weddings, ordinations, and funerals simply because of his official position. At the time of the local New Year's celebrations *(Songkran)*, headmen and villagers from all parts of the commune come to pay respects to the *kamnan*. At weddings, the *kamnan* usually is one of those tying strings around the wrists of the bride and groom and, more often than not, delivers the wedding address. When meetings are called at the district office, for whatever purpose, the *kamnan* is expected to attend. When United Nations International Children's Emergency Fund (UNICEF) lectures were held on the subject of delivery and care of infants, the *kamnan* as well as the midwives were present. When the *nai amphœ* has a special project, such as raising funds for erecting a building or a fence around a compound, he turns to the *kamnan* and headmen for contributions. At the annual winter fair in Saraphi, the *kamnan* and headmen gave financial support to one of the booths and even sponsored one of the beauty contestants. When the *nai amphœ* visited Ku Dæng, the *kamnan* called a village meeting and presented the *nai amphœ*. At one time the representative to the national parliament for Chiang Mai wished to start a teak company. He offered to sell shares at 25 baht each. This offer was transmitted to the *kamnan*, who passed it on to his headmen for consideration.

Efforts were made in the early 1950s to have more popular representation of the rural villages through the provincial assembly. Such attempts took a long time to materialize. In 1982 the provincial council was for the first time elected by popular ballot throughout the province. In 1950, a representative from the Nong Fæk commune was sent to be a member of the provincial assembly in Chiang Mai for a term of four years. This man was the *kamnan*'s older brother; he was selected in a way similar to that of other village and commune officials described above. In those days the assembly did not have much effect on the affairs of the rural community. In 1972, when M. R. Kukrit Pramoj was Prime Minister of Thailand, stress was laid on rural development through the communes. Some of this emphasis was delegated through the provincial councils, but on the whole they were bypassed.

The *kamnan*, then, is the principal representative of the people when dealing with the world outside the village. He is suited for this job by temperament and personality, at least in the cases that we were able to observe. When the *kamnan* nearly won first prize in the national lottery, he told us that if he had won, he would have built a new road from Ku Dæng to the district for 10,000 baht.[7] With the rest of the money he would have bought himself a house in Chiang Mai and some land.

The *kamnan* is courageous and fearless. However, his value judgments are not always those of someone raised in a more sophisticated environment. He told us he had visited many of the old ruins of temples and pagodas that abound in the neighborhood of the village. He found earthenware pots in many of the ruins, some of them containing black ashes or bones. He smashed all of them without any ill effect on him or his family. He found two very small Buddha statues made of bronze or brass, which he is keeping in his home.

The examples cited above support our conclusion that the system of government through the person of the *kamnan* or the individual headman is ideally suited for the village system as exemplified by Ku Dæng. The individual farmer is almost entirely free to conduct his own business, except when he comes into contact with his neighbors. The villagers feel confident that their affairs are in good hands, since they have had a voice in electing their leader. Though dissatisfied occasionally, they feel that they could not find a better man or one who would be willing to carry the heavy burden and responsibility of the office. It seems to have been a wise decision on the part of the national government to retain the services of the *kamnan* and the headman in their traditional roles with only gradual change of or additions to their responsibilities according to a rapidly changing social environment.

General Development

Before 1967, the Thai government had not initiated any official program of development for the village of Ku Dæng. Some progress had been achieved through programs at the district or provincial level. Officials in such fields as public health, agriculture, economics, or social welfare visited villages, including Ku Dæng, which were under their jurisdiction or within their areas of responsibility. Village meetings might be held, and the officials would make suggestions to the villagers on how to improve their way of carrying out particular activities. The actual expertise rested in the distant government officials, who attempted through example and instruction to convey ideas of progress to the villagers. However, there was no concerted effort to inaugurate a plan of development for the village as such.

In 1967, the Ministry of Interior chose Ku Dæng as a "Development Village Class A." There were three classes: a) those villages in which the farmers were considered receptive to modern technological methods and procedures; b) the vast majority of villages, whose populations were considered to be neutral as far as expected results were concerned; and c) those

---

[7] Then worth about U.S. $555.

villages that were considered unreceptive or "hopeless" with regard to introduction of measured change. The program of the Ministry of the Interior for selecting villages to be classified as category "A" was modeled closely on the method employed by us in choosing the village of Ku Dæng as our field of study in 1954.[8] Development officials from the Office of Community Development in the Ministry of the Interior were delegated to carry out the development program in the chosen villages by introducing the villagers to new methods and new ideas for the benefit of their village. This program was inaugurated in Ku Dæng in 1971.

To carry out the development of the village, three committees were elected from among the villagers: a village development committee; a social affairs committee responsible for a youth group, a center for small children, and an adult group; and an economic affairs committee to deal with vocational matters and capital investment.

Special development programs were devised to support and improve agricultural methods. Plant improvements were initiated for the growing of mushrooms, soybeans, and peanuts. Animal husbandry concerned itself with improvements in the raising of pigs and fish. Agricultural improvements of this type tended to be academically oriented, with the agricultural official of the commune instructing the villagers in the profitable and efficient use of their spare time.

Support of other vocational activities included work with and improvement of such home industries as basket weaving, candle making, and the production of cigarette lighters. Spare time agriculture as well as spare time home industries were encouraged in order to produce extra income for individual families. In conjunction with such an expected improvement of their financial situation, the villagers were urged to begin systematic savings of extra cash.

Development of the environment included improving the infrastructure of the village through cooperative efforts of the people. Other development programs included a center for small children, a program for practical public health, and a proposal for establishing a community government.

The village development, then, was dependent on and carried out by three main groups of individuals: the village development committee elected by the villagers themselves; government officials assigned to work alongside the villagers; and other villagers, who were not on specific committees, but whose cooperative involvement was essential for the successful implementation of the program.

---

[8] See the introduction.

Development Projects from 1971-1984

Development projects in Ku Dæng were initiated in 1971. Each project was proposed to the village development committee for consideration. This committee, in turn, submitted the proposal to the commune council, who studied it and passed it on to the district level for approval. Some projects were completed within a given period of time, while others are still in operation today.

In 1972 one of the first projects to be initiated was the improvement and development of cigarette lighters. At that time a number of Ku Dæng villagers were successfully involved in the manufacture of such lighters and had a reasonably good business going. It was considered a worthwhile undertaking to promote a home industry indigenous to the community. A number of villagers participated in improving the manufacturing process. The new method proved so successful that the industry spread to other nearby villages. Consequently, the Ku Dæng villagers lost interest and, for all practical purposes, discontinued manufacture of this particular item.

In the same year another project was initiated, namely, the establishment of a small children's daycare center. This was fully supported by both professional developers and villagers. The purpose was to help parents with the care of their children before they reached school age. The parents were thus free to engage in vocational activities. As a by-product, the children would receive an early start prior to entering regular school. A room in the village school was made available for implementation of the project, which continues in operation to the present day.

Additional projects, related to youth, were initiated in the same year. A youth group was established in the village to instill leadership skills in the young people and prepare them for adult responsibilities.

Two important projects saw their beginnings in 1973. A training program for pig raising was established. Its purpose was to train the farmers in modern, scientific methods of improving pig breeding, so that the farmers would be in a better position to improve their cash income. Interested villagers formed a pig-raisers club. A pedigreed boar was made available to service the sows owned by the farmers. When the pigs thus produced were sold, 10% of the sale price was returned to the boar's owner; the remaining profit was divided among the members of the club.

The other project was the establishment of a similar group for fish-raising purposes. The village development committee was responsible for the supervision of this group. The provincial fisheries consultant gave expert advice as required.

In 1974, another two projects were initiated: the improvement of soybean production and insect control for *lamyai* fruit trees. Both projects showed positive results within a short period of time.

During the two-year period from 1975 through 1976, emphasis was laid on training and encouraging young people to use their spare time productively and to enhance their interest in agriculture as a professional option.

A public health project begun in 1977 was designed to support government emphasis on cleanliness and proper disposal of human waste. One village developer and one information officer were assigned to each village during this period. These two volunteers gave their time for this purpose for a specific period of time. They had been trained by the Ministry of Public Health in basic health practices and in methods of dispensing such information to the rural people of Thailand. The villagers were instructed in the proper use of medicines and herbs available to them. A supply of medicines was provided for use in the village.

At present, Ku Dæng continues to be involved in several development projects. The women of the village are encouraged to develop more effective methods for coping with the myriad tasks in the home. Villagers are urged to participate in savings projects, which were initiated in 1972 and are continuing to this day. The village security system is being strengthened and the daycare center improved. Projects for upgrading public health practices and better mental health are being established.

The savings group, for example, was set up to encourage the villagers to work together for better basic living conditions. As they build up their savings accounts, an economic foundation is laid that can provide security for possible loans for agricultural enterprises. They are encouraged to coop-erate so that they can undertake more ambitious projects based on mutual responsibility and inter-relation of their efforts. As a self-help group, this indigenous organization does not depend on financial assistance from the outside.

The purpose of the public health group is to improve health practices among the villagers, especially in the areas of disease prevention, first aid, community health, and the proper use of drugs. A village cooperative pharmacy was set up to provide standard medicines at reasonable cost with possible profit sharing as a by-product.

The mental health project for young people concentrates on instruc-tion aimed at dealing with individual religious and secular matters as well as community concerns. Yearly seminars bring young people together to help them cope with the various problems encountered during the past year. This endeavor does not only help the young people, themselves, but through them influences the attitude toward mental health of the entire village.

These locally organized public health, savings, and village security groups all continue to function in the same manner to this day. It seems very likely that organizations of this type will have an impact on the whole village for some time to come.

Village Administration

The headman of each hamlet has full authority with regard to civil control of the village population. He is responsible for law and order to the *kamnan* and the *nai amphœ*. In 1971 a law was promulgated through the Ministry of the Interior providing for an elected council of eight members for each hamlet. This village council was set up with direct line of authority to the commune council. Each member of the hamlet council was delegated specific responsibility in one particular field in which he or she was then expected to help other villagers. The hamlet council coordinates relationships with the village and with the various village groups in order to present problems or reports to the commune council.

7

THE BASIC ELEMENTS
OF BUDDHISM IN KU DÆNG

Everybody in Ku Dæng is Buddhist. This fact is not so much the product of choice as it is one of tradition and childhood upbringing. While there are Christian communities within reach of Ku Dæng, in the village itself there are no Christians. Other religions are practically unknown. A few villagers have heard of Islam but identify it primarily as the religion of the Indian traders seen in the *amphœ* or in the city.

The concept of belonging to a church or a religion is something alien to the Thai culture as expressed through the Thai language. Here, a person does not belong to a religion but rather "respects" the religion. Thus, one can respect many religions without having to pay allegiance to any or all of them. Frequently, one finds Buddhists who respect Christianity as well as Buddhism. This was observed especially among the Buddhist monks who have the time and inclination to read books on other religions. In the pre-test of our schedule on religious knowledge, a question was included on whether the person interviewed believed that there are religions other than Buddhism that are also "true" or whether Buddhism was the only true religion. This question had to be dropped because it was impossible to phrase the question in Lanna Thai without instructing the people in a new concept, namely, that of a unique religion.

The Buddhist Temple

Since all the people of Ku Dæng are Buddhists, the temple is the most important institution for the spiritual welfare of the villagers. The temple is the center not only for religious activities but also for social and community affairs of the entire village. In addition, the temple is the center for education, as it has been throughout the history of the village. The village school is built on land adjacent to the temple.

The temple, then, lies at the center of the village, both geographically and functionally. It occupies a major portion of the time, energy, and devotion of the villagers. In as much as the temple is "there," right in the middle of village life, it must be taken as something inevitable, something as normal to the village as the rice fields, water buffaloes, or coconut trees.

There seem to be two diverse aspects of religion in the village that merit separate treatment: first, there is the appearance that the temple presents to the villagers; all the external aspects of Buddhism—the temple, the monkhood, the religious teachings and writings—are presented to the villagers to be taken or ignored according to individual preferences. Second, there is the reception of the religious presentations by the villagers, their understanding of what is taught, their reactions to the laws and commandments—in short, the effect these teachings have on their everyday life.

In the past, the role of the temple in the community was probably even more inclusive than it is today. The temple then was school, hospital, spiritual and community center, all combined into one. Today, the temple still is the village center, with the abbot the spiritual counselor of the entire village. The temple serves as a type of government center when officials come to the village to distribute new strains of plants or explain new methods of cultivation. It also acts as a health center when public health nurses come to visit to give injections, distribute medicine, or give general advice on health practices. The temple, however, has not kept pace with the rest of the village in the promotion and innovation of educational development.

To a stranger, the temple is the outward sign of the Buddhist religion. Visitors to all parts of Thailand are usually first impressed by the purely external aspects of temple architecture. Ku Dæng is no exception. The temple is the village center of expression of decorative art. Although there is a certain amount of carving and color in the decoration of the village houses, approaching the temple is like stepping from deep shadows into the sunlight.

Physically, the temple stands on a large plot of land in the center of the village; it can serve as a meeting place for village gatherings, whether for political purposes, such as election of local officials; or for religious purposes, as in the ordination of a novice into the monkhood; or for business or professional purposes, such as for the vaccination of all cattle in the village; or for recreational purposes, such as the holding of fairs.

The temple is dominated by the *wihan,* or place of general meetings and devotions. The present structure was built in 1951 and torn down for reconstruction in 1986. The *wihan* was modeled after a temple in Lamphun province and designed by one of the villagers of Hamlet 6, who gives his profession as "housebuilder." This man was a novice and later a monk for a total of nearly twenty years before he left the monkhood to resume lay status.

The pillars on the east porch of the temple are decorated with painted cement and glass designs. This work was done by four men from Lamphun. The *thewada* over the doors and windows were made in Chiang Mai, and the big Buddha statue at the west end of the *wihan* was made by a man from Doi Saket, a village ten miles east of the city of Chiang Mai.[1] The roof of the *wihan* is the usual Thai design for temples with two or more overlapping layers, giving the impression of steps leading to the top. The corners of the

---

[1] A *thewada* is a being in a realm higher than that of man. See Henry Alabaster, *The Wheel of the Law* (London: Trubner, 1871), p. 98.

roof are decorated with serpents' heads and tails. The roof is held up by two parallel rows of six pillars each.

The total cost of the *wihan* was over 60,000 baht, raised mostly by subscriptions from the villagers and through huge temple fairs to which members from sixty-two different temples as far away as seventy-five miles were invited.

The *wihan* is usually open throughout the day. Villagers may come at any time to bring offerings to the Buddha or gifts to the monkhood or the temple. Apart from the normal times of presenting food, such as in the early mornings and just before noon, little use is made of this opportunity. Monks and novices use the *wihan* at least once during daytime for devotions. At other times they read, practice chants, or just lounge in this large hall.

Precept Day sees the greatest activity in the *wihan*, at least during the rainy season, which is usually referred to for religious purposes as *phansa* and rendered in English as "Lent."[2] During this time, as many as 150 villagers come each morning to present food to the monks and receive the precepts in the *wihan*. In the afternoon a preaching service is usually conducted. For this period of Buddhist Lent, many of the older villagers stay in the *wihan* the entire "Precept Day."

The west end of the *wihan* is occupied by the Buddha statues. In the center, on top of a high pedestal, sits a ten-foot Buddha made of brick and plaster. He is flanked by four smaller Buddhas, one made of brass, the others of stone and plaster.[3] In front of this major array of figures stand some smaller tables with three more Buddha statues made of bronze and a gold leaf-covered miniature *cedi*, representing the tomb of the Lord Buddha. Behind the big Buddha, covering the entire west wall of the *wihan* and extending to a portion of the ceiling, is a colorful painting of village life, which centers on a Bo tree shading the Buddha statue in front of it. This painting was done by a Chinese artist from Pa Düa, a neighboring village.

In the southwest corner of the temple, to the right of the Buddha statues, stands a preaching pulpit, the *thammat*, which is built in the form of a temple with multiple roofs extending to the ceiling of the *wihan*. According to the monk, this pulpit is richly decorated with precious stones of Burmese origin. Steps, flanked by two serpents, lead up from the rear to a preaching platform. The front of the pulpit is covered with wooden lattice work, so as to conceal the novice or monk while preaching. In actual practice, the novices like to pin old newspapers to the inside of this lattice work so as to be completely hidden from view. The head monk asserted that the pulpit was several hundred years old. An old woman told us, however,

---

[2] "Precept Day" is a direct translation from the Lanna Thai term *wan sin*, which is the same day as *wan phra* in Thai, or the Buddhist Holy Day, which falls on the eighth and the last day of the waxing or waning moon. For more on Precept Day, see p. 210.

[3] When the base of the large Buddha statue was rebuilt early in 1954, the smaller Buddhas were removed, some of them taken to the priests' quarters, some to the *sala*, where food is received at times other than Lent.

that her father was the artist who built it. If the latter is true, it is an example of the disappearance of creative art in this particular area of the country. Nothing found in temples in the 1950s and 1960s was made by contemporary artists. On the other hand, since that time, the tremendous growth of international tourism in Northern Thailand has stimulated a revival of many of the traditional handicrafts and arts, carving among them.

Apart from these major furnishings of the *wihan*, there are also several large armchairs that serve as preaching chairs for extemporaneous sermons or when the pulpit is not used. Along the south wall of the *wihan*, a platform six inches above the floor serves as sitting area for the monks and novices when they lead the congregation in chants or devotions. In the back, the east end of the *wihan*, a set of comfortable chairs and a table are stored to be moved to the east porch on special occasions such as visits to Ku Dæng by monks from other temples. The entire floor of the *wihan* is covered with bamboo mats for use of the congregation during services or village meetings.

The oldest building of the temple is the *kuti*, the living quarters of the monks and novices. This is a typical local house constructed of wood with a tiled roof. The monks' rooms lie off a common gathering place in the center of the building. Here, the monks and novices live, eat, read, and practice their devotions.

Along three walls of the temple compound are long *sala* that serve as shelters for travelers who wish to stay in the village overnight. Here, also the older villagers use bamboo mats for partitions to build themselves small rooms for the *phansa* period, when they sleep in the temple the nights before and after Precept Day. During the greater portion of the year, the east *sala* is used for most religious functions, since not enough villagers attend the various activities to use the larger *wihan*. Under the west *sala*, the head monk has his carpenter shop where he builds simple furniture. Here, also, the big drums are kept that are beaten to signal the beginning or the end of religious festivities, thus telling the villagers and the *thewada* what is going on.

In the northeast corner of the compound is the *ho thamma*, the upper story of which is designated for storage of scriptures and sermons. Since there is no staircase leading up, this building is practically not used at all and has become a general storeroom.

Next to the *kuti* there is a small kitchen built under a straw roof. Here, the temple boys cook food for themselves for the evening meal and for the monks and novices at times when the villagers have failed to supply a sufficient amount of food, which occurs only rarely. In 1954, the villagers built a new and bigger kitchen to replace the old one and to have a place where they could prepare food for temple activities attended by large crowds.

Other major structures found in many temple compounds throughout Thailand, but absent in Ku Dæng, include the *bot* and various kinds of *cedi*. The *bot* is a structure similar to the *wihan* except that it is usually smaller. It serves primarily for the ceremonials of the monkhood, in which the laymen do not participate. If it is desired to build a *bot*, permission must be requested through the proper ecclesiastical channels from H. M. the King of Thailand. Some of the temples near Ku Dæng had such a building. Whenever special ceremonies were required of the monks, such as at the beginning of Buddhist Lent, the monks—but not the novices—had to go to other temples where they met with monks from six to ten other communities. In the Chiang Mai-Lamphun area of Northern Thailand, the *bot* is restricted to the male population. This practice was probably derived from Burmese Buddhism that was dominant in this area during long periods of history. Elsewhere in Thailand, it has been reported that many of the *wan phra* activities are taking place in the *bot* with both men and women participating.[4]

The other type of structure absent in Ku Dæng is the *cedi* or stupa. This is a circular or square structure with a pointed spire. Occasionally, relics of famous monks or even of the Lord Buddha are kept in the *cedi*. In general, however, the *cedi* is a structure built in remembrance of the Lord Buddha. It is supposed to resemble his tomb. Occasionally, a temple will also have a tomb, but this is the exception rather than the rule. One of the oldest temples in Chiang Mai has a large number of such tombs, where the remains of members of the royal family of Chiang Mai are kept.

The Buddha and Buddhist Statuary

The Buddha statue dominates the scene in the *wihan*. In fact, it dominates the external aspects of the religious activities of the villagers. The Buddha is revered as the center of the religion. He is the first element of the Buddhist Triple Gems *(tiratana)*, which consists of three elements: 1) the Lord Buddha, 2) the Law, Dhamma, or *thamma*, and 3) the monkhood, Sangha, or *phra song*.

The Buddha is considered to be the final authority in everything pertaining to Buddhist teaching and tradition. He is referred to again and again, both in religious writings and sermons, as the author of laws and regulations. Many rational arguments may be used in a dispute, but the matter can always be safely concluded by a reference to the Buddha. Thus, in a guide for teaching Buddhism to children several pages are devoted to a discussion between a Buddhist child and someone who is trying to present the case for a creator of the universe.[5] In the end, after all arguments have been exhausted, the child is represented as clinching the argument with the statement that the Lord Buddha taught us that it is not good to argue with

---

[4] See B. J. Terwiel (1975), pp. 186-217.

[5] Phon Rattanasuwan, *Kanson phutthasatsana to dek prathom 1-4* [Teaching Buddhism to elementary school children] (Chiang Mai: Buddhist Association, 1952).

other persons when we disagree; therefore, following the Buddha's advice, he discontinues the discussion.

Sayings of the Buddha based on texts from Buddhist scriptures usually form the basis for sermons presented in the temple, either in Thai or in Lanna Thai. Many sermons consist of stories—frequently Jataka tales—supposedly first told by the Buddha himself.

The statue in the *wihan* is considered to represent the Buddha. In no way is it thought to represent a living being or a spirit or to have any power whatsoever. It is an object of veneration to remind people of the real Lord Buddha, his life, and his teachings. The people as well as the monks bow to the Buddha statue whenever they enter the *wihan*, whether as part of a religious service or not. If any comparison to Western religious practices were to be made, we might say that the attitude of the people toward representations of the Lord Buddha is similar to that of members of the Roman Catholic Church toward representations of Christ and of the saints.

A small Buddha statue or a picture of the Buddha is usually found on shelves serving as house shrines and located in a corner of the main part of each house of the village. As far as house shrines in Ku Dæng are concerned, they are certainly among the most neglected of their kind. Except for special occasions, such as the blessing of a new house, a funeral, or a special *thambun*, these shrines are not especially cared for at all. Once a week during Buddhist Lent, an offering of candles and flowers is made to the Buddha image on the shrine. Apart from this, the paper flowers, which probably date back to the time when the house was built, are allowed to gather dust and fade and provide a favorite spot for spiders to spin their webs. There are no prescriptions or taboos with regard to these images. In the house where we lived the Buddha image and the shelf with paper flowers were in the room used for our office. My desk was directly underneath the Buddha picture. The only time during our year in the village that the flowers were replenished and especially arranged was when we asked permission to take a picture of the shrine.

The Dhamma or Buddhist Law

The second element of the Buddhist Triple Gems is the Law. This is generally represented as consisting of two parts: 1) the precepts or commandments, and 2) the holy writings, or sermons written on palm leaves. Of these two, the precepts seem to have the greater impact on the villagers.

There are five precepts for laymen, eight for laymen who wish to be especially devout for a specific period of time, ten for novices, and 227 for full monks. The precepts are stressed and presented to the villagers constantly. When designated villagers bring food to the temple each morning, the monks, in turn, present the five precepts. Whenever there is a religious ceremony or gifts are offered to the monks, the villagers request the five precepts, which are then graciously bestowed upon them by the monks. The five precepts are always given in Pali. The congregation, led by a lay leader, asks three times in unison for the precepts: "Honored teachers, we humbly request the five precepts together with the Triple Gems."

The head monk then invites the laity to take refuge in the Triple Gems and asks them to accept the five precepts: "I take refuge in the Lord Buddha; I take refuge in the Law; I take refuge in the monkhood *(sangha)*."

Each of these three refuges is repeated three times by the congregation before the five precepts are said in like manner:

1. I reverently promise not kill animals nor order others to kill them.
2. I reverently promise not to steal nor order others to steal.
3. I reverently promise not to follow lustful love.
4. I reverently promise not to speak lies, rude or frivolous language, or words that will cause quarrels.
5. I reverently promise to abstain from drinking, smoking, or eating anything that is intoxicating.[6]

These five commandments are repeated over and over on every conceivable occasion. Every villager knows the chants as well as their translation. The precepts form the theoretical basis of the life of the community. It is, perhaps, significant that in the North the Buddhist Holy Day is almost always called "Precept Day" *(wan sin)*, whereas in other parts of Thailand it is commonly referred to as "Lord's Day" *(wan phra)*.

During *phansa*, or Buddhist Lent, the older villagers sleep in the temple for the nights immediately before and after Precept Day. For this occasion they accept to obey an additional three commandments, making a total of eight precepts. In effect, they promise to live for one day in a manner similar to that of monks. They will take food only in the mornings, none after noon; they will not enjoy music or fragrant flowers; and they will not lie on soft beds. These extra precepts are not presented to the villagers as a whole and are not extolled as guides of conduct for all to follow.

One of the best discussions in English of the five, eight, and ten precepts is given by Terwiel in his analysis of religious ceremonies in Central Thailand.[7] Basically, his observation that "the scope and meaning of the five precepts are aggrandized for ritual purposes, [and] cannot retain much practical meaning for daily non-ceremonial life" is confirmed by our study in Ku Dæng.[8]

---

[6] Translated from a Thai translation of the Pali in Bhikkhu Panyanantha (1953).
[7] B. J. Terwiel (1975), pp. 186-217.
[8] B. J. Terwiel (1975), p. 198.

In Central and Northern Thailand there seem to be different customs involved in observing the five and eight precepts, especially as they relate to activities on Buddhist Holy Day *(wan phra)*. In Ratchaburi much of the day's activity is taking place in the *bot*, with both men and women participating. In Ku Dæng, the activities are limited to the *wihan* and the *sala*. Moreover, in the Chiang Mai-Lamphun area of Northern Thailand, the *bot* is restricted for use by men only. This practice was probably adapted from Burmese Buddhism, which has influenced local Buddhist expression dating from the various historical periods when Chiang Mai and Lamphun were under Burmese suzerainty. Whether or not the eight precepts consist of the five plus an additional three is discussed at considerable length by Terwiel.[9]

---

[9] B. J. Terwiel (1975), p. 212. The evidence from our study in Ku Dæng is not clear since the wording and translation of the precepts are open to different interpretations. A religious encyclopedia published in Bangkok lists the precepts as follows:

The Eight Precepts
1. Today and tonight we will abstain from killing, we will put down our weapons, and we will sustain living beings.
2. Today and tonight we will abstain from stealing, we will accept only freely offered gifts.
3. Today and tonight we will abstain from all sexual conduct.
4. Today and tonight we will abstain from falsehood, speak and uphold the truth.
5. Today and tonight we will abstain from drinking intoxicating liquids, which cause carelessness.
6. Today and tonight we will abstain from eating after noon.
7. Today and tonight we will abstain from dancing and decorating ourselves with flowers and fragrant substances.
8. Today and tonight we will abstain from sitting or reclining on thick seats or mattresses.

The Ten Precepts
1. Abstain from killing animals.
2. Abstain from stealing.
3. Abstain from unchaste conduct.
4. Abstain from lying.
5. Abstain from drinking intoxicating liquids that are addicting drugs and are cause for carelessness.
6. Abstain from eating after noon.
7. Abstain from dancing, singing, playing musical instruments, or watching entertainment.
8. Abstain from decorating oneself with flowers or fragrant substances or make-up.
9. Abstain from using plush mattresses or cushions.
10. Abstain from receiving money.

For references to these precepts, see Major Thawit Plengwitthaya, *Khoptham* [An Ecclesiastical Encyclopedia] (Bangkok: Buddhist Association, 1972), pp. 721-729, 554.

It should be noted that the eight precepts differ from the five and the ten in the opening phrase, "Today and tonight...." This could be an indication of the general use of the eight precepts for those of the faithful who spend the Buddhist Holy Day within the precincts of the temple. The recital of the eight precepts, then, binds them only for a period of twenty-four hours. For any successive periods of similar duration, the ritual is, presumably, repeated.

Apart from the five precepts, the Law is generally referred to as consisting of holy writings, which, as far as the villagers are concerned, are the sermons written on palm leaves and kept in the *ho thamma*, the scripture storeroom. When one goes to the temple to listen to a sermon, one goes to "listen to the Law." The content of these sermons is considered to be the word of the Lord Buddha and, hence, closely tied up with the first element of the Triple Gems.

The Precepts as Perceived in Ku Dæng

The precepts are among the basic tenets of Buddhism that are repeatedly hammered into the community. A person's status in the religious structure is largely determined, at least in the eyes of the villagers, by his or her observance of the precepts. Thus, a person who frequently visits the temple for offering of food to the monks, and thereby receives the five precepts, is considered a "good person" or a "good Buddhist." Older people, who sleep in the temple compound the nights before and after Precept Day during the season of Lent, and there receive and keep the eight precepts, are considered "very good" or "very religious." One who keeps the ten precepts is called a novice (or, conversely, a novice is the person who keeps these particular ten precepts). Whenever a novice is unable or unwilling to keep the ten precepts, he ceases to be a novice. Similarly, a monk is one who keeps the 227 precepts until he can no longer observe them.

This, at least, is the theory. As in the case of most laws, there are infractions of the rules. In the first precept, the faithful Buddhist promises to abstain from killing animals or from ordering others to kill them. Here utilitarian reasoning plays an important role.[10] If it is expedient to kill an animal, it will be done, and the deed will be rationalized. We did not meet anyone who was not willing to admit that a little sinning would do him or her no particular harm, provided the person makes plenty of merit to offset the transgression. We did not encounter any vegetarians in the village; indeed vegetarianism is not one of the dominant characteristics of the Thai people. All the monks of our acquaintance partook of meals that included meat or fish dishes. Of course, it is rationalized, eating meat is not the same as killing animals. If the animal is dead already, there is no law against eating the flesh. But someone must kill the animals first, since not enough die of natural causes to satisfy the needs of all the people. Most of the butchers living in the district are of ethnic Chinese or Indian background, but there are also a number of Thai engaged in this profession.

In 1951, the Thai government issued a regulation forbidding the slaughter of cattle or swine on Precept Day. This did not, however, prevent the sale of pork on that day, since the butchers could kill the animals the

---

[10] Theme 1: Utility.

previous day. Beef, however, was unavailable on Precept Day, since slaughtering of cattle was strictly regulated at one per day because of a shortage of draft animals in the country dating back to World War II.

Most villagers are unwilling to sell a chicken or a duck on Precept Day if it is to be used for food that same day. There is no objection to selling it the day before, even if it is known that it will be killed on Precept Day.

During the rainy season, fish are caught at all times and serve as one of the main sources of food in addition to rice. Of course, fish are seldom "killed." They are caught and left in the sun to "die." Whatever killing needs to be done is in most cases accomplished by the younger people, frequently at the request of an older person. Thus, if a housewife is planning to prepare chicken curry for the harvesting crew, she asks her son to kill the chicken. It is expected that young people will live many more years giving them plenty of time to make more than enough merit to offset the demerits of killing.

There are other special cases concerning the first precept. It is not evil or wrong, for example, to kill rats in the house or in the field. One villager told us that the Lord Buddha himself permitted the killing of rats, after they had been nibbling at some of his sermons. He then created cats to rid himself of all the rats. It is, perhaps, for that reason that cats have always been honored as highly as monks—as we were told by one informant. Killing a cat is as serious a sin as killing a monk.

The World Health Organization initiated a malaria eradication program in one of the villages of Saraphi District in 1949. This was later extended to all the villages in the district as well as elsewhere in the province. The program met very little, if any, opposition on the part of the villagers other than that it made their houses look unsightly. One villager was observed "going after" mosquitoes with a lighted candle to cremate them near walls or windows.

The second precept, "Thou shalt not steal," is seldom violated overtly. It is respected as the law of the land and of the community, and violators are prosecuted by the civil authorities. The concept of private property is much the same as that found in the Western world. Unauthorized "borrowing" seldom takes place.

At an evening "bull session" in one of the village homes, three men were discussing which of the five precepts is the most important. The two older men agreed that the last precept, the one that prohibits partaking of anything intoxicating, is the most important one, at least in as far as it refers to drinking liquor. Both of these men smoked and chewed betel regularly; one of them used to drink heavily, but by the time of the discussion he took a drink only occasionally. They argued that drinking is the beginning of all evil. When a person is intoxicated, he or she will break all the other precepts. The third man, a younger person, who claimed he had never drunk a drop of liquor in all his life, maintained that the third precept was paramount: every man loves his wife and will defend her against improper advances by other men, which in turn leads to quarrels and killing.

The fourth precept, "Thou shalt not lie or use rude language," like the second, causes little difficulty. Just as the second is seldom violated overtly, so the fourth is seldom kept in the strictest sense of its meaning. Few people are able to restrain themselves so completely as to abstain from all frivolous or rude language.

Many people hold that Precept Day is a special day that should be kept "holy." This has various interpretations. Some villagers believe the Lord Buddha proscribed work on Precept Day for both man and beast. Thus, the village blacksmith did not open his shop on Precept Day. Other work is permitted, but one's regular occupation should not be pursued on that day. One of the monks told us that the Lord Buddha said nothing about working or not working on Precept Day, either for people or for animals. Here, in this part of the country, he said animals are not used for work on Precept Day because of an old custom. Moreover, people should not work on that day so that they are free to attend the temple. Elsewhere, the monk said, a different custom was observed: people work on Precept Day with as well as without animals. Other villagers made similar statements with regard to work on Precept Day.

Certain types of work are proscribed on Precept Day. For example, one should not take rice to the mill nor pound it in an old-fashioned rice pounder. However, we observed both activities occurring on that day. The rice mill is not closed on Precept Day. We once counted fifteen persons using the mill on such a day, which is more than half the average daily number of customers.

Other work observed in the vicinity of Ku Dæng on Precept Day included: oxen used for drawing carts for various purposes; people working in the fields at their ordinary tasks, with the exception of plowing; a hired mason working on the new base for the Buddha statue in the temple; and several men building new houses or rice barns.

The practice of asking for and receiving the five precepts at frequent intervals is directly related to the observance or non-observance of some or all of the precepts. The precepts are not given once and for all, as were the Ten Commandments when Moses came down from the mountain. Rather, the precepts are given as a special privilege that the monks bestow upon the faithful whenever requested. Thus, a Buddhist can make a new start periodically, each time acquiring some new merit to offset the sin that may have been committed a short time before.

Other Literature

In addition to external manifestations of Buddhism such as temple architecture and the yellow wardrobe of the monkhood, there are two ways in which religious ideas and concepts are impressed upon the people: one is through sermons and lectures by the monks, and the other is through religious pamphlets and magazines.[11] Of these, the former is by far the more influential since relatively few people have read or will read literature of any kind.

There are two kinds of sermons delivered by the monks and novices: sermons that are read from written texts on palm leaves, and extemporaneous sermons given by those monks who are able to lecture to a congregation on matters pertaining to religion or ethics.

Written sermons are by far the more prevalent types. Each temple keeps a whole series of sermons in the *ho thamma*. Villagers buy these palm-leaf sermons for specific, merit-making occasions to present to the temple, where they are kept for future use. Today, copies written into school notebooks with pen and ink are sometimes substituted for the palm-leaf variety that are increasingly difficult to secure. According to a list prepared by the Ku Daeng head monk in 1953, his temple had at that time thirty sets of sermons in Lanna Thai, consisting of a total of 116 sermons. Several copies of the same sermon are often available, since different members of the congregation may give copies of the same sermon to the temple. In addition to sermons in the local language, the Ku Daeng temple had at the time one set of sermons in Thai, which had been given through the combined efforts of some forty villagers "many, many years ago."

The sermons in Lanna Thai contain mostly Jataka tales. These have been passed on from generation to generation and are generally known by the name of the Lord Buddha in one of his incarnations prior to his Enlightenment. The most important one of these is that of Wetsandon (Vessantara), his last life before becoming the Lord Buddha. This story is also known as *Maha chat*, or "The Great Life." It consists of thirteen sermons, all of which are read on the full moon festival of the second month, by Northern reckoning, which usually falls in November.

All sermons of this type are written in the same general form. There is a brief introduction, saying that this is a story told by Lord Buddha, thus putting every word under his authority without any doubt as to its veracity. It is supposed to be an easy way for the lay people to understand the teachings of the Lord Buddha. Invariably, the stories contain romance, adventure, and magic. They generally have a happy ending. At the end of the sermon, morals are drawn (still in the words of the Lord Buddha), relating the events to *kamma*, merit, the Four Noble Truths, rebirth, and, in some cases, to the persons in the final life of Siddhartha, the Buddha.

---

[11] The word "sermon," like most other words pertaining to religious expression in this study, must be carefully defined so as to avoid misinterpretation by the reader familiar with Western connotations of such words. The word "sermon" is used here to refer to the oral presentations by religious functionaries in front of a congregation of believers. In the Western sense, a sermon implies that some message or instruction is imparted to the listener. This is not necessarily so when we talk about "preaching" or "delivering a sermon" in the present context.

These Lanna Thai sermons are always delivered in singsong chanting style. Usually, the task of presenting them is assigned to novices. They preach from the pulpit in front of the congregation and to one side of the Buddha statue. The preacher sits in a pulpit that can be entered from the rear. The sides and the front of the pulpit are enclosed by fancy woodwork. In order that the novice may be completely shielded from view, some old newspapers are stuck to the inside of the wooden lattice work on the side facing the congregation. The preacher, thereby, can concentrate on reading his sermons without having to be bothered with disturbances from the congregation.

Some monks and novices are especially versatile in a special form of delivery of these sermons. They present them with what could be called musical variations, dwelling on certain syllables and words for a considerable length of time, letting the voice range from normal to the highest falsetto according to some traditional prescription. In these cases, the local poet may add some parts to the sermon or change certain passages to be more suitable for presentation.

One of these musical presentations was given at Ku Daeng during the marathon preaching on the full moon festival of the second month (November) as part of the above mentioned *Maha chat* story. The sermon lasted over two hours, or more than twice the normal time of delivery. The monk, who was expected to preach this particular sermon, practiced nightly for three weeks prior to the festival. Villagers came to the temple to listen to the practice sessions. Several old men, including the village poet, listened critically, making notes to correct the monk when he had finished. On the actual day of the festival, the monk had also been invited to preach the same sermon at a temple some five miles distant from Ku Daeng. It so happened that he did not return to Ku Daeng until late at night. One of the Ku Daeng novices was asked, therefore, to take the monk's place. This boy had been learning the sermon as an "understudy" to the monk. Only a limited number of monks and novices are willing to spend sufficient time training for correct delivery to preach this type of sermon.

Villagers travel great distances to hear such a performance. Early in 1954 a young novice from a temple in another village came to study at the Ku Daeng temple for several weeks to learn this particular type of preaching from the second monk.

On some occasions, especially when merit is made for a deceased relative, a number of monks and novices are asked to participate in the preaching. The villagers usually are not willing to spend all day in the temple unless the occasion happens to take place on a regular Precept Day during the period of Buddhist Lent. In order to compromise between having as many sermons by as many monks as possible so as to obtain the greatest amount of merit, while spending only a reasonably short time in the temple, the villagers ask the monks to read the sermons simultaneously.[12] It is more expedient to have the sermons delivered in this fashion, but it is more profitable to have many sermons by many different monks. Some monks recommend reading each sermon individually and separately, but this is usually overruled by the villagers. At one time we had seventeen monks reading seventeen different sermons at the same time. To our untrained ears it seemed impossible to understand the content of a single sermon. Furthermore, in situations like this, the monks seldom read the entire sermon, but preach for only ten or fifteen minutes, cutting most of the content except for the beginning and the end. Normally it takes about an hour for one monk or novice to preach a whole sermon. There was unanimous agreement among those asked, whether they were laymen with little experience or education, or the best educated and highest ranking monks in Chiang Mai, that one could obtain merit simply by listening to the presentation of sermons, even though one did not understand a single word. One monk told us that listening to seventeen monks reciting seventeen sermons simultaneously would give a person seventeen times as much merit as listening to one monk delivering a sermon by himself. Our informants maintained that the important aspect of listening was the attitude one had toward preaching. As long as one's heart and mind were directed toward the goodness of the Law, one could not fail to make merit by being present at the delivery of the sermon.

Sermons delivered simultaneously, if given in the *wihan*, were always recited from the monks' platform along the south wall of the hall, with the senior monk sitting nearest the Buddha statue and the other monks continuing in descending order according to age and seniority. If only a group of novices were preaching alongside the head monk, the novices would sit immediately next to him ahead of the other monks.

During the period of Buddhist Lent, some sermons were delivered in the Thai language, as noted above. These sermons are of an entirely different nature from those in Pali or Lanna Thai. They are written by monks in the Bangkok area of Thailand; they usually consist of an exposition of ethical principles in Thai context. Thus, there were sermons on "Wisdom," "Evil," or "Perseverance." In each case, the pro and con of the main topic would be presented alternately, repeated in many different forms and fashions. Throughout the sermon, sayings of the Lord Buddha are liberally inserted. These quotations are usually in Pali, then translated directly into Thai, and finally explained in general terms. Great stress is laid on the concept of cause and effect. Again and again, the people are told that good deeds by necessity result in reward and bad deeds in punishment. Reward is usually described in terms of worldly wealth and honors, culminating in happiness. A happy person is one who is rich. An unhappy person is one who has no money.

---

[12] Theme 1: Utility and Theme 2: Profit.

121

Reference to patriotism is made at least once in every sermon. Thus, one characteristic of a diligent person is that he will accumulate wealth, and one of the five uses that he can make out of this accumulation of wealth is "to give to King and country, such as pay respect to the King, pay one's taxes, help one's country in times of trouble, and share one's wealth with the nation for progress." On only very rare occasions is a story included in these sermons.

Thai sermons are much shorter than those in Lanna Thai. They seldom last more than twenty minutes. Such sermons are not delivered by popular demand but rather by order of the Buddhist Ecclesiastical Organization regional headquarters for the northern part of Thailand. All the temples in the area were told to preach at least one Thai sermon each Precept Day during Lent. It was permitted to substitute extemporaneous preaching by a visiting monk. Consequently, Thai sermons were preached at Ku Daeng on only about half the Precept Days of Lent. Since these sermons are supposed to be lectures for the benefit of the people, they are delivered by the preacher sitting cross-legged on the preaching chair—a large, wooden armchair placed in front of the congregation. The delivery is in plain language, without any embellishments. It was noted that most of the monks and novices in this part of the country found Thai sermons more difficult to read than those in Lanna Thai.

The third kind of sermon heard in Ku Dæng, and seemingly the most popular one, is the extemporaneous sermon, usually delivered by visiting monks. On some Precept Days during Lent, or on some other special occasions for *thambun* in private homes, well-known monks of the area were invited to preach to the villagers. Sometimes the head monk of the Ku Dæng temple invited one of his colleagues from a neighboring temple, and sometimes individual villagers invited monks whom they wanted to hear. At the ordination service of a new novice described elsewhere, one of the best-known and most widely respected preachers from Chiang Mai was invited to preach.[13]

Extemporaneous sermons are always given from the preaching chair in front of the congregation, or, sometimes, from right in the middle of the *wihan* with the people sitting all around the monk. If the sermon is delivered in a home, a chair is usually found somewhere and placed in the middle of the room for the monk to sit upon foreign—Western—style. On a few occasions visiting monks chose to stand up for preaching.

If the occasion is a special one, such as a *thambun* for the dead, or the ordination of a novice, the preacher will speak on a subject related to the event. He may explain why it is good and proper to make merit and then transfer it to the dead, or what is the meaning and origin of the ordination service. At other, more general occasions, such as on Precept Day, the preacher often speaks on any subject he feels should be of interest to the

---

[13] See pp. 137-144.

villagers. Such sermons are usually on a moral subject and are similar in content to that found in the printed Thai sermons.

Extemporaneous sermons are almost always delivered in the collo-quial language and usually include references to local situations, which the people understand and love to hear. Some of the best visiting preachers embellished their sermons with stories here and there, some of which caused considerable mirth and merriment. Sometimes a visiting monk criticizes the customs prevailing in the host village. One monk told the Ku Dæng villagers that it was improper to offer food to the monks in the *wihan*, since this was not the place for food to be eaten. It should be offered in one of the *sala* or in the monks' living quarters. This admonition had little effect on the villagers, who preferred their customary routine.

Not all the monks in the Chiang Mai area are necessarily Northern Thai by birth. Some come from the central plains, others from the South, and, therefore, usually preach in the Central Thai language. Such sermons were generally found to be less effective than those in the vernacular.

An older monk from a neighboring temple preached frequently in Ku Dæng. More than once he talked to us afterwards and explained that he always had to mix Lanna Thai with his Thai (actually he always preached in near-perfect Lanna Thai), so that the people could understand what he was saying.

The monk who preached at the ordination service referred to above was a Southern man who knew only very little Lanna Thai. He preached in Thai with only a few words of local usage thrown in here and there. This sermon was a rare exception and should be classified with simultaneous preaching of Lanna Thai sermons already described, benefit from which accrues to those present simply by being there, whether the contents are understood or not.

On several occasions, such as the *thambun* for the dead in one of the Ku Dæng homes, or at a special *thambun* during the Lenten season, villagers spontaneously requested one of the monks to tell them a story or preach a sermon. This usually happened when a monk well known for his speaking ability happened to be present at the regular service.

Of all the local monks and novices only the head monk was ever observed to give an extemporaneous speech, and that happened only once on Precept Day, before the presentation of food. This was one of the first Precept Days during Lent, and the head monk tried to explain the meaning of Lent to his congregation.

He traced the observance of Lent back to the time of the Lord Buddha who ordered all of his disciples to stay in one place during the rainy season and not to walk through the rice fields so as not to damage the farmers' newly-planted rice seedlings. But there is also practical meaning in Lent for the lay person. During this time the roads are in bad condition, so that the farmers cannot attend to much business away from home. This is an excellent opportunity for becoming better acquainted with the monks and for meditating and thinking about religious matters.

Then he urged the young people to attend the temple more regularly, because they, too, will die one day of an as yet unforeseen cause. To delay making merit and going to the temple until one is old and approaching the end of one's life may be a losing gamble. From this he went on to say that all people ought to help the temple when it is in need of something. Right at that time there was a need for financial help for the rebuilding of the base of the Buddha statue; and so, he used the opportunity to urge everyone, and especially the young people, to contribute their share.

During our stay in the village, both the head monk and the second monk of Ku Dæng preached extemporaneous sermons to the school children at times set by the school authorities. These sermons were supposed to be given in Thai. When no observer was present, the preferred language was Lanna Thai. At one time we attended such a session, when the second monk was lecturing to the school children rather haltingly in the Thai language. While he was still speaking, I was called back to our house to welcome some visitors. My assistant reported that as soon as I had departed, the monk breathed a sigh of relief and said, "Ah, now we can talk in our own language!"

One Precept Day during Lent the senior novice preached extemporaneously to the Ku Dæng congregation. He spoke about the desire for goodness within a person. Everybody wants to be good in the same way that one wants to eat and work. Evil comes upon a person without his or her specific desire, for one knows that doing evil can only result in evil for oneself. One should, therefore, protect oneself from evil consequences by doing no evil, thinking no evil, and speaking no evil.[14]

In general, there did not seem to be a very great demand for the Ku Dæng monks to preach extemporaneous sermons. At no time did one of the villagers invite a local monk or novice to preach other than written sermons. If a special preaching was desired, a preacher from another temple was invited.

Buddhist literature within the village was practically non-existent. The monthly magazine *Buddhist News*, published by the Buddhist Association of Chiang Mai, was regularly received by the temple for the monks and novices to read. Some villagers who came to the temple leafed through any issue that happened to be lying on the table. We failed to observe any determined or systematic reading on the part of lay persons in the village.

A typical issue of *Buddhist News*, that of July 26, B.E. 2496/1953, contained the following articles:

    1. an editorial on the difference between jealousy and evil;

---

[14] Theme 6: "Do good, receive good—Do evil, receive evil."

2. a reprint of an article on Buddhist Lent from the magazine *Buddhist Religion;*
3. a discussion on consciousness;
4. a reprint of a section of a book by a monk, *Where is Peace?;*
5. "Buddhism and World Peace," by Clay Lancaster of Columbia University (translated into Thai);
6. the last in a series on cause and effect by one of the leading monks in the Chiang Mai Buddhist Association;
7. second in a series, "Bear Yourself According to Your Name," by another well-known monk from Chiang Mai;
8. "Looking Through Glasses," a monthly column on everyday problems; and
9. miscellaneous poems, letters, and short announcements.

The temple also has a series of books on the various chants used by the villagers for morning and evening devotions. Before receiving food and offering the precepts on one particular Precept Day during Lent, the head monk scolded the congregation for not chanting more enthusiastically and louder during their part of the service. In fact, most of the chants are sung primarily by older men or those who have previously been monks or novices. A few older women move their lips as if they were participating, but there is little sound coming from their section in the *wihan*. On this particular day, the head monk suggested that the villagers make an effort to learn the chants. He told them that he had the books in the monks' quarters, so that anyone desiring to learn the chants could borrow the books. Those villagers unable to read could get help from the novices, who would teach them the chants. As far as we could determine, only one or two villagers were willing to borrow the books from the monks, and none came for instruction to the novices.

One day the monks distributed a booklet by a Chiang Mai monk, *Khrai kha khrai næ* [Who really kills whom?], an essay about various vices and their effects on a person.[15] Free-will offerings of 1 baht per book were collected for a total of sixty copies.

Some villagers own copies of sermons or booklets that they copied from other monks' books when they themselves were ordained and stayed in the temple. On some nights, when friends have gathered in a house, someone with a good voice, usually an ex-monk or ex-novice, reads part of a sermon or a passage from a book. Here again, emphasis seemed to be placed on delivery rather than on content.

The monks' handbook are always written in Lanna Thai, copied from copies of books that some other monk may have owned. No references or credits are given in these books, except an occasional listing of the name of

---

[15] Thammanantha Bhikkhu, *Khrai kha khrai næ* [Who really kills whom?] (Chiang Mai: Buddhist Association, 1953).

the monk who owned the book from which the present copy was made. One such book was translated in the course of our study.[16] The first section deals with directions for the layman on how to conduct a simple offering of gifts in the temple; it also explains the purpose of meditation in some detail. This is followed by a listing of thirteen kinds of evil intentions, which are recorded as demerits *(akuson)*. A large section of the book is devoted to instructions for the use of a "watch" table, a system designed to foretell the future according to the year and the day of a person's birth. The final part of the book contains ninety-seven proverbs attributed to the Lord Buddha.

Some poetry has been produced in Ku Dæng. The father of one of the village elders was a poet of considerable renown, according to one of our informants. He was a nobleman who spent much of his time composing poetry. This he sold to the villagers, who were eager to buy it. Some of the poems were even printed in Chiang Mai, although we could not find any actual examples of his writings. The poet's nephew, the Ku Dæng temple leader at the time of our stay in the village, followed in his uncle's literary tradition. He wrote poetic eulogies for the memorial services of deceased villagers—even the dead of other villages.

The Sangha or Monkhood

The third element of the Triple Gems, and perhaps the most evident one in Thailand, is the Sangha or monkhood.[17] One can go nowhere in Thailand, whether in the cities or the country, without coming upon the yellow robes of the monkhood. The yellow robe, the shaven head, and, to a lesser extent, the red umbrella are the hallmarks of the Buddhist monkhood in Thailand. According to the villagers, the shaven head and the yellow robes are signs to the people that a person is a monk and, therefore, should behave like a monk and keep the 227 precepts. Furthermore, these outward symbols make it rather difficult for someone to impersonate a monk.

From an early age, village children are conditioned to the presence and the role of the monks. When mothers or grandparents go to the temple to present food or receive the precepts, they usually take the little children with them. While the early childhood years prior to school attendance are marked by freedom and permissiveness, an exception occurs on temple

---

[16] See below, p. 185, for example.

[17] Many arguments have been advanced for using either the terms "priest" and "temple" or the terms "monk" and "monastery" with reference to the Buddhist ecclesiastical order. While the evidence in Ku Dæng shows that the members of the ecclesiastical order perform certain functions in conducting religious rites and services normally associated with the functions performed by priests in other religions, still the term "monk" has been used in current scholarship on Buddhism in Thailand because monks renounce the world. Since "monastery" in Western usage usually refers solely to the residence of a community of "monks," the term monastery has been discarded here in favor of "temple"—with the term "temple" standing for the *whole* temple complex and its various buildings and their associated functions.

visits. The children are admonished to fit into a set pattern by sitting quietly and holding their hands in the *wai* position, just like grown-ups. To the child, the monk appears as an exalted person who resembles the big stone figure of the Lord Buddha inside the temple.

From earliest school days, religion is included in the curriculum. One of the monks is invited to teach the children from time to time, bi-monthly according to a government directive. Even in the home, the importance of the monkhood is made manifest to the children. Is not the best food and the sweetest dessert *(khanom)* prepared the day before Precept Day to be presented to the monks the following day?

For the pupils of the elementary school, a special profession of the Buddhist faith was held near the end of the first term of school on July 31 of the 1953 school year. Only 63% of the children were present, since it was nearly the last day of school. About sixty boys and girls were led by their teachers into the *wihan*. The boys sat in front, the girls behind according to the usual division of the sexes inside the temple. The head monk entered and prostrated himself three times in front of the Buddha statue. Then, the head teacher led the children in a similar observance to pay respect to the Buddha image, the Buddhist Law, and the monkhood. He bowed *(krap)* three times from a kneeling position by sitting on his heels and touching the ground with forearms and forehead. He continued as leader in a Pali responsive chant of veneration to the Lord Buddha. At this time three of the Ku Dæng novices entered, bowed to the Buddha statue and the head monk in the same manner as that mentioned above, and then sat down on the monks' platform along the north wall of the *wihan*. The chant was followed by a single bow on the part of the pupils, who then recited a profession of faith in Thai.

> Oh our most respected monk! We have come to show our desire to worship the Lord Buddha, who died and went to *nipphan* long ago.
> We also wish to worship the Law of the Lord Buddha and the Holy Monkhood and promise allegiance to them for our support.
> We beg thee, our most respected monk, to acknowledge us as belonging to the Buddhist community.
> We venerate the Lord Buddha with this our offering.
> [Here follows one bow *(krap)*.]
> We venerate the Law of the Lord Buddha with this our offering.
> [One bow.]
> We venerate the Holy Monkhood with this our offering.
> [One bow.][18]

---

[18] Translated from the head teacher's notebook.

Then, the head teacher presented a tray of flowers, candles, and incense to the head monk. At the chanted request of the head teacher, the head monk gave the five precepts to the children, who repeated each one after him. All of these formal chants were recited in the Pali language.

Once more the head monk did three bows and seated himself on the preaching chair in front of the children. The head teacher then chanted a request for preaching, to which the head monk replied with a chant of praise and the following extemporaneous sermon in Thai:

> I am glad to have this opportunity to preach to you on the occasion of your profession of the Buddhist faith, which means that you wish to accept the Lord Buddha as your refuge. All of you were born into Buddhist families. It is, therefore, your duty to comport yourselves as faithful members of the Buddhist community.
>
> We venerate the Lord Buddha because we know that the Lord Buddha became enlightened through his own efforts and came to know and understand every creature in the world and to lead them to eternal peace and happiness.
>
> You were sent to school by your parents, who want you to learn to know the world. While you are in school, you must pay good attention and try to understand the lessons. How is it that your classmate, who is learning the same lessons as you and is taught by the same teachers, knows more than you? The reason is that he is paying better attention to what is taught than you are. If you do not pay attention to your lessons, you will fail in your examinations, and if you fail in your examinations, you will never succeed in your studies. On the other hand, if you pay good attention to your lessons, you will pass your examinations, and then your parents will be very happy when you have finished your studies. You will have a chance to take care of your parents as they have taken care of you.
>
> Very soon school will be closed to give you time to help your parents with their work in the fields. Each day, when you have finished helping your parents, you should not spend all of your spare time playing games, but you should study what you have been taught in school, so that you will better understand your lessons and not forget them. You must try to understand. If you are in doubt, ask someone to explain, so that you can remember. If you are, therefore, diligent during your vacation, you will not be far behind your classmates when school begins again next month.
>
> Before ending this sermon, I beg all the most respected things in the world to come and protect you

during your school vacation from every kind of illness and
inspire you to pay attention to what you have learned.

When the monk had finished, once more the children prostrated themselves
three times, and the monk dismissed them with a Pali blessing.

Many parents consider it an honor to have one or more of their small
sons become a temple boy for a time. There seem to be two ways in which a
temple boy is chosen. One is by his own desire or through the gentle
pressure of his parents. The second way is at the request of a monk or
novice. We were told on many occasions that no one could become a temple
boy against his will. Usually, boys ask their parents for permission to go to
the temple, which is always granted. Smaller boys frequently play in the
vicinity of the temple grounds. This is quite natural, since the local school is
built on temple property adjacent to the temple itself. The entire temple
area, then, becomes the children's playground. If a monk or novice takes a
special interest in a boy, he may ask him to become his temple boy. Such a
boy will then help this particular mentor in a variety of tasks, especially
those which the monk or novice is not ordinarily permitted to do. This
method of selection of temple boys does not seem to be the usual custom in
Ku Dæng; throughout our stay in the village, there were usually only four or
five boys living with the monks. The temple boys receive their subsistence
from the monks. They also are instructed in the writings and readings of
Lanna Thai and Pali. In return, the boys serve as general factotums for the
monks while they are in their own temple or when they are traveling.

Temple boys do not seem to come from any one particular type of
home or economic strata. Since a novice usually must have been a temple
boy before entering the monkhood, we can assume that the distribution of
types of homes from which temple boys have come is the same as that for
novices. According to our survey, the kind of home a novice comes from is
not related to the economic circumstances of that particular household.

There are a variety of incentives to become a novice or a monk. First,
there is the mass appeal of the religion as such. Since everybody in the
village is a Buddhist, religion and its external expressions are taken for
granted as part of village life. The community of monks and novices occupies center stage on the village scene. All members of the order live together
in fellowship as one big family—or at least that is the impression one gets
from the outside. They are respected and honored by the villagers. As soon
as a person puts on a yellow robe, he will be venerated by the rest of the
villagers, who prostrate themselves before him at the proper time. There is,
then, an appeal to the desire for recognition and prestige.

Those who wish to enter the monkhood in Ku Dæng as novices must
become temple boys first. This gives them the chance to learn from the

novices and monks how to read Lanna Thai.[19] A boy must have finished fourth grade in the village elementary school before he can become a novice. In actual practice, this does not necessarily mean that he has passed the final examination; he must at least have attended fourth grade for a full year. Before becoming a novice, he must pass an examination for new novices given at Wat Pa Kæyong, one of the bigger temples in the Saraphi district. The novice-to-be must, of course, also have the approval of the head monk of the temple in which he wishes to be resident. As a result of the educational requirement, most novices today do not enter the temple before they are 14 or 15 years old. In former days, when there was no school requirement, boys became novices as early as age 10.

In many parts of Thailand, especially in the cities and among the more highly educated groups, it is customary for boys to enter the monkhood as novices for a weekend or for seven days, or, at most, for one three-month period in Lent. In Bang Chan, near Bangkok, young men who enter the monkhood announce before their ordination how long they intend to be monks. In Ku Dæng, on the other hand, we were told by the villagers as well as the head monk, that according to their own recollections monks and novices never specified their length of stay ahead of time and usually remained in the monkhood for a number of years. The shortest residence within memory of our informants was for one year. Our own census figures revealed the case of a 64-year-old man who said he had been ordained as a novice for just seven days before he reached the age of 20.

Students in the bigger schools in Chiang Mai rarely have had experience in the monkhood. A survey of one hundred students in Chiang Mai, whose homes were located in more than thirty provinces in the North, the Northeast, and the Bangkok area, and who were studying in eleventh or twelfth grade, indicated that only one, whose home was in Lamphun, had been a novice for as much as a whole year. Two other students, from Central Thailand near Bangkok, said they had been novices for three and seven days, respectively.

Merit and Demerit

Closely related to the concept of the precepts is one of the fundamental tenets of Buddhism as understood in the village: the idea of merit and demerit—*bun* and *bap*.[20] These words are constantly on the lips of the villagers. At frequent intervals, something or other will be done to *thambun* or "make merit." Each person has something like a personal account in

---

[19] This is not necessary in Central Thailand, where the common language is the same as that taught in the schools.

[20] Since for Western readers the word "sin" is usually associated with "transgression against the law of God," which is also Webster's definition, I have chosen to translate the Thai word *bap* as "demerit" in order to pair it off with "merit," which is the usual translation for *bun*.

which his merit is recorded. To a lesser extent, but quite as realistically, the people talk about demerit. If a person has committed an act that results in demerit, the account should be evened up by making merit.[21]

To define merit in precise terms is as difficult as defining "happiness." The dictionary of the Royal Institute defines merit *(bun)* as a "means to purify one's habit; goodness; *kuson;* happiness."[22] This does not convey the impression one usually gets of acquiring a certain amount of merit for the future. A new word appears, *kuson,* which seems to be paired with *bun* and is frequently synonymous with it. When we asked villagers or monks what merit is, they usually answered, after some thought, that it means *kuson.* A visiting monk, educated in the South of Thailand, told us that merit is happiness, which brings bliss *(phongsai)* to the mind *(cit-cai)* whereas *kuson* has a higher connotation than merit. He continued as follows:

> Merit and *kuson* are always a pair, *kuson* being the higher of the two. *Kuson* comes first, followed by merit; that means, merit is the result of *kuson.*

> In making merit in Buddhism, a person who has great faith *(sattha)* but little wisdom *(panya),* receives more faith as a result. But a person who has little faith and much wisdom, receives *kuson.* In doing good *(tham di)* one receives *kuson;* in receiving good *(dai di)* one gets merit. Conversely, in doing evil *(tham chua)* one receives *akuson*— the negative of *kuson;* and in receiving evil *(dai chua)* one obtains demerit *(bap).*

Few of the villagers would have been able to follow this reasoning. To them merit means what they receive as reward for being good or for carrying out certain religious prescriptions.

"Demerit" *(bap)* is defined in the dictionary of the Royal Institute as "wickedness, fierceness, wretchedness."[23] It is a word used much less frequently in Ku Dæng than the word "merit." People always speak about the merit they are making or planning to make. Demerit is seldom discussed. Nevertheless, whenever an act is committed that is thought to bring demerit in its wake, the person concerned is sure to try to make some merit as soon as possible, whether it is at the regular offering of food or at a special merit-making occasion.

---

[21] See also Phon Rattanasuwan, *Guide for Teaching Buddhism to Children* (1952).

[22] *Royal Institute Dictionary* (1950); also see *Pru's Standard Dictionary* (1955). It is noteworthy that the official dictionary of the Royal Institute of 1982 defines *bun* as "doing good according to the principles and teachings of religion; goodness." No reference is made to *kuson.* However, the entry for the latter gives *bun* as a synonym.

[23] *Royal Institute Dictionary* (1950). The 1982 revised edition defines *bap* as "doing wrong according to principles of teaching or prohibitions in religion; evil; guilt."

A book used by the Ku Dæng monks in their bi-monthly instruction of school children gives the following discourse based on a *sutta* in the Buddhist canon on the relationship between merit and demerit:

> You will easily understand the following example. Suppose we have a handful of salt, which we put into a glassful of water. Will the water be quite salty? If we put the same amount of salt into a small water jar, won't this water be somewhat less salty than the water in the glass? Finally, if we pour the salt into a river, the water will not taste salty at all. Isn't that right?

> Some people make demerit (that is, commit an evil deed) like a handful of salt. Their merit, which is the same as their good deeds, is very small, just like a glassful of water. The demerit of such persons is quite obvious to everybody; they will receive evil consequences, just as the water in the glass became very salty.

> If a person's merit is great, like the water in the water jar, and his demerit is still only like a handful of salt, the evil result of this demerit will be insignificant, like the saltiness of the water in the jar. If a person's merit is exceedingly plentiful, like the water of a river and his demerit only like a handful of salt, the demerit will have no result whatsoever, as long as the person is protected by his merit; but if one's merit dries up, even a little demerit will show its consequences.[24]

There are a variety of ways in which a person can obtain merit. The most common method, of course, is through gifts to the monks or novices. Occasions for this are plentiful.

Every morning the villagers bring food to the monks. The village of Ku Dæng is divided into eight sections to facilitate the preparation and presentation of food for the temple. On the day before a particular section's turn, a gong is sounded in the neighborhood to remind the villagers to prepare extra food. The theme of utility is once more in evidence here. It is much more convenient to prepare food for the temple on certain days than to send it irregularly.[25] It is likewise much more convenient, both for the monks and the villagers, to have the food brought to the temple. The monks thereby do not embarrass those villagers who have no food for them, nor do they need to remember to what section of the village they should go on a particular day. On the villagers' side, they can take the food to the temple more or less at their own pleasure. The food will be much more inviting

---

[24] Phon Rattanasuwan (1952), pp. 98-99.

[25] Theme 1: Utility.

when it is not all mixed up in a dozen monks' bowls. We were told that the monks in Ku Dæng never go out to receive their own food in the fashion of monks and novices resident in city temples. One excuse given by the villagers is that the roads are so bad during the rainy season that the people could not ask the monks to go out. However, even though the roads were much improved during the development period in the 1960s, the custom of taking food to the temple continued unabated throughout the thirty-year period of observation. On the rare occasion when the villagers do not bring sufficient food for those in the temple, the temple boys either cook some extra food or will go to nearby houses, where they know that extra food is always available. It is generally understood in all Buddhist communities that the monks are graciously providing the villagers with the opportunity to make merit, rather than the villagers merely giving alms to the monks.

Gifts other than food also provide merit for the donor. A monk told us that the Lord Buddha taught that we should present gifts to all living creatures, not only the monks, but to all those in need, even animals. Thus, merit can be made by giving gifts to anyone. We experienced this personally on a number of occasions. From time to time we desired to buy fruit for our breakfast. We found that the villagers were generally not willing to sell us anything. When we asked our landlady for the reason, she told us that they would like to give us the fruit, for by so doing they would make merit. There is no merit in selling something, even if it is sold cheaply.

Opinions differ as to what kinds of gifts make merit and what kinds do not. One old man, an ex-monk himself, said that many people do not know how to make merit. They do not know what to give to the monks. It should be something useful. Frequently people give ordinary blankets, clothing, household utensils, and other "worldly" goods. This man always gave candles or robes or other items that a monk can use in the temple. He felt he would get more merit for this. The old man had obviously forgotten that monks in this area can sell what they have received and then use the money for something more "useful." Thus, even if his critique of "usefulness" were true, almost any gift would make merit for the giver.

Giving has taken such deep roots in the minds of the people that in many instances villagers give without realizing that it is for merit. One day while we were visiting the kamnan at his house, a young girl appeared on his steps asking for rice. Without any ado, the kamnan called his daughter to give the girl half a pint of rice. Together with others from the same village, she had left early in the morning from her home in a district in the neighboring province of Lamphun. They were poor people who did not have enough rice to last them all year. At that time the new crop of rice had not yet been harvested, and, therefore, the people had to go out begging. The kamnan told us he always has to give them a little rice when they come to his house, "because otherwise they wouldn't have anything to eat." Sometimes people ask him for money; he will give them 1 baht or 50 satang. If the person looks well-fed or seems to be strong, the kamnan may ask him why he is not working. In such cases, the *kamnan* told us, the beggar will leave on his own accord. If the *kamnan* has some work around his house, he may ask such a person to work for him. To the question whether or not he makes merit in cases of this type, he answered, "I don't know. It doesn't matter. The important thing is that the person would have nothing to eat if we did not help." He voiced a similar attitude toward beggars in the market place. He always gives such people 25 satang, if he has some coins in his pocket. If he has already given them something that day, he will tell them so. In 1952 a big flood destroyed the entire crop of another village in the Saraphi district, which happened to be a Christian community. Villagers from Ku Dæng as well as from other villages in Tambon Nong Fæk, collected rice to send to the stricken people. The religious affiliation of the needy villagers was not relevant. If a home burns down, the villagers collect rice, household goods, and money to help the destitute family. In all of these cases, the *kamnan* said, the question of merit is secondary.

Some of the older people give things to the temple at every conceivable occasion, for they wish to accumulate as much merit as possible before their death. One old lady worked hard at various tasks to make a little extra money, which she invariable gave to the temple. One of her pastimes was collecting feathers that ducks had shed while sleeping in their pens. She made about 3 baht per pound—then worth 15 cents. One day she received an invitation to attend a wedding in another village. We asked her whether she would go. "No," was the answer, "I don't have any money. I just sold two pounds of duck feathers for 6 baht. I have given five of them to the temple, so that I have only 1 baht left, and that is not enough to go to a wedding." At other occasions this woman gave sets of sermons, trays of food, screens to cover the food, buckets for drawing water, and other useful articles to the temple. She told us that for her remaining years—she was then over 70—she would give every penny she made to the temple for merit.

Gift-giving is not the only means by which one can acquire merit. Obeying the five precepts is meritorious. By the same token, transgressing the precepts will bring demerit. Just being present for a religious occasion provides one with merit. In the villagers' eyes we acquired tremendous merit by our regular attendance at temple functions, even though we did not participate in any of the overt actions of the various ceremonies.

On most occasions involving participation of monks or novices, sermons will be read. During the season of Lent, sermons were preached every Precept Day. At funerals, at merit-making ceremonies for the dead, or at new-house-blessing ceremonies, the monks were always invited to chant sermons and occasionally to deliver extemporaneous speeches. All of these occasions bring some merit to those who organized the particular ceremony and also to those who presented gifts to the monks or novices. In addition, every person who came to listen to the sermons made merit simply by being present.

There seems to be merit involved in listening to a sermon per se, even without understanding a single word. Some of the sermons were preached in Thai, especially during the Lent period. Few of the villagers understood very much of these sermons; yet, we were told, they made merit by just listening attentively.

When Lanna Thai sermons were chanted, often several monks chanted the sermons simultaneously. But they would neither read in unison nor start or finish together. Furthermore, on many such occasions the monks chanted different sermons altogether. We once heard seventeen monks chant seventeen different sermons at the same time, we inquired as to the value of such peformances. Monks from different parts of Thailand told us that the value of a sermon depends only on a listener's attitude. A person might understand every word of a sermon, but if he feels no happiness in his heart, he will receive no merit. Conversely, if a person listens with an appreciative heart, full of happiness and bliss, but does not understand a single word, he will still gain the full amount of merit. We were told that seventeen monks preaching seventeen different sermons simultaneously provide the listener with seventeen times as much merit as if he were listening to one monk preaching a single sermon. Elsewhere, we heard that this custom of simultaneous preaching is practiced only in Northern Thailand. One villager, an ex-novice, told us that we could listen to any one of the sermons or to none, if we wished; it would make no difference. Actually, he said, the sermons were intended for the listening pleasure of ghosts (phi).

In making merit, whatever is done must be done cheerfully. One of the books used for instructing elementary school children in Buddhist tenets states that a person offering gifts for merit must do so with a cheerful heart, otherwise he will gain no merit.[26] One of the monks, whom we interviewed, gave us a list of four conditions that must be fulfilled in order to make merit through gifts: 1) through the offering of the gifts we must be released from our innate greed; 2) we must give cheerfully; 3) we must not begrudge the monks our gifts; and 4) the gifts must be useful for the monks. The only tangible condition is the last one, and that, as we have seen above, can be interpreted according to the giver's pleasure.

Closely related to merit and demerit is a proverb attributed to the Lord Buddha, found in the same textbook for school children: "As the seed is sown, so the fruit will grow; do good and receive good, do evil and receive evil."[27]

Again and again, we have heard the second half of this saying quoted in sermons and religious discussions. It is, in fact, the basis of the solid trust in the law of cause and effect that provides the people with merit and

---

[26] Phon Rattanasuwan (1952), p. 104.

[27] Phon Rattanasuwan (1952), p. 134; Theme 6: "Do good, receive good—Do evil, receive evil."

demerit. By this law they can explain every condition in which they find themselves; they can admonish their children and fellow citizens to practice good behavior; they can have comfort in their own future life, provided they have done "good" now.

Most of the Buddhist ethics of the villagers can be traced back to this axiom, "do good and receive good, do evil and receive evil." It is perfectly suited to the profit theme of village life. The villagers will do something only if it can reasonably be expected to show some profit.[28] A good deed, they are told, will invariably bring good reward or profit, while a bad deed brings nothing but misfortune in its wake.

Elaborate stories are told in sermons and in textbooks to illustrate this law of cause and effect. The most common example is that of the thief or killer who gets away without being caught by the authorities. He takes up abode in a different province, where no one knows him. He may even marry again and raise a family. But within him his guilt is gnawing away until he loses all his property (loss of property is usually given as the prime example of evil consequences) and is visited by sickness and other misfortunes until eventually he is driven to death. The moral of the story is that there is no escape from inevitable punishment. Therefore, one should do good in the first place so that one will be rewarded only with good consequences.

---

[28] Theme 2: Profit.

8

THE BUDDHIST MONKHOOD IN KU DÆNG

The Ordination of a Novice

The ordination of a young boy into the monkhood as a novice serves as an occasion for a big village festival. Since it is a relatively rare occurrence in this part of the country, the villagers rejoice to have this opportunity for entertainment and merit-making.

A 15-year-old temple boy, the son of a poor farmer, desired to become a novice during the year of our study. He had been in the temple for some time, where he had studied reading and writing Lanna Thai with the novices and monks. He had gone through fourth grade for one year and was repeating this grade at the beginning of the school year. He had passed the examination of qualification for becoming a novice and had obtained permission from the head monk as well as from his parents to become a novice. With all prerequisites thus fulfilled, he requested the Ku Dæng head monk to set an auspicious day for the ordination.

Since the boy's father was not well off, an uncle undertook to sponsor the boy's ordination. About two weeks before the event, the *kamnan* called all the villagers together in the temple. He informed them of the date of the ordination festival and of the fact that there would be a temple fair at which a *like* troupe from a neighboring village would come and play for two nights.[1] Since the leader of the troupe was a relative of the family that sponsored the ordination, there would be no fee for the performance. The *kamnan* also said that he hoped that on one of the two nights they could get a movie from United States Information Service (USIS) in Chiang Mai, for which he solicited our help. Since the festival was entertainment for the entire village, each villager was asked to help the parents and the uncle of the boy to be ordained by contributing one liter of rice and 1.50 baht per household, thereby making merit for themselves as well as assisting in the community project.[2]

A few days later, the *kamnan* went to Chiang Mai to request a well-known monk to come to Ku Dæng to deliver a sermon for the ordination on May 26th. Sermons by good preachers are among major attractions for the elderly and devout at fairs and celebrations.

Preparations for the ordination started on Saturday, May 23, 1953. All day and long into the night a bustle of activities took place both at the house of the parents and that of the sponsor. In the evening some fifty people were

---

[1] A popular type of unmasked folk opera with both male and female performers.
[2] Theme 5: Communal responsibility.

gathered in the parents' house. The mother was busy in the kitchen preparing food for the monks, to be taken to the temple in the morning for a special *thambun* ceremony. Some women were helping with this task, others just sitting in the kitchen, watching or talking. The men and some young people were gathered in the main room of the house, where a phonograph was playing Northern songs. Everybody seemed to be enjoying the occasion, chatting with friends and neighbors and listening to music. The following morning the parents took the food to the monks, thereby officially initiating the ceremonies.

On Monday morning the scene shifted to the uncle's house, where some seventy or eighty men and women were milling about. Most of the women were inside the house, busy with a myriad of activities, such as preparing flowers, making *miang*, and rolling cigarettes out of local tobacco, to have everything ready for the many guests that were already beginning to arrive.[3] In the banana grove behind the house a temporary kitchen had been erected, where one of the men of the village presided over huge frying pans ready to prepare the curries for the crowd.

At three o'clock in the afternoon, the gifts for the temple were taken out of the house and placed on a bamboo litter to be carried in procession to the temple. There were more than thirty earthenware jars—*khontho*—each decorated with a money tree consisting of five 1-baht notes, all kinds of clothing, shoes, a suitcase, bedding, a mattress, and a four-poster bed—all of which were either presents for the temple or things which the new novice would need for his stay in the monkhood.

An hour later, the boy was carried out of the house by an older relative. His head and eyebrows had been shaved; he was dressed in a pink sarong, a white, long-sleeved shirt, and a pink headdress; and he was wearing dark glasses, rings on his fingers, lipstick, and face powder. Most villagers, responding to questions, were vague as to the reason for this type of appearance. From information gathered outside the village, it was clear that the ordination ceremony is supposed to represent a re-enactment of the story of the Buddha from the time he left his princely home (therefore the type of dress) to the time he reached enlightenment under the Bo tree. Only one person in Ku Dæng, one of the monks, was able to give as much as a hint that that was the purpose for this imagery. Many people, including influential lay leaders of the temple, said that the boy was supposed to be dressed as beautifully as possible, since this was the last time that he could wear clothing other than the yellow robes of the monkhood. One or two persons said that this was a Burmese dress and custom, but they could not give a reason for the choice of such a dress. Burmese dress for men is generally of this same type. The dark glasses, perhaps, are to indicate that the young prince is fleeing his home in disguise.

---

[3] *Miang* consists of fermented tea leaves wrapped around a lump of salt or sugar, eaten like chewing gum; it is used only in Northern Thailand.

At the foot of the stairs leading from the house, the boy was put on a bicycle provided by another villager. Two other men then guided the bicycle to the temple. The village band led the procession of nearly one hundred people, followed by gifts and offerings heaped on the four-poster bed. The boy on the bicycle was in the middle of the crowd. The villagers said that this type of transportation was used because he was too heavy to be carried the long distance to the temple. It also gave several people a chance to make merit by assisting him to reach the temple. Some villagers said that he could have ridden on a horse or an elephant, if one had been available. An ox or a buffalo would not have served as means of transportation—that would not have been sufficiently dignified. When the slow-moving procession reached the temple, many more villagers came to crowd around the band and the gifts. The boy, who should have been the center of attraction, seemed to be lost in the middle of the crowd. The monks and the novices watched the procession from the temple. They had no part in that day's activities. Since there were no further activities scheduled for this day, the boy was permitted to get down from the bicycle and walk the short distance to the monks' quarters, where he stayed until the next day.

Several days earlier, the villagers had built a hut in front of the temple compound to serve as headquarters and stage for the *like* troupe. The players showed up quite late on Monday evening, and the performance did not start until after ten o'clock. That night only a few hundred people were at the temple. Several enterprising villagers had opened food stalls in the temple area. One villager had obtained permission from the *kamnan* to sell liquor. He had opened a little shop in the school building, where he sold Chinese noodles as well as liquor. A large number of monks and novices from other temples had come to watch the *like* or, as some of them told us, to see the movie, which, however, was not shown until the following night.

Carrying a stick as sign of his authority, the *kamnan* patrolled the temple grounds throughout the festivities, both day and night. An energetic *kamnan* with the help of one or two assistants is usually able to keep the crowds at temple fairs under control. At this particular occasion, two policemen from the district seat stood around to help the *kamnan* if necessary.

On Tuesday morning, the novice-to-be was taken to the neighboring temple at Nong Fæk, from where another procession was led back to the Ku Dæng temple. This time the boy was dressed in the style of an Indian prince—wearing a long-sleeved, white shirt, a pair of red pantaloons—*pha toi*, and a golden, pointed crown—as frequently seen in the *lakhon* plays.[4] Once more he was sitting on the bicycle, pushed by two villagers.

---

[4] One type of Thai classical drama, usually dealing with romantic stories of kings and giants, and often inspired by Jataka tales of the Lord Buddha. See Phya Anuman Rajadhon, *A Brief Survey of Cultural Thailand*, Thailand Culture Series no. 2, third printing (Bangkok: National Culture Institute, 1955), pp. 11-13.

The monk from Chiang Mai, Phra Thammanantha, arrived by jeep in the middle of the morning. He had brought an electric generator and an amplifying system with microphone. Phra Thammanantha started his extemporaneous sermon in the *wihan*, even though the procession from Nong Fæk had not yet arrived. The sermon lasted for an hour and a half. Many of the villagers who were in the *wihan* complained that they could not understand what he was saying, because the amplification was too loud. Other villagers, who had stayed home, could hear the sermon better than those in the temple.

The monk preached on the subject of the novicehood. The first boy ever to be ordained as a novice was the son of the Lord Buddha, Phra Rahun (Rahula). One day, seven years after he had attained enlightenment, the Lord Buddha returned to his native town. When his wife, whom he had forsaken, heard of his coming, she sent their son, Rahun, to ask the Lord Buddha to make him a king. However, the Lord Buddha, who had abandoned all covetousness of worldly property, refused the request. So that the boy would not be disappointed, he offered to let him become a novice, instructing him to keep and obey ten precepts chosen from the 227 for full-fledged monks.

The Lord Buddha, thus, instituted the novicehood with his son, Rahun, who was too young to be a monk and could not yet be expected to follow the 227 precepts. In this way, the boy could start keeping some of the precepts and at the same time learn to become a monk when he grew older.

In conclusion, Phra Thammanantha explained that there are three kinds of disciples of the Lord Buddha. First, there is the layman, who keeps the five precepts; second, there is the novice, who keeps ten; and third, there is the monk, who keeps all 227 precepts. If anyone has never been a novice or a monk, he does not need to be sorry, because he can be one of the number of faithful who hold firmly to the five precepts. The Buddhist religion wants only people who believe in and hold to the Law of the Lord Buddha.

After the sermon, the monk bestowed his blessing upon the congregation. Then, all the monks and novices had their midday meal in the monks' quarters. An hour later, Phra Thammanantha returned to Chiang Mai. Before he left, he gave the money that had been given to him for the preaching—50 baht—back to the temple, to be applied to the fund for rebuilding the pedestal for the Buddha statue in the *wihan*.

While the preaching was still in progress, the procession from Nong Fæk arrived at the temple and stopped at the *sala*. The boy was carried up to the monks' quarters, where he remained until the ceremonies continued in the afternoon.

At two o'clock in the afternoon the congregation reassembled in the *wihan*. Several monks from other temples, who had been invited to participate in the ordination, were seated in front of the Buddha statue at the west end of the *wihan*. The head monk from Wat Ku Süa, acting as the preceptor (Pali, *upajjhāya*) of the rite, sat at the center.

Accompanied by his father, the candidate for novicehood came into the *wihan* and sat down in front of the preceptor. The boy was now dressed in white robes similar to the yellow ones of the monks and novices. The candidate prostrated himself three times before the Buddha statue, lit a candle stuck on a coconut, and placed it in front of the statue. Then, he paid respect to his father by prostrating himself three times in front of him, simultaneously asking permission to enter the novicehood. The father gave his consent by presenting his son with a tray containing a set of yellow robes. The boy took another tray with three coconuts, each bearing a candle, placed it in front of the preceptor, and prostrated himself three times, thereby asking the preceptor for permission to become a novice. The preceptor touched the tray and the three coconuts and asked whether the boy was really willing to enter the monkhood. The preceptor explained the rules of being a novice, his obligations, and the difficulties he would have to face as a new novice. Finally, he asked the candidate once more whether he was willing to become a novice; this the boy answered in the affirmative.

The preceptor then took the robes from the tray and showed the candidate how to use them. The boy took the robes and went to one side of the *wihan*, where one of the Ku Dæng monks helped him put on his new attire. When he had dressed, he returned to the preceptor, prostrated himself three times, and requested the ten precepts of a novice. The preceptor granted them sentence by sentence, repeated by the candidate. The new novice then took another coconut with a candle, which had a prayer-bead necklace (a "rosary") wrapped around it, and placed it in front of the preceptor, who took the beads and hung them around the neck of the novice. The new novice then turned and placed a candle on a coconut in front of the head monk of Ku Dæng. The monk touched the coconut to acknowledge receiving it, and the novice sat down beside him.

Immediately after the ordination, the new novice's father presented gifts of money trees in water jars to all the monks, who acknowledged receipt of the gifts by touching them. The assembled monks then blessed the congregation, thereby concluding the ceremony.

The new novice stayed in the *wihan* for three days after the ordination, so that he could learn to live frugally like the other novices. His bed was put into the *wihan*, and his food was brought to him. His uncle, who had sponsored the ordination, stayed with him during these three days, so that he would have someone to comfort him in his loneliness. During this time the novice wore the beaded necklace to help him say his chants and devotions.

The night after the ordination the temple fair continued with the USIS movie from Chiang Mai as one of the attractions. Most of the crowd of several hundred people had come from neighboring villages. The Ku Dæng residents stayed home to guard their property from troublemakers.

In January 1954, we witnessed another ordination at one of the neighboring temples. This time both a novice and a monk were ordained. The ordination ceremony of the novice proceeded generally along lines similar to those described above. There were minor variations, such as the absence of a beaded necklace or the use of rice-filled, glass tumblers in place of coconuts to hold the candles.

Properly, an ordination ceremony for a new monk should take place at a temple that has a *bot*. After ordination in the *wihan*, the new monk is taken into the *bot* by fellow monks for further initiating into the ceremonial of the monkhood. There, the preceptor teaches the new monk the ways of meditation. This particular ordination, witnessed by us, was held at a temple that had no *bot*. However, expediency overruled prescription.[5] A portion of the *wihan* was demarcated to be the *bot*. The congregation was warned not to cross the line into the imaginary *bot*, an action that would invalidate the ceremony. As soon as the ceremony was over, the special area reverted to its original use without any special ritual.[6]

A novice may remain as such until he has reached his twenty-first birthday.[7] He must then either advance into the monkhood or leave the temple. Most novices leave the temple at that time or before. In order to advance to the monkhood, a novice must pass the examination for *naktham* third class, which is a considerable achievement or obstacle for some of them. A different behavior pattern can be observed for novices in the Northern part of the country as contrasted to those living in Central or Southern Thailand. In the Bangkok area, many temples have ten, twenty, or more monks in residence, with only a sprinkling of novices. In Ku Dæng and vicinity, as well as in other parts of Northern Thailand, according to informants from such communities, most temples house many novices but only one or two monks. Thus, at Ku Dæng there are two monks and ten novices. According to villagers who have spent time in the monkhood, the relative number of monks and novices has varied only slightly over the years. Indeed, by 1985 the proportion was practically unchanged: there were still only three monks and eight novices. One of the neighboring temples has four monks and six novices, another has one and six, and another has two and nine. Advancement from novice to monk is, then, a relatively rare occurrence. During our stay in Ku Dæng we heard of only two novices actually advancing to monkhood. Both cases were reported from temples a considerable distance away from the Ku Dæng area.

---

[5] Theme 1: Utility. See p. 7 above.

[6] For a detailed description of the various parts of the ordination ceremony, see Kenneth E. Wells, *Thai Buddhism: Its Rites and Activities* (Bangkok: Church of Christ in Thailand, 1939), pp. 118-131.

[7] Normally a Thai adds a year to his or her age at the beginning of the first month of each year; however, for ecclesiastical purposes, age in Thailand is reckoned exactly as in the West.

Most men leave the monkhood because they are "fed up" with life in the temple, according to their own testimony. At first, there is a certain amount of pleasure in the relatively easy way of life. The added prestige in the community that the yellow robe lends its wearer is an incentive that is important in the early stages of a monk's career. However, this prestige soon wears off. The keeping of the ten precepts for novices is relatively simple. The 227 precepts of a full monk are much more difficult to keep. Ex-monks have told us again and again that the reason for leaving the temple was that they were not able to keep the precepts. There appeared to be no hesitance at all to "confess" that the reason for leaving the monkhood was their inability to lead a "sin-free" life according to the 227 precepts. It was simply a matter of fact that they were not the type of person who could continue to live a perfect life indefinitely. In short, it was no longer "fun" to be a monk.[8]

A monk is generally accepted by the villagers as a person in a class by himself, because he is willing and able to keep this large number of prohibitions in his life. For that he is respected and supported.

"It was not very enjoyable" is the second reason for leaving the monkhood most frequently heard from those who left before they had attained full status as monks. Older men said they went into the monkhood when they were young to get more education than would have otherwise been possible.[9]

One man, now 57, was a novice for four years. He had finished all his studies in Lanna Thai by the time he was 18. If he had wanted to study further in the curriculum, he would have had to go to Chiang Mai, the nearest place for such instruction in those days. He was not willing to go that far away from home. His only alternative was to stay in the Ku Dæng temple without continuing his studies, as, indeed, some of the monks have done to this day. If he had stayed in the temple—in effect doing nothing—the villagers, he said, would have formed a bad opinion of him. They would have thought he was lazy and without ambition. He, therefore, left the monkhood. Furthermore, this informant continued, there was no future in studying while in the monkhood, unless a person wished to remain a monk the rest of his life—this seemed to him a possibility not worthy of consideration. Studying in the temple does not assure a man of anything in the future. A person studying in secular schools can go home when he has finished and be assured of rice and money. Our informant thought that students outside the temple were fortunate; when they were through studying, which admittedly was a difficult task, they could get a job where all they had to do was sign a few papers and draw their salaries each month.

Before a novice or a monk can leave the monkhood, he must ask permission from the head monk and tell him when he wishes to leave. He

---

[8] Theme 3: Fun.

[9] Theme 1: Utility.

will then get a regular certificate of honorable discharge from the head monk. On the day he is to leave the temple, he must get up early, sweep the temple and the monks' living quarters, draw water, and perform any other chores normally carried out by all the novices and monks. He must have his head shaved once more just before leaving. Then he must ask the monks' blessings before changing into ordinary clothes to go home. For the next three days he must come back to the temple every morning to work for the monks. Public opinion in the village forces him to do this. The only other method for leaving the temple is to run away, but this just is not done; a person would not only jeopardize receiving a certificate of honorable discharge, he would also lose the respect of the community. The head monk could also expel a novice for unsatisfactory conduct; as far as Ku Dæng villagers can recall, this has not happened.

The Daily Routine of Monks and Novices

The daily routine of monks and novices varies only little in the course of a year. Depending on the season, the monks and novices get up between five and six o'clock in the morning, usually as soon as it is bright enough to see without artificial light. The temple area and the monks' quarters are cleaned within half an hour; then the monks and novices read, study, or meditate. Between seven and half past seven, the head monk goes down to the east *sala* to receive food from the villagers and to give the five precepts to those who have brought it. After the precepts, the second monk or one of the senior novices comes down to help accept the food, which is later carried to the monks' quarters by the temple boys and the younger novices. If the head monk is absent, the second monk substitutes in giving the precepts. On the rare occasion when both monks are away, one of the senior novices fills in. As soon as the villagers have left, the monks and novices gather in one of the rooms of the *kuti* for breakfast. The temple boys eat immediately afterward, usually on the front porch. Breakfast does not take much more than ten or fifteen minutes. All monks, novices, and temple boys then gather in the head monk's room at the east end of the *kuti* for their morning chant before of a small Buddha statue facing west on top of a cupboard. The head monk sits in front of the others with the temple boys at the sides of the room. Discipline is not very strict at the Ku Dæng temple. Novices may come in late or leave in the middle of a chant.

After the morning devotions, the monks and novices take care of any assigned or necessary tasks. The older novices go to monks' school for a couple of hours in the middle of the morning. If one of the monks or a novice has business in town, he may go at this time. Sometimes the villagers come to the temple for a visit with the monks. The head monk has a carpenter's shop under the west *sala,* where he often works in the mornings. Occasionally, novices visit their homes.

144

Sometimes villagers bring food again in the late morning, but customarily the monks save food from breakfast for their second meal. According to the precepts governing the life of monks, they have to abstain from food after twelve o'clock noon.[10] The second meal is, therefore, taken about half past eleven in the morning. The same procedure is followed as in the morning: the monks and novices eat first, followed by the temple boys, who are not bound by the before-noon rule.

After lunch some of the monks rest in their quarters or in the *wihan*. The younger novices soon go to monks' school for their studies. Later in the afternoon the carpenter shop may be busy again. No organized activity takes place until after six o'clock, when the monks and novices gather in the *wihan* in front of the Buddha statue for their evening chant in remembrance of the Lord Buddha. This service lasts about twenty minutes. The remainder of the evening is spent by the novices and temple boys in reading, studying, and practicing recitation of sermons. The head monk sometimes turns on his radio, reads a newspaper, or watches the others read. Some villagers may come to visit the monks and novices. Some time between nine and ten the monks, novices, and temple boys gather once more in the head monk's room for a twenty-minute chant prescribed by the ecclesiastical authorities in Bangkok. The content of the Pali chants, according to the monks, consists of verses written in memory of the Lord Buddha. Shortly after ten o'clock everybody goes to bed.

There are, of course, variations to this routine according to special days or events. Thus, on Precept Day more people than usual bring food to the temple. During Buddhist Lent, the reception of food on Precept Day and the subsequent bestowing of the five precepts takes place in the *wihan*. During this season some of the people sleep in the temple compound. On those days the head monk goes to the *wihan* at daybreak to give the eight precepts to the old folk who'spent the night in the temple. There may be special requests for the monks to chant or give the precepts at the homes of villagers on the occasion of a wedding, a merit-making ceremony for the dead, or for a house-blessing ceremony. These events usually take place in the mornings and generally include the monks' first or second meal of the day. Funerals, which may require the presence of monks or novices, are usually held in the afternoon. Except for the period of Buddhist Lent, monks may go on trips to other temples, where they may spend a night or two. During Lent, the only extra regulation the monks and novices have to follow is not to sleep outside their own temple. They may go out during the day and return in the evening, except in cases of sickness, when the head monk may grant them permission to stay in their own homes.

The livelihood of the monks and novices depends entirely on the good will and sense of obligation of the villagers. Theoretically, when a person enters the monkhood, he gives up claim to any and all property.

---

[10] According to local interpretation, this "food" does not include fruits or liquids.

While he wears the yellow robe, he is available as recipient for the villagers' gifts. Such gifts may be given to any one of the three parts of the Buddhist Trinity—or the Three Jewels—or to all three of them: the Buddha, the Dhamma, and the Sangha. The part that is given to the monkhood becomes the personal property of the individual monk to whom it has been offered. Each monk or novice is allowed to take home the gifts that were given him while he was in the temple. This practice is in decided contrast to those reported from the Bangkok area, where all the gifts become the property of the temple. There are only a few prohibitions of things that a monk may not own, such as land or food (for a period longer than seven days after it has been offered). Apart from these, he may deposit the gifts that were given to him in his home, where his relatives keep them for him until he leaves the monkhood. Gifts, such as ordinary clothing or household utensils, may be sold by the monks if they are no use to them.

Each day the villagers bring food to the temple. Actually the monks are not the recipients but the granters of a favor. They provide an opportunity for the villagers to make merit through their gifts. In the morning, the villagers usually bring enough food to the temple to provide for two ample meals for all the monks, novices, and temple boys. But there are certain times when the giving becomes rather lax. Then, the temple boys perform the additional duty of doing for the monks what they are not allowed to do for themselves: namely, to find and prepare food. In general, however, the villagers take good care of the monks and novices. After all, they are members of their own community. The best cakes and candies are prepared on the day before Precept Day. During the period of Lent, a large surplus of rice is generally brought to the temple each morning. This rice the temple boys save, dry, and sell back to the villagers to feed their chickens.

The fact that the monks and novices are allowed to keep their gifts as personal property causes some resentment among the villagers. One old woman told us that she always made merit by giving to *pa cao*—the Lord Buddha—or *pa tam*—the Law—but never to *pa song*—the Sangha or monkhood. This same woman was always very much concerned about the well-being of the monks and novices. She provided screen covers for their food, small buckets, so that the novices did not have to use the heavy ones in the temple for drawing water, and plates and silverware for the temple. Her objection was to the monks taking along all of her gifts when they decided to shed the yellow robe. According to conservative estimates, in the 1950s a monk or novice received from 300 to 700 baht in cash per year, which does not count the value of gifts in kind he also received.

Monks as Community Leaders

The monk is in a position of being—at least in theory—one of the village leaders, both in religious and secular affairs. However, this potential was not realized in Ku Dæng. The monks were respected and honored by

146

the villagers, but the village leadership was decidedly in the hands of the secular officials and the lay leaders of the temple. In a prestige rating of over thirty prominent villagers, the monks were almost always placed on top of the list.[11] In many cases, the persons doing the rating did not wish to include the monks in the ratings at all. They belonged into a class by themselves, they maintained. When we asked where the monks would be if they laid aside their yellow robes, the almost unanimous answer was that in such a case their position would be considerably lower.

This situation, however, is not necessarily typical for this part of the country. It depends on the local situation and personalities. In two neighboring temple communities where we visited frequently, the head monks definitely appeared to be leaders in village life. In a "new" temple, built in the 1930s, the head monk was instrumental in establishing the village as a separate community. He built the temple and the school, of which he was initially head teacher.

In another village, the head monk is energetic and aggressive. When we visited his temple for the first time, he was away for a religious ceremony in another community. We sat in the *wihan* listening to some of the novices preach until the head monk returned. He greeted us immediately, went up to the novice in the pulpit, told him he had preached long enough, and then introduced us to the whole congregation. Elsewhere, we observed similar leadership roles of monks in their communities, very much in contrast to the minor role played by the Ku Dæng monks in secular village affairs.

In former days, one of the incentives for entering the monkhood was the possibility of obtaining an education beyond what would otherwise have been possible. Today, this incentive is absent, since free education can be obtained through regular, secular government channels. The villager who left the temple because he could not progress any further in his education is probably the product of a bygone day.

Today, all novices are required to study. There is is a novice school in one of the neighboring temples attended by the Ku Dæng novices two or three hours each day. At this school, the novices may study the second or third grade of *naktham*. If they wish to go higher, they have to go to another temple about five miles from Ku Dæng. The second monk of the Ku Dæng temple was studying there two or three times a week during the year of our stay in the village. Once in a while we encountered a monk from the Saraphi district who was ambitious enough to advance to the higher grades. One was even desirous of learning English sufficiently well to be able to use it.

In some areas of Thailand the monks perform a variety of functions other than those inherent in their ecclesiastical office. We have already referred to their role as community leaders, a role not much in evidence in Ku Dæng. Monks often have knowledge of herbs and medicines or sacred words to cure villagers of a variety of diseases. Most of the local healers in

---

[11] See appendix F, "Prestige Rating."

Ku Dæng have learned their trade from other monks when they, themselves, were in the temple. At the time of our study, neither of the two Ku Dæng monks was renowned as a medical healer. The head monk had a few envelopes of Chinese medicine in a glass cupboard in his room, but he told us that he rarely made use of this, since the villagers generally do not come to him with their ailments.

Finally, some monks are called upon to play the role of astrologer. In Ku Dæng, the monks have astrological tables—called *yam*, which means "time" or "watch"—but there are also many other villagers who have such tables, especially if they have ever been in the monkhood themselves.[12] These "timetables" are consulted to determine auspicious days and hours for such occasions as weddings, funerals, the collecting of ashes after a cremation, or house-warming ceremonies. In some cases, we were told, the Ku Dæng head monk was consulted. However, it was more likely that the villagers would go elsewhere for this information. The Ku Dæng head monk might tell them one auspicious date; a more famous monk in one of the neighboring temples would give a different date, which was the one that prevailed. At one merit-making ceremony for a deceased girl there were 108 sand pagodas built in front of the *wihan*. We were told that the brother-in-law of the dead girl had gone to a famous astrologer in Chiang Mai to find out the exact number required; he did not even think of consulting the local monks. Thus, while there are potentially many roles that a monk can assume, in Ku Dæng his activities are almost exclusively confined to those of his religious office.

A monk in residence at a temple some thirty miles north of Chiang Mai acquired such fame through non-ecclesiastical functions that when he died in 1985 at the age of 98, he was honored with a royally sponsored cremation attended by 10,000 monks and novices and over half a million ordinary people from all over Thailand.[13]

Prestige and the Monkhood

The ideal in Thai Buddhism is for all males to spend some time in the temple, either as a novice or as a monk. This may be for as little as a few days or as long as for life. How far this ideal is from actual practice can be seen from the number of Ku Dæng villagers who have been members of the monkhood at one time or another. Our 1953 survey showed that only seventy-five men had ever worn the yellow robe, which was less than 30% of the eligible male population.[14] That it still remained the ideal was indicated

---

[12] See also below p. 185.

[13] Luang Pu Wæn Sucinno died in July 1985, and his nationally televised cremation took place on the 100th anniversary of his birthday on January 17, 1987, at Wat Doi Mæ Pang in Phrao District.

[14] This number included the twelve current priests and novices.

by the high prestige accorded those currently in the monkhood and those who had left the temple.

The results of the prestige rating of thirty-six leading villagers confirmed our observation of the high honor in which the wearers of the yellow robe as well as those who had left the monkhood were held.[15] Among the thirty men on our prestige rating list, only nine had never been in the monkhood. That means 70% of the "leaders" had at one time or another been monks or novices; this percentage is more than twice that for the entire male village population. The two monks were at the top of the list. All informants rated the head monk either first or second.

Twenty-three of the thirty-six persons interviewed rated the second monk in either second or third place. In contrast, the *kamnan* was rated among the first three places only nineteen times, including two firsts and three seconds. If only the first six ratings were counted, the second monk and the *kamnan* each received twenty-eight out of a possible thirty-five votes. Some villagers refused to rate the two monks together with the others, commenting, "Oh, the monks are in a class by themselves; we cannot compare them with ordinary people." In all those cases, when urged to place them somewhere in the listing, the informants placed them at the head of the list, "as long as I have to put them somewhere." Some individuals did not rate the monks at all or placed them in lower positions—one informant put them in twenty-second and twenty-third place, respectively. Invariably though, their position was readjusted, and they ended up at or near the top of the list. Those who rated the second monk low were ex-monks themselves; they considered him to be too young and not really a local man, since he had come from a neighboring village to be ordained in the Ku Dæng temple.

To spend some time in the monkhood, even if it is only for a few days, provides the person with a life-long title by which he is called unless he has some higher titular position such as headman or temple leader. Former novices are called *noi* and former monks *nan*. As the person grows older, these titles are adjusted to "Father *noi*" or "Father *nan*." *Noi* in the Thai language means "small" or "minor," while *nan* has no separate meaning in either Thai or Lanna Thai.

At religious functions it is the ex-monk who calls the tune, for he knows the procedure better than his lay brethren; furthermore, he has attained prestige through his period in the temple.

The foremost lay leader is the temple leader or *acan wat*, who presides over a lay temple committee. The Ku Dæng temple leader spent eight years in the temple as a novice and one year as a monk. He left the temple, he said, because he was "fed up" with the life of a monk and, furthermore, was unable to keep the 227 precepts.

---

[15] See appendix F, "Prestige Rating."

Members of the temple committee, who are elected by the congregation for a term of two years, do not necessarily have to be ex-monks, although in practice the majority of them are. In Ku Dæng, three of the seven members of the committee had been monks and two novices. The head monk calls a meeting of all the faithful and asks them to nominate those they think will make up a good temple committee. The number of committee members is flexible. There may be as many as ten. Apart from the nomination, there is no vote, just a general consensus of opinion. It is chiefly the old people in the congregation who nominate those who are, in their opinion, worthy of conducting the affairs of the temple.

A Sketch of the Life of the Ku Dæng Temple Leader

Early in the last century, the King of Chiang Mai appointed Cao Noi Panya to be ruler of a small region in the northern part of his kingdom. Some years later, back in the city of Chiang Mai, Cao Noi Panya had a son, who later became known as Cao Noi Luang.[16] The King of Chiang Mai sent Cao Noi Luang to be the *kamnan* of commune Nong Fæk.[17] He took up his residence in a village called Ku Dæng. In 1887 his wife gave birth to their first child, a son, whom they named Kham Tan, which means "a person rich in gold."

Like other villagers who wanted to have their children educated, Kamnan Cao Noi Luang sent his son to the Ku Dæng temple at age 7, where he became a novice in the same year. In those days the requirement of a fourth grade education prior to ordination as a novice had not yet been instituted. The head monk of Ku Dæng at that time was famous for his wisdom and knowledge of both the Thai and the Lanna Thai languages, and also of the Pali Law. Kham Tan studied the Buddhist Law diligently and learned all three languages: Thai, Lanna Thai, and Pali. When he was 20 years old, he was ordained as a monk. Two years later he left the temple, for he could not keep the monks' precepts.[18] Altogether he had spent fifteen rainy seasons in the temple.[19]

The knowledge that he had gathered during these many years in the temple helped him within a few months to obtain a good position as a district official in Saraphi. The district office at that time was at the same place as it is today, except that then it was a smaller building. Apart from the head of the district (*nai amphœ*), there were five more officers. Kham Tan

---

[16] *Cao* was a title bestowed by the King of Chiang Mai upon those of his citizens who had served him especially well. Since Chiang Mai has ceased to be an independent kingdom, and since the ruler of Chiang Mai lost all remaining power in 1932, these titles are no longer handed out.

[17] See map 2.

[18] Theme 1: Utility.

[19] In Thai Buddhist usage, the number of years is counted by the number of rainy seasons that has elapsed.

stayed at the district seat, in a house provided by the government. Occasionally, he would visit his home, using a horse for transportation. At that time bicycles were still very new in this area. The one belonging to the district head was the only one in the entire district. When he was not using it himself, he let Kham Tan ride it. He, thus, became the first man in Ku Dæng able to ride a bicycle.

While he was working at the district office, his salary was 20 baht per month, which then was as much as 600 or 700 baht would have been worth in 1953—more than the salary of the Ku Dæng head teacher at that time. When he went out on fieldwork, his allowance was 2 baht per day. That amount was then a very large sum of money for a person to earn in one day. He carried an ordinary pen on his trips, since they had not yet invented the fountain pen. Before he departed on one of his field trips, he put some ink in a tin can to take along and closed it carefully.

At that time the *kamnan* collected the taxes in the various villages of his commune and delivered them to the district office. What little work there was could easily be handled by five officials. In 1953 they needed twenty people to take care of the work; by 1984 the number had swollen to fifty.

After he had worked for one year at the district office, Kham Tan married Nang Kham Pæng, a 16-year-old Ku Dæng villager. He moved in with his wife's family in the village and commuted daily to work at the district office. After a few months, however, he left this job and took up farming in Ku Dæng.

A year later, after his wife had given birth to their first child, he gave up farming and became a trader. He bought silver bars in Chiang Mai and took them for sale to Lamphun and Lampang. He continued in this trade for seven or eight years, until his health deteriorated so that he could no longer travel from village to village.

Staying at home, Kham Tan spent his time learning medical skills. He obtained a book about local healing procedures from the Ku Dæng head monk. When he had learned everything in the book, he started to work as a medical practitioner in the village. Later, when he became famous as a doctor, he was called to many distant villages to help with their health problems. Instead of living quietly at home, as he had planned, he had to answer sick calls in such distant places as Müang Fang—a hundred miles north of Chiang Mai, Lamphun, or Com Thong. He could be at home only about one month out of the year during the rainy season. Kham Tan continued his medical career until 1941, the year when the Second World War began. In 1950, after living at home for about seven years and knowing that he was now too old to travel, he took up a new career, making fireworks, drums, and cupboards.

When Kham Tan was 44 years old, he was chosen by the congregation of the Ku Dæng temple to be their temple leader. This took place at the festival for the opening of the new *ho thamma* in the temple compound. The

151

temple committee had asked him to write a poem for the occasion, inasmuch as the temple leader in office at the time had no talent for this kind of activity. Kham Tan wrote an excellent poem, which he read at the opening ceremony. The response of the people was so enthusiastic that they elected him to the office of temple leader immediately after the ceremony.

In 1945, when he was 57 years old, he heard that the government was planning to build a new irrigation dam in the district of Mæ Fæk, thirty miles north of Chiang Mai. He thought that the projected dam would soon cause the land to rise in value and become very expensive. He gathered, therefore, about two hundred villagers from the Nong Fæk commune and traveled to Mæ Fæk, where he asked the district head for permission to settle on the land. This was refused, since the *nai amphœ* wanted the villagers of his own district to have the first chance at the land; and so Kham Tan and his followers had to return empty-handed.

Today (1953), Kham Tan lives contentedly in his old age at Ku Dæng. As temple leader, he has frequent chores at temple affairs. Occasionally, he is called upon to treat a sick villager who comes to him for help. He owns a rice mill in another village, operated by hired help. What time is left, he spends in making fireworks and drums and in writing poetry whenever there is demand.[20]

---

[20] This biographic sketch was written by Withun Leraman as told to him by the temple leader.

9

BUDDHIST VIEWS TOWARDS LIFE AND DEATH
IN KU DÆNG

Apart from the organized religious ceremonial in relation to the monks and the temple complex, the most evidence for the religious expression of the villagers can probably be gained from observations at times of sickness and death. During our year's study, we were able to observe long sicknesses, which, eventually, led to death; sudden, severe illnesses, resulting in death within a day or two; and sicknesses that proved not fatal.

Interest in the question of life and death is keen in Ku Dæng. Since each death and funeral becomes a public festivity, there is much talk about death and about the possibility of future life. The people are continually urged to make merit, so that they will be able to lead a better life the next time they are born, or so that someone else to whom the merit is transferred may have a chance for a better life. That there is some continuation after death of some part of what existed before the person died is generally accepted by the people. What kind of continuation it will be is less certain.

In general, the villagers have little idea of the more detailed Buddhist theories of rebirth and the final extinction in *nipphan* (nirvana). They would say that persons who had done much good in their present lives would go to a "good place," while those who had committed many sins would go to a "bad place." Some people would further identify the good place as heaven (*sawan*) and the bad place as hell (*narok*). The head monk said the good place was *nipphan* and the bad place hell. The locations of the good and bad places were unknown to the villagers. One old man referred to the good place as "up there" while at the same time nodding in that direction. One elderly villager thought that a good person could be reborn immediately as a man, whereas a bad person would have to suffer in the "bad place" for some time before being reborn. Others said they did not know what happened to the spirit of a person after death; they thought that sometimes the spirit (*phi*) likes to stick around and make friends with the people left behind. The people are, of course, afraid of this. One villager said that the reason nobody in the village had died during the previous three years was because the villagers were doing much good, only very few were still doing evil deeds. Apparently, then, death is some kind of punishment for demerit.

Nipphan is the place of highest happiness, according to one of the Ku Dæng monks. It is a peaceful place without birth or death. The spirits (*winyan*) of people are there, but not the persons themselves. The Lord Buddha is in *nipphan* and so are his disciples who are *arahan.* But today people are no longer good and cannot get to *nipphan*. Not even the monks go there, or at least, he added on second thought, one does not know. This view was supported by other monks and ex-monks. None believed that by being a monk a person would be assured or even able to reach *nipphan*.

A tendency toward a Buddhist humanism, quite widespread among the younger, educated Thai in the cities, was also observed in Ku Dæng. In a discussion about the concepts of heaven and hell, one villager said that he believed in the existence of heaven and hell, but that they existed right here and now in a person's own heart. Such a person has everything necessary and does not need to worry about tomorrow's rice. The implied conclusion was that life begins and ends with the present existence of a person. Other villagers who heard this discourse did not voice any disagreement.

The question of rebirth, however, is quite readily talked about, although it is less certain that the villagers have any firm conviction that they really will be reborn. One villager commented that I must have made much merit in my previous life, since I seemed to have more visible resources than the more well-to-do villagers. Another comment was that Americans are always reborn with plenty of hair on their legs, since a person who works much in the fields—which Americans obviously do not—has his body hair rubbed off, like a buffalo wallowing in mud. Thus, some of the villagers, who had more body hair than the rest, were thought to have been Americans in their previous lives.

The Death of Mr. Khieo

Mr. Khieo was one of the more prosperous Ku Dæng villagers. He was born in the Year of the Monkey in 1896 in the same house in which he was living at the time of his death, a house that had been built by his parents shortly after they were married.[1] When Mr. Khieo was 16, he entered the Ku Dæng temple as a novice. There he learned to read and write the Thai language as well as Lanna Thai and some Pali. When he was 21 years old, he left the temple, being unwilling to undertake the strenuous life of a monk. A year later his father died of tuberculosis. The following year Mr. Khieo married a Nong Fæk girl. He moved in with his wife's family, while his elder brother stayed with his mother in Ku Dæng. After two years he took his wife back to live at his mother's house, because his brother was not well and could not support the family. His father-in-law gave him two *rai* of land, which he sold four years later, because Nong Fæk was too far from Ku Dæng.

When they had moved back to Ku Dæng, his wife gave birth to a boy, who died a month later from "baby fever." When we first met Mr. Khieo, his family consisted of five daughters, three of whom were married, and a son. In 1925 his elder brother died, presumably from tetanus. Four years

---

[1] There is a twelve-year cycle of years in Thailand, each year having a particular animal as its symbol.

later his mother passed away and left all her property to him. He now had nine *rai* of land and the house with surrounding garden. In the course of the years he bought another three and a half *rai* and rebuilt his house twice. Being the owner, therefore, of over twelve *rai* of land, he had become one of the wealthier villagers.

When Mr. Khieo was 36 years old, he was chosen to be the assistant irrigation headman for the commune Nong Fæk, a position he occupied for three years until the then-*kamnan* died. A year later he was elected headman of Hamlet 7, but refused to serve because he felt that he did not have sufficient administrative ability required for this office.

We have here, evidently, an eminently successful citizen of Ku Dæng. Three of his children were still living with him; hence, he did not need to worry about supply of labor for his fields. At age 57, he himself had retired to the more leisurely tasks around the homestead. He was elected to the temple committee the year before our residence in the village. In the prestige rating of thirty-six persons, he ranked fifteenth.[2] No one ranked him among the top six, and only one placed him among the lowest four.

Early in August, when the rainy season had already set in, Mr. Khieo felt severe pain in his kidneys. He had heard from friends about Dr. Chinda's hospital in Chiang Mai, a private hospital of high medical standards. During his four-day stay there, he was examined by x-ray, and the doctor recommended immediate surgery for removal of a tumor in the kidney. The care received at the hospital apparently made him feel better, and he decided to return home without an operation. Whether it was fear of surgery or displeasure with the high cost of treatment at the hospital (from his point of view), we were never able to find out. Family and friends applied considerable pressure to help him come to a decision. Some people commented that he should come back immediately, otherwise he would be likely to die right in the hospital. Relatives usually were very much worried that the sick person might die in the hospital. If this happened, the body could not be brought back to the village or to the home for proper funeral rites, because it would be most likely that the ghost of the deceased would haunt the vicinity.[3] This aspect of cooperation on the part of other villagers is extremely important for making decisions when a relative is about to die. It requires considerable effort and expense to conduct a funeral; the help of friends is practically indispensable. Whenever a villager seeks treatment in one of the city hospitals, relatives and friends take turns going to Chiang Mai to live with the patient in the hospital to provide needed care and service for him. At first glance, this custom seems cumbersome to a Western observer: the hospital room is cluttered with relatives, often including children or even small babies. But this custom gives the patient a support

---

[2] See appendix F.

[3] Theme 5: Communal responsibility.

system of greater service and at lower cost than would be possible if the hospital provided for his entire needs.

Whatever may have been the real reason, Mr. Khieo returned to Ku Dæng. He had to be carried much of the way, for the road was so deep in mud that no vehicle could have covered the five kilometers from the highway to his house. The following day he felt worse and desired to return to the hospital in Chiang Mai. This time, however, he wanted to go to McCormick Hospital of the American Presbyterian Mission, thinking it would be cheaper. Relatives once again helped carry him on his way to the highway. When they reached a neighboring village, he was so weak and tired that he could not go on. After some rest, he was returned to his home in Ku Dæng. He did not leave the house again alive.

Now Mr. Khieo tried every conceivable remedy to relieve his suffering. He had some medicine from Dr. Chinda. A "doctor" from Lamphun had given him some herb medicine. He asked me whether I knew of any remedy that would restore his strength.

There were two kinds of local doctors in Ku Dæng. One of the elective offices of the commune is that of resident doctor. The one for commune Nong Fæk happened to be living in Ku Dæng. He was a doctor of traditional medicine. One of the villagers said that this kind of doctor is called a "medical doctor" (mo phæt) one who cures his patients with herbs made from roots of certain trees or from pieces of wood. He may also have some modern, "foreign" medicine, such as sulfa, quinine, or aspirin. These doctors must be licensed by the district office.

The other type of doctor known in the village is a kind of shaman, a man who uses sacred words to heal his patients (mo khatha). Such doctors usually dispatch food and gifts on banana leaf trays to the ghosts (phi) who supposedly cause sickness. With these gifts the shaman says some sacred words, either in Lanna Thai or in Pali, in order to appease the ghost and make it take the sickness back. This kind of doctor does not need to be licensed by anyone and is legitimized only through the trust and confidence of his patients. Several Ku Dæng villagers were renowned as such doctors, although most used their powers only for relatives or friends who specifically asked for their help. Generally there was no payment for this kind of service. If the patient got well, he or she would make the rounds of all those who had helped during the sickness, taking some presents, such as tobacco or betel nut. The doctor then would respond with a brief blessing over his former patient.

The general order of consulting healers is as follows: first, one calls upon those of one's relatives who have reputations as shamans. If there is no immediate improvement, the resident herb doctor is called in. If his remedies fail to help, an "injection doctor"—a person who is licensed to give injections, a mo chit ya—will be sent for from another villager, if none lives close by. The injection doctor often recommends that the patient enter a city hospital. In most cases he will give the sick person one or more injections.

At the time of our study, this was the only kind of doctor outside the big cities who earned his living from curing people. Thirty years later hospitals and clinics have spread to most of the district seats in the country. Since such doctors are more expensive than their local colleagues, they are usually consulted only as a last resort.

Here we have several themes at interplay. The profit motive forbids the villager to go initially to the most expensive doctor, even if it is felt that such a doctor could be of help.[4] The one that costs least will be tried first. After all, this person is a renowned healer, too. But it is better to play it safe.[5] After a very short time, other healers are called in, even at the risk of greater expense. Finally, one may go to the hospital. If it is not expedient to go, such as when the road is deep in mud, the patient stays at home to face the consequences.[6]

The resident doctor of commune Nong Fæk in 1953 was a man of 50 years of age, who was chosen thirty years earlier by the *kamnan* of that day to be the official doctor. As the second son of a Ku Dæng farmer, he became a temple boy when he was 12, because he wanted to learn the Thai language and receive some general education. At that time this was possible only through the temple, where the monks acted as teachers. When he had finished fourth grade, he was ordained as a novice, the first one in his family to enter the monkhood. Four years later he advanced to the status of a full monk. He became interested in studying local medicine through the head monk, who taught him out of an old book. Within three years he knew how to make many medicines out of local drugs and herbs. He was called upon to help some novices and other villagers when they were sick. Two years later, he left the temple because he wanted to build a future for himself in the world.

Although this man's main occupation was that of farmer, he still maintained a side interest in healing people. Luck was with him when an old medicine book, which had belonged to his grandfather, was discovered in his father's house. He proceeded to learn everything in this book and from this time on went out more and more on calls to sick people. He married when he was 28 and is living now on property that once belonged to his father-in-law. He owns nine *rai* of land, inherited from his father, part of which he rents out. Two years ago his daughter became seriously ill. When he could not cure her himself, he took her to a hospital in Chiang Mai, where he was told she had tuberculosis. After two weeks in the hospital, there seemed to be no improvement in sight. He took her back home, where she died four days later.

There was absolutely no indication that this doctor felt he knew all the remedies or that his methods were the only correct ones. The general

---

[4] Theme 2: Profit.

[5] Theme 7: Playing it safe.

[6] Theme 1: Utility.

attitude seemed to be to try anything that had previously worked. If other methods had also been successful, one could try them, too. This resident doctor said he mostly used the old type of medicine, even though he also had some modern drugs. He might use both types of medicine for a sick person.[7] Actually, the government does not permit the use of the traditional type of medicine without a license, but he used it nevertheless. Like some other villagers, he also knew how to use sacred verses and chants (*khatha*).

The resident doctor was called several times to see Mr. Khieo. He prescribed some traditional medicine. The doctor told us that a person who does not believe in this would have very little benefit from it.

To be on the safe side, all kinds of healers were called in to treat Mr. Khieo. Many of the villagers believe that there is something in a person that is responsible for his or her well-being called *khwan*. A monk from Chiang Mai told us that it had the same meaning as spirit or soul or heart (*winyan, cit-cai*). He said that the belief in *khwan* came from Brahmanism. The villagers believe that when a person is sick, his or her *khwan* has left the body, apparently because the person has become frightened. In order to recover, a *khwan*-calling ceremony must be held. This is a Brahman ceremony, which long ago became mixed up with Buddhism. The 1950 edition of the *Royal Institute Dictionary* states that *khwan* is

> a thing which does not have a body of its own, generally thought of as being associated with the life of a person from the time of birth; if the *khwan* is with the person, everything is in excellent condition, the person is happy and well, has a steadfast mind; if a person is frightened or sorrowful, his *khwan* has left his body—this is called 'loss of *khwan*' or 'escape of *khwan*' or 'flight of *khwan*'; this causes the person to receive all sorts of evil; a person who is easily frightened, like a child or a woman who is likely to lose her *khwan* easily is called a 'weak *khwan*'; an escaped *khwan* is recalled: 'Dear *khwan*, it is meritorious to meet the mother of the weak *khwan*.' It is customary to attribute *khwan* also to animals or things, such as elephants, horses, rice, or houses.

> It is in all ways considered as something excellent; like the *khwan* of a city, which means the excellence of the city. A man who knows the ceremony of *khwan* is called a '*khwan* doctor.' The ceremony of inviting the *khwan* means that of recalling the *khwan* of the body.

> The fine which a person has to pay for insult or libel is called 'to make *khwan*.' A string is tied around a child's wrist, and the *khwan* is called: 'Oh, *khwan* come back to

---

[7] Theme 7: Playing it safe.

flesh and body,' followed by the usual blessing; this is called 'tying the *khwan*.' To call or invite the *khwan* is called 'receiving the *khwan*.' Ceremonies like sprinkling blessed water, chanting sacred words, encouraging the *khwan* to be of fearless heart, are called 'promoting the *khwan*.'

Things that are given the owner of the *khwan* after the ceremony of 'making the *khwan*' or at other times for friendship's sake are called *khong khwan*—which means 'things of the *khwan*,' usually translated as 'gifts.'

One's favorite child is called '*khwan*-child.' A person very much in love with a girl is called *com khwan*—greatest *khwan*.[8]

One afternoon a *khwan*-calling ceremony was held for Mr. Khieo. Throughout the morning, friends and relatives helped make arrangements for the ceremony at the house. Food had to be prepared for those present, gifts for the *acan*—"learned teacher"—who was coming from a neighboring village. Several young men were molding clay figures to represent a variety of animals, men, and spheres. There were either nine or twelve of each kind of man or animal. Actually, each figure was made only once or twice, the spheres to be used to complete the number. Everything was placed on a hand-woven bamboo tray.

In the afternoon the *khwan*-caller came. The *acan* squatted down near the patient, who was lying on his mattress in an inner room. A few candles were lit on the tray with the clay figures. The *acan* chanted in Lanna Thai and Pali for about half an hour. Members of the family were in the room or just outside the door, paying respectful attention with their hands palm-to-palm across their chests in the *wai* position. Other people came and went, perhaps to watch the ceremony, perhaps to chat with someone in the room. There was no particular silence imposed on those present in the room. When the ceremony was over, the tray with the clay figures was taken outside the house, where it was left to decay. The *acan* received gifts of food, locally made cigars, flowers, candles, and 3 or 4 baht.

Opinion in the village varies as to the usefulness of ceremonies of this kind. Many villagers, even as long as thirty years ago, said that these are old methods that are no longer of any value; that a person should call at least an injection doctor or, better still, go to a hospital in the city. One villager told us that Mr. Khieo believed that he was sick because his "birth-father" and "birth-mother" (*pho kœt* and *mæ kœt*), who were his real parents staying "up there," were angry with him; that he had neglected to offer food for them.

---

[8] See Phya Anuman Rajadhon, *Chao Thi and Some Traditions of Thai*, Thailand Culture Series no. 6, third printing (Bangkok: National Culture Institute, 1955), pp. 11-66.

The birth-father and birth-mother give life to a person and have a book into which they write everything that must happen to the person at a given time. Hence, when someone is sick, he must send food to his birth-parents, so as to have them change his status and make him well. This informant told us that fewer than one in ten of the Ku Dæng villagers places serious stock in this type of ceremony.

A monk, who is one of the leaders of the Buddhist Association in Chiang Mai, gave us the following explanation of *khwan: khwan* is visible mind power that gives life to the thirty-two organs of the body. In one person, there are thirty-two *khwan,* such as the *khwan* of hair, the *khwan* of hands, or the *khwan* of legs. The *khwan* leaves the body when it dies. The *khwan* goes with the *winyan* of the dead person to whatever place the *winyan* goes. *Khwan* is not the same as *phi,* for *phi* is the *winyan* of one who has done much evil while alive. When such a person dies, his *winyan* becomes a *phi* and will live in the land of the ghosts *(müang phi).* On the other hand, if a person has done good things while alive, his *winyan* becomes a *thewada* after death. The ceremony of calling the *khwan* is performed when it is desired to gather one's mind. Popular belief is that on some days some parts of the *khwan* go to places that the person likes, to taste some favorite food, or to be with some thing or person whom he enjoys. In the ceremony, the shaman chants a passage to call all the *khwan* to come together and meet in the body of the sick person.

On another day, a ceremony by one of the local healers was held. This man was a respected Ku Dæng villager who was known for his knowledge of sacred chants for a variety of diseases. He had a monk's handbook.[9] Again a tray was prepared with a variety of flowers, fruits, and candles— nine of each kind. This tray was set on top of a blanket and clothes belonging to Mr. Khieo, who was seated to one side. The shaman came and bowed down three times in front of the house shrine, which was entirely empty. Candles were lit on the tray, and the shaman squatted down opposite the patient, put on his glasses, and proceeded to chant in Lanna Thai from the monk's handbook. The section that he had chosen apparently was rather lengthy, for in the middle of the recitation he stopped and muttered that it was too long. He turned several pages and read the last few sentences of the selection. When he had finished chanting, the shaman waved the tray over the patient's head. Then he gave it to one of the sick man's relatives, who took it outside the house, where it was placed on a small shelf near the fence of the compound. We were told that the purpose of this ceremony was to placate the gods *(thewada)* to come and help the sick man.

An injection doctor also came several times. He did not give injections, however, since the patient by this time was too weak. He left him some medicine in a bottle. Mr. Khieo was, therefore, well supplied with

---

[9] Similar to the one mentioned above.

different kinds of medicines. Dr. Chinda had given him some in Chiang Mai. The resident doctor of the commune had left some local herbs. The injection doctor had sold him his medicine. These bottles of vari-colored medicines were a prime topic of conversation when friends came to visit the sick man. Each person tried to read the labels or have someone else read out loud. The stopper would be removed and the contents smelled. If the liquid had a pleasant odor, the visitor took a swig out of each bottle. A medicine, by definition, so the reasoning went, must be good for a person, any person.

The theme of communal responsibility is quite evident when a person is sick or on his deathbed.[10] Throughout the period of Mr. Khieo's sickness, friends and relatives from all over the village and even from other communities came daily to be with the sick man and his family. During the day, generally only two or three guests were in the house at the same time. In late afternoon or during the evening hours, the house was considerably more crowded. In the early stages of his sickness, Mr. Khieo sat in the main room of the house, chatting with his guests. Later, as he grew weaker, he continued to lie on a mattress in one of the bedrooms, even when visitors went in to talk with him or about him. In the final stages of his suffering, he was again brought out to the main room, where he was put on a mattress under a mosquito net. There, he was cared for by his relatives until he died.

We were told that people came for friendship's sake to visit the homes of sick people or of those who had died. Many of the villagers stayed in the house all night. One goes there to help with any eventuality that may arise. For example, the only immediate relatives in the house may be women. There should always be some men available for heavier work. In case the patient needs some medicine or help of any sort, or if he should die, there should always be someone around who can run an errand or assist with whatever is needed. There seems to be no feeling of need of reciprocity or compulsion about these visits. It just is done. The more serious the sickness, the longer the visitor stays. During the days and nights before Mr. Khieo's death, a number of people were in the house at all times.

If an illness is protracted, as in the case of Mr. Khieo, it becomes a considerable burden on the family. Visitors must be provided with smoking and chewing materials; those who stay all day and night must be fed. Neighbors help with the preparation of these items, but the burden of expense falls on the household of the patient.

Young or old, men or women, alone or in groups, they troop in to visit the sick man. The older men among the visitors sit near the patient at the head of the bed. One of Mr. Khieo's daughters brings in a jar of water and a silver bowl. Cigars, fermented tea leaves, and betel nut are provided. Pillows are handed to the visitors so that they can sit more comfortably. Young men sit farther in the background; women stay mostly in the kitchen or in an adjoining room. Here is a good opportunity for the young men to

---

[10] Theme 5: Communal responsibility.

joke and flirt with the girls. Many of the boys come less out of sympathy for the sick old man than for the opportunity of meeting a pretty young maid.[11]

Mr. Khieo felt weaker and weaker as the days passed by. He was not able to hold any food, only a little water and orange juice. After about one month's sickness, he died on September 1, 1953, at 5:30 in the afternoon. Immediately a wail of lament arose from the older female relatives who had been attending the sick man. This wailing takes place as a sign of grief on the part of the bereaved relatives, as well as a signal to the village that someone has died. On other occasions, when we were not near the death house, we could hear this wailing clear across the entire village, from one end to the other.

Sometimes the big drums at the temple are beaten continuously from the time of death until cremation. We were told that this custom depends on the wishes of the relatives of the deceased. The noise of the drums is to inform the villagers for miles around, as well as the gods (thewada) of the departure of a spirit (winyan).

After a few minutes, the body was unclothed by young male relatives. It was washed with a bucket of water and the clothes put back on. The stomach was filled with honey to protect it from rotting—so we were told. The hands were folded over the chest and tied together, as were the big toes. An offering of a candle, a joss stick, and some flowers was placed in the dead man's hands. His face was brushed with white powder from a cosmetics can. A rope was suspended lengthwise about twelve inches above the body, and a blanket was draped over the rope to cover the corpse. The body was kept in this position until a coffin was ready.

A kerosene lamp was lit and placed at the head of the body, "so that the ghost of the deceased can see all that is going on in the room, including the gifts that are placed near the body for making merit." A monk told us that the purpose of this lamp was to light the way for the dead person so that he might find the way to the other world. The flame is used for lighting the fire at the cremation.[12] Also placed at the head of the corpse was a three-tailed white flag, the thong sam hang, which represents the Three Jewels of Buddhism (Lord Buddha, the Law, and the Monkhood) and publicly signifies that the deceased was a faithful Buddhist.

The following day an elaborate coffin was prepared by one of the village carpenters, who had been chosen for this task at the express wish of Mr. Khieo, himself, before he died. The corpse was put into the coffin and kept in the main room of the house until the day of the funeral. The lamp and the flag remained at the head of the coffin. In addition a number of other articles were placed on or near the coffin. The meaning of the various items was explained to us by a visiting monk.

---

[11] Theme 3: Fun.

[12] We actually never observed a funeral pyre being lit in this fashion.

A sack of rice *(thung khao)* is symbolic of the food that the dead person should carry to sustain him on his way to the other world. We were told that in many cases a dead cat is put on the coffin, but we, ourselves, did not observe this custom in Ku Dæng. The monk explained that the common belief is that a cat is a sign of good luck. An old story is told that the cat was created by the Lord *(pa cao)* out of the dirt from his hands. The Lord created the cat in order to rid himself of a mouse that had nibbled on his books. It is still believed today that the cat is a helper of the Lord. The corpse is covered with a cat to be of assistance to the dead person.

Flowers are placed on the coffin to represent the precepts of the Lord Buddha, which are fragrant and beautiful like flowers. The candles symbolize concentration of mind through their bright and steady flame. There is also a kind of popped rice representing wisdom, which is white like rice.

Finally, there are the golden and iron flags, consisting of small metal flags hanging from a circular wooden ring on a foot-high stand *(tunglek-tungtong)*. An old sermon, as related by the monk, tells that once upon a time there was a monk who worked as a blacksmith for his hobby. One day he went into the jungle to search for a big tree to make a new stove. When he finally found one that was big and strong enough for his purpose, he returned to the temple to fetch his ax to cut down the tree. However, he did not return to cut down the tree, because he was suddenly taken ill and died within a few short moments. After his death, his spirit *(winyan)* became a lizard (Thai, *tukkæ; Gekko verticillatus*) and stayed in the tree in the jungle, because he had been thinking of cutting it down before he died. One day a girl from the village went into the jungle to cut firewood, but she could not find her way home. And so, she went to the tree where the lizard was living and asked him to protect her from all danger. The lizard had mercy on her and did as she had asked. The next morning, after the lizard had shown the girl the way back to the village, she asked him whether there was anything he wanted her to do when she arrived back home. The lizard asked her to make an iron and a golden flag and offer them to the monk at the temple, so that he could be released from being a lizard watching the tree. When the girl had done as requested and transferred her merit to the lizard, the former monk was released from the shape of the lizard and reborn in the other world. Today, we believe, our informant continued, that by giving iron and golden flags to the temple at a funeral the merit thus made will help the spirit of the dead person to be reborn in the other world

The various customs related to death were described in detail in an article in one of the Chiang Mai weekly newspapers:

> Death is inevitable for human beings. While people are still living, they are surrounded by powers of wealth and beauty of the angels; or, on the other hand, they may have been born poor. Whatever the case may be, their life

will end some day. Few persons nowadays think about the lifeless body and the custom that goes with it. The more the world progresses in leaps and bounds, the more western customs come to our country, the less we think of our customs dealing with death, or, perhaps, we even forget them entirely.

Not long ago a foreigner came to attend a wake in a house in one of our villages. He became interested in the decorations on the coffin. He asked an interesting question: "What are those circles of wire and brass on the wooden stand?" He was told that they were called *tunglek-tungtong* in the local, Lanna Thai, language. However, no one could explain what was the meaning of the small pieces of metal. The writer of these lines went to see the head monk of Chiang Yün temple in Chiang Mai; he also read the book, *The Immortal Problems;* from these two sources he gleaned the following information:

Tunglek-tungtong is a native word meaning "iron and gold flags." They are symbols for the dead. In former days, if we wished to provide a house for the dead, we would build a real house and then present it to the temple. Or if we wished to give money, we would give it to the monks for use of the temple. Nowadays the situation has changed. We have to think about and deal with economic affairs. Goods are expensive; gold and silver are scarce. We cannot make offerings by giving real things to the dead. Therefore, the iron and golden flags have become a substitute for these properties. The little pieces of gold leaf are used as a substitute for gold, and the tin foil of a package of cigarettes can take the place of silver. Sometimes the whole is painted with mercury. Soil, rice, and other bits of material, making a total of twelve pieces, are put on the tray.

The old customs of dealing with the corpse are rapidly disappearing. In ancient times, when someone died, the relatives gathered in the house and wailed as loudly as they could. They did this as a sign to the villagers that a person had died. Then the neighbors would come to help with the ceremony. A fire would be lit to boil water in a pot for a period of time. Then the pot would be removed from the fire to let the water cool, because cold is the normal temperature. The lifeless body was then bathed in the water. Next, the corpse was dressed in the most beautiful clothes. They wound a white thread three times around the dead person's neck, hands, and feet. Then the body was put into the coffin together with a stick which had been used to measure the length of the corpse when the coffin was made. The bottom of the coffin consisted of three boards only.

Before they laid the corpse into the coffin, pieces of gold and silver were put into the person's mouth as well as a wad of ground betel, lime, and other ingredients for chewing. Then the coffin was covered and decorated with wreaths and vases of flowers. A lamp was lit on the coffin, and a monk's bowl was placed beside it; a glass filled with candles was set at the foot of the coffin together with the gold and iron flags.

In addition, they made a three-tailed flag and hung it over the coffin. They put a bag of rice, a ring with a real diamond, a coconut for cleansing the corpse just before cremation, dishes of food, threads, white cloth, and other goods on the coffin.

A temporary ladder with three steps was made to fit over the regular ladder (staircase) of the house. When the coffin was taken down, it was carried over this temporary ladder. Those left in the house then took pots of water to clean the ladder and the room in which the corpse had been. Upon completion of this task, all the pots were broken. When the funeral procession had passed the gate, a line of demarcation was drawn near the gate in order to divide the people in the house from the procession.

The author is not going to tell about all the ceremonies, such as the sermons in the wake house, for they are well known. But we as Northerners should try to understand these ceremonies in order to be prepared for death, which we all must meet some day.

The following passages are taken from *The Immortal Problems:* Once upon a time there was a country governed by an emperor. In the town of the Lord Buddha there happened to live a monk who wished to go on a pilgrimage. When he had obtained permission from the Lord Buddha, he started on the trip and soon reached the city of the emperor. When he arrived, he remembered that his robe was rather old and ragged. He, therefore, went to the cemetery hoping to find some yellow cloth left there by charitable persons.

The monk met a man and his wife who told him the news that the daughter of a rich man had just died. She had been a most beautiful girl, beloved by the whole town. All the people joined the parents in sorrow for their daughter. The monk, too, felt sorrowful; inasmuch as he was a member of the monkhood, he offered the couple, who happened to be the undertakers, to help reduce the people's sorrow. He told the man to inform the emperor that he would help with the ceremony. The emperor was no less sorrowful than the girl's parents, for at that time all the citizens of the realm were considered to be his sons and daughters. The emperor thus invited the monk to perform the ceremony, which became the origin of today's funeral customs.

When the corpse had been taken to the cemetery and everything was finished, the emperor asked the monk to explain the details of the ceremony, so that it could be passed on to later generations.

1) The boiling water. The sins in our body are like hot water; they are bad ideas, prejudice, deceitful minds, and anger, which emanate from six doors: the eyes, ears, nose, tongue, body, and mind. If we can draw these sins out and throw them away, everything cools down, like the hot water when left standing becomes as cold as the quiet mind of a holy monk.

2) Banding the body with three turns of white thread. The three turns of thread are passion, anger, and prejudice, which are bound in our bodies. This is called our burden (tra sæng). When the corpse is taken to the cemetery, the undertaker cuts the three turns of thread, thereby replacing the three burdens by the three wisdoms: charity, kindheartedness, and meditation. The four principles of Buddhist belief are: 1) life is burdensome, unhappy, and tragic; 2) the ambition of a person is to be this and that, thereby becoming indifferent to life; 3) the ability to know how to stay away from these ambitions; 4) the Middle Way to lead us to destroy unhappiness and tragedy.

3) Placing the measuring stick into the coffin. This is a sign giving warning of the dead person's size, thereby to act according to real conditions and real size, and not try to exaggerate.

4) The planks on the bottom of the coffin represent the three evil conditions: 1) the condition of passion-hell, the devil, brutes, human beings, and angels; 2) the bodily condition, the rupaphrom, the divisions of angels with bodily form; and 3) the formless condition—the four divisions of angels without form, arupaphrom. All creatures are confined in one of these three conditions. A wise person should pray to be absolutely freed from them. Success in this will bring hope of nirvana (nipphan).

5) The ladder with three steps. This is comparable to the three conditions mentioned above. The ladder is destroyed to show that the dead person is freed from these conditions and will never be born again.

6) Putting gold and silver into the dead person's mouth. All people are lovers of money. Some try to get it by any means, such as cheating or stealing. When a person dies, the money is put into the mouth to show

that the dead cannot eat, for money is a worldly thing; we cannot take it with us when we die.

7) Putting betel into the dead person's mouth. A person's mouth is dirty. It is used to gossip with one's neighbors. One eats everything, whether it is clean or dirty. When one dies, one cannot eat anything, even ground betel.

8) Lighting a lamp. Light represents wisdom. When the light is out, life meets death. Life without wisdom is hard and dark.

9) The vase of candles is a sign of gratefulness. The dead body is considered a sinless body, which we should recognize as being cleansed from sins.

10) The monk's bowl. A person still living is not much interested in the problems of sin or charity. When life is about to reach its end, we feel that we will die soon, and thus begin to learn how to be charitable to monks.

11) The three-tailed flag may be compared to the Three Refuges: the Lord Buddha, the Law, and the Monkhood. Buddhists are supposed to seek refuge in these three.

12) The three vases for flowers, candles, and joss sticks have the same meaning as the three-tailed flag.

13) The bag of rice consists of one hundred little packages of rice, which are supposed to be for the dead. However, they are given to the beggars at the cemetery.

14) The fuel pot containing charcoal is always used to light the funeral pyre at the cremation grounds.

15) Choosing a man wearing a diamond ring to lead the funeral procession shows that human beings are in love with living. When they die, they must get rid of this love. The man who wears the ring will not look back, but must look at the diamond ring until the procession reaches the cemetery. A diamond is a good thing to look at in order to forget all of the past.

16) The demarcation at the gate is to show that the dead person has been associated with the world long enough. One should forget about it absolutely, never to come back again.

17) The white thread with which the monks and novices lead the procession must be large enough for all the monks, so that they can lead the the dead person to a holy place, even to *nipphan*.

18) The white cloth on the coffin should be given to the monks who come to help with the ceremony.

19) The six girdles on the coffin represent the six divisions of heaven.

20) The bamboo grating and the thread are to give protection from evil spirits.
21) The lustral water is to be used by all the people in the procession to cleanse themselves when they return. It is considered holy water, which will protect a person from all kinds of evil.[13]

When comparing this article to actual practice, it is quite evident that many of the traditional customs of death rites are no longer observed by the people of Ku Dæng. Expediency is very likely the cause for abandoning certain customs.[14] For example, to place a lamp at the head of the coffin is relatively simple and does not require much effort. On the other hand, to build a special ladder over which the coffin is to be moved, or to wash the entire room after the coffin has been taken out, would cause considerable inconvenience; therefore, these parts of the ritual have disappeared. Of course, the extent or the completeness of the funeral rites depends mostly on the wishes of the relatives and on the financial circumstances of the family. A rich man, like Mr. Khieo, will have a much more elaborate and complete funeral than his poor neighbor, who owns no land and makes his living by laboring on others' fields.

Mr. Khieo's body was kept for several days in the house, first under the blanket that had been draped over the body soon after his death. When the coffin was finished, the corpse was placed inside. Elsewhere, we observed that the coffin containing the body was taken outside the house as soon as possible. This depends on the number of guests the family of the deceased expect to be present from the time of death until cremation. When the coffin was kept in the house, mattresses were placed on either side of it, so that the people who had come to stay with the family would have a place to sleep.

It is important for the villagers to determine an auspicious day for the cremation. A "watch" table was used for this purpose. The villagers usually consulted a monk for such information, although renowned astrologers among the laymen of the village could provide satisfactory data. The head monk of one of the larger neighboring temples determined the date for Mr. Khieo's cremation.

Not all deaths are followed by an elaborate funeral. When a 6-year-old boy died of tetanus at one o'clock in the afternoon, relatives, not his parents, buried him that same day. Responses to our inquiries about the reason for immediate burial varied. The father told us that parents were not allowed to cremate their own children. He did not know the reason, except that no one else in the neighborhood had ever done otherwise. The final

---

[13] Krai Krainiran, "Rüang thong lek læ thong thong" [The story of the iron flag and the golden flag] Khon Müang 1:50 (November 12, 1953); translated from the Thai by Amnuay Tapingkæ.
[14] Theme 1: Utility.

word as to the disposal of any corpse rests with the *kamnan*. In this case he told the father of the child to cremate or to bury the body immediately. It happened to be raining that day, so that firewood was difficult to find. The father told us that he would have burned the body had he been able to find dry wood. No ceremony of any kind was held when the boy died or when he was buried. A *thambun* (merit-making ceremony) was held three days later in the home of the parents.

On another occasion a man died at two o'clock in the morning on Precept Day in June. He had been sick with a swollen neck for only two days. General comment was that he had had a boil inside his neck that choked him to death. One person told us that the man had eaten *lap*, a dish of raw, pickled meat, washed down with a good helping of local liquor. This is considered a very dangerous combination and was blamed for the boil inside his neck. Whatever the cause, this was considered an unlucky disease and an unlucky kind of death. Hence, the body had to be buried immediately. Over several hundred friends and neighbors came to help put together a makeshift coffin of bamboo and reed matting. At noon the body was put into the coffin and carried without ado to the cemetery, where two monks and two novices were waiting for the small procession. They chanted and departed. Then twenty-odd men dug a grave under a big Bo tree. When the hole was about three feet deep, a blanket was spread on the bottom, the corpse was placed face down on the blanket, some of the dead man's clothes were put on top and covered with a bamboo mat; finally, the hole was filled with earth. A small tray was placed beside the grave with some rice and pork "for the birds," so as to make a little merit for the dead man.

We inquired about the reason for this hurried kind of burial. One man said that since the person had died on Precept Day, he had to be buried the same day. Cremation was forbidden. Another said, this death was caused by a special and unusual disease, an "unlucky" one. The body, therefore, had to be disposed of as quickly as possible. Actually, the corpse should have been lowered through a hole in the floor of the house, since taking it through the regular door would only perpetuate bad luck for the family. This custom seems to be similar to the one of the special ladder described in the newspaper article mentioned above. Here, again, the custom was not observed because it would have been "too much trouble."[15] It would not have been expedient to cut a hole in a wooden floor—this would have spoiled the appearance and value of a very good house.

A third reason for the quick burial was the time of year. It was the end of the harvest of the second crop of rice and the beginning of the planting of the main crop. Everybody was busy in the fields and could not very well take time off to participate in and help with an elaborate funeral

---

[15] Theme 1: Utility.

ceremony that would take several days. A fourth reason was that it was likely to rain the following day, and it would be difficult to find firewood.

The variety of reasons given for this uncommon kind of disposal of the corpse indicates that the villagers in general did not have a very clear concept of what should be done in the case of death. The older and more influential people in the village apparently determined what kind of funeral should take place in each case. They based their decision on precedent, without being able to rationalize their actions.

The days between the actual death and the funeral are days of great activity in the house of the deceased. In Mr. Khieo's case the funeral preparation lasted four days. Friends, relatives, and neighbors came to help with building the coffin, preparing the gifts for making merit, cooking food, rolling cigars, and packing chewing paraphernalia for the guests. The festivities continued day and night.

About forty men and women spent most of their time preparing trays that were to be offered to the monks and novices. Each set of gifts was put into a white, enameled wash basin—a big one for each of the monks, and a smaller one for each novice. Altogether, there were thirteen bowls, six for monks, six for novices, and one for the temple leader, who was expected to lead the ceremony. Each basin contained a variety of items such as a monkly robe, a coconut, bananas, cigarettes, candles, matches, tea, rice, and flowers. A money tree was placed in the middle of each basin. The trees are made of bamboo sticks, split so that paper money can be easily attached. The money trees for the monks contained 10-baht notes, those for the novices, 5-baht. While the men were making these gifts, the women were preparing *miang*— fermented tea leaves wrapped around a core of sugar or salt, ground coconut meat, peanuts, and bits of pork—to be used for chewing after and between meals. The women also rolled cigars and prepared betel paraphernalia for the guests. At night, when all the work was finished, two big kerosene pressure lanterns from the temple were lit, one inside the house and one outside, where several gambling games were in progress.

Gambling as well as the sale of liquor are actually illegal. However, at special occasions, such as a funeral, the *kamnan* may give permission for a few men to organize games and sell liquor for consumption on these nights. In Thailand, all liquor dealers must be licensed by the government. None of the shopkeepers in Ku Dæng had such a license. Only for special occasions was permission requested and granted. Many people drank homemade rice liquor, illegally acquired and illegally consumed. There seemed to be little effort on the part of the village authorities to enforce complete prohibition of liquor.

The *kamnan*, himself, usually was present at the big funeral festivities the night preceding the cremation. Although he did not participate in many of the games, his presence was sufficient to keep general order among the guests.

The older people, the honored guests, and most of the women were usually inside the house in the same room as the corpse and in adjoining rooms if the crowd became too large. Friends and relatives had come from distant villages and the city of Chiang Mai. Some of these visitors told stories or read from books to those present. When we were there, we invariably were asked to talk about other countries. One night a doctor from another village spent several hours reading the questions and answers about Buddhism that one of the Ku Dæng monks was using in his instructions of the school children.[16] About a dozen people were listening attentively. Since the book was written in Thai, they did not understand very much. Occasionally, one of them asked the reader to explain a passage, during which he was supported by several villagers, usually ex-monks. This discussion then was carried on in Lanna Thai, which everybody could understand.

The local Ku Dæng band played intermittently throughout the night. There were seven players. Two played on instruments resembling Western violins. These instruments are typical of Northern Thailand. The body consists of a coconut shell. One of the instruments had an open shell, the other a closed one. They were each strung with two metal strings. There were three guitars made of teakwood; we were told that other wood could be used just as well. Each instrument had four strings, tuned in pairs to two pitches. There were ten frets on the fingerboards. One person played on a kind of flute, another on a green leaf. The repertoire included a song called "The Dinner of a Foreigner" and another, "The Peanut Song." Both of these were modern Thai songs popularized through radio and public address systems. The remainder were Northern Thai songs, including some that were played for *ramwong*, the Thai adaptation of dancing by couples. On this occasion, though, the guests did not dance.

Festivities of this kind continued for all the nights up to the cremation. Here is one of the best opportunities for the Ku Dæng villagers to have "a good time."[17] The young people come together for talking and playing. It is their chance to get acquainted.

One reason for continuing the festivities throughout the night is the fear of the dead man's ghost. This fear is usually mentioned quite freely as one of the reasons for keeping the house noisy and alive all night, although all of our informants told us this as if it were a big joke.

I do not believe that fear of ghosts is the predominant reason for such large and expensive festivals, but it may well have been the origin of the custom. Two or three friends ought to be sufficient protection from ghosts; this was confirmed at other occasions. The wake nights seem to have developed into a time of general recreation for the villagers. The original

---

[16] Bhikkhu Panyanantha (1953).
[17] Theme 3: Fun.

purpose seems to have been lost, while few villagers would be willing to abandon this opportunity for a social gathering.

On the day of Mr. Khieo's funeral, the coffin was carried out of the house by a group of people led by the head monk, who held in his hand the end of a long, white thread fastened at the other to the coffin. Once outside the house, the coffin was placed under a canvas roof to protect it from rain and sunshine. Near the coffin, the band, now consisting entirely of percussion instruments, played for most of the morning, while gambling continued nearby.

At about ten o'clock in the morning, the invited monks and novices arrived and filed into the house where they were seated at one end of the main room. The villagers sat facing the monks in the usual order of descending age and prestige, with the men in front and the women in the rear. The gifts for the monks were put in front of them. One of the small Buddha figures from the temple had been placed on the Buddha shelf of the house above and behind where the monks where sitting.

The ceremony was led by the Ku Dæng temple leader. First, he asked for the five precepts in the same way as was customary for the regular Precept Day devotionals in the temple. The senior monk from another temple responded. This was followed by the presentation of the gifts. Some village elders, all ex-monks or ex-novices, pushed each tray of gifts in front of the monk who was to receive it, who then touched the tray, thereby indicating that he had accepted the gift. Then, the temple leader asked the monks to preach. Each of the monks was given a copy of one of the Lanna Thai sermons that had been chosen by the Ku Dæng head monk. Some of the sermons were written on palm leaves, others in ordinary school notebooks with pictures of Superman on the front cover. The monks preached part of their sermons simultaneously, finishing in less than fifteen minutes.

When the preaching had been concluded, the monks lit cigarettes and chewed *miang*. Some villagers requested the senior monk to preach an extemporaneous sermon. This monk was highly respected by the villagers and renowned for his preaching ability. After a few moments' hesitation, he stood up and preached the following sermon:

> Dear friends, I have been invited to deliver a speech to all of you who are attending this *thambun* ceremony for the dead Mr. Khieo. A good Buddhist presents his guests with two things: good food and accommodations, and a sermon by a monk to take back home. Today I will preach to you about death.
>
> Death is a common event that will come to everyone without exception. No one can live forever, rather everyone must die sooner or later. Some people say that a dead person is only a lot of trouble to his relatives and

friends who stay behind. Dead animals are more useful to us than dead people, because we can use their hide, bones, and meat. Dead people leave only their good deeds, which we can remember.

We go to the funeral of a dead person just as if we were going to see a good friend off who is leaving for another country. Now we have come to see Mr. Khieo off to another world. We do not like to see him leave, but when it was time for him to go, he had no choice. Nobody could stop him; all we are able to do now is to make merit and transfer it to him.

There are three kinds of death: 1) common death, which comes to every person. This is death of the body. The spirit *(winyan)* goes to another place *(pai yu thi ün)*; 2) death of good deeds that occurs when a person misbehaves; and 3) death of work comes to a person who abandons work. Out of these three kinds of death, we prefer only the first kind, which is better than the other two.

Everybody has been registered by Phaya Matcurat, the chief of death. We are now waiting for our turn to be called by Phaya Matcurat. Who is this Phaya Matcurat? Somewhere in an old sermon it is written that Phaya Matcurat is a big giant with two eyes; one is a ball of fire, and the other is a diamond. He has seven hands and thirty teeth. He catches his victims with his hands and eats them. He will kill everybody without exception, even the Lord Buddha or a king. The meaning of this Phaya Matcurat is as follows: the giant represents death; the two eyes are the sun and the moon; the seven hands are the seven days of the week; and the thirty teeth are the days of the month. Death comes to a person on any day of the week or the month, at any time, whether by day or by night.

Everybody must remember that we all have to die, not only the person whose funeral we are attending today. Before death comes, we must prepare ourselves. The Lord Buddha did not shed tears when death was approaching, because he knew the meaning of death. We cry when we see death, because we do not have the knowledge of a Buddha.

The Lord Buddha said, "Death is the change of the name and the body of a spirit *(winyan)* from one form to another." Nothing in the world can vanish, only change, not even life or matter. "To the question, where the spirit of a dead person goes, we can answer that it is reborn. In Buddhism we say that a person with an unclean spirit of greed, anger, and ill temper will be reborn again, but one who has a clean spirit will go straight to *nipphan*. The

Lord Buddha had a clean spirit; so after his death, his spirit went straight to *nipphan* without being reborn.

Some people believe that life is created by a married couple. That is not right. Buddhism teaches that life is created by the rebirth of a spirit. Some people do not believe in a spirit, because they cannot see it with their own eyes. I wonder why they believe that there is wind, when they cannot touch or see it. Life is formed by the following three things: the intercourse of husband and wife, the wife's period, and the rebirth of the spirit. Sometimes it is said that the wife is like the earth, the husband the fertilizer, and the spirit the seed. As a result, these three bring forth the tree, which is life.

I cannot speak any longer, because I have already taken a long time. Before ending, I want to stress again that death is not a strange event; it does not belong to any particular person, but to all of us. We will die when our time comes, the time being scheduled by Phaya Matcurat, who is the chief of death.

If I should receive any merit for this preaching, I beg to dedicate it to Mr. Khieo. I ask that this merit may help and support him in the right place, or give him a chance to be reborn in a good place. If his spirit should still be wandering around someplace, because of his attachment to his family or his property, I beg that this merit will lead him from these earthly attachments to some other place. Finally, I beg for the blessings of the Lord Buddha to come upon you and bring you long life, a light complexion, happiness, and good health.

With these words the monk sat down, and the men among the family and relatives brought large trays of food for the monks. The monks had brought their own spoons and forks, even though the rice served was of the glutinous type that is the kind usually eaten by the Northern Thai people, and for which no silverware is needed. The monks and novices sat in groups of five around the various sets of food. Shortly after the monks had started eating, the other guests were fed, first the men and then the women, all clustered in small groups of five or six people.

Shortly after noon a procession of about thirty men and sixty women was formed to take the coffin to the cemetery. The men came first, then an elderly Ku Dæng villager carrying the three-tailed flag. Behind him one of the undertakers carried a husked coconut, its water to be used to wash the corpse just before cremation. The novices were holding the white thread leading the litter on which the coffin rested. The litter was carried by eight men who were Mr. Khieo's close relatives. The women walked behind the coffin. The villagers carried firewood, which they had brought as a contribution toward the funeral.

When the procession reached the cemetery, the coffin was put inside a small building. Three pieces of white cloth were placed on top of the coffin for the monks to "find." There were also a few pieces of firewood on the coffin. The monks chanted briefly and then returned to the temple, taking the cloth with them. We were told that monks could stay to witness the cremation if they so wished. When the dead person is a relative of one of the monks, he usually stays. In general, however, the monks' duty is done with the last chant, and they prefer to return to the temple.

Now the coffin was cut open with an ax, and the thoroughly decayed corpse taken out. The man carrying the coconut cut it open and poured its water over the man's face. A bucket of water, which had been brought along, was then poured over the body.[18] The corpse was placed on the heap of firewood and the coffin and litter on top of the body, so that everything would burn better. The actual cremation was carried out by a group of seven, non-professional Ku Dæng undertakers, who had volunteered for this duty to make some extra merit.

The temple leader unrolled a fifty-foot long fuse that he had made out of paper and gunpowder. The fuse was lit with a cigarette lighter, and the flame sputtered along the ground until it reached a couple of rockets at the end of the fuse. The rockets shot up along a wire to the top of the coffin, where they ignited other rockets, which in turn lit the pyre. Elaborate fire lighting like this is done only for very special occasions, when the deceased is a village leader, a rich person, or, perhaps, a monk. For others the firewood is simply lit with the flame of the kerosene lamp, which had been standing on the coffin since the time of death. As soon as the fire was lit, most of the people returned home, leaving the stoking of the fire up to the undertakers.

Mr. Khieo's funeral was representative of most normal funerals in the Ku Dæng area. Of course, there were minor variations. Some of the funerals we witnessed were less elaborate than others. But on the whole, there was the same kind of careful planning and attention to detail as in the case of Mr. Khieo's funeral.

One wealthy villager's wife died later in the year. The husband chose to have her cremated in one of her own fields, which she, herself, had planted with peanuts some time before. We were told later that this unusual action would make it very difficult for the man ever to rent or sell this particular field.

Some of the coffins used for cremation are made simply and of cheap wood. Others are more elaborate. If the coffin is made of good wood, such as teak, it is usually not burned with the corpse, but rather given to the temple for the monks to use in their carpentry shop.

---

[18] Occasionally, the bones of the corpse are cut with a saw to prevent the limbs from shooting up during cremation.

The cremation of the corpse is, to a certain extent, the climax of the funeral celebrations. It is, however, by no means the end of all ceremonies related to the death of a particular person. The nights immediately following the disposal of the body are still critical ones. The family of the dead person does not wish to stay alone in the house. They invite friends and relatives to stay with them for several nights.

Mr. Khieo's son came to our house to ask our landlady's son and daughter to stay with them for one night. When questioned as to the reason for this, he did not give a specific answer. He said it was customary to invite friends to stay with the bereaved after his father's death.

The kerosene lamps are usually kept burning from three to seven nights after the cremation. Some villagers are quite frank about the reason for this: it is done so as to be somewhat protected from the ghosts.

The ashes and remaining bones are collected a few days after the funeral. Some villagers go out to the cemetery at an unspecified time, perhaps even as early as the morning following the cremation. Others consult one of the monks for an auspicious day or hour. Mr. Khieo's widow had planned to collect her husband's remains on the afternoon of the seventh day following the funeral. However, the Ku Dæng head monk told her it would be better to do it in the morning. So one of her sons and a son-in-law went to the cemetery early in the morning of the seventh day, put the ashes and a few remaining bones into an earthenware jar, and wrapped it all into a white cloth. They then took it to the temple, where the two monks and two of the older novices chanted over the remains. The sons then took the bundle back out to the cemetery, where it was buried in an unmarked spot.

The man who had his wife cremated in one of her own fields continued to be unorthodox regarding the method of burial of the remains. He wished to erect a small tomb in which to keep the ashes. This was not without precedent, since in former days the remains of members of the royal family or other influential persons were placed in small tombs or pagodas, some of rather elaborate design. These might even become landmarks, such as the old tomb that gave Ku Dæng its name. However, an old and respected monk from a neighboring temple, who was present at the funeral ceremonies, told the man that it would be improper to build a tomb, since the spirit *(winyan)* of his wife would then stay at the tomb and not have a chance to be reborn or go elsewhere. The remains of this woman were, therefore, placed into an earthenware jar and buried in the usual manner in an unmarked spot in the cemetery.

Elaborate funerals of this kind can only be carried out by the well-to-do. Mr. Khieo's funeral cost between 2000 to 3000 baht. For several days friends and relatives of the deceased and his family came from distant villages. All of these people had to be fed. Some of them stayed with friends in the village, who thereby helped Mr. Khieo's family meet part of the expense. Nearly every guest who came to the house for the cremation festivities brought an envelope containing a little money, identified with the name of the donor written on the face of the envelope. These sums varied from 50 satang to 20 baht and assured the giver of some merit. Other villagers helped with the preparation of food and the smoking and chewing paraphernalia. Firewood was donated by those who went to the cemetery grounds in the procession. However, all these donations amounted to only a small part of the total expense.

There is no consensus among the villagers concerning elaborate funeral ceremonies. An old lady, approaching the time when she, too, would face death, told us that she did not wish any big festivities. She wanted her family to put the corpse into an ordinary coffin, keep it at the house for not more than one day, and burn it at the cemetery as quickly as possible. She wanted no procession, because, she said, she was not an important person in the village. She did not want her relatives to keep the corpse for many days; it would only rot and cause inconvenience and great expense for her friends and relatives.

Thambun for the Dead

If a *thambun* ceremony is carried out on the same day as the cremation, as in Mr. Khieo's case, no other ceremony needs to be performed for some time thereafter. However, when the person is buried or cremated without benefit of special merit-making ceremonies, it becomes necessary to perform such a ceremony as soon as possible. This was done in the case of the man who had died from a boil in his neck. One of the village leaders, an ex-monk, told us that the *thambun* ceremony for the man would have to be held at least three days after death, but it could be delayed for seven days. The number of days was not significant, he said; these numbers were just easy to remember. Actually, it was over three weeks after the burial before this particular rite was held. The man organizing the festival told us that he was waiting for a convenient day, preferably another Precept Day, since the deceased had died on one. This day also would be a day on which work would not be too heavy, since this was rice planting season, when most of the villagers were busy in the fields on ordinary days. No astrologers were consulted in this case. In the end he had to postpone the ceremony another week, because everything could not be arranged in time for the first date set.

In another case, a *thambun* ceremony had been held in the temple at the time of the funeral of a young mother. An elaborate ritual was organized fifteen weeks and six days after death. The father of the dead woman told us that he had not consulted anyone, but had set the date himself.

In some cases, the *thambun* ceremony may be held several years after a death. One Ku Dæng villager sold all of his land in anticipation of emigrating to Müang Fang, a hundred miles north of Chiang Mai. After he had bought twice as much land there as he had sold in Ku Dæng, he still had enough money left to conduct a proper *thambun* ceremony for his father and his two sons, who had died some years earlier. He said this was the first time that he had had enough money and time to have this rite performed for them.

Preparations for the *thambun* ceremony were similar to those for other family festivities, including the funeral described above. All the gifts and offerings were prepared in the house of the family. In some cases the ritual was held in the house. Otherwise, especially in the case of smaller homes, the ceremony could be held in the temple.

In the case of Mr. Khieo, the day for the *thambun* ceremony was selected as an auspicious one by the Ku Dæng head monk. The night before the main part of the ceremony, one of the Ku Dæng monks preached in the home, where some thirty people came to listen. The men were sitting on the porch in the front section of the house, the women sat in an inside room, except for the *kamnan*'s wife, who sat in the lower section of the porch amidst all the men.

The monk preached in Lanna Thai, reading from palm leaves. It was the story of Malai, the fifth life of the Lord Buddha before he became the Enlightened One. He went on a tour of hell, where he saw many sinners being punished. This sermon was recited as an example to the living, so that they would know what punishments awaited the dead. When the preaching was concluded, a basket of offerings was placed under the sermon to designate the gifts for the temple. Another basket was given to the monk, who touched it as a sign of receiving the gifts, which were for his personal use. The monk poured a small amount of water from one cup into another while reciting a chant, and the merit acquired through the giving of the gifts was transferred to the water, which was poured on the ground outside the house simply by reaching over the railing of the porch. This act was done so that other ghosts could not benefit from it. Elsewhere, the reason given for this practice was that it enabled the ghost of the deceased to pick up the merit from the ground.

The main part of the *thambun* ceremony was held in the temple the following morning. Three sets of offerings had been prepared in addition to individual baskets for each monk. The three offerings were in the form of houses for the deceased. The largest one, for the dead father, was a large bamboo litter with a straw roof. On the litter was a mattress, sheets, pillows, blankets, a tray for betel paraphernalia, smoking utensils, a basketful of glutinous rice, a water jar, a spittoon, cigarettes, flowers, and candles. The two smaller ones, for sons who had died earlier, contained similar gifts in smaller numbers. We were told by Mr. Khieo's widow that these gifts would be given to the monks, so that the dead would receive them in the other world. On further questioning, she said that these things actually did not go to the spirit world, but that something equivalent would be provided for the ghosts there. We found this reasoning quite widespread, although few villagers would admit that they really believed it. Most of them would take an agnostic point of view: "We really don't know what happens in the 'other world,' but it is better to play safe and provide all of these things, so that one has as pleasant a life as possible when one gets there."

An even more complete set of personal property, including clothes and household goods, was given to the temple at the *thambun* rites for the dead woman mentioned earlier. We asked several people whether the woman actually received these gifts in "the other world." They laughed and said, no, of course not. She only receives the merit *(kuson)*. The litter was built like a house because her old father liked it that way.

A 70-year-old grandmother told us that she had provided herself already with everything that she might need for the time when she moves on to the spirit land *(müang phi)*. The more merit she made now, she said, the better life she would have in the next world. By "better life" she meant a life with more money than she has now. This old lady was quite certain that all the goods that she had given to the temple, or something equivalent, would be waiting for her in the spirit land. "Once in the sixth or seventh lunar month, I made merit by holding a *thambun* ceremony. That night I dreamed that I was accompanying one of the monks to the spirit land, and there I saw all the things which I had given to the temple that day."

The same old woman thought that *thambun* rites carried out more than five years after death, as in the case of the man emigrating from Ku Dæng, was rather late. The people involved were, most likely, already reborn, so that all of this merit would not do them any further good. Here, seems to be one reason why the custom of making merit for the dead does not lead to elaborate ancestor worship. The general feeling is that the spirit of a person who dies will wander around freely for some time before being reborn. Thus, it may haunt one's house, an event which usually occurs shortly after death while the ghost is still attached to his previous property and family. Or the deceased may go to the spirit land, where it must remain for some time before it is reborn, according to some villagers. The example of the spirit of the monk in the sermon quoted above also shows that there may be a period after death and before rebirth when ordinary people still can help the dead by transferring merit to them. As soon as the spirit is reborn, however, there seems to be no more danger from the *phi* and little need for making additional merit for this particular spirit. When the *thambun* ceremony for the man who had died from a boil inside his neck had been concluded, several villagers breathed a sigh of relief, and someone said, "Now we can rest in peace; he has been reborn."

The rite in the temple started in mid-morning. Not more than forty people were in the *wihan*. Two older monks from a neighboring temple came in first, did three prostrations *(krap)* in front of the Buddha image, and sat down on the monks' platform along the north wall of the *wihan*. They were followed by the two Ku Dæng monks. The head monk did two prostrations, one to the Buddha and one to the visiting senior monk, who returned the greeting with a *wai* in front of his chest. The second Ku Dæng monk did three prostrations to the Buddha and three more to the other monks; then he sat down with the others. The people did three prostrations to the Buddha and then one to three to the monks. The temple leader led the people in a chanted request in Pali for the five precepts. Some of the monks lit cigarettes during this part of the ceremony. The Ku Dæng head monk then led the chanting in granting the precepts. Then, the temple leader asked the monks to preach. The people did three more prostrations to the monks, who then read the same sermon that had been preached the night before. The people stayed attentive for a few minutes with their hands in *wai* position across their chests, then they relaxed, lit cigars or cigarettes, and engaged in light chatter.

One of the temple elders told the man making the merit to light three candles in front of the Buddha image. When the monks had almost finished, the temple leader addressed them while they were still chanting, asking them to accept the gifts. The people once more were attentive. Some of the older villagers, all ex-monks, helped in presenting the gifts to the monks, who had to touch each set of gifts as a sign of receiving them. A set of gifts was also presented to the temple leader. Then, the monks chanted acceptance of the gifts and a blessing on the donor. Each of the four monks and the temple leader poured a little water from one cup into another, while chanting. After the ceremony this water was poured on the ground in the temple yard. This is called *truat nam*, or transferring merit to the dead.[19] One monk told us that they use water because it represents something that is most pure. While the water is being poured, the monks chant to dedicate to the deceased the things that were given to the temple and the monks. The ghost of the dead cannot enter the *wihan* to receive this merit, which is now supposed to be in the water, hence the water must be poured on the ground outside.

This transfer of merit to the dead is very common in Ku Dæng. After every ceremony at which people make merit, some of the villagers can be seen kneeling on the ground outside the *wihan* in the temple compound, slowly pouring a little water out of a small bottle, while murmuring some Pali verses. On these occasions they are transferring merit either to some dead relative, or to the gods *(thewada)* who, thereby, are supposed to bestow favor on the donor of the merit. According to the Ku Dæng head monk, this is both a Buddhist and a Brahman custom, but is not necessary in Buddhism. One villager told us that sharing merit with the gods or with ghosts *(phi)* of dead relatives is like getting a bunch of grapes, eating only a few, and giving the rest to friends.

After the *truat nam* ceremony the monks lit their cigarettes, and the people engaged in light conversation. The temple boys from the neighboring temples came in to collect their monks' share of the gifts. They take out of the baskets only the useful items, such as money, clothing, or

---

19 *Yatnam* in Lanna Thai.

cigarettes. Larger items such as coconuts are left behind for the host temple to use.

The ritual lasted only a total of twenty-five minutes. The time for these merit-making occasions varies widely, depending on the number of monks present and the desire of the merit maker to have an elaborate ceremony or not. If it is held in the morning, lunchtime for the monks imposes a time limit on the official activities, since the monks are not allowed to partake of food after twelve noon.

Sometimes, when a renowned monk is present at a *thambun* ceremony, the villagers ask him to preach extemporaneously. At one such occasion, a monk talked about merit-making:

> I have been invited to preach at the occasion of the *thambun* ceremony for Mr. Kham, who died a few weeks ago. When he was still alive, he behaved very well and did many good deeds, so that he was beloved by his relatives and friends. After his death, these relatives and friends still remember his good deeds so that at the proper time they have come together to hold a *thambun* ceremony to dedicate merit to him who has already gone to another world. This merit may help him escape from his sins. This is quite different from other dead persons, who have misbehaved all their lives, and whom nobody liked. When such persons die they are not remembered by anyone, and no one will dedicate merit to them.
>
> When organizing a *thambun* ceremony, we follow Brahmanic principles, which teach us that the gift of merit for a dead person must consist of food, clothing, and water, because the belief is that the spirit *(winyan)* of the dead person who has gone to the other world will lack food, clothing, and water. Frankly, when we offer gifts to dead persons, it does not mean that they can take all of these gifts with them, because dead people have no bodies but only spirits which are not able to touch anything. Because of this, we have to offer the gifts to the monks first, and then we can transfer the merit which we have received to the spirit of the dead person by pouring water on the ground. In this way we can be sure that the dead person will receive the gifts which we have offered.
>
> Every merit-making ceremony must consist of three things: 1) the donor must be in a certain state of mind; 2) the gift must be correct in form; and 3) the recipient must be able to receive the gifts. Thereby the merit may reach the person to whom it is dedicated. We believe that only merit can take a person to a state of bliss. The Lord Buddha told his disciples to do good, for merit received for doing good will save them from suffering evil *(bap)* when they die.

One rule in Buddhism states that one who does good will receive good, and one who does evil will receive evil. This means that every person who does a good deed will always receive a good reward, and every person who commits an evil act will earn misfortune, just like a farmer who sows common rice in his fields can eventually harvest only common not high-quality rice.

There are three ways in which a person can prevent evil from coming upon him: 1) watch your actions; do not destroy others by what you are doing; 2) watch your words; do not destroy others by what you are saying; 3) watch your mind; do not destroy others by what you are thinking. Persons who can prevent evil in these three ways will succeed in life and will always be loved by others. When such persons die, their friends and relations will sorrow greatly and hold *thambun* ceremonies to dedicate merit to them.

There are four uses for making merit: 1) use for the donor, who will receive merit as a result; 2) use for the person to whom the merit is dedicated; 3) use for the monk who accepts the gifts; and 4) use for the friends and neighbors who come to help in the *thambun* ceremony and thereby also receive some merit. A result of all *thambun* will be to bring the fruit of merit *(anisong)* to the recipient when the donor makes merit and transfers it to the recipient in the right manner. We hope that this merit will help the recipient escape from suffering and be reborn in the next life.

The preaching is ended here. I beg for the blessings of the Lord Buddha to fall upon you and be with you, the listeners, forever.

10

"NON-BUDDHIST" RELIGIOUS EXPRESSION IN KU DÆNG

Non-Buddhist Religious Elements

Non-Buddhist religious elements are more difficult to divide into presentation and reception categories than are the more formal aspects of the Buddhist religious system. Casual observers frequently describe the rural population of Thailand, and specifically that of the North, as being "animistic" or one of "spirit worshippers." For all practical purposes, a village such as Ku Dæng must be called a "Buddhist" village, if we mean by "Buddhism" the actual and explicit religious expression evident in the people's relationship to the ever-present temple and monkhood. It is not the aim of this study to go into detailed analysis of the origin of certain religious practices, which are described by authorities on Eastern religions as purely Buddhist or Brahman in origin or animistic in principle. Locally, religious practices are classified by some of the more knowledgeable villagers as actually Buddhist or Brahman in origin, or as "ancient customs."

Most of the essentially non-Buddhist religious beliefs and manifestations are governed by an all-pervading sense of expedience.[1] Most such practices are carried out because they are ancient customs. The parents and the grandparents of the present villagers have done it this way; therefore, we should do it, too.

An example is the custom of not taking rice out of the rice barn or bin on Sundays. According to reports from other parts of Thailand, and even from other parts in the Chiang Mai Valley, this is definitely not a uniform custom. In some places special days are prohibited, depending on the particular month. No person in Ku Dæng was able to give us a reason for this practice. Some said that wise men had come to Ku Dæng a long time ago and instructed the villagers not to draw rice on Sundays. One woman suggested that rice would spoil if she did draw it on Sundays, although she was not too sure about this. It is of interest to note that this same woman was observed drawing rice from her barn on the Sunday previous to our interview. One old lady told us that she did not believe there was any reason for this custom. However, when confronted with the serious proposal to try it the following Sunday, she decisively refused to experiment.

---

[1] Theme 1: Utility.

A similar custom, that of not taking belongings out of a house on Mondays, could not be observed with equal ease, since people rarely moved from one house to another. The few times that this happened during our stay in the village did not give us sufficient statistical data to make a reliable statement.[2]

While many ceremonies and practices are based on ancient custom, others are simply the result of successful precedents. For example, local healers are called upon because it has become known that someone has been cured under similar circumstances. By this means, modern medicine and medical practices have entered the village without serious obstacles. Villagers who are sick will try everything: herbs from the resident district doctor, sacred words from a renowned healer, medicine from a traveling Chinese salesman, vitamin shots from an injection doctor, or going to a modern hospital and consulting a physician in the city when everything else has failed.[3] Through the courtesy of the World Health Organization (WHO) Malaria Control Unit in Chiang Mai, we obtained some anti-malaria medicine for distribution in the village. After we had distributed a few of the pills to villagers suffering from fever, we found ourselves besieged by others who had heard of the good results achieved in the earlier cases.

Most villagers still follow customs with regard to the selection of auspicious days for all kinds of ceremonies and celebrations, even though they usually deny that they actually believe in this practice. Here again we have an example of the underlying tenet that it is better to play it safe. In cases of old, it was known that a person who did not follow the advice of an astrologer *(mo du)* would be visited by bad luck. Hence, to be on the safe side, it is better to consult a monk or some other person skilled in reading astrological tables. Different persons, some of them monks, some of them ex-monks, are consulted for different purposes, depending on fame achieved in their specialty.

At the *tham bun* ceremony for a recently deceased woman, 108 small, two-inch-high sand pagodas, each decorated with a white flag, were erected just outside the front door of the *wihan*. One villager suggested that the woman had requested this number just before her death. But a relative told us that he had gone to consult a famous astrologer in Chiang Mai, who had told him, for 20 baht, to use 108 pagodas. Furthermore, the relatives consulted the local head monk to determine which would be the most auspicious day for the ceremony.

A villager who was an ex-monk owned a handbook written in Lanna Thai, which gave the fortune of a person born on a certain day. This he had copied from the book of another monk. Such books are to be consulted when one wants to build a house, make a trip to another village, or find a

---

[2] When we left the village at the end of our study, we were requested not to leave on a Monday. Any other day would have been satisfactory.

[3] Theme 7: Playing it safe.

day on which to get married. The owner of the book maintained that the people in the old days believed in this, but that it is of no use today. Yet this same man, when it came to the time for his own house-blessing ceremony, consulted a monk to determine the proper day.

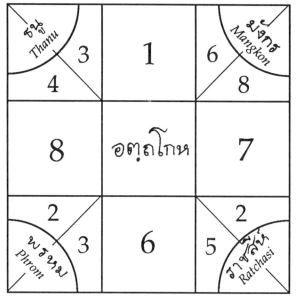

Figure 2

Figure 2 represents a copy of the "watch" table: *yam* or *atthakoha*.[4] Instructions for the use of this table tell the astrologer to count clockwise for men and counterclockwise for women:

> The diagram is used for predicting the future for any given year, so that the person can prepare himself or herself to fend off the predicted evil.
> Every person starts counting at the square marked '1' and then continues around the circle until he or she has reached his or her full age (that means, completed years). The number on which he or she stops will then give the fortune for the coming year according to the following list:
>
> 1. Cattle and buffaloes will get into trouble; it is not good to go west into the jungle; blood will flow out of one's mouth; one will lose things.

---

[4] Taken from a priest's handbook of one of the Ku Dæng villagers. Translated from Lanna Thai into Thai by Prayat Yananto and into English by Withun Leraman and Konrad Kingshill.

Countermeasures: Offer four trays of rice and food; six candles with red wicks; release captive birds.

2. He will quarrel with women or become angry because he has lost something he loves.
Countermeasures: Worship with a yellow and white flag; use fifteen candles with white wicks and fifteen candles with yellow wicks; release one white fish.

3. If you go out on trade, you will lose property; if at home, you will die; you will have a very serious quarrel.
Countermeasures: Offer a thousand flags, eight candles, and release fish.

4. You will be very lucky.
Offerings: One white flag; seventeen candles with white wicks; release fish. If these things are not offered, thieves will come to your house.

5. You will leave your house; you will get into a quarrel; you will be sick; you will lose four-legged and two-legged animals.
Countermeasures: Offer nineteen big (three-tailed) flags; candles with white wicks, with yellow wicks, and with red wicks; one yellow flag; release a turtle; move to another house.

6. You will have good luck and bad luck; someone will steal things from you.
Countermeasures: Offer twelve lumps of rice, candles with grey wicks or a yellow flag; release ten captive birds; offer candles with black wicks; release catfish according to how many have been caught that day.

7. You will have hayfever.
Countermeasures: Offer one black flag; ten trays of rice and food; ten candles with black wicks; release a snail.

8. (There were no predictions listed for this number.)

A person who uses this diagram should take rice and divide it into equal portions altogether equal in number to his or her age, offer it to the Three Jewels, and transfer the merit thus acquired—*truat nam*—to chase away all evil.

Here follows a list of the characteristics of men:

There are five kinds of lengths: long slits (tails) of eyes, long arms, long chins, long distance between breast nipples, long noses.

There are four kinds of shortness: short neck, short forehead, short waist, short legs.

There are four kinds of thinness: Thin fingers, thin toes, thin beard, thin hair.

All these characteristics bestow merit *(bun)* on the owner.

There are five kinds that are red: red insteps, red lips, red toenails, red fingernails, red eye lids—he who has these has happiness.

There are three kinds that are deep: deep navel, deep voice, heavy step—he who has these will be wealthy.

There are three kinds that are wide: wide head; wide forehead; wide chest—he who has these will have plenty of rice and property.

The characteristics of men were followed by the characteristics for women:

If a woman walks like an elephant, talks pleasantly, has a beautiful face, she will have many servants like a princess.

If a woman has a voice like a nightingale, like a swan, or like several other kinds of birds, she will have much rice, property, and servants.

If a woman has three wrinkles on her forehead, three folds on her neck, she will be a powerful woman.

If her hair is long and dark, like a certain insect flying in the air, she will be the owner of much property.

If toes and fingers are not spread apart, if hands are soft, she will be rich.

If she has soft flesh, a round waist, is leaning to the right, she will be rich.

If she has big ankles, short feet and hands, she will have no lover.

If she has moles and birthmarks on her feet, breasts, or earlobes, she will be very rich; if on her forehead, she will have much knowledge.

If she has much hair on her legs, it is not a good sign.

We have here undoubtedly a considerable residue of practices reflecting anxiety about the future from a time when everything in the villagers' daily lives must have been governed by such auspicious signs and portents. Attitudes of those who have attained a higher level of education have influenced other villagers sufficiently, so that they assume apologetic attitudes when questioned about these practices. Many of the younger villagers no longer participate in overt behavior of this kind. Oldsters, though still actively observing such propitiations, disclaim any belief in associated power but are hesitant to tempt fate by abandoning the ceremony.[5]

Results are all-important. After the rice had been transplanted in July, we observed a simple sign—*mai ta læo*—made by weaving strands of split bamboo into a star-like shape, placed on top of a stick in a corner or in the middle of a rice field. One villager told us that the purpose of this was to fend off insects that would damage the rice when it is in bloom. He said that many of the younger farmers no longer carry out this precaution but rather rely on insecticide that they may obtain at the district office. He admitted that such insecticide would kill the insects if sprayed in time. He maintained, however, that his bamboo star did the job just as well. Furthermore, he said, when other villagers first notice insect damage to their crops, they have to go to the district office to request insecticide. There could be a delay of several days by which time the crop would be damaged. His own method incurred no such delay.

Non-Buddhist Religious Expression

Casual observers of cultural expression in Northern Thailand often write that the people of this part of the country are predominantly animists rather than Buddhists. Landon maintains that mainland Southeast Asia is characterized neither by animism nor by Buddhism, but that the religion is rather a developed conglomeration of Hindu and Brahmin practices.[6] I would classify the villagers of Ku Dæng as Buddhists: a Buddhist temple lies at the center of village life, a Buddhist monkhood fulfills the function of religious leadership, and this monkhood is part of the national ecclesiastical

---

[5] Theme 7: Playing it safe.

[6] Kenneth P. Landon, *Southeast Asia: Crossroads of Religion* (Chicago: The University of Chicago Press, 1949).

organization of the established Buddhist religion. Each and every villager will answer, when questioned, that he is a Buddhist.

The term "animism" has been used to describe a number of interrelated religious concepts. According to Tylor's usage (that animism is the doctrine of the soul and other spiritual beings in general), Buddhism is certainly "animistic," just as all the other major religions of the world would have to be classified as such.[7] Other uses of the term "animism" include the belief that all objects may be inhabited by spirits or souls, or the belief in the activities of the spirits of recently deceased people. When the casual observer talks about "animism" of Northern Thailand, the word is usually used to mean the same as "spirit worship."

From the above description of the customs and beliefs with regard to the disposal of the dead, it seems quite evident that the people of Ku Dæng are animistic in the sense that they quite definitely believe in the activities of the spirits of the recently deceased. As for spirits residing in specific objects, only very little evidence was obtained. The story of the monk's ghost *(phi)* turned into a lizard and living in a tree was one of the few examples of this kind we encountered.

In some of the newly built houses we observed small pieces of white paper pinned to the top of the posts of the house. On each piece of paper some numbers or some words had been written. When we asked the owner of one of the new houses why there were papers at the top of each pillar, he replied, "Each pillar has a name, given because they are with us always, like good friends. There are sacred words *(khatha)* written on the paper so as to keep various spirits *(phi)* away." When we asked him whether the posts had life, he laughed and said, "No, of course not."

We found only one case of specific worship of a deceased ancestor. Behind a villager's house there was another house, nearly as large as the one in which the villager lived. This house was built by the present owner's father, who had prepared it as a place to stay for the spirits *(winyan)* of his grandparents. While his father was still alive, he saw him make offerings to the spirits of his grandparents with flowers and food every Precept Day. When his father died, he continued with this practice with the same conviction. This man believes that the spirits of his grandparents can protect his family from every kind of sickness.

Belief in the Supernatural

Belief in Spirits

Belief in spirits manifests itself predominantly in the belief in the spirits of ancestors *(phi puya)*. They are family spirits who contribute to the well-being of the living members of the family. Every household in Ku

---

[7] Edward B. Tylor, *Primitive Culture* (New York: Brentano, 1871).

Dæng has a number of these ancestor spirits who are honored and respected. When special family events take place, such as a wedding, building a house, or moving to another house, the family spirits must be informed and concurrence in the event requested. If this action is not taken, the family spirits are likely to obstruct the occasion, cause bad luck, or punish the family in some other manner, until or unless forgiveness is requested. This system of rewards and punishment is self-reinforcing, so that the reliance on family spirits continues and grows stronger with each passing generation.

In addition to family spirits, there are other spirits who may be benevolent or malevolent, such as house spirits, nature spirits, or village guardian spirits. These spirits are honored like gods; when they are propitiated, happiness, good health, and good luck will follow. In case of neglect, the spirits will cause punishment upon the members of the family. In some cases these spirits are given exalted honorary titles, such as Lord Father, Lord Mother, or Lord Uncle.

There are some spirits that cause evil rather than good. If such spirits are annoyed because of some action of one of the villagers, evil consequences will follow without doubt. A spirit doctor or shaman will be required to exorcise an evil spirit. Shamans are usually former monks or novices, who learned the art of exorcism when they were in the monkhood.

The Guardian Spirit of Ku Daeng *(Phi Cao Pho Ku Dæng)*

The villagers believe that the guardian spirit of Ku Dæng lives in or near the Ku Dæng spirit house. This spirit is the resident supernatural power who looks after the well-being of the village and its inhabitants. The villagers must carry out a propitiation ceremony every year. If this is not done, evil consequences, even possible death, may befall the villagers. One of the elders of the village related the following story: Once upon a time, a farmer went to cut grass in the vicinity of the village guardian spirit house. He did not pay proper respect to the spirit. Whereupon the farmer disappeared from the village without a trace for one day and one night. The villagers searched for him unsuccessfully until the second day, when they discovered his body near the spirit house. This frightened the villagers sufficiently to reinforce their belief in and respect for the guardian spirit. Henceforth, and to this day, no one has dared to come near the spirit house with evil intentions.

Lord Sænthong *(Cao Pho Sænthong)*

In addition to the guardian spirit of Ku Dæng, there is another group of spirits called "Lord Sænthong." This spirit inhabits Mrs. Khieo Phongkæw, a 66-year-old villager, who acts as medium for this spirit. Mrs. Khieo formerly was a very poor villager. Later, Lord Sænthong entered Mrs. Khieo and told her he wanted her to be his vehicle ("horse to ride on"). At first Mrs. Khieo was unwilling to oblige. But Lord Sænthong told her that she would be sick and even poorer if she did not yield to him. Mrs. Khieo sought help in the hospital and from the village doctor without results. In the end she yielded to ride on and reside in the Lord Sænthong's horse. Her health returned and she became better off economically. Through Mrs. Khieo, Lord Sænthong also healed other villagers and gave them good luck as well as continuing good health. This spirit was not willing to cast spells on or influence other villagers in an evil way, since this would be considered sinful. In addition to Lord Sænthong, three other spirits take turns inhabiting Mrs. Khieo.

There are two other houses in the village, each one the size of a small room, which could be described as "spirit houses." They are communal houses that are used only once a year for a special spirit ceremony. At other times these houses stay empty and uncared for. There are no taboos connected with them. At one house, a ceremony is conducted in June and at the other at the time of the Northern New Year's festival in April.

The Spirit Dance (fon phi)

On April 17, 1954, the third day of the Thai New Year's festival (songkran), a celebration was held at the neighborhood "spirit houses" in Hamlet 6.[8] The spirit houses had been repaired and cleaned for the occasion and decorated with beautiful flowers. The caretaker of the spirit houses, in whose backyard they are located, acted as the leader of the ceremony and his wife as the representative, or medium of the spirits (thi nang). Food was placed on woven mats with which the floors of the houses had been newly covered. Near the spirit houses there was a platform about two feet high on which a phonograph was placed to play local songs, both for the enjoyment of the spirits and the entertainment of the villagers. More than one hundred villagers attended the ceremony.

Several old women in the caretaker's house arranged flowers on trays, made miang, and rolled cigarettes to be taken into the spirit houses. The medium went up into the bigger of the two houses accompanied by several old women who sat down in a circle around her. The medium placed a tray of flowers in one corner of the house, prostrated herself three times (krap), and announced to everyone that she was inviting the spirit of Cao Ton Luang, the chief of the spirits, to visit her. Then she put her face on a pillow near her. After a few minutes her body began to tremble, and she took a few dancing steps, while her eyes were half closed. An old woman nearby gave her some face powder, a new shirt, and a sarong, which she put on. Suddenly, she jumped up and sat on the bamboo mat, still shaking as if with fever. She wrapped her head in a light blue scarf and put some flowers

---

[8] See map 3.

into her hair; then she announced that she was now Cao Ton Luang, who had come to the ceremony at the invitation of the villagers.

One of the old women told Cao Ton Luang that the people performed this ceremony every year at this time. Cao Ton Luang answered that this year the spirit world *(müang phi)* needed a lot of people, so that many people would die, but that those who believed in Cao Ton Luang and had always made offerings to him would be able to save their lives.

Then some people sent water jars up to the spirit and asked him to make sacred water for curing sickness. Cao Ton Luang took the jars, said some sacred words *(khatha)* over them, and blew into the water five to seven times. He said that if someone got sick, the person would have to drink some of this water to be healed.

A few minutes later, Cao Ton Luang said that he would have to leave, for he could not stay any longer in the people's world *(müang khon)*. The medium put her face into the pillow again and arose after a few minutes, no longer trembling.

After a short rest, the medium announced that she would now invite another spirit, Cao Noi, to visit her. He arrived in the same manner as the previous one. When the spirit was in the woman, some of the old women gave her different clothing to dress in, this time representing a younger person, since this spirit was not yet very old. The medium then went into the smaller of the two houses.

Cao Noi said that he wanted to listen to some folk songs that he named. The man at the phonograph put the records on as requested, and the spirit listened attentively. After the songs, Cao Noi asked for some food and liquor, which was given to him and which he consumed. When he had finished eating and drinking, he sang a song and performed a local dance *(fon phi)*, to the great amusement of the spectators. A little later, Cao Noi asked for a pillow and lay down to sleep for about an hour. When he awoke, he made some sacred water in the same manner as the previous spirit had done. After this activity he departed, and the medium became her normal self again. She tried to invite some other spirits, but none would come.

This ceremony was performed for some twenty people who lived in the neighborhood of the spirit houses. Others had come for the entertainment.[9] The caretaker of the spirit houses told us that such a ceremony cost about 300 baht, two-thirds of which had been given by the surviving member of the Royal House of Chiang Mai, because some ancestor of his, who had once lived in Ku Dæng, had promised to support this ceremony whenever it was held. The remainder of the money had been contributed by the twenty people of the neighborhood.

The Ku Dæng head monk told us that he could not say much about this ceremony. He had no idea whether Cao Ton Luang or Cao Noi actually

---

[9] Theme 3: Fun.

existed. He thought that this ceremony depended on the faith of those participating, who had either been taught by their parents or had seen the ceremony performed by others. As a monk he could only say that there was no use believing in spirits *(phi)*. The temple leader told us that he thought this ceremony was a great deception played on the people. Those who believe in it will get nothing but soon lose their faith in the Lord Buddha.

At the other end of the village, at the village guardian house, the ceremony performed on the same day was much simpler.[10] The people cleaned the house, decorated it with flowers, and offered food on the doorsteps. An old man chanted while presenting the food and poured water on the ground in the usual manner of transferring merit to the dead.

A monk from a nearby temple gave us the following information about belief in spirits *(phi)*:

> There are two kinds of people who believe in spirits: first, there are those who believe that all spirits are bad, bringing harm to those who do not believe in them; secondly, there are those who believe that spirits are benevolent beings who can give medicine to the sick and good luck to those who believe in them. Educated persons have never written or taught about believing in spirits. This belief came from the people themselves. It is believing in nonsense.
>
> Some books say that belief in spirits arose for the first time a long, long time ago, when some people went out into the jungle to collect firewood. Unluckily, they got lost in the jungle and could not find their way back home. Being afraid of the wild beasts, they found shelter under a big tree, which they asked for protection from danger. At night they all slept under the big tree. The following morning, when they found that they had slept very well under the tree, they came to believe that the tree really had protected them from the wild beasts. So when they returned to their homes, they made offerings to "something" in that tree, which had protected them the previous night. Other people, who heard this story, which was growing in detail with time, also came to believe in the power of that "something" in the tree. From that time on people began to believe in spirits.
>
> After some time, a dancing ceremony to please the spirits was developed. The people thought that spirits must be pleased to see dancing, because the villagers liked it themselves. Thus, when people were in trouble, they went to a place that was supposed to be the abode of a spirit and asked the spirit to help them get rid of their

---

[10] See map 3.

difficulties. If the spirit helped them, they promised to arrange a very enjoyable dancing performance near the spirit's abode. When they got help, a dancing festival was held for the spirit. The villagers found great pleasure in this ceremony; they thought it pleased the powerful spirit at the same time that it provided pleasing entertainment for themselves. This then developed into a custom of the people.

Actually, this ceremony came from a very clever deceiver, who wanted to make a lot of money from the villagers. He organized the festival and collected money from the villagers, which was supposed to be given to the spirit but actually went into his own pocket. Sometimes this same ceremony was performed for the sick. The results were found to be very good, for the sick persons recovered. The fact is, the sick who saw the dancing were pleased in their hearts by the performance. Their joy and satisfaction were the powers that then stopped the illness. Many people, like those of Ku Dæng, deeply believe in this kind of spirit propitiation, because they have no idea about the real values of life.

Not only monks, but also most villagers give sophisticated answers to questions about belief in spirits. They usually relate what others, or "they," believe, while the villagers, themselves, seldom admit real fear of or trust in spirits. We asked one man what a little hut behind his house was; it looked to us like a "spirit house." He laughed and said, "No, that is not a 'spirit house'; we keep our chickens there. We used to have spirit houses a long time ago, but nowadays we have none, because the Lord Buddha said one should not believe in spirits. Some people still have them, but most people do not."

There are really only two kinds of beings that enter into the vocabulary of the villagers. There are ghosts (phi) and gods (thewada). The spirits of the deceased seem to become either ghosts or gods, unless they are reborn immediately as humans. One man informed us that those who went to heaven after death became gods, while those who went to hell became ghosts. The gods, he said, were invisible; they are the result of making merit (phon bun). This means, if we make merit, we will receive help from the gods, who will protect us in our next life.

Belief in gods is quite widespread and readily admitted. Belief in spirits is much less overt. In one of our questionnaires we asked three questions: 1) Do gods (thewada) exist? 2) Do ghosts (phi) exist? 3) Are there any other beings more powerful than a person who can help or hurt you?

To the first question, 66.7% of the sample answered in the affirmative; 27.8% denied that gods existed, and 5.5% did not know. As for ghosts, 38.9% affirmed their existence; 55.6% denied it; and 5.5% did not know.

There were frequent responses that "in the old days 'they' believed in ghosts." When persons giving such answers were pressed for something more definite, they usually said, "No." For the third question, 66.7% answered that no beings more powerful than humans existed; 11.1% did not know; and the rest, 22.2%, listed the following: Giants (yak), Phra In or Indra who lives "up in the sky," and "the Buddha image." In the pre-test, the wording was found to be slightly ambiguous, when one of the informants answered, "Oh yes, an elephant is more powerful than a man."

The gods (thewada) are consistently mentioned in sermons and in discussions among the villagers. Pictures of the gods can be seen in the temple, and certain actions are specifically designed to reach the gods, such as the beating of drums at the conclusion of sermons or when a person has died, "to let the gods know."

A Chiang Mai monk, trained in Southern Thailand, who only recently had joined the leadership of the Buddhist Association in Chiang Mai, shed some light on the position of some of the upper echelon Buddhists concerning the question of ghosts and gods. He himself did not believe in ghosts, but he had read in some of the old scriptures that the Lord Buddha talked about ghosts. At the time of the Buddha, people generally believed in ghosts. The Buddha, who was very clever, did not wish to destroy the common belief of the people. He said that ghosts do exist: a ghost is the spirit (winyan) of a person who has done much evil while alive. Belief in ghosts arises from fear. Ghosts actually exist for a person who believes in ghosts; they do not exist for those who do not believe in them. A ghost will have power over those who believe in its existence, but no power over those who do not. In Buddhism, as in Christianity, the monk continued, there is much talk about ghosts, and, in his opinion, the meaning is about the same. Mostly the uneducated believe in ghosts, the educated do not.

Buddhism affirms the existence of gods (thewada), who live in groups in heaven (sawan). The gods are to human beings what a king is to his people, each belongs to his own kind. The Lord Buddha said that a person who is reluctant to do evil is a god in this world. There are at least three worlds (lok) in Buddhism: 1) phrommalok, the world for the best kind of gods, the phrom, or Brahma; 2) thewadalok, the world of the gods; and 3) manutlok, the world of humanity. The world of Brahma is subdivided into the world with body (rupalok), which consists of sixteen parts, and the world without body (arupalok) consisting of four parts for the very best kind of Brahma. Finally, there are six parts to the world of gods. Belief in these various worlds, the monk insisted, is an ancient belief, not necessarily held today. However, neither did he deny their existence.

He also commented on the giants (yak), who are a kind of people who live in Tibet. Buddhism teaches that the giants are people without mercy, who are always doing evil. The Lord Buddha said in one of the scriptures that a person who is very angry is a giant. The dictionary of the Royal Institute defines giants as "a non-human group, believed to have huge and fierce bodies with long, protruding buck teeth, who usually have the ability to fly and to change their body form at will. They are supposed to receive offerings and sacrifices."

In the central plains area of Thailand, little "spirit houses" can be seen in the yards of many homes.[11] Along the railroad and in the larger cities in the North, these little shrines are also in evidence. In Ku Dæng, their absence in 1953 was noteworthy. By 1985 we observed a considerable increase in the number of such "spirit houses."

During our original study, the only conspicuous center of religious expression in the home was the Buddha shelf in one corner of the main living room. During Buddhist Lent and on other special occasions, the head of the house where we lived made an offering to the Buddha picture on the shelf consisting of a few flowers and a little popped rice placed on a tray together with a lit candle. He did three prostrations in front of the Buddha picture and chanted the following request in Pali:

> *Sathu, sathu sa.* Thus on this occasion, Lord Buddha, who is the only Lord, who has the only truth in this world, and who has the Triple Gems in your hand, please come and give your blessings to us, your faithful followers. We have brought you some flowers and candles as offerings of veneration. Please accept our gifts and lead us away from evil. Please give us some merit, if we have performed good in your sight, so that the merit will take us to *nipphan* at the end of our lives.

Although the words in this chant are definitely addressed to the Lord Buddha, the man insisted that he was making his request to the gods.

The *Salak Phaya In* Festival

Toward the end of October, on the first Precept Day following the end of Buddhist Lent, one of the special festivals of the religious calendar of the year was held for the gods. This festival, called the *Salak Phaya In* ceremony, is given in honor of Phaya In (Indra), the head of the gods, who is living in the sky. This is a festival of thanksgiving, for he has given peace and happiness to the world at the request of the Lord Buddha.

In the middle of the morning on this Precept Day, the Ku Dæng faithful brought parcels of gifts to the temple. Each package contained some confectionery, food, fruit, cigarettes, betel nuts, and money in the form of money trees. Members of the temple committee assembled all the packages on the east *sala*, counted the various items, and divided them into equal parts. They agreed to give one part to Indra and his company of gods, one

---

[11] See Phya Anuman Rajadhon (1955c), pp. 3-10.

part to the temple leader, one part to the Buddha statue, one part to the Law of Buddha, one part to each of the monks and novices in the temple, and an extra part to the novice who had been designated to preach later in the morning.

When all the packages had been counted, all the shares except those designated to Indra and company were taken into the *wihan*. Those for the monks and novices were placed alongside the platform on the south side of the *wihan*; the share for the Buddha statue was placed at its base; and the shares for the Law and for the novice who was to preach were left at the foot of the pulpit. The temple leader's share was put in the front part of the *wihan*, were he would be sitting.

When the congregation had assembled in the *wihan*, the temple leader led the people in prostrations to the Buddha statue, and the monks and novices came in to sit down on their platform. One of the village elders presented a large tray of flowers to the head monk and made three prostrations. When the five precepts had been bestowed upon the people, the temple leader led the congregation in a chant to offer all the gifts to the Lord Buddha, the Law, and the Monkhood. The monks and novices then went outside into the temple yard to receive the gifts for Indra and the other gods by proxy. The monks and novices each chanted while pouring water on the ground. The villagers who had given these specific gifts were nearby, watching the proceedings in respectful silence and attention. The merit that they had made by giving the gifts was here being transferred to the gods, who, they hoped, would thereby be favorably inclined to help them and their families in the days to come.

When everybody had returned to the *wihan*, the temple leader invited the designated novice to preach a Lanna Thai sermon. The novice ascended the pulpit, where, hidden from the view of the villagers, he read the sermon from a set of palm leaves. Forty minutes later, when he had finished, the monks and novices chanted a blessing for the congregation who had brought the gifts. All the monks and novices, except for the head monk, left the *wihan* while the people were chanting in praise of the Lord Buddha. Outside, in the temple yard, the packages were sold back to the villagers, eight small parcels for 1 baht. The money was to be added to the repair fund of the temple. Some of the packages were given to beggars who had come for this purpose to the temple.

Life Cycle Ceremonies

Of the various life cycle ceremonies, that of the funeral is by far the most elaborate as far as Ku Dæng custom is concerned. A person is ushered out of this world with much greater ceremony than on arrival. There actually is very little ceremony or celebration when a new baby is born.

Childbirth

When the time for the delivery of a child arrives, the prospective mother usually goes home to her own mother, if she is not still living with her parents. Since in most cases a young couple lives with the wife's family, the first child or two will automatically be born in the mother's parents' home. If the couple lives with the husband's family, or if they live on their own, the wife usually returns home, even if they are practically neighbors. In some cases, when it is difficult for the prospective mother to move, or when her family has no room for her in their house, the wife's mother, and sometimes also her father, temporarily move to their daughter's home to be there at the time of delivery.

In the cases about which we have information, labor lasted from two to six hours, which seems to be a general figure according to the village midwife. Delivery always takes place in one of the inner rooms of the house. The child is delivered by one of two professional midwives of the village for fees ranging from nothing, in the case of a relative, to 15 baht. No other persons assisted in the actual delivery, although other people, especially the immediate relatives of the young mother, were present. In some cases the husband's father chanted sacred words (*khatha*) during the delivery, imploring the help of the gods.

Women usually delivered in a sitting position, leaning against a post or a wall. The midwife worked under the woman's skirt or under a cloth. She said she did not wish to be too close to the actual birth because of the odor. Usually, she received the baby on a cloth. Then she cut the umbilical cord with a bamboo knife and tied it. In most of the cases known to us, the father took the afterbirth and buried it at the gate of the compound. We were told it could also be buried at the foot of the stairs. "Custom" controlled the choice of place.

One old man told us that the afterbirth had to be buried in a certain place according to the day of the week: on Sundays in the north or south, on Mondays in the north, on Tuesdays in the east, on Wednesdays in the southeast, on Thursdays in the west, on Fridays in the northwest, and on Saturdays in the southwest. On each of these days, the spirits (*phi*) live in the opposite direction from that in which the afterbirth is to be buried; in that way, they cannot harm the mother through the afterbirth.

Immediately after the birth, both baby and mother are washed, in some cases with soap and warm water, in others just with warm water, and sometimes with a solution of a medicine supplied by UNICEF, which had been distributed to all the village midwives in the district. In most cases the new mother was told to take a "red Burmese medicine," which could be obtained in the market. This was supposed to strengthen her blood for some days after the delivery. One new baby was fed two hours after delivery. In all the other cases observed, the baby was given only water until three days after birth, when it began to be breast fed. The mother was usually put on a diet of rice, a spinach-like vegetable, and dried fish. After ten days, she could eat some pork with the vegetables. In all cases, confinement lasted for one month, although the young mother would be allowed to get up and walk around after five or six days. After a month, or at the longest forty days, normal life resumed.

In general, the parents desired a baby boy rather than a girl. One father, who already had two boys, told us when his third boy arrived that he would rather have had a girl. He liked to have girls, because they will stay at home and help with work, whereas boys will not.

We met the resident doctor one day just as he was returning from the house of a sick woman. She had had a miscarriage and was on the verge of death. She was now recuperating with medicine he had prescribed. He advised the family to bury the still-born child somewhere, so that it could not spread any disease. He said there was no ceremony since the baby had not yet had life. In other words, he believes that life begins at the time of actual delivery.

In a few cases of childbirth the villagers went to hospitals in Chiang Mai. The wife's mother always went along, and sometimes also the father. In general, however, the villagers preferred to have their babies at home.

There is no coming-of-age ceremony in Ku Dæng, unless one considers entering the novitiate as a life cycle ceremony for boys. The small number of boys entering the monkhood would make this an exception rather than the rule. The topknot cutting ceremony, described by some writers and still practiced in the 1950s by some people in the Bang Chan community north of Bangkok, is entirely unknown in Ku Dæng.[12]

Longevity Ceremony

An occasional ceremony in the life of a young man is that of *süp cata* (or Central Thai, *süp chata*). During our year in Ku Dæng we observed this ceremony three times: once for a 21-year-old unmarried man, who had been seriously sick and, after his recovery, wished to have this ceremony performed. Another time the ceremony was held for a 24-year-old married man, who was suffering from hepatitis. The third occasion was the case of a 35-year-old houseowner, who had the ceremony performed in conjunction with the dedication of his new house.

The ceremony for the young, unmarried man, the son of one of the richest villagers, took place the day before the second month full moon festival described below. One of the villagers told us that a long time ago every male villager had to submit to this ceremony when he reached his 20th birthday and every couple in their first year of marriage. It is a ceremony of offering gifts and sermons to the temple and of having the monks bless the

---

[12] Lauriston Sharp and Lucien M. Hanks, *Bang Chan: Social History of a Rural Community in Thailand* (Ithaca: Cornell University Press, 1978).

persons to give them good luck for the remainder of their lives. The ceremony always was carried out on the day before the second month full moon festival, as was done in this case. The head monk selects the sermons from his astrological tables, depending on the person's day, month, and year of birth. The young man presents these sermons to the temple on the day of the ceremony. There is a different sermon for each day, month, and year. A person is supposed to give three sermons to the temple at this time, one for his birthday, one for his birth month, and one for his birth year.

The young man's father helped him set up three pieces of wood (*mai kam*) in the temple. Each piece was approximately six feet long, and together they formed the skeleton of a tepee-like structure. Two bamboo tubes, one filled with rice, the other with sand, were tied alongside one of the wooden poles. Two other bamboo tubes, one filled with water and one with paddy, were attached to the second leg of the tepee. A bundle of reeds, equal in number to the years of the young man's age, was tied to the third leg. A white flag was fastened to the point of the tepee. A small "bridge" made of bamboo, string, and dried betel nut to represent continued wealth for the remainder of the young man's life was suspended between two of the bamboo tubes. A young coconut and a sprouting betel nut sapling were placed at the foot of one of the posts.

The young man squatted under the "tepee." A white thread, the *fai luang*, was passed across the top of the tepee to the hands of the young man on one end and to the monk, who was sitting on a preaching chair or on the floor beside the tepee, on the other. Elsewhere, we observed that the thread could be placed on the person's head instead of his hands. A tray containing the three sermons was placed beside the preaching chair.

The ceremony began when the head monk sat down in the preaching chair. The young man took flowers and popped rice in his hands and prostrated himself before the monk. Then the monk preached from one of the sermons for about twenty minutes. When he had finished, he sat down in front of the young man, took the white string, and tied two turns around the man's wrist. While tying the string, the monk chanted a blessing. Then the head monk returned to his usual place along the south wall of the *wihan*. Another monk and two novices came into the *wihan* to join the head monk in receiving gifts from the father of the young man. The ceremony ended with a chanted blessing of the monks for the donor of the gifts.

After the ceremony, the young man and his father took the tepee outside the *wihan* and placed it under the Bo tree in the back of the temple. This is another custom dating back to a time before Buddhism, when Brahmanism was the predominant religion in India, according to the explanation given by an old monk. The people then believed that gods were living in big trees, such as Bo or Banyan trees, because these trees had a long life. As Buddhism developed, it became mixed up with Brahmanism, including the belief about the gods in the Bo and Banyan trees. Uneducated people, the monk said, believed in these stories. Actually, a Bo tree was planted at every Buddhist temple in memory of the place where the Lord Buddha died. Today, the paraphernalia of the *süp cata* ceremony is taken to the Bo tree behind the temple and left there. A long, long time ago, they used much bigger posts for this ceremony. These posts were then used to prop up the cracking branches of the Bo tree. The people believed at that time that if one did a good thing, like propping up a Bo tree, one would certainly earn merit in return. Today, the monk continued, people are very lazy. They make only a small structure and place it under the Bo tree after the ceremony, hoping that they still will receive merit.

The young coconut and the betel sprout are similar in origin to the pieces of wood. When the temples first were built, there usually were no trees in the vicinity. Therefore, the people were encouraged to make offerings of young coconuts and betel trees, so that the fruits of these trees would be of use to the monks. Today, these same plants are still used in the ceremony. Afterwards, however, they are just thrown away outside the temple area, where they may or may not have an opportunity to grow up. Expediency seems to have outweighed other considerations in the performance of this ceremony.[13] It was too much trouble to make the symbols used the proper size; smaller replicas seemed to serve the same purpose. In fact, the whole ceremony seemed to have little positive value, and, hence, it has disappeared for all practical purposes. In some cases, when persons are sick or occupy a new house, they want to play it safe, and so the ceremony is performed.

Marriage Ceremonies

Marriage ceremonies are seldom performed. Although weddings are supposed to be registered in the district office, in many cases a young man just moves in with his wife at her parents' home. When the wedding is not registered, divorce is much simpler. Whether or not there is a ceremony depends on the financial circumstances of the bride's family and on how many times the participants have been married previously. We heard of a big wedding feast for a person getting married the fifth time. This seems to have been an exception to the general practice.

We attended a wedding in the middle of May. The ceremony took place at the bride's home. When we arrived we found more than fifty guests already waiting. As is customary at parties or celebrations in homes, the men were sitting in the front room, while the women were more inconspicuous in the kitchen and the inner rooms. It was late in the afternoon when the bridegroom finally arrived, followed by a large party consisting mostly, but not entirely, of men. One young man was carrying a large, wooden chest with the groom's belongings. The groom, a 23-year-old youth, wore short, blue pants, a white shirt, and a blue undershirt, multi-

---

[13] Theme 1: Utility.

colored striped socks, and brown canvas sneakers. The bride, wearing a plain, black, three-quarter-length skirt, a dark blouse, and no shoes, came out to pose for pictures with the groom. Then everybody went inside.

The *kamnan* presided over the ceremony. He directed the two young people to kneel down on two pillows. Nobody seemed to know the correct procedure. One man pointed the pillows in front of the couple in one direction, someone else pushed them into a different position. The *kamnan* told them to prostrate themselves first toward one old man, then another, presumably distinguished relatives. Then the couple knelt down on the pillows, the bride to the left of the young man. The commune doctor tied a white string about three feet in length to the groom's left wrist and to the bride's right. Then he tied a long string to the middle of the first one and gave the other end to the *kamnan*, who was standing before the couple. While the doctor was tying the strings, he murmured some sacred words of blessing.

With the string in his hands, the *kamnan* gave a ten-minute speech of advice to the newlyweds. He told them that they were now potentially mother and father. No longer did they have their parents to cling to, but from here on they were on their own. He admonished the girl to be a good housekeeper while her husband was working in the fields. At the conclusion of the speech everybody clapped his hands in applause.

The *kamnan* then led the couple by the string to the bridal chamber to the accompaniment of jokes and laughter. The boy's chest and a silver bowl containing the guests' wedding offerings were carried behind them. Everybody soon returned, the couple without the strings on their wrists.

Food was brought for all the guests. There was considerable consumption of liquor, sufficient to make the party noisy, but not enough for people to get drunk. When the general tumult had become rather noisy, the *kamnan* called in a loud voice for all to quiet down; this was temporarily effective. A few people asked the *kamnan*'s permission to return home. This was readily granted. A short while later the *kamnan* proclaimed the official conclusion of the wedding. He said that this was just a short feast and people should not overstay their welcome. Most of the guests thereupon left, although some of the younger people stayed around until late at night.

There is no official participation by monks at weddings in Ku Dæng. At this particular wedding, a woman told us, the monks had been invited in the morning to the house of the bride, where they preached and were fed their morning meal. However, the Ku Dæng monks did not corroborate this statement. They told us they had not been invited. From other, similar occasions we learned that this is the only function of the monks at a wedding. They may be asked to come to the house for special merit-making in the morning and bestow a blessing on the young couple. In former days the newlyweds would ask to have a life-blessing ceremony *(süp cata)* performed for them by a monk some time during their first year of married life.

For bigger wedding feasts, relatives travel long distances to participate, sometimes staying several days in the village of the bride's family. In other cases, no ceremony takes place whatsoever. In one house, where we visited during our initial census canvass, we found a young man who had no apparent relationship to other members of the family. After lengthy questioning, we were told that he would be married to one of the daughters "in a couple of weeks." In another case, a man who owned considerable property, and whose wife had died a few years earlier, suddenly was found living in the house of one of his neighbors. He had "married" their only daughter.

House-Blessing Ceremony

The house-blessing ceremony in Ku Dæng should be considered as a life-cycle ceremony, since it usually comes but once in a man's lifetime, and then usually only when he has reached middle age or more, and when his farming has been successful enough to enable him to marshal sufficient resources for a large wooden house. Smaller bamboo huts are regularly built and rebuilt, but there is seldom a house-blessing ceremony held for such abodes. A small, bamboo house suggests that the owner has limited means, hence an elaborate house-blessing ceremony would be financially impossible.

House-building of large, wooden structures may take as much as a year in Ku Dæng. This is in marked contrast to the small, bamboo structures, which can be put up in one day, and which are frequently moved from one site to another in half a day by a new owner. All new wooden houses are put on reinforced concrete pillars. Some of the teakwood posts from an old structure may be used for the rear part of a new house, provided it is built on the same site as the old one. In 1953, however, most of the posts for new houses were made of concrete. By 1985 new houses of the affluent segment of the village were built in brick and concrete with wood being employed only for the second story, if at all. When concrete posts were made right on the site, the builders liked to leave them exposed to rain and sunshine for several months, so that the concrete could harden and settle in the ground before the house was put on top.

When the time came for proceeding with the building, lumber was prepared according to the specifications of a semi-professional house builder, usually a villager acting in this capacity. Not more than two or three men were paid for working on a new house. By far the largest number of those helping with construction were volunteers, who, in turn, would receive help when they were ready to build a new house.[14]

When the wooden posts had been erected on top of the concrete pillars, coconuts and bananas were tied to each of the pillars. There was no

---

[14] Theme 5: Communal responsibility.

special ceremony accompanying this activity, and nobody could tell us the reason for doing so: "It is just always done this way." When parts of the roof beams had been put in place, a friend of the house owner, an ex-monk, held a ceremony for the gods *(thewada)*. Six banana leaf trays had been prepared, each containing food and candles. These trays were placed on little platforms sticking out of a banana stump, which had been erected on the ground behind the new house. The trays were arranged so that one was pointing in each of six directions, comprising the four compass points as well as up and down. When all the candles had been lit, the ex-monk read from a monk's handbook an invitation to all the gods to accept the food and protect the house that was being built. When he had finished reading, he poured water on the ground from a small cup, thereby transferring merit to the gods. Again the reason given for this ceremony was that it had been done by their parents before them, hence it was fitting to do so at this time as well.

All those who had been working at the house during the day were invited for a feast the same evening. After this no work was done on this particular house for several months, which happened to coincide with the main part of the rainy season. Wood was difficult to obtain at the time, and the villagers were busy with rice cultivation in their fields. There was little spare time for helping with the building of a new house.

When the house was finally finished, written invitations were sent out for the house-blessing ceremony. In most cases, this ceremony lasted only a few hours in the morning. Among the wealthiest house owners, however, it was customary to have large feasts with festivities continuing for an entire day or even two.

In some cases, prior to the actual house-blessing ceremony, a special offering was made to the old posts, which were now no longer in use, or had been, perhaps, relegated to the inferior task of holding up the rear part of the house. Trays of food similar to those used in the ceremony already described, were placed near the old posts, while a monk chanted. Again, no special reason could be given for this by the villagers other than that this was the usual procedure.

According to an old custom, when the ceremony lasts more than one day, monks from several temples are invited to the new house the night before the main part of the ceremony. One of the monks told us that they are invited to sleep there the first night in order to bring good luck to the house. On that night, the owner and his family are not yet allowed to sleep in the new house.

Over sixty villagers, more men than women, were present at the evening ceremony. Six monks and six novices sat under the Buddha shelf in the main room. A white thread had been strung completely around the house. One end passed through the hands of all the monks and novices, then through a silver bowl containing lustral water, and thence to the Buddha image on the shelf above. Two lit candles had been stuck to the rim of the silver bowl. The monks chanted the Law of Buddha to turn the water in the silver bowl into lustral water, so that it could be sprinkled around the house and thus prevent bad luck from entering. The white thread strung around the outside of the house was to prevent evil spirits or disease from entering. The monks were holding on to the thread in order to concentrate their minds in unison on the good things that should come to the house. The Buddha image was connected to the string to transmit the Lord Buddha's blessing.

After the monks had finished their chanting, one of them told us that they actually could not give happiness to anyone, for they do not have it to give. Happiness really comes to those who have done some good, and who thereby become happy upon seeing a monk who is the representative of goodness. In the same way, we receive benefit from asking a monk to chant a blessing. If previously we performed a good deed, we will become happy through the blessing. If we failed to do good, we will not be happy at all. In chanting, the monk does not have any powerful words but only praise for the Lord Buddha. This was written down by one of his disciple in remembrance of him, not for a blessing as they are used today.

After the chanting, the lustral water was sprinkled around the house. Sometimes the white thread is cut and bits are tied around the wrists of the house owner. In one such case, the oldest man present tied pieces of string around the wrists of the owners, both husband and wife. Then one of the village elders followed by tying strings in the name of all the guests present. With each tying a few words of blessing are murmured or chanted. The housebuilder frequently also ties a set of strings, thereby officially handing over the house or "giving" it to the owners. Finally, the *kamnan*, who is almost always one of the invited guests, ties strings around the owners' wrists and gives them his blessing.

Phya Anuman Rajadhon suggested an explanation for the wrist-tying ceremony.[15] He related the practice to the belief in various *khwan* of the body. Binding the left wrist with a string is done to call the *khwan* of the person back to his body; binding the right wrist is an exhortation for the *khwan* to remain in the body.

Sometimes, when the chanting is completed, one of the monks gives an extemporaneous speech. In the case of the evening ceremony, a monk spoke about how industrious the owner of the house had been, how he had built up wealth with his bare hands from practically nothing to become one of the richest men in the village. For comparison, he told the story of a woman who had achieved success because she also had been industrious and ingenious. Her parents had died and left her with nothing but a single coin, which was worth next to nothing. The woman tried to use the coin to buy vegetable seeds from a merchant, even though the price of seed usually was at least a hundred times the value of the coin. After long pleading, she

---

[15] Phya Anuman Rajadhon (1955c), pp. 15-22.

finally succeeded in melting the merchant's heart, and he would let her dip her finger into the pot of seeds to let her have all that would stick on her finger in return for her single coin. Using her wits, the woman dampened her finger and thus got a fairly large number of seeds. She planted them and sold the resulting crop of vegetables in the market. People who heard about this were sympathetic and bought everything from her until she became rich. Soon after, a rich man heard about the industrious woman, fell in love with her, and married her. Thus, by being industrious, the woman achieved a happy life.

After the extemporaneous preaching, the headman of another village, who was a native of Ku Dæng, gave a humorous conclusion to the monks' speeches. This man was a well-known speaker to whom the villagers liked to listen. He repeated in a somewhat more humorous fashion what the monks had said, eliciting considerable laughter from the audience.

By popular demand, one of the monks chanted a Lanna Thai sermon in the expanded musical fashion. Since there was no pulpit in the house, where he could be hidden from the view of his listeners, he took a monk's robe and hung it across a corner of the room, so that he could sit apart from the audience and not be seen. He continued with this sermon for some hours, while the guests were smoking, chewing betel nut, and chatting with each other. When he had finished, another monk continued with another sermon in which he was a specialist. The meeting did not break up until three o'clock in the morning.

The following morning more monks came to join those who had stayed in the house all night. Some lengthy chanting was followed by more extemporaneous sermons. One of the monks talked about the house-blessing ceremony. He implored the villagers to continue observing this ceremony since it was a worthwhile custom. It is not only a ceremony for the house but also to celebrate the success of the owner. After the preaching, the usual five precepts were requested and granted, food was offered to the monks, and everybody present participated in a hearty breakfast.

In most of the house-blessing ceremonies that we witnessed in Ku Dæng, the ceremonies lasted only a few hours and concluded with breakfast. Long, extended ceremonies were the exception. In the case described above, there was more to come after departure of the monks. The invitations for the morning ceremony had been issued in the name of the owners, husband and wife. Gold-engraved invitations for a special dinner in the afternoon had been sent out in the name of the 19-year-old daughter. This was an unprecedented step. Some villagers surmised that perhaps the parents did not know very many people; in order to have a well-attended house-blessing ceremony, they had to ask their daughter to invite her friends. The actual reason seemed to be that the owner, being one of the wealthiest villagers, wanted to have his house-blessing in as modern a style as possible, although he was still careful not to leave out any of the traditional parts of the ceremonial.[16]

The invitations called for the guests to arrive at 3:30 in the afternoon. At that time the daughter and her friends were still busy transforming the yard into a festive place. They had borrowed tables and chairs from the school. These they arranged in two parallel banquet rows.

The guests were mostly young people from elsewhere. Those from Ku Dæng had either not been invited, or, if they had, were too shy to mix with the "city folk" who were soon milling around the yard. Apart from the meal, there was no special organized activity. All of the guests wore modern Western dress, in contrast to the morning ceremony, when the village women appeared in their traditional, long sarong skirts. In the evening, non-glutinous rice was served to all the guests; this was another sign of attempted sophistication; at all other occasions for communal meals in the village, glutinous rice was the standard and preferred type.

The host had purchased fifty bottles of liquor. We learned later that only eighteen were consumed by the two hundred guests. A traveling medicine salesman had supplied a microphone in return for the privilege to sell medicine before dinner. A young man took charge of the microphone and asked various representatives from different villages or towns to say a few words of praise for the daughter of the house. Some attempt was made to interest the people in dancing, but no one was willing to be the first. With nothing else to do, the party broke up soon after dark.

All the precautions for insuring good luck for the owner of the house and his family seemed to have been of no avail, because three weeks after the house-blessing ceremony the owner's wife died following a three-day illness.

When household goods are moved into a new house, the owner will frequently ask a villager with a "good" name—such as Nai Ngœn (Mr. Silver), Nai Thong (Mr. Gold), Nai Nun (Mr. Support), or Nai Di (Mr. Good)—to help bring the things into the new house, so that some of the good luck inherent in the person's name be transferred to the house.

These house-blessing ceremonies are expensive, even if one counts the gifts brought by the guests. The feast described above cost the owner 2000 baht, while he received less than one-fourth of this amount in contributions.[17] This is the reason why such elaborate ceremonies are held only by the wealthier villagers.

Other Beliefs and Practices Observed

Gifts in a basket. When a baby is born, the doctor in attendance or the midwife hand the newborn baby to a person designated by the parents

---

[16] Theme 7: Playing it safe.

[17] 2000 baht was approximately equivalent to US $111 in 1954.

as an exemplary individual (godfather or godmother). This person must be well-behaved, of good character, and acceptable to the parents. The child is expected to grow up in the image of the person who first held it after birth. The person thus selected will have to give the baby its first bath. In the bathwater must be placed a piece of gold, silver, some jewelry, a gold chain, or something of similar value. It is believed that this will ensure that the child will grow up to be prosperous. After the bath, when the baby is dressed, it will be laid on a pillow in a winnowing basket *(kradong)*. In the case of a girl, needle and thread are put under the pillow to ensure that she will be a good seamstress. For a boy, pencil and paper are supposed to encourage him to become a sage.

Locating a new house. A new house should be built facing East, so that it does not obstruct the path of the sun.

Sleeping direction. Villagers should sleep with their heads toward the East or the North. West is the direction of the dead.

Prohibition on wedding day. It is considered inauspicious to break or tear anything belonging to the household. This would precipitate a breaking up of the marriage because of estrangement or death.

Dog urinating on a person. Although a very rare occurrence, this happenstance is considered a very bad omen. The person so showered with misfortune must carry out a special ceremony to restore his good luck; otherwise his business will not prosper, he will make no profit, and what he has will be eaten up by debts.

Sweeping the House at Night. In ancient times it was considered bad luck to have one's children or grandchildren sweep the house at night. This was because when it is dark something valuable, such as small pieces of gold or silver, could not be seen and could easily be swept away.

Sneezing. When a person sneezes three times in succession, it is believed that someone is calling his or her *khwan* or that the person is being slandered.

On the basis of our observations it is clear that traditional practices reflecting divination or propitiation of various real or imaginary powers are continually on the decrease, whereas reliance on introduced, technologically modern methods is increasing rapidly. At the same time, religious manifestations of a non-Buddhist nature tend to be incorporated more and more into the formal pattern of the Buddhism of the village temple.

11

THE RELIGIOUS CALENDAR OF KU DÆNG

During our twelve months' stay in Ku Dæng, which lasted from the Northern New Year's festival in April 1953 to the same festival in 1954, we observed one cycle of the annual religious events in the village. The following table is a summary of these events:

Precept Days occuring four times a month

April 13, 14, 15	New Year's Festival—*Songkran*
April-July	Temple fairs, ordinations of monks and novices
May 28	*Wisakha Bucha*—anniversary of Buddha's birth, enlightenment, and death
July 26	Beginning of Buddhist "Lent"
October	Mass merit-making festivals *(kin salak)*
October 23	End of Buddhist "Lent"
November	*Thot Kathin* ceremonies—not held in Ku Dæng in 1953
November 14	*Thot Pha Pa*—'jungle cloth' ceremony
November 21	*Loi Krathong*—Floating Lights Festival, not celebrated in Ku Dæng; Second month full moon festival
January-February	Seven-day cemetery ceremony
February 18	*Makha Bucha*—worship on the full-moon day of the third lunar month in commemoration of the great assembly of disciples; not held in Ku Dæng in 1953
February-March	Temple fairs; ordinations

Precept Days *(wan sin* or *wan phra)*

Precept Days occur at Thai temples four times a month depending on the lunar calender. This observance is especially lively during the period of Buddhist Lent, which is from the end of July to the end of October, when many people are residing at the temple.[1] On Precept Days during Lent, in addition to the people who slept in the temple the previous night, other devout villagers come to the temple any time after dawn, usually between six and seven o'clock. They bring glutinous rice in metal pots or rattan containers and a certain amount of accompanying dishes that are left outside in the *sala.* The rice is taken into the *wihan* and kept by the individual donors. Each villager also has brought a silver or lacquerware tray with flowers, popped rice, candles, and incense.

The faithful usually prostrate *(krap)* themselves facing the Buddha image when they first enter the temple. Some do this three times, others only once, some not at all. Each person is supposed to perform this ritual by touching the floor with "five points": the two knees, both forearms with palms flat on the ground, and enough space in between to touch the ground with the forehead as the fifth point. Actually, most villagers of Ku Dæng *krap* in the fashion of the monks and novices, who kneel and prostrate themselves with their hands flat against each other, touching the floor with the little finger side of the hands only, and placing their foreheads on the line of thumbs and first fingers.

When there seem to be no more villagers straggling in, the temple leader or some other elder beats the bell in the *wihan.* This is a sign for the faithful to *krap* once more, one to three times. The men then kneel, sitting on their heels, while the women, in the back of the *wihan,* sit sideways with their legs extended to one side. All present have a few flowers, some stalks of rice, candles, or incense, or sometimes some of each, in their hands held chest high, palms against each other—this is the *wai* or "Brahma" position. One of the elders, usually an ex-monk or ex-novice, then lights a few candles and some incense in front of the Buddha images at the west end of the *wihan.*

The temple leader—or the lay leader of the day, if the temple leader is not present—leads the congregation in devotions *(namatsakan)* to the Buddhist Triple Gems:[2]

> *The Blessed One is the purest one, free from all faults—
> *arahato* or self enlightenment; the Law is that which the
> Blessed One rightly proclaimed; the Monkhood consists of
> the disciples of the Blessed One, who follow his ways.

---

[1] See section below on "The Beginning of Buddhist 'Lent'."

[2] Translations of chants marked with an asterisk (*) follow in the main those given by Wells (1939), pp. 39-90. All other translations are taken from Thai and Pali texts found in booklets written by Thai priests.

We praise and adore the Lord Buddha, the Law, and the Monkhood by means of these offerings which we have presented. May the Blessed One who has reached *parinipphan* or *parinipphuttho* receive these offerings from us who are poor, having a heart willing to help us, in order that benefits and happiness may come to us all until the end of time.[3]

This introductory chant, which is repeated by the congregation after the temple leader, is frequently omitted. The following, short devotions are always carried out:

*The Blessed One who is far from desire, the self-enlightened.
I devote myself to him, Lord Buddha.
[Everybody *krap* once.]
The Holy Law, which the Blessed One proclaimed—I devote myself to that Holy Law.
[Everybody *krap* once.]
The Monkhood of the Disciples, who follow the way of the Blessed One—I respect the Monkhood.
[Everybody *krap* once.]

The temple leader reads each phrase, and then the congregation repeats after him. After the devotions to the Three Jewels, the men sit down, legs to one side of the body. Everybody continues holding his hands chest-high (*wai* position). Together with the temple leader the congregation then chants the Pali *"namo"* three times: *Namo tassa bhagavato arahato sammāsambuddhassa.* This may be translated as: "Homage to the Blessed One, the Perfect One, the Fully-Enlightened One."

Then the temple leader says, "Let us join in praise of the Lord Buddha," and all the congregation chants the *Buddhābhithuti* in unison.

*The Tathagata, the Lord Buddha, who is far from desire, is one who should be praised and adored. He is the self-enlightened, who has achieved the ultimate in wisdom and upward striving. He attained *nipphan* and omniscience. He taught those who were teachable, no one more than he. He was the teacher of the gods *(thewada)* and human beings. He achieved bliss. He proclaimed the Law, making it clear with his own supreme wisdom. He taught the world together with all the gods, devils *(man)*, Brahmas, and human beings. He proclaimed the Law

---

[3] For a discussion of *parinipphan, nipphan,* and *parinipphuttho,* see Konrad Kingshill, "Some Notes on Theravada Buddhism in Southeast Asia" (unpublished manuscript, 1952).

which is sweet in its beginning, sweet in the middle portion, and sweet in its conclusion. He proclaimed ascetic conduct in its entirety, in its ramification and in all purity. We reverently adore that Blessed Lord. We give highest adoration to that Blessed Lord.

At the conclusion of this chant all *krap* together once. Then the temple leader gives the invitation to the passage of praise for the Law, the *Dhammābhithuti*, which is chanted in unison.

*The Holy Law which the Glorious Lord uttered is that which people should see for themselves. It is timeless. It is a thing to call others to come and see. It is that which people should bow to and enshrine in their hearts. It is that which thoughtful people should know for themselves. We humbly adore the Law. We reverently bow our heads to the Holy Law.

Again all the people *krap* together once. After giving the invitation, the temple leader leads the congregation in the unison-chanting of *Sanghābhithuti*, the praise for the Sangha or Monkhood of Disciples.

*The Monkhood of Disciples of the Blessed One consists of those who behave according to his teaching; the Monkhood of Disciples have behaved well; the Monkhood of Disciples have been virtuous; they have been truly righteous. The four stages of men, with the eight steps, are followed by the Order of the Monkhood of the Disciples of the Blessed One—it is fitting that they should receive gifts offered through our devotions. It is fitting that they should receive offerings. It is fitting that they should receive adulation. They comprise the extent of merit—*bun*—of the world. There is no greater extent of merit. We humbly respect and adore the Holy Monkhood. We reverently bow our heads to the Holy Monkhood.

This chant, like the preceding ones, is followed by one *krap* by the people. The final chant to the Three Jewels is that in praise of the Three Jewels, the *Ratanattayapanāma gāthā*.

*The Lord Buddha, who was pure and good, has mercy as boundless as the ocean. He has eyes, namely precious wisdom, and means of knowing purely and well by his own power. He has slain the sin and lust of the world. We devoutly bow to the Lord Buddha.

The Law of the Great Teacher, that gives light like a lamp, the Law that is laden with the Way, the Fruit, and *nipphan,* that Law transcends the world. It sheds light on the meaning of the highest Law. We devoutly bow to the Holy Law.

The Monkhood reveals itself as that which is good and great. They have attained serenity, clear and calm, and know how to follow the Holy Law. They have escaped from the enemies of lust and vacillation. They have true wisdom. We devoutly bow to the Holy Monkhood.

The merit that we have made in praising the Three Jewels, which are worthy of praise in themselves—may that merit avert all evils by means of fruit—*kuson*—which arises from merit.

This chant is followed by a variation of the same theme, according to local custom. The content of the remainder is similar to the foregoing; it continues in praise and adoration.

Then all the congregation joins in chanting a passage for offering of food to the monks. During the chant, one of the young men of the congregation places a bowl of rice at the feet of one of the Buddha images. At the same time, the head monk (or the second monk, or the senior novice, when the head monk happens to be absent) comes into the *wihan,* prostrates himself three times before the Buddha image and sits down on the monks' platform along the south side of the *wihan.* All the people then prostrate themselves toward the monk, one to three times, and one of the elders, usually an ex-monk or ex-novice, offers candles and flowers on a tray to the monk, who accepts the gift by touching the rim of the tray.

The congregation then asks three times in unison for the five precepts: "Honored teachers—*bhante*—we humbly request the five precepts together with the three refuges."

The head monk responds by chanting the *namo* three times, each time repeated by the congregation in unison, followed in the same manner by the three refuges and the five precepts.[4]

After the five precepts, the temple leader leads the congregation in another chant of offering food to the temple. While this chant is in progress, the second monk and two or more novices come in, prostrate themselves three times toward the Buddha image, and sit down on the monks' platform below the head monk.

The monks and novices reply to the chant of offering food with a chant of thanksgiving, to bless the congregation and bestow merit upon them for their gifts. While this is in progress, the villagers file out onto the

---

[4] Refer to p. 114.

steps of the *wihan*, still carrying the rice in their individual containers. This then is put into the monks' bowls, one for each of the monks and novices participating in the service, one for the Lord Buddha, and one for the Law. When the bowls fill up, someone empties the rice into large vats put on the porch for that purpose. The villagers divide their individual portions, so that a little can be put into every one of the bowls provided, whereby merit is made from each of the monks as well as from the Lord Buddha and from the Law. The men of the congregation deposit their rice first, followed by the women, approximately in descending order of age. When the last person has placed her rice in the bowls, young men of the congregation take the bowls of rice back into the *wihan* to be placed in front of the monks, the novices, the Buddha image, and the pulpit (for the Law).

The temple leader now leads the congregation in another chant of offering food to the monks. While this is in progress, one elder offers a tray of flowers and candles to the head monk, and two or three other elders present trays of food to each of the monks and novices. The monks touch the bowls of rice; simultaneously, the trays of food are placed in contact with the rice bowls, so that the monks' touch can "flow" through all of them; all of the gifts, then, can be said to have been "received" with proper credit given to the donors.

When the monks have received all the food, the villagers prostrate themselves once more one to three times. Then the head monk makes necessary announcements, such as for special pilgrimages to ceremonies at other temples, or for a request for money for improvement of the *wihan*.

The monks conclude the service with a blessing *(anumodanā)*, while the temple boys and some of the younger novices (if there is a great amount of food) come in to carry the food to the monks' quarters:

> *As all rivers finally reach the Great Ocean, so do all the gifts you have given in this world reach those who have departed from it. May the wishes that are yours be achieved quickly. May all your plans reach fulfillment like radiantly shining jewels.
> [Here the novices join in the chant.]
> May all evils vanish, may all disease disappear, may danger not come to you. May you have happiness and old age. May all evils vanish, all diseases disappear, may danger not come to you.
>
> May the four laws, namely those of old age, of health, happiness, and strength come to all who bow down and prostrate themselves before the eternally Great One.

The congregation concludes with two chants. While this is in progress, the second monk and the novices prostrate themselves three times toward the Buddha image and depart. The head monk leaves after the chanting is concluded. The people then gather the candles out of the flower offerings, which are bought from the temple for future use, at a cost in 1954 of one *satang* per candle.

All the chants in this ceremony are in Pali. Most of the people questioned did not know the meaning of the chants, although they could identify individual words. One old villager knew a special chant in the Thai language. He would lead the congregation in this chant whenever he was present at food offering ceremonies. The villagers seemed to know even less of this chant, however, than of the ones in Pali; they were unable to attribute any meaning to particular words.

The New Year's Festival *(Songkran)*

Since times before records were kept, the Thai people have celebrated the passing of the old year and the beginning of a new year with play and frolic, mixed in with some observations of religious ceremony.[5] This is a solar festival, falling on or about the 13th of April and the days following. On that day, the sun leaves the House of Pisces and enters that of Aries. It is obvious that neither in Central nor Northern Thai reckoning the numbering of the months corresponds to those in the Gregorian calendar culminating in the New Year's celebration on January 1st. In modern times, announcements of the exact timing of the *Songkran* observation are published in most diaries sold in the market before the beginning of any given year. Different experts seem to base their calculations on different sources, since announcements found in these diaries are not always identical. One of the more reliable versions is published by the Public Relations Department of the Government Savings Bank and distributed to customers before the New Year. For the year 1986/2529 the announcement read as follows:[6]

Songkran Announcement for the Year 1986/2529

Songkran Day of the year of the tiger, the eighth in the cycle of ten years of the Lesser Era 1348, or the Buddhist Era 2529, a year of normal months and dates on the lunar calendar, a common year on the solar calendar, falls on the 14th day of April.

On the lunar calendar, the *Maha Songkran* Day falls on Sunday, the 13th of April, the 5th day of the waxing moon of the 5th month of the lunar calendar, starting at 2

---

[5] For a discussion in some detail of this festival see Richard B. Davis, *Muang Metaphysics* (Bangkok: Pandora Press, 1984), chapter 4. Two articles on the same subject, written by Phya Anuman Rajadhon, were published in *Journal of the Siam Society* 41, pp. 153-178 and 42, pp. 23-30.

[6] Translated by Vachara Sindhuprama.

hours 26 minutes and 27 seconds after midnight. (A day by lunar reckoning begins at 6 a.m. and ends at 6 a.m. the following morning.)

On the solar calendar, the *Maha Songkran* Day falls on Monday, the 14th of April, starting at 02 hours 26 minutes and 27 seconds.

The *Songkran* Princess, Thungsathewi, arrives astride a garuda (fabulous bird in Hindu mythology) with her eyes closed. She wears bracelets, carries the blossom of the pomegranate behind her ear, has rubies as ornaments and figs for food, a disk (*cak:* a spoked wheel) in her right hand and a conch shell in her left.

The new year of the Lesser Era, 1348, starts at 6 hours 16 minutes 12 seconds on the 16th of April B.E. 2529, which is Wednesday, the eighth day of the waxing moon of the fifth lunar month.

This year, the Lord of Saturday (in Hindu mythology called Sanivara) is the Chief of Rain, providing 400 *ha* of rain (a mythological measure of rainfall) from the mouths of 6 serpents *(nak):* 160 *ha* on Cakkrawan Mountain (located at the Center of the Universe), 120 *ha* on Himmaphan Forest (surrounding the Center of the Universe), 80 *ha* on the ocean, and 40 *ha* on land.

The measure of the harvest is 7, called *papa:* rice in the field will be one part good and nine parts bad; water for agriculture is in the sign of fire *(techo),* indicating a small amount of water.

The observation of this festival in Thailand, as well as in other countries influenced by Hindu-Buddhist tradition, always includes the use of water to bestow one's blessings on friends and strangers alike. On the first day, the 13th of April, called *wan sangkhan luang,* the villagers clean their houses and do their laundry in the river to cleanse everything of bad luck from the previous year.

The next day, the 14th of April, called *wan naw,* is devoted to preparation of food for the monks to make merit for ancestors. In the afternoon sand is brought up from the river and taken to the temple. Mutual blessings involving sprinkling or throwing of water is an integral part of the activities.

On the 15th of April, *wan phaya wan*—or "Princely Day"—the villagers make merit at the temple. This includes flowers, incense, candles, and small flags to be attached to the sand stupa *(cedi)* built the previous day in the temple compound. Later in the morning birds and fish are released for additional merit to cleanse away the previous year's sins. In the afternoon the Buddha statues are given a ceremonial washing.

On the 16th of April, *wan pak pi*—"Mouth of the Year"—considered the beginning of the new year, the *dam hua* ceremony is performed for one's elders (parents and grandparents) as well as respected village leaders. This ceremony is performed to express one's respect and gratitude to the elders for all they have done for us. Fragrant flower petals are floated on scented water in a silver bowl to be poured over the hands of the persons to be honored, thereby wishing them good luck and asking for their blessing. In some rural areas a similar ceremony called *long cao nai* is performed for spirits to request their intervention to receive good luck for oneself and others.

Songkran is celebrated in most parts of Thailand. The following account consists of those features of the festival that are characteristic of the celebration in Ku Dæng.

The New Year's Festival in Ku Dæng

The first two days of the festival, the village remains rather quiet. Occasionally, a villager from Ku Dæng or from some other village comes to visit some older person, apologizing for some evil that has been committed during the past year. Early in the afternoon of the first day, April 13th, one such man came from a distant village to see the *kamnan*. He wished to apologize for evil actions he had committed against some Ku Dæng villagers (not including the *kamnan*) the previous year. He sat down in front of the *kamnan* and handed him a tray with flowers, candles, and other offerings. The *kamnan* chanted a brief passage of absolution for a few minutes, which was the entire ceremony. This man, apparently, was going from village to village to set his accounts straight before the start of the new year. Apart from this type of visiting, not much out of the ordinary occurred on either of the first two days, even though major celebrations took place in the city on the second day.

On the morning of the third day, April 15th, the villagers went to the *wihan* for a special service. There were, perhaps, a hundred middle-aged and older people in the temple, more men than women. Since this was our first appearance at an official function in the village, the *kamnan* stood up before the start of devotions and told the villagers about our coming to the village.

After some time, when no more people seemed to be coming, the temple leader led the congregation in the usual request for the precepts, which the head monk, who was the only monk present at that moment, readily granted. At the conclusion of the chanting, a man beat a big bell as a signal for four novices to enter the *wihan*. The youngest went up to the pulpit, where he preached a Lanna Thai sermon about plentiful grain for the new year and a plentiful harvest. The other novices sat down beside the head monk. When the sermon was concluded, the monk and the novices chanted, while holding a white thread stretched all the way over the big Buddha statue. At the end of the service, this thread was cut into many pieces, which the villagers took home for good luck. Gifts—consisting

217

mainly of flowers, scented water, incense, candles, popped rice, and money—were then presented to the monk and the novices.

At the end of the service, some men went forward to bathe the Buddha images with lustral water. First they took the small ones and dipped them into water. Then they splashed some water on the larger ones. When they came to the big Buddha statue, others called out not to use the water, since it would spoil the color wash.[7]

A general holiday mood prevailed in the village. We noted several groups of young men playing kickball (takro), while others gambled with dice. In the afternoon groups of villagers—mostly young people, but also some middle-aged ones—went to various houses to "bless" the families with water and to be blessed in return. There were two reasons for selecting particular houses: first, homes were visited where daughters of marriageable age were to be found; here is one of the occasions when young people of opposite sex can meet in informal, jocular circumstances, even though it is in the midst of a big crowd; secondly, the people visit village leaders, such as the kamnan or the headman. At the kamnan's house, groups from the other villages in the commune, usually led by their respective headmen, came to pay their respects. They usually went right into the main room of the house, where water was poured over the house owners and their daughters, who responded in kind. Water was splashed all over the living room floor, which, however, dried quickly when the water ran through the cracks onto the ground below.

Most of the bigger temple fairs, organized for promoting new buildings or some other special projects, are held from April to July. During this time, the Ku Dæng temple and individual villagers receive invitations from other temples to attend their festivals. Usually, a temple community invites guests from villages where they have relatives. Once a temple community has been invited, it will remain on the other's "mailing list" indefinitely. Ku Dæng had such a reciprocal relationship with sixty-two other temples in more than ten different districts in Lamphun and Chiang Mai, as far away as Müang Fang, 150 kilometers north of the city of Chiang Mai.

When a major project is planned, such as the building of a new wihan, all of the sixty-two temple communities are invited. Since each village delegation will bring considerable amounts of gifts, such a large festival contributes considerably toward the cost of the new structure to be built. Normally, a temple is not allowed to solicit gifts or subscriptions from other communities. However, for special purposes, permission may be obtained from the district temple. As in the case of house-building by villagers, or weddings, or funerals, where large expenditures are required, and where invited guests are expected to contribute, this system is, in effect, a means of obtaining long-term, interest-free loans. Sooner or later every one of the

---

[7] Theme 1: Utility.

sixty-two temples will be building a major structure and invite the other temples to share in the occasion. For smaller events, such as the ordination of a novice or a monk, only the neighboring temples are invited. In some cases, individual villagers are invited by special printed invitations. The usual procedure, however, is to invite the temple and the temple community. The head monk then will make an announcement on Precept Day or on some other occasion when a large number of villagers is gathered together. On the appointed day, a procession is formed at the temple, villagers being called together by the beating of the big drums in the temple yard. Anywhere from ten to fifty people, both young and old, male and female, may heed the summons. Occasionally, there may be very little response, especially when the festivity falls in the middle of a heavy work season. At such times, the head monk will send a message to three or four villagers to be representatives of Ku Dæng at the particular fair. The people do not like to be coerced in this manner, but usually follow the desire of the head monk.[8]

There was no major temple festival at Ku Dæng during the period of our original study. The ordination ceremony and accompanying fair have been described elsewhere. A temple fair for dedication of a new base for the Buddha statue in the *wihan* and a new temple kitchen was planned for May 1954, but this was to be a modest affair to which only neighboring temples were invited.

Wisakha Bucha

According to tradition, the Lord Buddha was born, reached Enlightenment, and died (that is, he achieved *nipphan*) on the full moon night in May. This convenient lumping of anniversaries has made the *Wisakha Bucha* festival one of the most important ones in the Thai religious calendar. We were told that the festival actually should have taken place at the end of April. However, since *Songkran*, another major religious festival, is fixed by the solar calendar in April, the Thai government postponed *Wisakha Bucha* until May.

Festivities for *Wisakha Bucha* were planned by the Buddhist hierarchy of the fifth district, which encompasses several northern provinces. Each commune was to have only one joint ceremony at one of the larger temples. The commune Nong Fæk, therefore, went to the Nong Fæk temple on the evening of May 28th to observe the *Wisakha Bucha* festival. The seven hamlets of the commune, comprising altogether four temple communities, came together for the occasion. Ku Dæng was represented by over a hundred villagers, including all the monks and novices, as well as the foreign anthropology student and his assistant.

---

[8] Theme 4: Individuality and Theme 5: Communal responsibility.

At dusk, several hundred devout villagers gathered in front of the steps of the *wihan*, where the monks had already assembled. All the villagers and the monks had flowers and popped rice in their hands and were each holding a lighted candle. One of the Nong Fæk monks read a *Wisakha Bucha* message from Buddhist scripture, translated from Pali into Thai, and printed and issued by the district headquarters located at Wat Phra Sing in Chiang Mai:[9]

> We know that the Lord Buddha is our support. He is the teacher of mankind. He was born among the Aryan people in the country. He is a king. He is a son of the Sakaya tribe. He escaped to become a monk. He did good things and was very diligent. He is the greatest in the world. He became enlightened as others never had. He was greater than heaven or satan, Brahma or Brahmin, god or man, without a doubt. He knew everything in the world. He knew everything by himself without a teacher. He was full of knowledge and wisdom. He is the charioteer of men. No one is better than he. He was a teacher of gods and men. He was awakened and was lucky. His teaching is very good. It is a great truth that people should know. There is no time element.
>
> His disciples are good and just. There are four pairs of disciples, which represent eight kinds of men. It is the disciples whom we ought to respect. They are the field of merit in the world. No greater field of merit exists, whether *bot, wihan,* or *cedi*. The temple, Buddhist holy days, pagodas, and so on, were instituted to be dedicated to the Lord Buddha to be seen forever. We all remember the Lord Buddha. On this *Wisakha Bucha* day we celebrate his birthday, his enlightenment, and his death. We all come to this place with candles and with incense. We have done all of this in deep respect and in remembrance of the Lord Buddha. We will go around the temple three times, starting at the right. We worship with deep respect. We petition the Lord Buddha and his disciples. Though they have been dead for a very long time, it looks as if they were still alive, having real bodies, as we have known of old. Please accept our offerings, for happiness for all of us, from here on for a very long time.

---

[9] Translated from Pali into Thai by Phra Thamma Rachanuwat and from Thai into English by Nopphadon Sombun and Prathan Nimanhemin of The Prince Royal's College in Chiang Mai.

The monk read each short phrase, and then the assembled faithful repeated after him. Since the message was in Thai, many of the older people were unable to follow the words or understand their meaning.

Following the reading, the Nong Fæk monks led the other monks and novices, and those villagers who had candles in their hands, three times around the *wihan*, keeping the Buddha image on their right, walking clockwise. Some of the oldsters in the procession were quite slow in making the rounds; some of them finished their second round only just ahead of the monks on their third. This evoked ridicule on the part of the bystanders. Some small children also joined in the procession. They thought it was a great game to play.

At the conclusion of the circumambulation, the monks, followed by 150 to 200 villagers, entered the *wihan*, where the monks sat down in front nearest the Buddha statue. Then came the men, while the women sat in the rear of the temple. Various verses were chanted by the monks, the congregation, or both together. Toward the end, all the people prostrated themselves, keeping their heads on the floor while chanting. This was done three times. For the last chant, a white thread was stretched from the monks through a window to the top of the pagoda *(cedi)* outside. One of the headmen standing near us explained that this was done to bring the *cedi*, which is a memorial to the Lord Buddha, into the *wihan*. While the chanting was still in progress in the *wihan*, processions from other hamlets and villages arrived carrying fireworks to be displayed later in the evening. Each group was accompanied by drum and cymbal bearers beating their instruments vigorously. Others were dancing around the fireworks and shrieking at the top of their lungs, reminiscent of American Indian war whoops. There was no consideration whatsoever for the religious ceremony going on inside the *wihan*. The fireworks displays were carried once around the *wihan*. When the ceremony inside was concluded, the fireworks were taken into the *wihan* and placed in front of the Buddha image. There, they remained for a little while, until it was time to take them outside again for the actual shooting of the fireworks.

There were thirteen entries contesting in the fireworks display. The head monk of Nong Fæk was the judge to award prizes of more than 100 baht. Each contestant was permitted to light his fireworks three times. If they still did not go off, the display would be disqualified. The *kamnan* was in charge of security arrangements. Before the first event he went up to the firework embedded in the soil, waved his stick above his head, and ordered everybody to clear a circle of fifty feet.

When the fuse had been lit, one or two men, who had had more than enough to drink, danced around the bamboo tube containing the gunpowder and iron filings waiting for the sparks from the fuse. The men tried to coax the fire out, especially, if the fuse did not seem to fulfill its function. When the firework was finally lit and in full progress, the men jumped under the sparks to demonstrate their courage. They were applauded by laughter; when they got burned or showed signs of fear, the crowd roared with delight.

At the conclusion of the fireworks display, more than two hundred people crowded into the *wihan*, while an equal number stood around the doors trying to catch some of the melodious preaching going on inside.[10] The monk who preached the three-hour-long sermon added humorous variations by holding a note very long and then stopping abruptly, causing laughter to ripple through the crowd.

During the preaching a fight broke out near the temple gate. Crowds of people who had been listening near the *wihan* were quickly drawn away by this distraction. The *kamnan* came running and separated the opponents with his stick. No further trouble was observed during the evening, even though considerable drinking was going on. The younger people, as at most of the religious festivals in temples, stayed on through the major portion of the night, while their elders returned home before midnight or whenever the preaching was concluded.

The Beginning of Buddhist "Lent"

When the Lord Buddha was still living, his disciples traveled about the country teaching and preaching wherever they could find an audience. One year, after the rains had started, some farmers came to complain to the Lord Buddha that his disciples had walked across their fields and damaged the rice seedlings. The Buddha ordered his disciples, thenceforth, to stay in one place for the duration of the rainy season. This period, *phansa*, has been fixed ever since at three months, from the end of July to the end of October. In Western literature, it is generally referred to as "Buddhist Lent," even though it can hardly be considered as a period of "springtime."

In 1953, the first day of Buddhist Lent *(wan khao phansa)* fell on July 26th, which was the day of the full moon of the tenth lunar month, Lanna Thai reckoning. In order to keep the lunar months relatively in step with the solar year, an extra month must be added from time to time. Alternate lunar months have thirty and twenty-nine days, respectively. In 1953, the tenth month occurred twice, and the beginning of Lent fell on the full moon of the second tenth month. There is a two-month difference between the Thai and the Lanna Thai lunar calendars. The first Thai month usually is concurrent with December, whereas the first Lanna Thai month occurs in October.

On this day, the regular Precept Day activities in the temple shifted into high gear. We have already described the ceremony of offering food to the monks in the morning. During the main part of the year this takes place under the *sala*, with only a handful of people present. During Lent the average attendance was nearly one hundred. The older people, who, during Lent, sleep in the temple area the nights before and after Precept Day,

---

[10] See above, p. 120.

receive the eight precepts from the head monk at daybreak. An additional fifty villagers come to stay in the *wihan* for the major portion of Precept Day. In the afternoon, monks or novices preach from two to four hours, each sermon being accentuated by the beating of drums "to let the gods *(thewada)* know what is going on." An average of one hundred villagers, mostly men, attend the afternoon services. At night other villagers come to the temple area to sit and chat with the oldsters or with the monks, smoking cigars or chewing betel.

On every full and new moon, the regular monks have to attend a special ceremony in the nearest *bot*, which for the Ku Dæng monks means walking a mile to the temple in Nong Fæk. On the first and last days of Buddhist Lent, the seventeen monks from nine temples in the area have to attend the ceremony at a more distant temple, which is somewhat higher up in the temple hierarchy.

The twenty-minute ceremony, called the *plong abat* ceremony, begins with the monks pairing off and confessing their faults to each other. Any infraction of the 227 precepts that they may have committed has to be confessed to one's fellow monks. After this confession, all the monks face the Buddha statue at the west end of the *bot* and join in chanting. The two oldest monks, who had been sitting nearest the Buddha image, then turn around and the other monks chant toward them. The two monks, in turn, answer with a general blessing. One of the younger monks then sits down on the preaching chair in the middle of the room and chants while the other monks sit attentively with their palms held together over their chests. Sometimes the chant is followed by recitation of the 227 precepts. At the conclusion of the chant, all the monks join in chanting led by one of the Nong Fæk monks, who read the words out of a book. Apparently, the proceedings and the chant were not well known by the attending monks. Thus ended the ceremony in the *bot*.

The monk who presides at this ceremony is chosen each time by the other monks. He must have been a full monk for more than five years and must be a *phahusut* monk, one who is widely read in the law of Buddha. A different monk presides each time.

Women are prohibited from entering the *bot* while a ceremony is in progress. One monk told us that they may enter at other times. Other informants said that women are never allowed to set foot inside a *bot*. There seemed to be no prohibition against laymen being present during the ceremony. We were invited to sit anywhere in the *bot*, so that we could take pictures of the proceedings.

The flowers that the monks bring to the ceremony as offerings of devotion are afterwards taken back to their respective temples to distribute to the villagers, who attribute special power to them. Flowers from the *bot* are put into water to be used for bathing boys with weak brains. A newly pregnant woman will be delighted and joyful of heart, if she bathes in water containing some of the flowers.

During Buddhist Lent, monks and novices are supposed to stay in their temples for meditation and study. Their life is not much changed in actual practice during this time. They are not supposed to sleep outside the temple, unless they are sick, in which case they may go home and have their families take care of them. From casual observation, it seems that there are just as many monks traveling through the countryside during Lent as during the remainder of the year.

Mass Merit-Making Festival *(than salak phat)*

During the twelfth or first month of the Northern Thai year—in about October—a major festival may be held in one of the temples of the area. There are a number of names given to these festivals, all of which include the word for "lot" or "stake." The *kin salak* festival is described in detail below. Other names are *tan salak, tan kui salak,* or *tan salak phat. Tan* (Northern Thai) or *than* (Central Thai) refers to gifts or donations that are customarily presented to the monkhood or the temple. These are mass merit-making occasions. They come at a time when there is little labor in the fields, the weeding of the rice fields having been finished, and the harvesting not yet begun. People have not had any major festivities since the temple fairs prior to the beginning of Lent, and there are plenty of fruits and food available for gifts to the monks. These festivals seem to be special occasions for the monks themselves to make merit by giving gifts to each other.

The basic idea is that a variety of small gifts, such as toiletries or kitchenware, are elaborately prepared and packaged. At some time during the festival, monks and novices will draw lots for these gifts. To each basket of gifts is attached a message, traditionally written on palm leaves, but today slips of paper are made to serve the same purpose. A blessing together with the name of the donor and the name of a relative who has recently died are written on the slip of paper, which often is cut in the shape of an animal, such as an elephant, a water buffalo, or a horse. When a monk or novice receives the gift, the merit thereby bestowed upon the donor is automatically transferred to the deceased relative. This slip of paper is called *kan(t)* (the "t" is silent in Thai usage), a word derived from Pali and actually meaning "a section of a sermon, or part of scripture." The Latin derivation of the word canto may well have come from the same Pali root. The gifts and the slips of paper are prepared the previous day, called *wanda.*

There were three *kin salak* festivals to which Ku Dæng was invited. I shall describe the one at Wat San Ton Kok, about three miles from Ku Dæng. The big drums at the Ku Dæng temple were beaten beginning at seven o'clock in the morning of October 16th. About one hundred villagers, four-fifths of them women, together with the monks and all the novices, formed a procession to the host temple. The villagers carried three big litters of gifts *(salak yai)* and more than twenty smaller baskets of gifts *(salak noi).* One of the big litters had been prepared by the head monk of Ku Dæng, the second

224

by the novices, and the third by the villagers. A four-foot-high bamboo structure, in the shape of a tepee or a small tree, towered over the litters. The bamboo frame was wrapped with colored paper, and paper flowers were stuck into the wood. Various gifts were hung on the structure in Christmas tree fashion, including notebooks, pencils, rulers, cans of fish, milk, and crackers. At the foot of the "tree" lay various kinds of food and fruits such as pomelo, coconut, sugarcane, and rice. The apex of the bamboo frame was crowned with a reed into which paper money, amounting to 20 baht, had been stuck. The small baskets, containing presents similar to those in the big litters, were carried by the donors. The baskets were covered with colored paper and crowned with "money trees" of about 10 baht each. Each gift, whether large or small, was labeled with the name of the donor or the group of donors. It is these labels that are called in Thai, "salak."[11]

The procession left the temple about eight o'clock. Some twenty older women walked ahead, carrying their baskets of gifts. They were followed by the monks and novices, who carried nothing but their small shoulder bags and umbrellas. Then came a number of men carrying big litters, followed by six members of the Ku Dæng band, who played drums and flutes all the way to the other temple.[12] School children followed the band, and the remainder of the villagers brought up the tail of the procession.

Processions from other temples varied somewhat from this order. One was led by two dancers, a man and a woman, with powdered faces and painted lips like actors in local theater productions. They danced to the beat of a percussion band accompanied by hand-clapping villagers. Other processions arrived to the explosion of firecrackers thrown in their path, usually by novices from their own temple.

All the processions reached Wat San Ton Kok some time during the morning. There the gifts were placed in rows in the temple yard. A set of labels, furnished by the villagers, was collected by the host temple committee. The sala around the temple well had been divided into sections with the names of each of the fifteen participating villages written on signboards. There the villagers gathered. Some groups had special little ceremonies with certain monks of their choice, to whom they gave some presents as a group, and from whom they received a blessing and the five precepts.

On the south side of the wihan seventeen trays were set up along the wall. Many older villagers, mostly women, went there to present offerings of flowers and candles to the Three Jewels inside the wihan. The devout placed their offerings on trays, then knelt, facing the Buddha statue inside the wihan, said a short chant, and performed three prostrations. This was

---

[11] The Thai word salak is usually translated as "ticket" or "label." Salak kin pæng means "lottery."

[12] However, we observed women in processions from other temples carrying big litters as well.

similar to the usual offering of flowers, incense, and candles when people come for regular ceremonies to their own temples.

A running score of the number of gifts brought to the temple was kept on a big blackboard at the foot of the steps leading into the *wihan*. The final count was 2,066.

The labels from the gifts were taken into the *wihan*, where they were put into a big pile. The temple committee and the monks from Wat San Ton Kok then divided the labels into bundles as follows:

19 labels for each of 30 monks	570
10 labels for each of 111 novices	1,110
19 labels for the local temple leader	19
184 labels for the Lord Buddha	184
183 labels for the Law	183
Total	**2,066**

The bundles of labels were given to the head monks of the participating temples, who divided them among their monks and novices after the ceremony in the *wihan* was finished.

About eleven a.m., the monks and novices were fed in the *wihan*. Villagers brought food to the *wihan* steps, where some of the younger monks took the trays and served the other monks and novices. Apparently, the villagers themselves were not allowed to serve the monks. This was the only time that we observed such a procedure but were unable to obtain a satisfactory explanation.

While the monks were being fed in the *wihan*, local villagers brought big baskets containing small packages of ready-to-eat cooked rice or other items of food wrapped in banana leaves. Some thirty beggars, many of them suffering from leprosy, were squatting on the ground outside the temple compound with their begging baskets in front of them. The villagers walked down the line of beggars and dropped a package into each basket. This is sometimes done as part of the *kin salak* ceremony and is called *than khao roi ho* ("100-bundles-of-rice offering").

After lunch the monks and novices chanted for some time in the *wihan*. Only a few older people were present, since the *wihan* was already nearly filled with monks and novices. The villagers, in the meantime, milled about outside, waiting impatiently for the monks to come out. Finally, the labels were distributed to the monks and novices, who then came outside accompanied by their temple boys or some helpful villagers. They set up "shop" along the wall of the temple or in some other shady spot, spreading the labels out on the ground in front of them, where the villagers could come to find their own names. The temple boys held up the labels from time to time and called out at the top of their lungs the names of the donors who could not read. The people walked about from monk to monk until they found their names. Then they hurried to get their gifts to present to the monk or novice who, in turn, chanted a short passage and, if requested, transferred the merit thus obtained to some deceased relative by pouring water on the ground. From time to time the monks and novices also walked around to find the recipients of their own gifts.

Much merit was acquired that day. Not only did the donors make merit with the gifts that they presented, but later the monks turned back to the villagers much of what had been given to them, especially food and condiments, which the villagers ate as their lunch. This form of giving also bestowed merit on the giver, in this case the monk or the novice.

This festival is undoubtedly one of the biggest single sources of income for monks and novices. We were told that in some temples the novices pool their gifts and then divide them evenly. In general, we found both monks and novices reluctant to divulge the amount they had been give. One novice told us that he had received 156 baht. This, of course, would vary according to the luck the novice had in drawing good labels. The festival, itself, we were told, dates back to the time of the Lord Buddha. There is no prescription as to holding it regularly, or as to the details of the procedure. The three *kin salak* festivals we witnessed differed in some detail according to the wishes of the local temple committee.

The *Thot Kathin* and *Thot Pha Pa* Ceremonies

The *Thot Kathin* ceremony—the giving of robes to the monks after Lent—was not celebrated in Ku Dæng in 1953.[13] There seems to be no regularity about this festival as far as the village temples are concerned. Some hold the ceremony one year, some another.

A similar ceremony, the *Thot Pha Pa* ("jungle cloth" ceremony) was held on the night of November 14, 1953, a Precept Day. In the early days of Buddhism, the monks were supposed to clothe themselves with discarded cloth that people had either thrown away, or that kind-hearted citizens had left in the jungle, where the wandering monks could find it. The Ku Dæng villagers decided to take a set of new robes to the oldest monk in the neighborhood. The cloth, taken in a nighttime procession to the village where the monk lived, was "abandoned" at the foot of the monk's living quarters. Firecrackers were set off to wake up the monk, who, of course, had been warned beforehand. The monk cautiously approached the cloth, asking whether it belonged to any man or spirit. When no answer came, he could rest assured that it was abandoned, and that he could take possession of it, while, simultaneously, bestowing a blessing upon the donor.

Like most of the festivals and ceremonies described in this chapter, this was an occasion for entertainment and diversion for the villagers.[14] Here, it took the form of an excursion on a full moon night. Of course, this

---

[13] See Kenneth E. Wells (1939), pp. 99-102.

[14] Theme 3: Fun.

type of activity is especially popular with the young, unmarried villagers, who thereby have a good opportunity to get better acquainted with each other. Often some of the young people do not return home until the early hours of the morning.

The Second Month Full Moon *(wan düan yi peng)* Festival

The *Loi Krathong* ("floating light") ceremony that has been described by many authors, is not celebrated in Ku Dæng for the simple reason that the village is not located alongside a river or large canal.[15] Together with *Loi Krathong* there is celebrated, however, another festival usually and mistakenly overlooked as part of the *Loi Krathong* ceremony. This is the Second Month Full Moon Festival, which in 1953 fell on November 21st.[16] It was actually the final, big religious festival of the season that began shortly before the end of Buddhist Lent. After this festival harvesting is in full progress, preventing villagers from attending major celebrations. For example, in December the annual Winter Fair is held three miles from Ku Dæng at the district seat in Saraphi. Although some villagers went once or twice, most of the people did not go at all. They had to take care of their rice in the fields, which was either in the cutting or the threshing stage.

The second month full moon festival consisted essentially of two days of merit-making and listening to sermons. From the afternoon of the day before until late at night of Precept Day, twenty-one sermons were preached by monks and novices. At an average of forty minutes per sermon, this was a marathon of fourteen hours of preaching. All the sermons were part of the *Maha Chat*, also known as the Vessantara story. Those villagers who wished to make merit during these two days so notified the head monk, at the same time indicating their selection of a particular sermon title. The head monk then made out a schedule for the two days, assigning time and novice or monk to the respective villager.

The *Maha Wetsandon* (or Vessantara) is the story of the tenth life of Buddha, the last and most important life before he was born the Lord Buddha. There are altogether ten *chadok* (or Jataka) tales, which are tales of the Buddha's ten former lives. Of these only two are of special importance: the fifth, when he was Phra Mahasot, the excellent doctor; and the tenth, which is customarily preached only on the Second Month Full Moon Festival.

The Lord Buddha preached the Maha Vessantara Jataka first to his disciples on the day when he went to see his parents and relatives at

---

[15] Such as, Kenneth E. Wells (1939), pp. 104-106; or Phya Anuman Rajadhon, *Loy Krathong and Songkran Festival*, Thailand Culture Series no. 5, third printing (Bangkok: National Culture Institute, 1955), pp. 3-12.

[16] Lanna Thai: *wan düan yi peng* = Full moon day of second lunar month, Lanna Thai reckoning.

Kabinlaphat City many years after his enlightenment.[17] At that time his parents and relatives had come to see him at the city gate. When the Lord Buddha arrived, his parents prostrated themselves before him three times, but his relatives, who thought they had more prestige and were older than he, refused to pay respect. Realizing their pride, the Lord Buddha wanted to give them a lesson. He floated up in the sky and shone with rays of six different colors of light emanating from his body. The relatives were sorely afraid and quickly paid their respects.

The gods (thewada) were so well pleased with this display in the sky that they poured a special, red-colored rain (bok khoraphat) over the people. The Buddha's disciples sat down at the city gate and loudly called his praise. Afterwards, Phra Anon (Ananda), the Buddha's right-hand disciple, asked him about this rain. The Lord Buddha answered that this special rain had been poured out only once before, when he was born in his tenth life as Phra Wetsandon. Phra Anon, who was not familiar with this story, asked the Buddha about it. Therefore, the Lord Buddha preached the story of his tenth life as follows:[18]

A long time ago the Lord Buddha was born as Phra Wetsandon, the ruler of Siwirad City. Phra Wed married Nang Matsi, and they had two children, a boy named Kanha, and a girl Chali. Phra Wet loved to make merit by giving gifts, for he wished to attain nipphan at the end of his life. One day trouble came to him when he lent his rain-producing elephant to another city, which was experiencing drought. The people of Siwirat were very upset, for they thought that the rain-producing elephant should have remained in their own city. Therefore, they exiled Phra Wet, who took his wife and children to live in a deep jungle, called Pa Himmaphan.

Firm in his resolve to give away whatever people asked of him, he soon gave his children to an old Brahmin, named Chuchok, who had asked for them. This action nearly caused his wife to die of heart-break. When Phra In (Indra—the head of the gods) heard of this, he thought that Phra Wet would be in trouble if he continued in this way, for people never have enough and always ask for more. He therefore suggested that Phra Wet go back to Siwirat, since his people had already forgiven him and wanted him back as their ruler. When Phra Wet returned to the city, the Brahmin returned to him his children. At the reunion with his children, wife, and parents, the gods poured special rain, fon bok khoraphat, over them as a sign of the gods' pleasure. As a result of his unfailing

---

[17] See E. J. Thomas, The Life of the Buddha (New York: Knopf, 1952, reissue), p. 16.
[18] This account of the Maha Wetsandon sermon was written by Withun Leraman.

generosity, Phra Wet was reborn as the Lord Buddha in his next life.

There are thirteen chapters in the *Maha Vessantara Jataka*. Any person giving a hand-written copy of one of these chapters to the temple must do so according to the month in which he or she was born:

Chap.	Thai Name	Content	Month of birth
1	Thotsaphon	The early years of PW[19]	First
2	Himmaphan	PW's exile to the jungle	Second
3	Than Kan	PW's last merit-making before exile	Third
4	Wanna Pawet	Arrival in jungle and making a home	Fourth
5	Chuchok	Brahmin's desire to take children	Fifth
6	Cunlaphon	A hunter tells Chuchok the story of PW's jungle exile	Sixth
7	Mahaphon	Chuchok's arrival in jungle	Seventh
8	Kuman	PW gives his children to Brahmin	Eighth
9	Matsi	The suffering of Matsi	Ninth
10	Sakabab	Indra's visit to PW and the latter's offer of his wife to Indra, which he refused	Tenth
11	Maharat	PW's children redeemed by citizens	Eleventh
12	Chao Kasat	Meeting of PW and his family	Twelfth
13	Nakhon Khan	PW's return as ruler of Siwirat	Seventh

The *Maha Vessantara Jataka* has been translated from Pali into several languages, including Thai and Lanna Thai. The story in Pali consists of only 1,000 stanzas *(phan khatha)*. In translation, however, it has been enlarged many times. A translation into Lanna Thai was completed in 1821 A.D. in the time of King Phra Cao Luang Setthi Khampan, ruler of Chiang Mai. Later, it was rendered into at least seven different poems by Phaya Phün, Pukam, Hing Kæw, Tang Lo, Phra Maho Pathe, Pa Kuimüt, and Wing Won.[20] The translations by Hing Kæw and by Pukam are the most prominent in Lanna Thai temples. The Ku Dæng temple owns one of the latter.

As a special part of the second month full moon festival, each of the two Ku Dæng monks had prepared a huge, six-foot-high paper balloon made of multi-colored crepe paper. In mid-morning, when there was a lull in the preaching, the monks and novices with the help of the villagers tried to fill the balloons with smoke. Fires were lit in small holes in the ground,

---

[19] "PW" will stand for Phra Wetsandon.

[20] Taken from an article in *Khon Müang* newspaper by Phra Lanna Siho, head monk of Wat Phra Non Pakethi, November 30, 1953.

and the smoke channeled through bamboo tubes into the opening at the bottom of the balloons. It was a cold day with rain drizzling intermittently, which made the release of balloons difficult. The head monk's balloon rose only enough to clear the roof of the *wihan* before it settled into the temple yard on the other side. The second monk's balloon floated a little higher but dropped down at the far end of the central rice field half a mile away. Each balloon carried a tail onto which the monks and villagers had tied a few baht notes. As soon as the balloon was airborne, a group of teenage school boys raced after it to catch the tail when the balloon descended.

Throughout the day, other balloons, apparently more successfully launched, were seen drifting high over Ku Dæng, evidence that many temples were following the same custom. One villager had also made a balloon, which he set adrift in the evening. He tied sticks dipped in oil near the opening at the bottom of the balloon so that there would be a continuous supply of hot air for lift. This balloon rose higher than the other two but caught fire and burned before it had drifted out of sight. Small specks of light could be seen moving across the sky for hours, showing the greater success of other temples.

The Ku Dæng temple leader told us that a long, long time ago there lived a monk who had a magic dog *(ma wiset)* with which he could fly in the air. Every year on the day of the full moon in the second month, the monk would fly to heaven on his dog to receive the most precious presents from the king of the gods *(thewada)*. Another monk in a nearby temple grew jealous of the very unmonk-like behavior of the monk with the magic dog and in secret prepared a balloon of his own with which he, too, hoped to be able to fly to heaven to obtain gifts from the king of the gods. When the full moon of the second month approached, he brought out his balloon, filled it with smoke, and ascended to heaven, thereby breaking the monopoly of the monk with the magic dog. Ever since, monks build paper balloons to set adrift on the day of the full moon in the second month of every year.

The *wihan* and the temple yard had been decorated with Chinese lanterns for this festival. Candles inside the lanterns were lit at night. In addition there were rows of candles along the banister of the *sala* and in the *wihan*. Many villagers lit candles at the gates, at the door posts, and in the windows of their properties. This was a specific part of the second month full moon festival, rather than of *Loi Krathong* to which it has been attributed by others. The reason that the villagers gave for lighting candles, other than that it was tradition, was that it was a sign for the gods and spirits to know that the village was holding a special festival and that they were invited to join in the rejoicing of the villagers.

In the evening some three hundred villagers milled around the temple yard, while the more devout were inside the *wihan* listening to sermons. Many of the older villagers had brought blankets to wrap around their shoulders since it was a rather cold night. The young men were also cold and shivering but did not want to wear blankets, "because then the girls would laugh" at them. The novices were amidst the crowd in the temple yard with towels draped around their shoulders to give a little protection from the cold. Whenever it was their turn to read a sermon, they went into the *wihan*, to join the head monk who was the only member of the monkhood to stay inside all evening. Whenever a sermon had been concluded, the novices and school boys joined in setting off firecrackers and beating drums until the temple yard was filled with eye-stinging smoke and ear-splitting noise. The people returned home as soon as the preaching was finished, because it was too cold to make an all-night affair out of it.

Seven-day Cemetery Ceremony

One other ceremony of special interest in the religious calendar of Ku Dæng and vicinity is the cemetery ceremony *(khao kam)*, which is held for seven days in the second half of January or the beginning of February. This ceremony is not so much a popular festival as it is a gathering of monks and novices for meditation *(phawana)*. We were told by a monk that this ceremony was held when there was a need for some special public works, such as a new well or the repairing of a road.

The monks call all the faithful to meet at the cemetery, where some sermons are preached in order to lead the villagers into thinking about the Law of Buddha and good things in general. When the people have thus been softened, the monks ask their help for the particular project. The *kamnan* usually makes a speech in support of the monks. The villagers, who have been led to think in terms of the Buddhist Law, then usually carry out what they are asked to do.

The monks choose to meet in the cemetery because it is a place for all, not belonging to anyone in particular. It is a quiet place for meditation, far away from the hustle and bustle of the village. The main purpose for this seven-day retreat is to provide special time and opportunity for the monks and novices to meditate.

During the seven days at the cemetery, the monks have to meditate in four different ways: sitting, standing, walking, and lying down. They have to do it in this manner so that they will not tire of meditation, which could happen if they remained in a single position. The place where the monks meditate while walking is called the *thi dæn congkrom;* it is marked by a white string stretched between bamboo posts. The "walk" is paved with straw so that the monks' feet will not get too cold. At each end of the "walk" there is a little platform where the monks light candles during meditation. Novices are not allowed to meditate while walking, because they are too young to know what they are doing.

The cemetery ceremony is held in the cold season, because at this time the villagers are relatively free from work and can spend some time in the cemetery listening to the preaching. One monk told us that the ceremony originated in Brahmanism and has since become mixed into Buddhism. It used to be held under a big tree and was then called *ruk khamun*, which means a ceremony of praying to the gods under a tree.

Fourteen monks and fifty-one novices stayed at the cemetery when we observed this ceremony. Little straw and bamboo huts had been built for the monks and novices to sleep in, an individual one for each monk and larger ones to accommodate two or three novices. None of the Ku Dæng monks or novices had been invited. We were told this particular ceremony was never held in Ku Dæng, nor did the Ku Dæng monks attend those organized elsewhere, because they were afraid of ghosts. In the morning, when the villagers bring food to the monks, someone may place pieces of white cloth on the path where the monks will approach during meditation. This is "jungle cloth" similar to that described above.[21] The monks for whom the cloth is intended (and they are always informed as to who is supposed to "find" it) sit in a circle around the cloth on the ground. Then they ask three times for the owner of the cloth. When nobody answers, the monks pick up the cloth and take it to the place where the food is being offered by the villagers.

---

[21] See p. 227.

12

ACCULTURATION AND DEVELOPMENT

The dynamics of culture change in Ku Dæng, which is caused by the contact between the local culture and that of Western origin, is conditioned by two seemingly opposing influences, which are among the themes proposed in chapter one. Both of these themes, the one referring to utility, or to the adaptation of almost any means in order to obtain the desired results, which is usually one of material gain, and the theme of profit motive expedite culture change. This is evident in many innovations in the fields of agriculture, education, medicine, and village administration, some of which have been discussed in previous chapters. On the other hand, the theme of "playing it safe" would seem to be a stabilizing influence and work toward retarding culture change. This influence is especially evident in medical practices and religious expression, where certain unknowable factors play upon the fears of the villagers. When a person is sick, it is best to try every possible remedy, from that provided by the spirit healer to that of the modern physician. Of course, this also tends to further the acceptance of innovations, since it permits the active participation in traditional ceremonial as well as modern practice without disadvantaging the participants.

Dress

Visitors to Thailand usually express astonishment to see the people in Western dress. While this is more readily evident in the cities, it also holds true for villages like Ku Dæng, where the people wear clothes distinctive of village life. They are readily recognized as rural people whenever they come to the city, but there is very little that is "traditionally Thai" in their garb. For work in the village, the women wear long, dark-colored, wrap-around skirts, which reach from the waist to just above the ankles. Older women wear the same type of skirt when going to town, while the younger generation has changed to dresses of Western style and length. As far as we could ascertain, women had never worn any kind of trousers in the village when we first began our study. One or two girls, who had had more than usual contact with the city, had begun to wear slacks occasionally. By 1985, trousers were worn by some for field work as well as for trips to the city.

Before the Second World War, one informant told us, the men used to wear traditional Thai *pha congkaben*, a rather expensive piece of cloth wrapped around the body with the end brought up between the legs to give an effect of trouser legs and a baggy body. An elderly woman from the Central Plains of Thailand still wore such a garment in 1954. The villagers gladly abandoned the *pha congkaben* for Western-style trousers during World

War II, when the government so ordered because of a shortage of cloth during the war. The cost of trousers was then only one-sixth or one-seventh the cost of the traditional type of garment.

The men enjoy wearing a Burmese-style sarong, especially after work, when they are at home. Some men wear these "skirts" to the temple as well, but they are not allowed to appear in public places outside the village in this traditional dress. For work and at home, many of the younger men and some of the older ones wear short pants, popularized as the prescribed uniform of school children throughout the country. These pants are cheap and easy to keep clean. Sometimes a *phakhaoma*, a piece of cloth one yard wide and two yards long, is wrapped around a man's hips, provided there is some kind of pants worn underneath. While at work, young men frequently discard their upper garments, consisting usually of a shirt or a thin denim jacket. Old women, likewise, like to leave their upper bodies bare, but it is universally considered impolite to show much of the skin of the body to guests in the house. One villager told us that the body is usually dirty from perspiration and tanned from the sun, hence it should be covered for honored guests. While they and their familes are alone at home, such covering is not needed, although women under fifty in general conform to the Western custom of pectoral modesty.

Hairstyles are increasingly conforming to Western style. Most women under forty have permanents, either done in the village beauty parlor run by some local girls, or in town, where more professional results can be obtained. Older women wear their hair in a knot at the back of the head, the front part being brushed straight back. Older men wear their hair crew-cut, which is the traditional style throughout Thailand. This also used to be the custom for women in Central Thailand and is still being adhered to by some of the older, mostly rural people from that part of the country.

School children have to have their hair cut short according to government regulations. As a reaction to this compulsion, young men no longer in school wear their hair as long as possible. In the 1950s, the hair was treated with a generous supply of oil, a custom which, for all practical purposes, had disappeared toward the end of the 1970s. One person suggested that the hair style for young men in those days was set by Tyrone Power and Johnny Weissmuller, both then popular movie idols. The movies, especially through the medium of TV and video, continue to have a marked influence on types of dress and styles of hairdo even in the remotest parts of the country.

Among the older men a great deal of body tattooing could still be seen in the 1950s. One man told us that tattooing was done when he was a young man in order to be protected from all kinds of evil. Nearly all the men born before 1900 had their thighs tattooed from above the knees to just below the waist. This was done as a sort of puberty rite for adolescents: a young man could not go out with the girls unless he was tattooed; he would not be considered dressed. A Thai author writes:

Northern men in former days liked to have themselves
tattooed from the legs to the neck. From the waist to the
thighs they were likely to be tattooed completely black.
Tattooing frequently reached almost to the head; but on
the back, on the chest, and on the arms, tattooing was in
the form of Lanna Thai letters, pictures of animals, or
astrological tables, which were held to protect the wearer
from physical harm on those parts of the body. When a
man undressed to bathe in the river, he looked from a
distance as if he wore black pants. At the present time
very little tattooing is done, so that one sees examples only
on old people.[1]

A considerable test of endurance was involved in the tattooing of the
hips. We were told that the young men were given opium in order to help
overcome the pain. In a couple of cases, according to one informant, death
resulted from either the opium or from the tattooing itself. A few young
men today still have a small amount of tattooing on arms and chest, somewhat similar to that found among Western people of certain professions. In
most cases, these younger men were tattooed when they served in the Thai
armed forces.

For special occasions, such as a big temple fair, a wedding, or a
funeral, the people like to dress up as much as possible. One old grandmother admonished my assistant not to wear his old clothes for the kin salak
festival we were planning to attend, for everyone would be wearing his or
her best for such an occasion. At another time, a monk, who had seen me
pass by, sent word that I should not be wearing a jacket with short sleeves
over a long-sleeved shirt, for the villagers would laugh at such a reversal of
tradition.

The kamnan was invited to the opening of a new health center in the
district seat. He took his daughter along to the ceremony and the tea that
followed. It had been arranged to meet the other headmen of the commune
on the way to Saraphi, so that they all could travel together. The group had
to wait a long time until the kamnan's daughter caught up with them,
making the party late for the opening ceremony. At the amphœ, the daughter
went to a friend's house to get dressed in Western style, complete with all
the aids and props invented by modern fashion experts. She made her
appearance at the tea only a few minutes before everybody left, but at least
she was dressed for the occasion. This same young lady had placed second
in the provincial beauty contest in Chiang Mai the year previous to our
study. While we were in Ku Dœng, she was chosen by the Department of
Agriculture to be their representative at the Constitution Fair Beauty Contest

---

[1] Boon Chuey Srisavasdi, *Samsip khati nai Chiang Rai* [Thirty tribes of Chiengrai]
(Bangkok: Prachachon, 1950), p. 24.

in Bangkok in December 1953. The *kamnan* accompanied his daughter to the national capital, from where he brought new clothes for himself to set a new style in the village. The daughter, of course, also brought new fashions and new styles back to the village. Western type beauty contests, perhaps more than anything else short of movies, TV, and video, have tended to set the pace for acculturation as far as feminine fashions are concerned.

Language

One phase of acculturation is making steady though slow progress. This is the acculturation of the local, Lanna Thai language to the national Thai. Lanna Thai has a written form that developed separately from Thai. According to one of the monks in a neighboring temple, who is an expert on local history, there were two forms of writing that came into the Lanna Thai kingdom:

> One form of writing, the one which is still in use today, came from India in the time of Cao Küna in B.E. 1331 (788 A.D.), when Indian monks brought Buddhism to the Lanna Thai kingdom. The king, Cao Küna, adapted the Indian letters brought by the monks for use in the Lanna Thai language. This language was called *thewanakhi* or *tua pom* ("rounded figures").

The second kind of writing, called *khün* type or *tua liam* ("square figures"), was introduced into the Lanna Thai kingdom in 1442 B.E. (899 A.D.) by monks who brought a different kind of Buddhism, that of the *Langkawong* type, from the south, the part of the country called Suwannaphum, which is present-day Nakhon Pathom. This form of writing closely resembled the present-day Thai letters. For some unknown reason, this type of writing did not take solid roots in the Lanna Thai area, leaving the rounded letters in use for the written language to the present day.

Today only a few people remain who know how to read and write Lanna Thai. A boy wishing to enter the temple as a novice has to know Lanna Thai before he can be ordained. Indeed, the temple is the only place where this form of writing is still practiced. Almost all the writing of texts and sermons has been done and is still being done by hand. A metal stylus is employed, which is rotated around the thumb to form the rounded letters. The only type that ever existed for use in a printing press was brought into the country by the American Presbyterian Mission at the turn of the century and could still be found in a private printing shop in 1954. With the death of the owner, printing in Lanna Thai vanished from the scene. Parts of the printing press and font can be seen today (in 1985) on display at the Faculty of Humanities at Chiang Mai University.

Sermons continue to be copied on palm leaves with ink and stylus by novices in some of the temples where this art is perpetuated. Some monks copy ancient books for their own use. Reading knowledge of Lanna Thai is confined to ex-monks and novices. Occasionally, a student of the culture of Northern Thailand sits down to learn the language, but such cases are rare.

Children in all government and private schools are required to learn the Thai language. Instruction is always supposed to be in Thai, although both teachers and students prefer to talk in the local language. A mixture soon becomes evident. Many Thai words have made their way into the vocabulary of the villagers. Plants and fruits are usually known by both local and Thai names. Sentence construction and pronunciation also may differ. However, the frequent contact between city and district officials, who as likely as not may be Thai, tends to increase the knowledge of Thai words and usages on the part of the local population.

Central Thai is still difficult to understand for the majority of the people in rural areas. When monks come to preach in Thai, the villagers seldom make the effort to follow the sermons. In 1953 we made a follow-up study after one such sermon. Most people questioned said they could understand only a little. ("What I could understand, I understood; what I could not understand, I did not understand!")

Travel in and out of Ku Dæng in 1954

There was not a great deal of movement in and out of the village. Most of the older people seldom moved beyond the vicinity of Ku Dæng. The most frequent traveling was done to Chiang Mai, which, in 1954, could easily be reached by bicycle or bus from the highway. One indication of the extent of this type of traveling was the small number of bicycles in Ku Dæng: there were only forty-two in the entire village, averaging one for every four households. Many women walked every morning to the market at the district seat, a distance of five kilometers from the village. During the dry season, when agricultural work was slack, some young men commuted daily to the city for work, for which they usually contracted in groups. Otherwise, the villagers stuck mostly to their home territory. Only a few of the younger villagers ventured forth to participate in seasonal events, such as the Winter Fair in Saraphi or the *Loi Krathong* festival in Chiang Mai. Some special occasions for travel already have been described: the group of villagers going to Khun Tan for work on the railway tunnel; the *kamnan* making a trip to Bangkok to accompany his daughter to the national beauty contest; villagers traveling to Müang Fang, north of Chiang Mai, to visit relatives who earlier had migrated to that part of the province.

We questioned a number of villagers of different ages as to how far they had ever traveled in their lives. Most of them had been at least once to the city of Chiang Mai, to Lamphun, climbed up to the temple at Doi Suthep, or, perhaps, had gone to one or another of the temples that extend invitations to Ku Dæng villagers. All of those questioned had traveled at least once by car or bus. This was the usual means of transportation to Chiang Mai. Fifty percent of the informants had never been on a train. Trains are much more inconvenient for the villagers as far as their needs are concerned. There were two trains per day in each direction, which could be taken for travel either to Chiang Mai or Lamphun. Bus service was much more regular, with seventy-five buses passing daily through the district seat, as reported by the district office.

Only one villager, the *kamnan*, had ever ridden an airplane. In 1953 the Thai Airways Company had a plane at the airport in Chiang Mai for the duration of the Winter Fair celebrations. Anyone could take a ten-minute ride for 20 baht. Later in the same year, the *kamnan* accompanied his daughter by plane to Bangkok for the beauty contest.

Most villagers expressed interest in traveling, but showed little desire to do so on their own. Our presence in the village stimulated a number of people to voice their desire to travel to America. However, such dreams arose out of the general desire to learn more about the foreigners rather than wishing to travel and see different places. Usually, villagers commented that if they won first prize in the lottery, they would make a trip to America. Some said they would take their families, others that they would go alone. The reaction of most men to the question of whether they would like to travel to America was that it would cost as much as the value of three or four *rai* of land, and they would rather keep their land or buy more than waste the money on such a journey.

A few exceptional persons have traveled more than other villagers. When the *kamnan* was young, he told us, he had climbed most of the high mountains in the Chiang Mai area. He said he had done this merely for pleasure. He also visited many temples where there are famous or unusual footprints of the Buddha. The head teacher was another one who had traveled somewhat more frequently. Perhaps he had more spare time and more ready cash than others. Apart from these men, however, there was general satisfaction with staying at home in Ku Dæng. This was the environment they knew best and it is where they were known. There seemed to be no urge toward seeing other places or people, or to learn about other customs, except in so far as they were introduced into Ku Dæng by strangers or visitors.

External Communications in 1985

Knowledge of and communication with the world outside the village should be an indication of the presence or absence of a world view of the people of Ku Dæng. This knowledge could conceivably be an influence on their daily lives as well as their well being, and it could well be a factor of their ability to adjust to problems arising out of social and economic changes in their immediate environment. From observations and data collected during the present study, we were able to identify five different types of such communication with the external world.

Travel to and from the City of Chiang Mai

The reasons for travel to and from the city of Chiang Mai were found to be 1) to seek temporary employment, such as in construction work or sewing clothes, 2) to find steady employment, usually in civil service, the military, or the police force, 3) to sell vegetables or livestock in the market, 4) to study, 5) to go shopping, 6) to go sightseeing, or, very rarely, 7) to go to the movies or other places of entertainment.

Travel to and from other Provinces

Occasionally, villagers travel to other provinces, such as Chiang Rai or Lampang, for recreation, sightseeing, or participation in religious festivals. One villager has gone to Mæ Hong Son to visit a younger sister, another to Uttaradit to visit a son. One teacher travels daily to Lamphun, where she is employed in one of the schools.

Even rarer is the person who has traveled to the nation's capital: one villager went there for sightseeing, another to visit a younger sister who had followed her husband to Bangkok.

Group Travel

School children may travel together with their classmates. Those who travel to Chiang Mai for business, usually travel alone. If there are some who have business in the same vicinity, they may, as likely as not, travel together. Travel to other provinces or to Bangkok is usually not undertaken alone. A husband or wife or some other relative will usually accompany the traveler.

Means of Transportation

School children attending school in the district seat usually go by bicycle. Those going to the city drive their motorcycle or catch a ride with a friend who owns one. Others take regularly scheduled minibuses. Those working in the city as well as those selling goods in the market use motorcycles, public transportation, or private vehicles. Travelers to other provinces go by regularly scheduled buses or private cars, while travel to Bangkok is usually by tour bus or railway.

In summary, we may say that improved roads and readily available means of transportation have been of considerable influence on Ku Dæng villagers, causing an increasing number of them to travel beyond the geographical limits of their community. The nearness of the city of Chiang

Mai continues to exert a pull of which more and more villagers take advantage. As a result their knowledge of and attitude toward the world outside their immediate environment has taken on a considerably broader scope than was true thirty years ago.

News of the World

News of the world reached Ku Dæng only sparingly in the 1950s. "The World" here refers to everything outside the district of Saraphi and the city of Chiang Mai. There was only one radio in the village, owned by the temple and operated by the head monk. It was given to the temple by the villagers more than ten years prior to our study, so that they could turn in to sermons preached on Precept Day during Buddhist Lent. However, the villagers mainly came to hear the results of the weekly lottery drawings. Not once during our period of study was the radio used for listening to sermons. One of the novices told us that they listen usually to news in the morning and evening, sometimes to music and to *lakhon*, the Thai classical drama. He, himself, liked most do listen to news from other countries, especially about the war in Korea.

Newspapers were bought for much the same reason that people listened to the radio: results of the national lottery. *Khon Müang*, a news magazine issued every five days in Chiang Mai, was subscribed to by the *kamnan*, by the head monk, and by ourselves. The copies were then read primarily by a number of young villagers, who came to visit for this specific purpose one or the other of the three places to which the magazine was delivered. The head teacher once asked us what would be the best newspaper for him to subscribe to so that he could enlarge his knowledge of things that went on outside the village. He thought that a newspaper would be able to supply him with a great deal of knowledge.

The Thai storekeeper, mentioned before, one day attended a meeting in the temple, called by the *kamnan* for the entire village. Before the meeting started, the storekeeper was reading a four-day-old newspaper and explained to a group of young men a headline story about Luang Pridi, the self-exiled leader of the opposition to the then-ruling regime of Thailand. The story related to 20,000 Red Chinese soldiers and the Free Thai movement in Yunnan province of China.

Apart from these few occasions for dissemination of information on national or international events, the villagers showed very little concern for or knowledge of what happened in the world around them. The following summary of a survey made in Ku Dæng in 1954 will illustrate the extent to which villagers were unfamiliar with external affairs or even with the events that should affect them directly.

The original plan was to take a random sample of villagers and present them with the questions in our schedule. A pre-test was carried out on a number of leaders in the community including one young woman. It was soon noticed that none of those tested could answer a large number of the questions. It would have been of little use to present this questionnaire to a random sample of all the villagers. In addition we felt that a general questioning of this kind would generate a certain amount of ill-feeling. It would involve loss of face for those who were interviewed in the presence of others, a circumstance that could not be avoided under the conditions in which we lived and worked in Ku Dæng.

Certain questions were found to be irrelevant to the problem on hand. Everybody in the village, for example, knew the name of their headman or the *kamnan*. In other villages, where there was no *kamnan*, this might have been different. For Ku Dæng we felt we could eliminate the question from our schedule.

The question, "Where is Korea?" was found to be useless, since locations are almost impossible to determine through a simple question in Lanna Thai. "*Pun,*" accompanied by pointing with the chin and an outstretched arm, is the almost universal answer to a question on location. Furthermore, most of the people who answered knew practically nothing of Korea.

The question of religion of the Thai people was found to be generally answered correctly. The people know that their own religion and that of the Thai people as a whole is Buddhism. What they did not seem to know, in some cases, was that this religion is also practiced outside Thailand, or, conversely, that there are many other religions.

The large number of "don't know" answers on the pre-test convinced us to use a selected rather than a random sample of villagers. We tried to choose, by and large, those in the village who, according to our observation, had more knowledge of outside places and events than the average villager. Thus, we chose some who had achieved the highest level of education in the village (equivalent to seventh grade, or *matthayom* 4), or those who were leaders in the community (such as, the *kamnan* and the headman of Hamlet 6), or those who had frequently been outside the village (for example, the daughter of the *kamnan*, who is employed in Lamphun). In addition we tried to sample some of the older people, generally considered wise in local knowledge.

Some people were very uncooperative or refused to answer. The Thai storekeeper, who used to be a soldier and undoubtedly could answer most of our questions, refused to cooperate and gave no answers to many of the questions. The woman teacher refused to give any answers. The *kamnan's* daughter was reluctant, but eventually did answer the questionnaire. It seemed that those who had the reputation of knowing many things were reluctant to participate, probably because they were afraid of possible loss of face. Those who knew only a little, and those who could answer well, were willing to talk freely.

The name of the district official, Nai Amphœ Kæw Nethayothin, was given correctly by 38% of those questioned. He was a relatively new man, having been in office only four months when our survey was made.

Nobody gave a wrong answer, and many inferred that they would have known the name of the former district official.

An even smaller percentage (22%) could identify the governor of Chiang Mai province. Again, some people said he was a new man (in office for more than one year at the time of the questionnaire), and again nobody gave a wrong answer.

The head of the Thai Governnment, Marshal Phibun Songkram, was correctly identified by 44% of those asked. He was mostly referred to as "Comphon Po" ("Marshal P."). Wrong answers were given by 11%, including the answers that he was a new man, and that he was Dr. Sanguan, who is one of the Chiang Mai representatives in the National Parliament.

The King was identified by name by 50% of those questioned, the Queen by 44%. One wrong answer was given for the name of the King, which is a little surprising, since most of the houses in the village that had pictures hanging on the walls included at least one of the King and Queen. Some people knew only the name of one. In most cases, if they knew the name of one, they were able to identify that of the other as well.

The capital of Thailand was identified correctly by 61% of the sample. Only 33% did not know its name. The remainder gave Si Ayutthaya, the previous capital, as the answer. Of those who identified the capital correctly, 45% named it "Krungthep," while the other 55% called it "Müang Kok." This is signifcant inasmuch as in Thai writing and on Thai maps Bangkok is always referred to as Krungthep. Bangkok, or Müang Kok, is undoubtedly the older name, the one used by "foreigners" for the city. This could well be an indication of resistance to acceptance of the "new" Thai regime as the national government in contrast to a holdover allegiance to Lanna Thai as an independent country.

Knowledge of the names of foreign countries turned out to be meager. America is listed by more than 80% of the people, Japan by 77%. Other countries that were named by more than half of those questioned included England, China, France, India, and Burma in order of frequency. Other countries listed more than once were Germany, Russia, Malaya, Indochina, American (in addition to America), Australia, Switzerland, and India. Single mention was made of Vietnam (in addition to Indochina), Holland, Austria, *farang*, Soviet (in addition to Russia), Thailand, Canada, Europe, U.S.A. (in addition to America), South America, Ceylon, Hong Kong, Denmark, Africa, Iran, Egypt, Turkey, Singapore, Philippines, Greece, Norway, Panama, and a country called "Lesowiya." The countries listed only once each were largely the answers of two persons who gave six each. The countries mentioned most often first were America (5 times), Japan (5 times), and India (3 times). Those mentioned most frequently for one of the first three places were America (11 times), Japan (10 times), England (9 times), and France (6 times). People varied considerably in the number of countries they listed: from fourteen (two participants) to one (one respondent).

243

The United Nations was identified correctly by 17% of the respondents as an "Association of Nations." Forty-four percent did not know the meaning of the term. Other answers were America, Moral Nations, some country, soldiers of sixteen countries combined in alliance, and World Court.[2]

At the time of the questionnaire in August 1953, the armistice had been in effect in Korea for one month. Thirty-eight percent of those questioned answered correctly that Thailand was not at war with any country. Half the people did not know. Those who answered Thailand was at war gave Red China or "the Communists" as opponents.

Responses to the question, "Who is fighting in Korea?" varied. The largest group, 38%, did not know. North Korea against South Korea was given by 22%; 11% stated the Communists were fighting the United Nations. Six percent each gave the following: Red China against the United Nations; Red China; Red China against Thailand and America; the Communists against Thailand; America and sixteen countries, including Thailand, against Korea. Most people (77%) did not know why there was fighting in Korea. Those who answered gave as reasons, 1) because the Communists attacked, 2) because of Red China, 3) because America also fights, or 4) because America and the sixteen countries want more territory. Only 28% did not know whether or not Thailand had sent troops to Korea, the other 72% affirmed this definitely. The reason given for sending troops varied: 1) to help the UN, 2) to fight, 3) to help North Korea, 4) to help South Korea, 5) to help, 6) to fight Communists, and 7) to watch the border.

In the question referring to knowledge of world personalities, living or dead, only two persons were identified correctly by more than 50% of those questioned; they were 1) the King of Thailand and 2) Luang Phibun, the Prime Minister. Malenkov, Churchill, and Ho Chi Minh were either completely unknown or identified incorrectly by a few persons. Only one person identified Stalin correctly as dead. Another, one of the villagers with more education than the rest, said he was the prime minister of Italy. Eisenhower was identified as the president of the UN by one person and as the president of Korea by another. Chiang Kai Shek was identified correctly by 17%, incorrectly by 6%, and had never been heard of by the remaining 77%. Mao Tse Tung did not fare much better: 6% identified him correctly, 11% incorrectly, and 77% had never heard of him. Nehru was known by 11%, misidentified by 6%, and unknown to the remainder.

The results of identifying world personalities suggest several interesting interpretations. Propaganda from either the West or the Communist countries seemed to have little impact on rural areas like that of Ku Dæng. Although Eisenhower's picture, distributed by the United States Information Service, adorned many of the village homes, he could not be

---

[2] There were actually sixteen member countries of the United Nations who had sent troop contingents to fight in Korea.

identified correctly by more than 11% of the villagers. There seemed to be little interest in personalities or leaders of other countries. Propaganda, to be effective, would have to be undertaken differently to leave a lasting impression on Ku Dæng.

The remaining questions dealt with the concepts of democracy, monarchy, and communism. In each case, the people were asked to identify the concept. Those who were able to give an answer then were asked to state what country came to mind when they were talking about the particular form of government; they were to state whether they thought it was a good or a bad thing.

Democracy could be defined by 55% of those questioned as 1) the government of a country, 2) a new form of law, 3) the people, 4) moral people, 5) the Thai nation, or 6) might. The others did not know what the word meant. Those who had answered, listed two countries as representative of democracy: 1) Thailand, named by 73% of those responding, and 2) America, named by 13%. Only a positive answer was given by 72% of the respondents to the question whether democracy was a good or a bad thing. An equal number said communism was something bad. Two people did not know, including one who expressed himself to the effect that some said it was good, while others said it was bad. One man said, "People talk about being afraid of communism," but he, himself, did not know.

Explanations of communism were given by 44% of those questioned: 1) Red China, 2) people who have no morals (*sintham*), 3) an enemy without religion, 4) destroyer of nations, 5) those who rob people of money, 6) dictatorship. Countries mentioned as representative of communism were the following in order of frequency: 1) China or Red China, 2) Russia, 3) Yunnan, 4) Korea or North Korea.

The people were less certain about the term "monarchy." Those who claimed they did not know amounted to 61% of the informants. The remainder defined it as 1) when the king is above the law, 2) the old (Thai) government, 3) the government, and 4) a Buddhist country. Examples of monarchies were, Thailand (38%), Old Thailand (15%), and 8% each for America, Japan, Russia, Red China, Korea, and "don't know." The informant who defined monarchy as a Buddhist country gave Thailand and America as examples of such countries.

When a list of countries was presented to the informants, and they were requested to state what form of government each country had, the majority of respondents said they did not know for all countries except Thailand and China. Thailand was listed by 68% of the respondents as a democracy, by 27% as a monarchy, and by 5% as "don't know." China was listed by 11% as a democracy and by 50% as a communist country; the remainder did not know.

From the above it is quite evident that propaganda from abroad does not seem to have been very effective in acquainting the people either with particular countries or their leaders. On the other hand, Thai propaganda,

245

such as that presented through the medium of local school textbooks, has had the effect of disseminating some knowledge as well as positive evaluation of such terms as democracy, monarchy, and communism.

Knowledge of national affairs, though greater than that of other countries, is nevertheless very meager. While people have heard of Field Marshal Phibun, they have difficulty identifying him. One man told us that he had seen him during the war when he had stopped at one of the villages along the highway. He said he looked more like a foreigner than a Thai. He was dressed like the King, so that it was not possible for our informant to identify him. He thought he must still be alive; if he had died, it certainly would have been mentioned in the newspapers.

On National Day in June, school was closed for two days in memory of the 1932 establishment of the constitutional monarchy.[3] The *kamnan* was the only person questioned who knew what day it was and why it was being celebrated by closing the schools. Others could name it but could not give a reason for the observance. Perhaps it was the King's birthday, or, perhaps, the King was planning to make merit. Even school children, who were free from school, did not know the reason. The head monk avoided an answer by saying it was a celebration "of the world" not of religion.

The attitude toward other nationalities and races in general is one of indifference in Ku Dæng, since no outsiders live in the village. The case of the two Thai has already been described. One villager told us that the people of Ku Dæng welcome any person, regardless of race or religion. If they knew someone in the village, they could come and visit the girls, otherwise they would have a difficult time establishing contacts. The villagers of Ku Dæng welcome immigration from anywhere. However, this same informant continued, at present the people do not wish their children to marry Chinese, Indians, or *Ho* (Yunnanese) because those people always make trouble. Chinese and Indian traders come frequently through the village and are always received cordially with great hospitality. There was no evidence of overt antagonism toward people of different ethnic backgrounds.

Americans are held in high esteem, although the reason for this is not exactly clear. United States Information Service leaflets reach the village in large quantities, and pictures of the American President hang in many bamboo huts, sometimes being the only picture on the wall. Such a receptive attitude facilitates introduction of new techniques, especially in the field of agriculture. When an American MSA official came to visit Ku Dæng, the village leaders gave him a welcome reception and listened to his suggestions with regard to various problems related to agriculture and animal husbandry. When tilapia fish were introduced into Thailand, the villagers

---

[3] Observance of this day was discontinued when Marshal Sarit was head of the Thai government (1958-1964). Since then the King's birthday (December 5th) has been celebrated as Thai National Day.

learned about it through USIS pamphlets, with the response already mentioned.

In general there seemed to be a great desire on the part of the villagers to obtain more information and education—at least in so far as it did not interfere with their regular tasks.[4] Many of the older men repeatedly asked us questions about America, which, at least in part, were prompted by questions we had asked them about Ku Dæng or Thailand. They also wanted to know about religion in America and expressed the opinion that the Americans, like they themselves, had a "good" religion.

Many ceremonies were allowed to fall by the wayside when they no longer seemed to fulfill any need or did not show evidence of results.[5] Thus, the calling of the *khwan* before the first rice is brought in was practiced by only a handful of people. Any means is acceptable to reach a desired end, but when there is no end in sight, the means, which may at one time have produced results, is discarded. New things and new methods are rapidly accepted. Two small rice mills were introduced into the village after World War II. Today no villager will hand mill his rice. We tried to get our own rice milled in the old-fashioned manual way, but we encountered tremendous resistance. Each time there was some excuse or other; and so the rice would be taken to the mill, and we were presented with a *fait accompli* when we sat down for lunch. Even the rice mill operator would not mill the rice less than usual: we were told he would lose his reputation for doing a good job of milling rice. An old woman was suffering from beriberi. We suggested she should eat some bran from the rice mill. She actually took bran three times a day, much to the amusement of her neighbors, who soon asked her to let them try some, too.

There seems to be a general trend toward further acculturation to various aspects of Western culture, as well as to those aspects of Thai culture not found in this Lanna Thai village. As there is continued and increased travel to the provincial capital, more new things will be brought to the village. One girl bought a new bicycle; it was a Raleigh sports model, one of the most expensive that could be bought in those days. When asked why she did not buy a cheaper one, she said that she bought this type because she had saved up enough money and because a more expensive one ought to be of better quality than the cheaper ones. Prestige seems to be a factor in buying bicycles in Thailand just as it does in the purchase of automobiles in America.

With acquisition of the new comes distaste for the old. The milling of rice already mentioned is an example. Another one concerns the 70-year-old grandmother who had gone to the wedding of one of her grandsons in a village north of Chiang Mai. When she returned, she told us that she did not

---

[4] Theme 1: Utility.
[5] Theme 2: Profit.

like to stay in that particular village, because there were no toilets or bathrooms: the people used the jungle and the Mæ Ping River instead.

The steady though small emigration from Ku Dæng has undoubtedly played an ever increasing role in adaptation to newer agricultural methods in the village. The people who moved to Müang Fang were primarily those who owned little or no land in Ku Dæng. It was these people who supplied the extra labor needed to bring in the rice for the wealthier farmers. As they left, the richer people bought up their land, thereby increasing their need for extra labor, which became progressively less available. This process inevitably led to mechanization, involving changes in methods of farming. The advent of tractor plowing for the dry season crops, though not readily accepted as a permanent innovation in those days, was one of the signs pointing in the direction of culture change.

In 1954 it seemed to us that Ku Dæng would be ideally suited for establishment of an experimental station in applied anthropology. We thought that controlled changes could be introduced with little difficulty. Agricultural improvements, which would give a greater immediate yield, seemed to have a good chance of success and, thus, be accepted by many of the villagers. Changes in other phases of village life, such as in public health or diet, could be expected to be slower in taking effect, since they would not be able to show immediate results of a material nature.

Our predictions were largely fulfilled in a manner not necessarily anticipated. Rather than establishing an anthropological field station, the Thai government decided to choose Ku Dæng as a model village for development. Their criteria for selection of suitable villages as well as their methods of operation could well have fit into a university-related project in applied anthropology.[6]

---

[6] Also see chapter 6, pp. 103-104.

CONCLUSION

Ethnographic and anthropological studies of village life in Northern Thailand have over the years been weighted consistently in favor of diverse ethnic groups, usually referred to as "hill tribes." One of the first village studies of lowland agricultural people of Northern Thailand was undertaken by the writer in 1953-54. Follow-up studies at ten-year intervals indicated only minor changes in the lifestyle of the villagers. In 1984 the writer carried out a third, somewhat more thorough, study to determine what if any changes had taken place in the socio-economic lifestyle of the villagers of Ku Dæng.

Changes in social characteristics of the village of Ku Dæng over the thirty-year period from 1954 to 1984 parallel development of rural areas in Northern Thailand, which in turn has followed the general development of the country. The population growth of Thailand is reflected in the growth of individual villages in every region of the country. This growth has been tempered in recent years by the successful introduction of family planning, which has influenced the social structure of most rural communities, including those in Northern Thailand.

Changes in population of Ku Dæng follow in general the demographic pattern found in Northern Thailand. While the number of households increased steadily at an annual rate of approximately 1.5% over the thirty-year period covered by the study, the change in total population of the village showed quite a different pattern. During the first ten years there was a 50% increase in the number of people living in Ku Dæng. There was a 12% decline the following ten years and a further 16% decrease during the decade ending in 1984. The population of Ku Dæng at that time was only 6% larger than it had been in 1954. Since the emigration pattern seemed to have remained much the same during the thirty-year period, stability in size of the village of Ku Dæng must be attributed to successful family planning.

While the general educational structure of the village school did not change over the period under consideration, it was evident that increased contact with the outside world had a marked influence on the general level of knowledge of the villagers and increased the educational expectations of each succeeding generation. Educational institutions outside the village were able to fill the needs of the villagers. Educational opportunities and expectations, together with economic development and changing social values, have influenced the family structure in villages like Ku Dæng. The trend seems to be moving away from extended toward preponderantly nuclear families. At the time of the first study in 1954, movement in this direction was already observed. Such change toward nuclear family lifestyle is tempered, however, by continued cooperative living within the family

249

structure and a continuing vitality of neighborhood bonds for maintenance of belonging to a particular village community. Respect for older persons and involvement in each other's happiness and sorrow continue as major values for villagers of all ages. Divorce in Ku Dæng is still a relatively rare occurrence.

The economic life of the village continues to be rooted in agriculture. However, reliance on traditional methods of rice cultivation is being supplemented by an increased awareness of the importance of cash crops like *lamyai* as well as by utilization of modern technologies in rice planting, new strains of seed rice, crop rotation, use of tractors, and the systematic application of fertilizers. This development, in turn, has resulted in a higher standard of living, manifest in such material possessions as radios, television sets, motorcycles, and cars. The water buffalo and the bullock, thirty years ago essential participants in agriculture and mode of transportation of the village, have for all practical purposes been replaced by tractors and pickup trucks.

Religious expression and practice has seen the least change in Ku Dæng over the thirty-year range of the study. The temple remains the focal point of village life. The participation of the abbot in every activity of the village continues to be an indisputable factor for success or failure. The teachings and moral directives of Buddhism continue to be of influence in the spiritual life of the villagers. The various ceremonies and festivals comprising a mixture of Buddhism, Brahmanism, astrology, and simple social togetherness continue much as before. Observance of the New Year's festival and mass merit-making are good examples of unchanging attitudes in this respect. Informal religious practices and expressions, such as belief in or fear of ghosts, seem to be less overtly accepted or defended than thirty years ago, especially among the younger villagers, perhaps due to contact with new educational approaches and changing social situations outside the village.

The administrative structure of the village has shown very little change. The office of *kamnan* has returned to the village of Ku Dæng after having been exercised by one or another of the headmen living in hamlets other than Ku Dæng. The power and influence of this office has not changed substantially. Methods of selection and election of village officials have remained much the same over the thirty-year period.

For more than ten years prior to the final restudy, a number of development projects were introduced to Ku Dæng by various government agencies above the village level. Some of these projects have been completed or abandoned, while others continue to be operative. Those activities that have been integrated into the structure of village life have lost their novelty and no longer pose a threat to the old way of doing things.

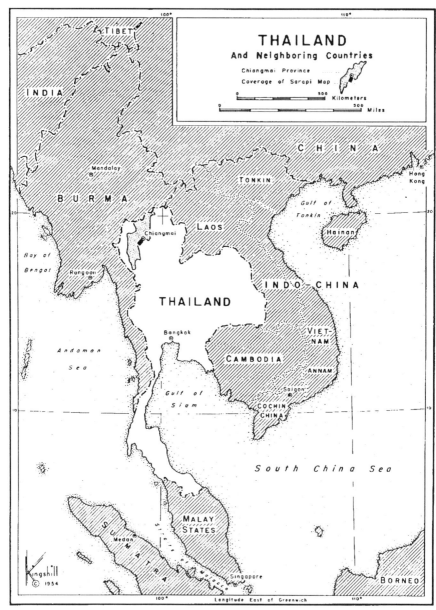

THAILAND

And Neighboring Countries

Chiangmai Province

Coverage of Sarapi Map

0   500

Kilometers

0   500

Miles

TIBET

INDIA

CHINA

Mandalay

TONKIN

Hong Kong

BURMA

Gulf of Tonkin

LAOS

Chiangmai

Hainan

Bay of Bengal

Rangoon

INDO-CHINA

THAILAND

VIET-NAM

Bangkok

Andaman Sea

CAMBODIA

ANNAM

Saigon

Gulf of Siam

COCHIN CHINA

South China Sea

MALAY STATES

Medan

SUMATRA

Singapore

BORNEO

Kingshill

© 1954

Longitude East of Greenwich

Map 1

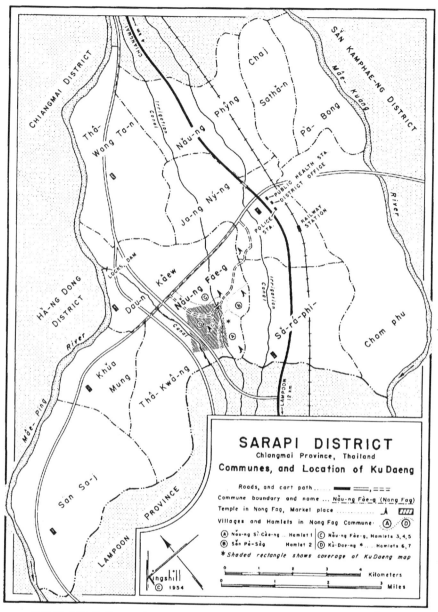

SARAPI DISTRICT

Chiangmai Province, Thailand

Communes, and Location of Ku Daeng

Roads, and cart path	▬▬ ══ , ═══
Commune boundary and name	Nǎu-ng Fàe-g (Nong Fag)
Temple in Nong Fag, Market place	⅄ ▦
Villages and Hamlets in Nong Fag Commune	Ⓐ ⓒⒹ

Ⓐ Nǎu-ng Sǐ Càe-ng ... Hamlet 1 | ⓒ Nǎu-ng Fàe-g, Hamlets 3,4,5
Ⓑ Sǎn Pà-Sàg   Hamlet 2 | Ⓓ Kù-Dae-ng ✳ ... Hamlets 6,7

✳ *Shaded rectangle shows coverage of Ku Daeng map*

0   1   2   3   Kilometers
0   1   2   3 Miles

Kingshill
Ⓒ 1954

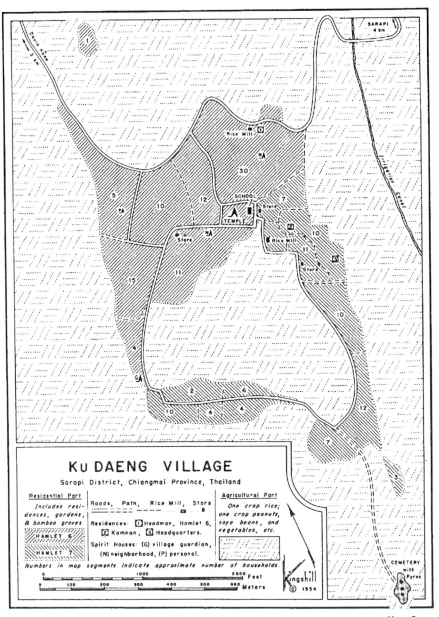

KU DAENG VILLAGE

Sarapi District, Chiangmai Province, Thailand

Residential Part

Includes residences, gardens, 8 bamboo groves

HAMLET 6

HAMLET 7

Agricultural Part

One crop rice; one crop peanuts, soya beans, and vegetables, etc.

Roads, Path, Rice Mill, Store

Residences: ① Headman, Hamlet 6, ② Kamnan, ③ Headquarters.

Spirit Houses: (G) village guardian, (N) neighborhood, (P) personal.

Numbers in map segments indicate approximate number of households.

Feet

Meters

Kingshill © 1954

SARAPI 4 km

CEMETERY with Pyres

Drawn by James R. Wray

Map 3

253

APPENDIX A

THE TWELVE COMMUNES OF SARAPHI

Commune	# of Hamlets	# of Families 1951[1]	1986[2]
Tha Wang Tan	12	976	1,958
Nong Phüng	7	935	2,357
Chai Sathan	7	418	978
Pa Bong	6	428	698
Don Kæw	7	606	985
Nong Fæk	7	689	1,341
Yang Nüng	7	1,016	2,156
Chom Phu	8	665	1,669
Khua Mung	10	836	1,289
Saraphi	8	922	1,775
San Sai	10	905	1,342
TOTAL	96	8,793	17,320

[1] David H. Bau, *Agricultural Economic Survey of Sarapi District* (Chiang Mai: Food and Agriculture Organization of the United Nations, 1951), p. 2.
[2] Population census figures obtained from the District Office in Saraphi.

AGE AND SEX STATISTICS

DISTRIBUTION OF POPULATION BY AGE AND SEX
IN KU DÆNG, 1953

Age Group in Years	Frequency Male	Female	Total	Percent
Young				
0-4	61	62	123	14.6
5-9	26	34	60	7.1
10-14	41	3	78	9.3
Total	**128**	**133**	**261**	**31.0**
Adult				
15-19	47	44	91	10.8
20-24	48	63	111	13.2
25-29	40	33	73	8.7
30-34	29	28	57	6.8
35-39	16	15	31	3.7
40-44	17	22	39	4.6
45-49	29	31	60	7.1
50-54	24	17	41	4.9
Total	**250**	**253**	**503**	**59.8**
Old				
55-69	14	14	28	3.3
60-64	12	15	27	3.2
65-69	10	4	14	1.7
70-74	2	4	6	0.8
75-79	3	0	3	0.4
Total	**41**	**37**	**78**	**9.3**

TOTAL SEX DISTRIBUTION

	419	423	842	100.1

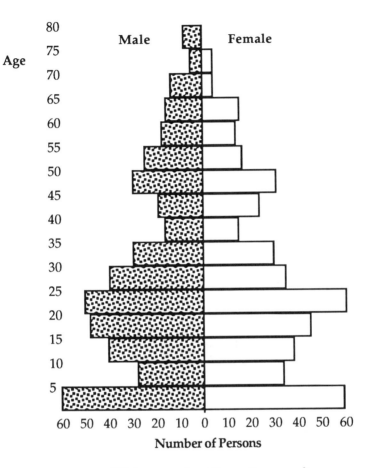

Histogram: Age Group Frequencies

SUBDIVISION OF AGE DISTRIBUTION
FOR AGES 0-8 YEARS

Age in Years	Frequency (Both M and F)	Percent
0-1	34	4.04
1-2	21	2.50
2-3	27	3.21
3-4	25	2.97
4-5	16	1.90
5-6	15	1.78
6-7	6	0.71
7-8	11	1.31
TOTAL	**155**	**18.42**

POPULATION STATISTICS FOR SARAPHI DISTRICT
AND KU DÆNG, 1938-1984[1]

| Year | Population of Saraphi | Ku Dæng Statistics | | |
		Persons	Households	Persons per household
1938	41,219			
1947	40,289			
1952	40,371			
1954	43,366	848	168	5.05
1964	56,897	1,222	194	6.3
1974	49,821	1,008	210	4.8
1984	48,889	956	272	3.5

---

[1] Source: District Office and *kamnan*'s tabulation adjusted for part of Hamlet 7 not included in village of Ku Dæng.

AGE GROUP FREQUENCIES FOR 1954 AND 1984[2]

Year of Birth	1954 Age	% of pop.	1984 Age	% of pop.
		1.1		
1884	70			
		4.9		
1894	60			
		8.4		0.5
1904	50		80	
		11.8		2.9
1914	40		70	
		10.5		5.3
1924	30		60	
		21.9		13.1
1934	20		50	
		20.1		11.2
1944	10		40	
		21.7		9.2
1954	0		30	
				29.1
1964			20	
				16.5
1974			10	
				12.1
1984			0	
TOTAL		**100.2%**		**99.9**

[2] The 1954 statistics were taken from a census of the entire village. The 1984 statistics represent a sample of 206 persons (21.5% of the population) from 48 households (15.9% of the total).

APPENDIX C

WEIGHTS AND MEASURES

Thai Name	Lanna Thai Name	Equivalent	Unit of
rai	*rai phasi* ("taxed rai")	1 acre-2.5 *rai* 1 hectare = 6.25 *rai*	area
	rai	a small square field (of almost any size)	
thang		20 liters	capacity
	tang	24 liters	capacity
	khit	100 grams	weight
baht	baht	5 cents[1]	money
satang	satang	1/20 cent	money

One *thang* of rough rice or paddy equals twenty liters, which weighs approximately 10.2 kilograms.

One *thang* of mixed bran weighs approximately 7 kilograms.

One *thang* of rice husks weighs approximately 5.2 kilograms.

Two baskets, each holding exactly one *thang*, constitute one *hap*, which are carried over the shoulder with the help of a bamboo stick.

---

[1] Money equivalents as of 1954.

APPENDIX D

KINSHIP TERMINOLOGY

Kinship terminology has been listed for six generations, from Ego's great-grandparents to Ego's grandchildren. For further generations, names do exist, but they are not in general use. Small letters indicate terms used in the Thai language; capital letters indicate terms used in Lanna Thai.

1. Ego's Paternal Great-Grandparents: The same names are used for both branches:
   a. great-grandfather: *pu thuat, PO MON*
   b. great-grandmother: *ya thuat, MÆ MON*

2. Ego's Paternal Grandparents:
   a. grandfather: *pu, PO UI*
   b. grandmother: *ya, MÆ UI*

3. Ego's Paternal Grandparents' Siblings:
   a. grandfather's older brother: *pu yai, PO UI LUANG*
   b. grandfather's younger brother: *pu lek, PO UI NOI*
   c. grandfather's older sister: *ya yai, MÆ UI LUANG*
   d. grandfather's younger sister: *ya lek, MÆ UI NOI*
   e. grandmother's siblings: (same as grandfather's)

4. Ego's Father: *pho, PO*

5. Ego's Father's Siblings, their Mates and Children:
   a. Ego's father's older brother: *lung, LUNG*
   b. a's wife: *pa, PA*
   c. a and b's sons: *phi (chai),*[1] *AI*
   d. a and b's daughters: *phi (sao), PI*
   e. Ego's father's younger brother: *a (phu chai), A*
   f. e's wife: *a (saphai), A (YING)*
   g. e & f's sons: *nong (chai), NONG (CAI)* or *NONG KHOEI*
   h. e & f's daughters: *nong (sao), NONG*
   i. Ego's father's older sister: *pa, PA*
   j. i's husband: *lung, LUNG*
   k. i and j's sons and daughters: (same as c and d)
   l. Ego's father's younger sister: *a (sao), A (YING)*
   m. l's husband: *a (chai) A (CAI),* or *A KHOEI*
   n. l & m's sons and daughters: (same as g and h)

---

[1] Words in parentheses are sex indicators, which are not used unless specific sex differentiation is required.

260

6. Ego's Maternal Great-Grandparents:
   a. great-grandfather: *ta thuat, PO MON*
   b. great-grandmother: *yai thuat, MÆ MON*

7. Ego's Maternal Grandparents;
   a. grandfather: *ta, PO UI*
   b. grandmother: *yai, MÆ UI*

8. Ego's Maternal Grandparents's Siblings: (same names are used for the siblings of both grandfather and grandmother)
   a. grandparents' older brother: *ta yai, PO UI LUANG*
   b. grandparents' younger brother: *ta lek, PO UI NOI*
   c. grandparents' older sister: *yai yai, MÆ UI LUANG*
   d. grandparents' younger sister: *yai lek, MÆ UI NOI*

9. Ego's Mother: *mæ, MÆ*

10. Ego's Mother's Siblings, their Mates and Children:
    a. Ego's mother's older brother: (same as father's older brother)
    b. a's wife: (same as father's older brother's wife)
    c. Ego's mother's younger brother: *na (chai), NA (CAI) or NA KHOƐI*
    d. c's wife: *na (ying), NA (YING)*
    e. Ego's mother's older sister: (same as father's older sister)
    f. e's husband: (same as father's older sister's husband)
    g. Ego's mother's younger sister: (same as d)
    h. g's husband: (same as c)

The terminology for the children of Ego's mother's siblings is the same as that for Ego's father's siblings' children.

11. Ego's Wife: *phanraya (or mia), MIA*

12. Ego's Wife's Paternal great-Grandparents: (same as those for Ego's paternal great-grandparents)

13. Ego's Wife's Paternal Grandparents: (same as Ego's paternal grandparents)

14. Ego's Wife's Paternal Grandparents' Siblings: (same as Ego's paternal grandparents' siblings)

15. Ego's Wife's Father: *pho (ta), PO MIA*

16. Ego's Wife's Father's Siblings, their Mates and Children: (same as Ego's father's siblings, their mates and children)

17. Ego's Wife's Maternal Great-Grandparents: (same as Ego's maternal great-grandparents)

18. Ego's Wife's Maternal Grandparents: (same as Ego's maternal grandparents)

19. Ego's Wife's Maternal Grandparents' Siblings: (same as Ego's maternal grandparents' siblings)

20. Ego's Wife's Mother: *mæ (yai)*, *MÆ MIA*

21. Ego's Wife's Mother's Siblings, their Mates and Children: (same as Ego's mother's siblings, their mates and children)

22. Ego's Siblings and their Children:
    a. Ego's older brother: *phi chai, PI AI*
    b. a's wife: *phi saphai, PI PAI*
    c. Ego's younger brother: *nong chai, NONG*
    d. c's wife: *nong saphai, NONG PAI*
    e. Ego's older sister: *phi sao, PI*
    f. e's husband: *phi khoei, PI CAI*
    g. Ego's younger sister: *nong sao, NONG*
    h. g's husband: *nong khoei, NONG CAI* or *NONG KHOEI*
    i. children of Ego's siblings: *lan, LAN*

23. Ego's Wife's Siblings and their Children:
    a. wife's older brother: *phi khoei, PI CAI*
    b. a's wife: *phi saphai, PI PAI*
    c. wife's younger brother: *nong khoei, NONG CAI*
    d. c's wife: *nong saphai, NONG PAI*
    e. wife's older sister: *phi saphai, PI PAI*
    f. e's husband: *phi khoei, PI CAI*
    g. wife's younger sister: *nong saphai, NONG PAI*
    h. g's husband: *nong khoei, NONG CAI*
    i. children of wife's siblings: *lan, LAN*

24. Ego's Children: *luk, LUK*

25. Ego's Grandchildren: *lan, LAN*

APPENDIX E

AGE AND SEX ROLES IN KU DAENG

The following table was prepared from observation and from information obtained from villagers. The tabulation follows that first used by Kingshill in 1954. The new data obtained in 1984 is placed side by side with each of the three categories for easy comparison.

0 = Activity absent	M = Men
x = Activity present	W = Women
xx = Activity strongly present	Ch = Children under age 15
	b = Boys
	g = Girls

Activity	Men		Women		Children	
	'54	'84	'54	'84	'54	'84
Attending temple rites	x	xx	x	xx	x	x
Barbering	xx	x	0	x	0	0
Basketry	xx	x	0	x	0	0
Being tattooed	xx	x	0	0	0	0
Buying and selling land	x	x	x	x	x	0
Buying and selling buffaloes or cattle	x	x	0	x	0	0
Buying pigs	x	x	x	x	0	0
Buying household goods, clothes, etc.	x	0	xx	xx	0	0
Bicycle riding	x	x	x	x	x	x
Caring for babies	x	0	x	x	x	x
Caring for buffaloes, cattle	x	x	x	x	x	x
Carpentry	x	xx	0	0	0	0
Cleaning or digging ditches	x	x	0	0	x	0
Cleaning house	0	0	xx	xx	x	0
Carrying women's used undergarments	0	0	xx	xx	x	x
Climbing tall trees	xx	xx	0	0	0	0
Cock fighting	xx	xx	0	0	0	x
Coffin bearing	xx	xx	x	x	0	0
Cutting firewood	x	x	x	x	0	0
Cutting hair short	xx	x	0	x	x(b)	x(b)

263

Activity	Men '54	Men '84	Women '54	Women '84	Children '54	Children '84
Drawing water	x		xx		x	
Drinking alcoholic beverages	xx	xx	x	x	0	0
Driving oxcarts	xx	0	0	0	x(b)	0
Fishing with net on bamboo pole	x	0	xx	x	x	0
Fishing with rod	x	x	xx	x	x	x
Fishing with throw-net	xx	x	0	0	0	0
Fishing with traps	xx	xx	0	0	x	0
Fishing with spears	x	x	0	0	x	0
Fishing with bamboo shovels	0	0	x	0	x	0
Gambling (dice, cards)	xx	x	0	x	0	0
Gambling (lottery)	x	x	xx	x	0	0
Guns and crossbows, Use of	x	x	0	0	0	0
Headman or *kamnan*	xx	xx	0	0	0	0
Hoeing fields	x	x	x	x	x	0
Keeping pigs, poultry	0	x	x	x	x	x
Loaning money	x	x	xx	xx	0	0
Laundry operating, general	0	x	xx	x	x	0
Making mats	0	x	x	x	x	x
Midwife	0	0	xx	xx	0	0
Operating farms	xx	xx	x	x	x	0
Ownership of land	x	x	x	x	x	x
Contact with a priest's robe	x	xx	0	0	x	x
Piercing ears for earrings	x	0	xx	xx	x	x(g)
Playing in an orchestra	xx	xx	0	0	x	0
Playing takro, checkers, etc.	xx	x	0	0	x	x
Plowing, harrowing	x	xx	0	0	x	0
Polygamist	x	x	0	0	0	0
Preparing fish	x	x	xx	xx	x	x
Preparing food	x	x	xx	xx	x	x
Preparing food for temple rites	x	xx	x	x	0	0
Presenting food to priests	xx	x	0	x	x(b)	x
Priest or novice	xx	xx	0	0	x(b)	x(b)

Activity	Men		Women		Children	
	'54	'84	'54	'84	'54	'84
Reaping (cutting) rice	x	x	x	x	x	0
Selling surplus rice	xx	x	x	x	0	0
Selling (milled) rice in market	0	0	x	x	x	0
Selling pigs	0	x	xx	x	0	0
Sewing cloth	x	0	xx	xx	0	0
Sewing netting	xx	x	x	x	0	0
Shoveling water	x	x	x	0	x	0
Slaughtering poultry	x	xx	x	0	x	0
Sowing rice	xx	xx	x	x	x	x
Storekeeper	x	x	0	x	0	x
Sweets seller	0	x	xx	x	x	x
Taking care of household Buddha shrines	x	xx	x	x	x	x
Taking food to temple	x	x	x	x	x	x
Taking rice to market (paddy)	x	xx	0	0	0	0
Taking rice to rice mill	x	xx	xx	0	x	0
Teaching school	xx	x	x	x	0	0
Temple committee, Member of	xx	xx	0	0	0	0
Threshing	xx	x	x	x	0	0
Traditional doctor	xx	x	0	x	0	0
Undertaker	xx	x	0	0	0	0
Vegetable garden tending	xx	x	x	x	x	0
Village meeting, attending	xx	x	x	x	x	x
Wearing charms	xx	x	0	x	0	x
Wearing jewelry	x	0	xx	xx	0	0(g)
Wearing shoes	x	x	0	x	x	x
Wearing wrist watches, fountain pens	xx	x	x	x	0	0
Weeding rice fields	x	x	x	x	x	x
Winnowing (throwing rice in air)	xx	x	x	x	x	x
Winnowing (fanning)	xx	x	0	x	0	x

APPENDIX F

PRESTIGE RATING

One of the tools employed in our community study was that of a "prestige rating."[1] After some experience in the village, we made a list of some twenty men, who, we thought, were the leaders in the community. Then we approached some of these leaders for comments on the list, explaining that we were trying to get a list of all those in the village who were respected by others, and whose advice was usually followed. The names of a few women were added to the list. Together with all suggestions we finally arrived at a total of thirty-six names. On a six-inch card each person's first and last names were written in Thai on one side and in Lanna Thai on the other. Then the cards were shuffled and presented to each of the thirty-six ratees in turn. They were requested to put the cards on the floor in descending order according to the general respect in which the people were held by the villagers. We did not include the ratee's own card in the pack he was to rate. Notes of any comments the ratee made were duly recorded. Wives or husbands were not asked to rate their spouses, nor were the two monks asked to rate each other.

The following table is a summary of the prestige rating results obtained. The first column gives the average rank obtained by each of the thirty-six persons. The second column indicates the range of the ratings obtained by any one person, that is, his highest and his lowest ratings. The third column indicates the person's rank according to the frequency of high and low ratings he obtained: for this column the first six positions were counted as high ratings and the last four positions as low ratings. The fourth column gives the age of each ratee. The average age was 47 years. The fifth column gives the number of *rai* of land owned by each of the thirty-six persons. The last column gives other factors that may have influenced the prestige of that particular person.

---

[1] See Lauriston Sharp et al. (1953), p. 101.

Rank according to average rating	Range	Rank according to frequency of high and low ratings	Age	Land owned (rai)	Other prestige factors
1	1-2	1	42	—	Head monk
2	1-9	2	52	18	*kamnan*
3	2-27	2	24	—	Monk
4	1-20	4	55	11	Headman, rice-mill owner, ex-novice
5	1-32	5	66	9	Temple leader, drummaker, doctor, ex-monk
6	2-28	6	53	25	Ex-monk, ex-headman
7	3-24	7	63	11.5	Temple committee member, ex-headman
8	3-21	8	64	20	Temple committee member, ex-novice
9	4-33	11	50	6	Commune doctor, ex-monk
10	3-23	8	52	9	Temple committee member, ex-monk
11	4-34	8	61	3	Temple committee member, house-builder
12	5-26	12	57	14	Ex-novice, doctor
13	3-34	14	56	32	Ex-novice, "most diligent man of 1953"
14	3-27	12	48	12	—
15	8-32	16	57	12	Temple committee member, ex-novice

Rank according to average rating	Range	Rank according to frequency of high and low ratings	Age	Land owned (rai)	Other prestige factors
16	7-30	25	50	10	Tobacco headman
17	5-31	15	57	12	Ex-novice, our landlord
18	7-32	16	42	—	Assistant irrigation headman
19	4-34	18	47	—	Kamnan's wife;[2] makes and sells sweets
20	6-35	18	31	2	Headteacher, ex-novice
21	5-34	20	48	—	Wife of no. 10
22	6-35	20	38	—	Assistant kamnan, ex-novice
23	5-33	20	52	—	Husband owns 12 rai of land
24	5-34	25	44	3	Assistant kamnan, storekeeper, ex-monk
25	6-34	29	42	—	Wife of commune doctor (no. 9)
26	5-34	20	24	—	Ex-novice
27	9-34	27	33	—	Assistant kamnan, ex-novice, ex-policeman
28	10-35	29	41	8	Makes and sells sweets, wife of no. 22
29	12-35	20	39	13	—
30	10-33	27	47	6	Ex-soldier
31	17-35	29	53	4	—

---

[2] Subject of 1984 biographical sketch; see appendix I.

Rank according to average rating	Range	Rank according to frequency of high and low ratings	Age	Land owned (rai)	Other prestige factors
32	8-35	34	66	—	Ex-novice, kamnan's messenger, wife owns 13 rai, "drunkard, immoral"
33	10-34	32	30	8	Ex-novice, ex-soldier, assistant irrigation headman, bicycle repairman
34	9-35	33	26	—	Assistant kamnan, ex-novice
35	10-35	35	30	1	Ex-monk
36	17-35	36	57	—	Midwife, trader, Thai

APPENDIX G

BRIEF BIOGRAPHIES OF THE TEN KU DÆNG NOVICES

During the 1953-54 study of Ku Dæng, there were ten novices in residence at the Ku Dæng Temple. Brief biographies were collected for each of the ten novices. In 1964 a follow-up study included an update on each of these then-former novices. This was again carried out in 1984. The year of data collection is indicated at the beginning of each paragraph for each novice.

1. Duangcan Yongkæo, age 17.

1954: Nen Duangcan is the third child, second son of a 44-year-old farmer who owns 12 *rai* of land. No other member of the family has so far spent any time in the monkhood. He finished fourth grade of primary school at Ku Dæng when he was twelve years old. When he was in third grade, at age 11, he became a temple boy at the Ku Dæng temple. When he had completed fourth grade and learned the novices' rules from the head monk, he was ordained a novice in the Ku Dæng temple in February 1949. He started to study the primary Buddhist law in 1950 and was graduated from the primary course in 1951. At present he is studying the secondary course. He does not know how long he will stay in the temple as a novice or monk.

1964: Noi Duangcan left the temple about five or six years ago.[1] Since he was 17 years old when we made the original study, he would have left when he reached the age of 21, at which time he would have had to become a fully ordained monk if he had wished to remain in the temple. At first he farmed for his mother-in-law, but now he is working in a *lamyai* orchard for his family. He passed the second degree course in Buddhist Law before he left the novicehood. He is married and has three children. He is no longer living in Ku Daeng, but has moved to his wife's village a few miles away.

1984: At age 49 Noi Duangcan is living with his wife Kham Noi, age 42, in Pan Tan village in Tambon Don Kæo. A son, Wanlop, age 20, lives with them. He has finished technical school in Chiang Mai with a certificate equivalent to completing grade thirteen. He is helping his parents at home and looking for work elsewhere according to his qualifications. No report was available concerning the other children.

---

[1] A person who has been a novice retains the title *noi* for life, while a former priest is addressed as *nan*. See p. 149.

270

2. Kham Noi Yano, age 19.

1954: Nen Kham Noi is the second child, the only son in addition to three daughters of a 61-year-old farmer, who owns one and a half *rai* of land. His father has never been in the monkhood. Kham Noi became a temple boy at Ku Dæng temple when he was studying in third grade at age 14. After completing fourth grade, he became a novice in the Ku Dæng temple in 1950. He started to study in the primary class of the Buddhist Law at the Nong Fæk temple school in 1951 and passed the examination for that grade in the same year. At present he is studying in the secondary class at the same school. He wants to become a monk before he leaves the temple.

1964: In 1955 Nan Kham Noi reached the age of 21 and received higher ordination to became a fully ordained monk. He remained at the Ku Dæng temple until 1957, when he left the monkhood after passing the second degree course in Buddhist Law. He now lives with his wife's family in the section of Hamlet 7 that is not part of Ku Dæng. At first he farmed with his parents-in-law but later built his own small house and works now as hired farm labor, making a satisfactory living for himself, his wife, and their daughter. He owns his house and one buffalo.

1984: Nan Kham Noi and his family now live in a different village in another commune, still in Saraphi District. His wife, Candi is 43 years old. Their oldest daughter, Aphinya, age 23, has finished the higher teacher's certificate (equivalent to grade fifteen) and is now a government teacher in Sukhothai province. A second daughter, Sukanya, is 6 years old and presently enrolled in first grade at the Ku Dæng school.

3. Bunsi Kanthawong, age 17.

1954: Bunsi is the third of four children and the youngest son of a 49-year-old farmer, who owns one *rai* of land. Neither Bunsi's father nor his brothers have ever been in the monkhood. Bunsi became a temple boy while he was studying in fourth grade. When he finished fourth grade in 1949 at the age of 12, he became a novice. In 1951 he graduated from primary Buddhist Law and continued to study the secondary course at the Nong Fæk monks' school. He is not sure how long he will be staying in the temple.

1964: Noi Bunsi earned the second degree in Buddhist Law before he left the monkhood in 1956 at the age of 20. He has been living with his parents in Hamlet 6 and helping his mother after his father died three years ago. He married in 1960 and has a 10-month-old daughter. Their first child, a boy, died as an infant. Noi Bunsi rents four *rai* of land for rice cultivation and two *rai* for growing vegetables each year. He also raises pigs, ducks, and chickens.

1984: Noi Bunsi moved from Ku Dæng to Fang District, where he died in November 1984. His family continues to live in Fang District.

4. Bunma Thongma, age 17.

1954: Bunma is the younger of two sons of a 50-year-old Ku Dæng farmer, who owns three *rai* of land. Neither his older brother nor his father has ever spent any time in the monkhood. At the age of twelve, when Bunma was a third grade pupil in the Ku Dæng elementary school, he became a temple boy. In June 1950, after he had graduated from elementary school, he was ordained as novice in the Ku Dæng temple. At present he is studying the primary Buddhist Law at Nong Fæk. He wishes to receive higher ordination as a monk before he leaves the temple.

1964: Noi Bunma reached third grade in Buddhist Law while still a novice. At the age of 21, instead of receiving higher ordination, he left the temple. He now lives with his wife and three children in Lamphun province, farming for his mother-in-law after his father-in-law's death. His mother-in-law owns a little over three *rai* of land. Noi Bunma also bought a buffalo from his own parents and works some time each year as hired farm labor for others. Some additional income derives from vegetable gardening and a small *lamyai* orchard.

1984: At age 47, Noi Bunma now lives in Sai Mun village, Hamlet 3, Nong Changkün commune, city district, Lamphun province. His wife, Nuansi, is 44 years old. They have three children. The oldest, a girl, Phikun has finished the higher teachers' certificate from the Teachers College in Lampang and is presently studying for a bachelor's degree at Sukhothai Thammathirat (open) University. The second child, Wiraphon, a son, graduated from the agricultural college in Chiang Rai with an advanced certificate. Presently he is studying for a bachelor's degree in agriculture at Mæjo Institute of Agriculture in Chiang Mai. The third child, Rataphon, a girl, is taking an accountancy course at the Technical College in Lamphun.

5. Sombun Kæwprasit, age 16.

1954: Sombun was born in Lamphun province. When he was in third grade, his parents separated, and he came to live with his elder brother, a

30-year-old farmer in Ku Dæng. His brother owns eight *rai* of land, works as a bicycle repairman in the village, spent five years in the novicehood, and was a soldier in the Thai army for two years. Sombun finished fourth grade in the Ku Dæng primary school and became a temple boy the same year. After he was graduated from primary school in 1950, he became a novice in the Ku Dæng temple. He studied and completed the primary course in Buddhist Law at Nong Fæk temple in two years and is now studying the secondary course at the same place. He does not know how long he will stay in the temple as a novice.

1964: Noi Sombun studied and passed his third degree of the Buddhist Law before he left the novicehood at the age of 20 in 1957. His mother is dead; his father lives in Chiang Mai; and Noi Sombun, himself, is now working as a driver in Bangkok.

1984: Noi Sombun no longer lives in Ku Dæng but moved to Pa Sang district in Lamphun province. Address unknown.

6. Intha (or Inta) Fongsi, name later changed to Niran Fongsi, age 17.

1954: Inta was born in Ku Dæng in the family of a poor woman.[2] His father was a native of another village. While a fourth grade pupil, Inta became a temple boy in the Ku Dæng temple. When he graduated from fourth grade in 1952, Inta became a novice and is presently studying the primary course in Buddhist Law at Nong Fæk. He wishes to become a monk before he leaves the temple.

1964: At the age of 21, Nen Inta received higher ordination as a monk. He stayed in the monkhood until 1963, when he was 27 years old. By that time he had attained first degree in Buddhist Law; and for the last two years in the monkhood he was a teacher of the Buddhist Law at the Ku Dæng temple at a salary of 100 baht per month. He also took a correspondence course in accounting and received a "middle class" certificate. When he left the monkhood, he changed his name to Niran and worked in a bank for half a month. Then he returned to Ku Dæng to take care of his uncle. Nan Niran owns four and a half *rai* of land, which he rents out to others to farm; from this he receives enough rice for his own and his uncle's needs. He owns thirty-six ducks and a vegetable garden. His cash income per year is 4-5,000 baht, which he uses as capital for business transactions

---

[2] Our census data listed this woman as single, living with her younger sister and her husband. It is possible that Inta is actually the son of this couple, rather than of the older woman.

during the harvest season and for purchasing additional land. Nan Niran is not married and has no particular plans for the future.

1984: Nan Niran is now 47 years old and resides at Hamlet 7 in Ku Dæng village. He is married to Fongsi who is 43. They have two daughters. Rungthiwa, age 18, finished tenth grade in the Saraphi secondary school; she is presently applying for work in the Warorot market in Chiang Mai. The second daughter, Ræmcan, age 11, is a fifth grade pupil at the Nong Fæk temple school.

7. Winen Kawicha, age 16.

1954: Winen is the son of a 60-year-old Ku Dæng woman who owns eight *rai* of land. His father was a native of a neighboring village and is no longer living. In 1951, at the completion of fourth grade, and after he had been a temple boy for seven months, Winen became a novice. He is now studying the primary Buddhist Law and would like to stay in the temple as long as possible.

1964: Noi Winen left the temple in 1954 at the age of 17 after attaining third degree in Buddhist Law. He was married in 1960 and now has two children. He farms his mother-in-law's twelve *rai* of land and works a vegetable garden.

1984: At age 46 Noi Winen continues to live in Ku Dæng, where he now is headman of Hamlet 6. His wife, Buppha, is 45 years old. They have two children: a son, Prasit, age 24, who is an enlisted man in the air force; and a daughter, Amphai, age 23, who finished tenth grade at the Saraphi secondary school. She is married and has a 1-year-old daughter.

8. Unrüan Fonglao, age 16.

1954: Unrüan is the fourth of eight children, all boys except the oldest. Their father is a 42-year-old Ku Dæng farmer, who owns seven *rai* of land. Unrüan's oldest brother spent seven years in the temple as a novice. Unrüan became a temple boy when he was in the fourth grade. In 1951 he was ordained as a novice when he had completed fourth grade education. He is now studying the primary Buddhist Law at Nong Fæk temple. He wishes to receive higher ordination as a monk before leaving the temple.

1964: Unrüan stayed in the temple until six years ago. He received higher ordination as a monk and reached second degree in the Buddhist Law before leaving the monkhood. He now lives with his parents in Amphœ Fang. He is married and has one child.

1984: At age 47 Nan Unrüan continues to live in Amphœ Fang in Lo village, together with his family. He is working in the oil field near the district town.

9. Mi — (surname not recorded), age 15.

1954: Mi is the oldest son and third child out of five children of a 48-year-old Ku Dæng farmer. His father owns no land and has never been in the monkhood. At the age of 12, Mi became a temple boy while still in second grade in the Ku Dæng village school. Upon completing fourth grade, he became a novice in 1951 and is now studying primary Buddhist Law at Nong Fæk. He wishes to stay in the temple as long as possible.

1964: Noi Mi left the temple before attaining monkhood and drowned shortly thereafter.

10. Ai Yünbun, age 15.

1954: The youngest and newest of the Ku Dæng novices, Ai was ordained in 1953 after he left primary school. He could not pass the final examination, which had been made more difficult by government order during his final year in school. He had been a temple boy for one year before he was ordained as a novice. He is now studying the primary Buddhist Law and wishes to become a monk before he leaves the temple. He is the oldest son and second of five children of a 34-year-old Ku Dæng farmer, who owns four *rai* of land. His father was never in the monkhood.

1964: Noi Ai left the monkhood as a novice after attaining third degree in the Buddhist Law. He was married this year and is living with his in-laws, working their land. He also owns a vegetable garden.

1984: At age 48 Noi Ai still lives in Ku Dæng, Hamlet 7, and is married to 41-year-old Wanphen. They have two daughters: Sangwan, age 18, has finished seventh grade and is presently working as a seamstress in a local store; Chophet, age 11, is a pupil in the Nong Fæk village school.

1964: At the time of our original study in 1953-54, there was only one fully-ordained monk in addition to the head monk (abbot) in the Ku Dæng temple. Nan Si Hinyæng left the monkhood in 1959 and was married the following year. He has no children. Nan Si helps his in-laws with their twelve *rai* of land. Some years he has to rent a tractor to prepare his land. In addition he raises ducks and pigs and grows peanuts and garlic during the appropriate seasons.

1984: Nan Si is now 52 years old and lives in Hamlet 6, Ku Dæng village. His wife Siriwan is 57 years old. They have two children: a son, Mongkhon, age 18, who is presently in twelfth grade in the Saraphi secondary school; and a daughter, Ariwan, age 16, who is in tenth grade in the same school.

APPENDIX H

AN AUTOBIOGRAPHY OF A 73-YEAR-OLD WOMAN
(written in 1953)

My childhood was normal, like that of other children. I did not have very many neighborhood friends, since there were very few other houses near our own. My friends at that time have all died by now and left me here alone. Every day, from early morning, my friends and I liked to play near our homes or in the nearby woods. I am quite sure that we had a greater variety of games than children have today. My favorite game was "hide and seek," which was usually the first of our day's games. When we were tired of running in the woods, we usually went to play on a swing in the banyan tree near the Ku Dæng temple. The swing had been hung on the tree with an iron chain by the villagers for their children.

At that time we had meals only twice daily: once in the morning, and again in the evening when our parents returned from work. Often we returned home a little earlier than our parents. Sometimes I did some cooking: easy jobs, such as roasting fish or preparing peppers, to help my parents who came home late in the afternoon.

Children of my generation continued to play around their homes until they were 14 or 15 years of age. They seemed to be reluctant to accept the changes in their lives leading toward adulthood. I remember that I collected some fruits and vegetables and took them to the market when I was 18 years old.

I was very slender at that time. When I was 16, I was as tall as my mother, which was lucky for me, for I could wear some of my mother's clothes. They fitted my body perfectly. Other children had to wait for a long time to get one extra dress in addition to the one they were wearing. There was nothing more expensive than cloth at that time. Usually the villagers bought thread in the market, which they wove into cloth from which they then made their clothes. Most of the cloth was black or gray in color. There were no bright colors as we have today. Children of 18 years of age as well as those who were big and strong, would try their best to sell things in the market. There in the city they would see people dressed in beautiful garments. They would see other beautiful clothes as well as jewelery in the shops. Even if these young people had no money, just seeing the beautiful clothes would make them happy and let them dream of having some of their own one day.

Young people usually started work at the age of 20, since they were then strong enough to undertake heavy tasks. This is one reason why people in the country married very young, so that they would have children early to help with work.

I am the oldest daughter of my parents, and, therefore, my parents named me "Bunpan," which means "gift of merit." As the oldest daughter, I received good care and was beloved by my parents. I had to watch my younger sisters instead of running up and down in the woods. This annoyed me very much, but I had no choice. I had more trouble when my parents went to work in the fields, for then I had to take complete charge of my sisters. At that time I was only 15 years old, but I knew how to take care of children and also how to cook at home. Occasionally, I even had to clean our very big house while taking care of my sisters at the same time. My sisters were sometimes so naughty that I wanted to cry; I felt that I had too many duties for one day and saw no way out for a long time to come.

I married when I was 21 years old. My husband was a 40-year-old widower of Ku Dæng, who had two children from his first wife. We stayed together for about thirty years, when my husband died and left me with our four daughters. At the time of our marriage, there was no wedding ceremony. The parents of both young people simply went to the houses of their friends and told them that the young people were living together. After that the groom collected his bag and his sword and came to live with the bride at her house. After staying for three years with my family, we moved to another place where we built our own house.

At that time, communication between Ku Dæng and Chiang Mai was not as good as it is today. We had to travel along the bank of the river down to Lamphun, from where we could go up to Chiang Mai. There were never any cases of highway robbery in those days as there are today.

My first son died at the age of 17 because a witch ate him. He had fallen in love with a girl in the village. People believed that the girl was inhabited by devils. When my son broke his word to this girl, she was very angry and sent the worst devils to kill him. He fell suddenly sick and died the same day. Finally a shaman from another village was called in to drive the devils away from the girl, imprison them in a pot, and throw the pot into the Ping river. This girl is still living in Ku Dæng today, but I do not wish to mention her name.

My son died, because he was killed by a *phika* who had been his girlfriend. My son loved her because he was too young to know better. The same girl had already killed a number of other villagers. When a renowned shaman was called in to chase away the *phika* that was eating people, he used some powerful sacred chants *(khatha)*, and the *phika* had to flee from its victim. Just before she left, the *phika* told the shaman her name; that is why we know the name of the person who has a *phika*. The *phika* herself would tell everybody that she was not a *phika*, but she would know, herself, that she was one. When she became angry with any person, she would send her *phika* into the body of that person and try to kill him by eating everything inside his body.

I heard that a woman who has a *phika* in her body must be related to the owls. Someone told me that the owls have excellent eyes, which can see through the body of a woman and see the *phika* inside her. The owl will carefully watch at the *phika*'s house until a man comes to visit the girl. The owl will follow the man to his own house, where it will hoot as a warning to the man that the woman he has just visited is a *phika*. If the man heeds this warning, he will never go to see the *phika* woman again. A *phika* woman never wants to see owls; she always chases them away whenever she has a chance.

When my son died, everybody in the village agreed to get rid of the *phika*. My husband, who was the headman of the village, sent one of the villagers to call the shaman from another village to come to Ku Dæng and perform the ceremony to kill the *phika*. The woman did not want to have the ceremony held, but she had to submit since it was the will of the majority of the villagers. Otherwise, she would have had to leave the village, which would have made it difficult for her to find another place to live.

My first house was made of bamboo. It was located near the temple. When it burned down, I sold the land to the present temple leader and moved to the place where I live now. The bamboo house had been a big one, as big as one of the teak houses today. When it burned, many villagers came to help put out the fire, but to no avail. While the villages were busy pouring water on the flames, I suddenly remembered that I had left my golden necklace, weighing forty-eight grams, on a cupboard in my bedroom. I told my husband about it; he tried to get back into the house through the door, but was prevented from doing so by the flames. He tried again by cutting a hole into the floor of the bedroom, through which he managed to crawl and bring out the necklace. This was the only thing we saved from the fire. Later, through the kindness of the villagers, we received much food, clothing, and other necessities.

The fire was the first reason why we sold that piece of land and moved to our present site. The second reason was because our land was close to the tracks of *phima bong*, the ghosts of horses. I always heard them galloping up and down the pathway behind our house. However, I dared no go out and look at them, as I was very much afraid that they would kill me. These ghosts robbed our family of happiness. We always had at least one person down with sickness. Even today, the family which lives on that land always has someone sick.

When I was young, girls never dressed as beautifully as girls do today. We tried to weave cloth ourselves, but were not able to produce any fancy colors as can be done today. We dressed mostly in the style of the Burmese with coats and skirts—*phasin*—down to the ankles. We wore no shoes. Our hair was darkened with coconut oil and rolled up on the head like that of Japanese women.

In those days the Cao Luang of Chiang Mai sent his elephants to be kept at Ku Dæng. Each elephant had a bell around its neck. Some of these bells were made of wood, others of iron. In the evenings the elephants always came to eat leaves from the bamboo trees in the village.

At that time there were still many bamboo trees in places where today there are houses. Elephants love to pull down the bamboo trees, strip off all the leaves to eat, and then let the poles snap back up.

At that time many wild rabbits and mongooses could be found around the village. There have almost never been any other wild animals in Ku Dæng. One day I heard that a lemur had been seen. The villagers caught it and sold it in Saraphi. Since that day I have not heard of another lemur in the neighborhood.

My grandfather was an architect, working for the King *(cao luang)* of Chiang Mai *(cao chiwit ao)*. The Cao Luang gave him a palanquin with four carriers to bring him to the city whenever he wanted to see him. He built various houses as well as Wat Phra Sing for the King of Chiang Mai.

From time to time, when the Cao Luang got a new elephant, he sent it to a friend of my grandfather in a neighboring village for training. I still can remember the elephant pen, which had poles as big as the posts of our houses today.

I was afraid of the Cao Luang's elephants. He sent five at a time to bring back his paddy to Chiang Mai. The mahouts always tied the elephants to the bamboo forest near Ku Dæng. In the afternoon they untied them and let them bathe in the Ping River. After that they loaded the paddy and returned to Chiang Mai.

The temple of Ku Dæng was built during the lifetime of my grandfather. I have seen it repaired twice since then. The first time was when Nai To, a villager from Doi Saket, had become a priest in the Ku Dæng temple. Priest To was a former house builder. He repaired the temple when he saw that it was not in very good condition. About two or three years ago, the present head priest, Phra Kong, repaired the temple again. The number of buildings in the temple compound is the same today as it was before, except that a *sala* has been built around the temple area. The Ku Dæng temple is about 70 years old.[1]

Until twenty years ago or so, we planted rice only once a year. We started planting two rice crops annually after the irrigation dam at Don Kæw was completed. This dam brought enough water to Ku Dæng for a second planting. A long, long time ago, the rice fields of today were just jungle. Later, when a person wanted to work this land, he informed the *kamnan* of his desire, cut down the vegetation, and laid claim to the land.

About forty years ago, when rice was planted only once a year in this area, my father and I planted a different kind of rice, called "red rice," which today is no longer raised. We worked very hard from daybreak until dark to plant this rice. At harvest time one liter of this rice sold for five *thæp*.[2] This rice was very expensive, because people treasured it for its

---

[1] Built approximately in 1880 A.D.
[2] One *thæp* = 80 satang (.80 baht) at that time.

fragrance when cooked. Because of the great demand, we had to mix it with regular rice so that there would be enough left over for our own family.

Once every two or three years, the villagers held a big festival to pacify the spirit of the village, called Nong Fon Phi. This festival was held in the third or fourth month after the rice harvest.

A long time ago, when villagers wanted to go to Chiang Mai, they had to wake up at two a.m., cross the big rice field south of the village, and then cross the river to walk to Chiang Mai. At that time robberies never occurred along the way, even in the deepest jungle. If it had been like today, people would have lost much of their wealth to robbers. There was a robbery that took place just a month ago in broad daylight with many people passing by the spot where it occurred.

When I was 30 or 40 years old, I was known as the best fisherwoman in the village. The end of November is the egg laying season for fish. During this time fish will keep in hiding. All the fishermen stop fishing during this period, but I went out as usual. I took my fishing rod and basket for storing the fish. On the way I met a villager who advised me not to go fishing, since no one had ever caught fish during this season. I did not believe him and continued as planned. Late in the afternoon I surprised all the villagers with a big basketful of fish. This was the cause for my reputation as the best fisherwoman in the village. I stopped fishing many years ago, when I found myself too old to sin against the precepts.

Once, about thirty years ago, I nearly had a chance to go down to Bangkok. At that time my youngest daughter was living in Chachœngsao Province with her husband. I had been invited to go to Bangkok by a villager from Don Kæo who owned a boat that took goods on the Ping River from Chiang Mai to Bangkok. I would have had to pay only ten *thæp*—about eight baht—for food on the trip. I wanted very much to see my daughter, but my husband would not allow me to go, because he was afraid I would get into trouble. At that time Bangkok seemed very, very far from our village.

1964, Ten Years Later

In 1964, at age 84, Grandmother Pan still lived in her old house in Ku Dæng. She had lost the sight of one eye and was hard of hearing. She could not work very much or go visiting other than her immediate neighbors—as much as she would have liked to. But she still gathered palm branches to make brooms and split firewood for use in her house. She told us she did not want to sit still and be idle.

Noted in 1984

Grandmother Pan Yongkham was born in B.E. 2423 (A.D. 1880) and died on the 19th of September B.E. 2511 (A.D. 1968) at the age of 88.

APPENDIX I

BIOGRAPHICAL SKETCH OF KAMNAN MONG'S WIDOW

Grandmother Mun was born in the Year of the Horse, B.E. 2449 (A.D. 1906), in the village of Ku Dæng, the fourth child of five of Father Kui and Mother Bun Pan Yüntham.[1] Her father was called by the villagers "Caonoi Kui," indicating that he was descended from the Royal Family of Chiang Mai.[2]

During Mun's childhood, Ku Dæng was still in the middle of a jungle. There were many kinds of valuable trees in the jungle, but only small animals, such as mongooses, snakes, and so on. Communication with other villages in the neighborhood was by foot path through the jungle. There were not very many people residing in the village, and the few houses that did exist were far apart. In order to build a house, the owner first had to clear a piece of jungle. The villagers planted coconut trees and vegetables, such as peppers and eggplants, for their own consumption. They had two rice crops per year and raised such animals as pigs, ducks, and chickens.

The village was under the administration of a headman. Mun's father was the village headman, probably because he was of royal descent, which was at that time an important factor. Titled descendants were highly honored and respected in those days. The villagers seldom disputed an opinion voiced by Mun's father. When she was 19 years old, when her father had already died, Mun was married to Mr. Mong Namwong, the son of the Prince of Nong Fæk (Pho Khun Phai Cit). Her husband moved to Ku Dæng to live with Mun's family according to custom. Because of his ability, he was elected headman, irrigation official, and eventually *kamnan* of the commune. During Pho Mong's term of office as *kamnan* the village of Ku Dæng developed in many ways: roads were built in the village, so that the people could visit each other without having to pass through other people's property; irrigation ditches were built, enlarged, and inter-con-

---

[1] The following biographical sketch of Mrs. Kham Mun Namwong, widow of Kamnan Mong Namwong, was written in 1984 by two Payap University history students, Nitinan Thitinan and Khancit Khumson. Interviews were conducted with Grandmother Mun during the 1984 follow-up study by Kingshill, Bhandhachat, Renard, and selected Payap University instructors and students. English translation by Konrad Kingshill.

Since we are dealing here with a person who is today a great-grandmother, we will use the following terminology in referring to her: "Mun" (without a title) for the period of childhood until she was married; "Mæ Mun" (= Mother Mun) during adulthood from the time of her marriage until the time of our original study in 1953; and "Ui Mun" (= Grandmother Mun) for the period since 1953 to the present. While her given name is "Kham Mun," it is customary to refer to people by a nickname, which in this case is "Mun."

[2] Her mother was the person whose autobiography is recorded in appendix H.

nected, so that the farmers would be able to sprout their rice more effectively; and a cemetery was developed from land cleared and set aside for convenience of villagers to cremate those who had passed away. When Mæ Mun was about 40 years old (B.E. 2489 or A.D. 1946), her husband introduced *lamyai* (longan) trees into Ku Dæng. He obtained saplings from a village on the bank of the Mæ Ping river in Lamphun province. He cleared part of his land formerly used to raise coconuts. When results proved good, other villagers asked for saplings from Pho Mong. Thus *lamyai* spread throughout the village until today it has become one of the major cash crops for Ku Dæng. In addition, as a result of improved irrigation, water became available for the entire village the year round, while at the same time preventing flooding during the rainy season. Other cash crops profiting by this were garlic, tobacco, and a variety of vegetables.

As growth and development continued, a road was built to connect the village with Saraphi district in one direction and the district of San Pa Tong in the other. This helped communication of the villagers with their neighbors and with officials in the district. Finally, about ten years ago, electricity was introduced into Ku Dæng, enabling the villagers to have electric lights as well as television, both black-and-white and color, amplifiers, and refrigerators.

When comparing the state of the village sixty or seventy years ago with that about thirty years later, it is quite evident that major changes occurred more or less as of the time that Mæ Mun's husband became *kamnan*. Improvements in communications with the outside world, methods of agriculture including improved irrigation, and the introduction of electricity, brought progress until today it can be seen clearly in the style of living of the villagers and in the type of houses that are being built. In Hamlet 7 most of the newer houses are built of brick and mortar with little wood, perhaps only in the upper stories. Older houses in more traditional style continue to exist side by side with these newer ones, although the older ones are mostly found in Hamlet 6. The life of Mrs. Kham Mun Namwong is best divided into three periods, paralleling the changes that took place in the village.

First Phase: Age 1-19

This period covers Mun's life from the time of birth until she got married. As a small child, Mun helped her parents at home. When she was 12 or 13 years old, she gathered vegetables that were grown in the vicinity of the house, such as pepper or eggplant. She also looked for wild vegetables in the fields and irrigation ditches to be used for food at home. If she was able to gather more than could be used at home, she tied them together in bundles to sell in the market at Saraphi or in the city. She earned about one satang for every six or seven bundles sold. She also helped her parents take care of livestock: they had about fifteen to sixteen head of cattle and water buffaloes that were kept in the fields, while at home they had two sows, as well as some ducks and chickens. During the proper season she helped her parents with rice planting and harvesting in the fields. Mun's father took care of her education in these years. He taught her to memorize the Thai alphabet by writing a letter at a time on a piece of paper and then covering it up with a wooden ruler. When she had reproduced the letter from memory, she could check on it by lifting up the ruler. She learned only to read and write in Thai, not Lanna Thai.

When Mun was 13 years old in 1919 many of the Ku Dæng villagers went to work to build the Khun Tan railway tunnel (Tham Mæ Yon Wai). According to official records, the railway reached Chiang Mai in 1921, but there is no mention of the date when the line was completed to Saraphi. Many of the workers died from jungle fever. Mun's oldest sister carried food, such as coconuts, rice, fish, and other kinds of food, to the mouth of the tunnel to sell to the workers. She usually made 70 to 80 satang profit each time. In 1921 the work was finished, and the first train pulled into the Saraphi station. Most of the Ku Dæng villagers went to attend this event, together with a number of priests who blessed the first train with holy water. When Mun was 17 years old, her second oldest brother passed away, followed two years later by her father.

Second Phase: The Middle Years, Age 19-40

When Mun was 19 years old she was married to Pho Mong Namwong, who moved in with her in her parents' home in Ku Dæng. During this period they had ten children—five boys and five girls—the oldest, a girl, was born when Mæ Mun was 20 years old, and the youngest, a boy, when she was 37. In 1934, when Mæ Mun was 28 years old, the first airplane landed in Chiang Mai. Mæ Mun joined other Ku Dæng villagers to go by bicycle to the airport at the southern edge of Chiang Mai city. The plane had two wings, one of which was painted almost completely with the emblem of the Royal Family. A ceremony to tie strings around the wrists of the pilots was held when they first landed.

Mæ Mun's life during these years was mostly preoccupied with the raising of her large family. When she was 30 she helped clear a piece of jungle so that they could expand their house which now had fourteen people living in it: Mæ Mun and her husband, their ten children and two nieces and nephews. She had to cook ten liters of rice each day to satisfy her family.

Mæ Mun was in her mid-30s during World War II (1939-45). Many Japanese passed through the village. Some of them asked to buy foodstuff such as ducks, chickens, or fruit. Those people who traded with the Japanese became quite rich. The villagers had to build air raid shelters in the village. They dug holes in the ground and lined them with house posts, which then were covered with earth, so that the shelters would be water tight. When food had been cooked in the morning, everything was taken into the shelters in order to be ready for the time when the siren in Saraphi sounded. Then everybody would scurry into the shelters. Some observers were assigned to build lookouts on the taller trees in Ku Dæng and two other localities in the neighborhood to observe the flight of the planes. When her husband became *kamnan*, Mæ Mun was about 35 years old. During this time she had to be separated from her husband, because she had to take her children into town so that they could attend school. They did not have great treasurers to leave for their children, so they decided to give them as much education as possible. She rented a house near one of the city gates of Chiang Mai for 100 baht per month and sent her children to the government school. While her children were in school, she sold vegetables in the city market or anything else she could get hold of from villagers who came in from the rural areas early in the morning. In this way she could earn 30 to 40 baht per day, enough to keep her children in school and feed them throughout this period. After seven years she returned to Ku Dæng.

Third Phase: From Age 40 to the Present

Mæ Mun returned from the city when she was about 42 years old, after having suffered all sorts of hardships trying to make ends meet to send her children to school. This was the time when they still had coconut trees and could sell coconuts for some cash income. At the same time, Kamnan Mong had started planting *lamyai* trees, which soon started producing crops. Middlemen came to the village to buy their fruit as well as to bargain for their rice crops.

As her children grew older, they were married and left home. Her husband died when Ui Mun was 65 years old, and ever since she has lived alone in her house. Some of her children come to visit her and stay with her for brief periods of time. Those children who are still living in Ku Dæng bring food to Ui Mun for every meal. In 1982 her second son passed away.

At the present time Ui Mun continues living happily at home in Ku Dæng as usual, taking one day at a time. She cleans her house and yard and weaves mats for use by her family or friends. She is content with life and happy that she is still living.

Glossary

acan	อาจารย์	(venerated) teacher
acan wat	อาจารย์วัด	temple leader
æo sao	แอ่วสาว	to court women (Lanna Thai)
akuson	อกุศล	demerit, the opposite of *kuson*
akusonthamma	อกุศลธรรมะ	doing evil; evil things
Alawakayak	อาละวะกยัก	demon in the Yakkhasangyut
amphœ	อำเภอ	district
Anon	อานนท์	disciple of the Buddha, Ananda
anisong	อานิสงม์	merits, meritorious deeds
anuban	อนุบาล	kindergarten
anumothana	อนุโมทนา	a blessing
arahan	อรหันต์	*arahanta* (P.), enlightened person, disciple of the Buddha
arupalok	อรูปโลก	formless world, a subdivision of the Brahman world
arupaphrom	อรูปพรม	formless state, one of the evil states of man
athibodi krom saman süksa	อธิบดีกรมสามัญศึกษา	director of secondary education
bai tong	ใบตอง	banana leaves
Bang Chan	บางชัน	village north of Bangkok, site of early Cornell study
Bangkapi	บางกะปิ	former (1953) district north of Bangkok, now a borough of the city
bap	บาป	demerit, "sin"
bat	บาท	baht (monetary unit)
bhikkhuni (P.)	ภิกบุนี	"nun," female counterpart of a fully-ordained monk
bok khoraphat	โบกขรพรรษ	red-colored rain of Buddhist legend
bot	โบสถ์	consecrated ordination hall, part of the temple complex
bun	บุญ	merit
cai	ใจ	heart/mind
cakkri	จักรี	Chakri dynasty
cangwat	จังหวัด	province
Cao Chiwit Ao	เจ้าชีวิตอ้าว	a prince of Chiang Mai

Cao Küna	เจ้ากือนา	King of Chiang Mai, 788 A.D.
cao luang	เจ้าหลวง	chief, prince, king
Cao Noi	เจ้าน้อย	name of a spirit
Cao Phraya Kalahom	เจ้าพระยากลาโหม	title of a leader of the Thai army during the reign of King Rama IV
Cao Ton Luang	เจ้าต้นหลวง	name of a spirit
cedi	เจดีย์	pagoda or stupa
chadok	ชาดก	*jātaka* (P.), Buddhist "birth stories" (of the former lives of the Buddha)
Chai Prakan	ไชยปะการ	older name for the district of Fang
chan	ฉัน	first person pronoun, I
Chiang Sæn	เชียงแสน	ancient Northern Thai Kingdom (14th cent.) near present Lao border
Chiang Yun	เชียงยืน	temple in Chiang Mai
chit	ฉีด	to inject
Chulalongkorn	จุฬาลงกรณ์	name for King Rama V (1868-1910)
cit	จิต	mind, "soul"
cit-cai	จิตใจ	mind/heart
com khwan	จอมขวัญ	a man very much in love with a woman
comphon	จอมพล	Field Marshal
Com Thong	จอมทอง	town and district about 50 km. SW of the city of Chiang Mai
congkrom	จงกรม	walking meditation
dai chua	ได้ชั่ว	to receive evil
dai di	ได้ดี	to receive good
di	ดี	good, goodness
Doi Saket	ดอยสะเก็ด	district ten miles NE of the city of Chiang Mai
Doi Suthep	ดอยสุเทพ	lower peak on 5,500 ft. mountain west of the city of Chiang Mai
Don Kæo	ดอนแก้ว	commune in Saraphi district (see map 2)
düan	เดือน	month
failuang	ฝ้ายหลวง	name of white thread used in Buddhist ceremonies

Fang	แฟง	district in Chiang Mai province bordering Burma
farang	ฝรั่ง	Caucasian foreigners
fon	ฟ้อน	dance
fon phi	ฟ้อนผี	spirit dance
ha	ฮา	first person pronoun, I (Lanna Thai)
ha	ห่า	mythological measure of rainfall
hæk na	(พิธี)แฮกนา	(annual ceremony of) field preparation
Hang Dong	หางดง	district adjacent to Saraphi
hao	เฮา	I or we (Lanna Thai)
hap	หาบ	measure of weight (see appendix C)
Ho	ฮ่อ	Yunnanese
ho thamma	หอธรรมะ	storehouse in temple compound for scriptures and sermons
Hua Fai	หัวฝาย	part of Hamlet 7 along irrigation canal
i-lung	ถี่ลุง	you (Lanna Thai)
Kabinlaphat	กบิลพัสดุ์	Kapilavatthu, the city of Lord Buddha's princely family
kam	กรรม	*kamma* (P.); karma (Skt.)
kamnan	กำนัน	commune headman
kathin	กฐิน	ceremony of giving robes to monks after the rains retreat
kha	ค่ะ	polite particle spoken by women
kham	คำ	gold; common proper name
khana	คณะ	group, area, portion of time
khanom	ขนม	dessert, candy, sweets
khao kam	เข้ากำ	cemetery ceremony
khatha	คาถา	sacred verse
Khieo	เขียว	proper name ("Mr. Green")
k(h)ing	คิง	you (sing., Lanna Thai)
khon	คน	person, people
Khon Müang	คนเมือง	name of weekly newspaper in Chiang Mai; way of referring to Northern Thai people
khong	ของ	things, "stuff"

khong khwan	ของขวัญ	gifts
khontho	คนโท	earthenware waterjar made and used in Northern Thailand
khrap	ครับ	polite particle spoken by men
khru	ครู	teacher
Khua Mung	ข้วมุง	commune in Saraphi district
khuba/khruba	ครูบา/ครูบา	venerated teacher (as *acan*)
khun	คุณ	you (Central Thai)
Khuntan	ขุนตาน	mountain between Lamphun and Lampang
khün	ขืน	square figure-type of Lanna Thai writing, introduced in 899 A.D.
khwan	ขวัญ	spirit (often responsible for one's well-being)
kin salak	กิ๋นสลาก	mass merit-making ceremony
krap	กราบ	to prostrate oneself
Krungthep	กรุงเทพฯ	"City of Angels," Bangkok
kuson	กุศล	merit, good deeds
kuti	กุฎิ	hut or living quarters for monks
lap	ลาบ	a North/Northeastern Thai dish of raw, pickled meat
lakhon	ละคร	a type of Thai classical drama
lamyai	ลำไย	longan (*Dimorcarpus longan*), a sweet tropical fruit
Lampang	ลำปาง	name of city and province in Northern Thailand
Lamphun	ลำพูน	name of city and province in Northern Thailand
Langkawong	ลังกาวงศ์	a type of Buddhism brought to Chiang Mai in the 14th century
Lanna Thai	ล้านนาไทย	name of former Northern Thai kingdom, also the name of the Northern Thai language, sometimes erroneously referred to as "Lao"
like	ลิเก	a popular type of Thai musical production
linci	ลิ้นจี่	lychee (*Litchi chinensis*)
Loi Krathong	ลอยกระทง	"Festival of Floating Lights"
lok	โลก	world

luang	หลวง	great, royal; a title formerly bestowed on deserving citizens
Luang Pu Wæn Sucinno	หลวงปู่แหวน สุจิณโณ	famous monk who lived north of Chiang Mai
lung	ลุง	uncle
mæ	แม่	mother
Mæ Fæk	แม่แฝก	site of irrigation dam north of the city of Chiang Mai
mæ kœt	แม่กิด	"birth-mother" in the spirit world
Mæ Kuang	แม่กวง	tributary of the Mæ Ping River
Mæ Phosop	แม่โพสพ	the spirit of rice planting
Mæ Ping	แม่ปิง	main river flowing through the Chiang Mai Valley
Mæ Rim	แม่ริม	district north of Chiang Mai city
Maha Chat	มหาชาติ	"The Great Life," most important of Jataka stories, the Maha Vessantara Jataka
mai kam	ไม้กรรม	three pieces of wood used in the long-life ceremony
mai talæo	ไม้ตาแหลว	woven bamboo charm placed in newly-seeded rice fields
Makha Bucha	มาฆะบูชา	Magha pūjā (P.), worship on the full-moon day of the third lunar month in commemoration of the great assembly of disciples
malæng mao	แมลงเม่า	a kind of insect
Man	มาร	Mara, the devil or temptress
manut	มนุษย์	people, human beings, mankind
manut lok	มนุษย์โลก	one of the three Buddhist worlds
Matcurat	มัจจุราช	name of the King of Death
mathayom	มัธยม	secondary school
Mengrai	พญามังราย	King of Chiang Mai (1239-1317/1323 A.D.)
miang	เมี่ยง	fermented tea leaves used for chewing as a stimulant in Northern Thailand
Minburi	มีนบุรี	former (1953) district north of Bangkok, now a borough of the city
m o	หมอ	doctor
mo chit ya	หมอฉีดยา	"injection doctor"

mo du	หมอดู	astrologer, fortune-teller
Mongkut	มงกุฎ	name for Rama IV (1851-1868)
m u	หมู่	group
mu ban	หมู่บ้าน	hamlet, village
nai	นาย	mister; master, boss
nai amphœ	นายอำเภอ	district headman
nak	นาค	serpent
nakhon	นคร	*nagara* (P.), city
Nakhon Pathom	นครปฐม	city and province SE of Bangkok
Nakhon Ratchasima (Korat)	นครราชสีมา	city and province NE of Bangkok
Nakhon Si Thammarat	นครศรีธรรมราช	city and province in S Thailand
naktham	นักธรรม	Buddhist studies
nan	หนาน	title used for ex-monks
nang	นาง	Mrs. (also Lanna Thai, Miss)
narok	นรก	hell
Neranchara	เนรัญชรา	other name for Yamuna River
ngœn	เงิน	silver
nipphan	นิพพาน	nirvana, the goal of Buddhism
noi	น้อย	small (amount); title for ex-novices (Lanna Thai)
Nong Fæk	หนองแฝก	commune in Saraphi district (see map 2)
Nong Si Cæng	หนองสีแจ่ง	village in Nong Fæk commune
pa	ป่า	forest, jungle
Pa Dua	ป่าเดือ	village near Ku Dæng
Pa Kong	ป่ากอง	village near Ku Dæng along the Lamphun-Chiang Mai Highway
panya	ปัญญา	wisdom, intelligence
Panyanantha	ปัญญานันทะ	name of Buddhist monk in charge of the Buddhist Association of Chiang Mai (1953)
parinipphan	ปรินิพพาน	the death of the Buddha
pathom	ปฐม	primary (school)
pha	ผ้า	cloth
pha bangsukun	ผ้าบังสุกุล	cloth draped over a coffin to be given to priests

Pha Cao	พะเจ้า	the Lord (Buddha) (Lanna Thai)
pha congkraben	ผ้าโจงกะเบน	traditional Central Thai "trousers"
phæt	แพทย์	medicine, doctor
phahusut	พหูสูตร	a priest who knows the Buddhist suttas well
phakhaoma	ผ้าขาวม้า	all-purpose, wide loin cloth
phansa	พรรษา	rains retreat, "Buddhist Lent"
phante	ภันเต	honored teacher
phasin	ผ้าซิ่น	sarong for women
phatoi	ผ้าด้อย	pantaloons worn by novice-to-be in procession prior to ordination
phawana	ภาวนา	*bhāvanā* (P.), meditation
pho	พ่อ	father
phokœt	พ่อเกิด	"birth-father" in the spirit world
phi	ผี	spirit, ghost
phi mabong	ผีม้าบ้อง	ghost of a horse
phi puya	ผีปู่ย่า	ancestor spirits
Phibun Songkram	พิบูลสงคราม	name of the prime minister and field marshal (1953)
phika	ผีกะ	a kind of spirit that may possess a person
phiksu	ภิกษุ	*bhikkhu* (P.), a Buddhist monk
phiksuni	ภิกษุณี	see *bhikkhunī* (P.), a Buddhist nun
phithi	พิธี	ceremony, ritual
phitphi	ผิดผี	sexual activity between two people of opposite sex (lit. "transgress against custom")
Phisanulok	พิษณุโลก	name of city and province in Northern Thailand
phom	ผม	first person pronoun, I (male)
phon bun	ผลบุญ	the fruits of merit
phothiyan	โพธิญาณ	the knowledge necessary to attain nirvana
phra	พระ	monk
Phra In	พระอินทร์	Indra
phrasong	พระสงฆ์	*sangha* (P.), monkhood
phra tham	พระธรรม	the Dharma, the Buddhist teachings
phra trirat (or		

292

phra ratanatri)	พระไตรรัตน์	*tiratana* (P.), the Three Jewels of Buddhism—Buddha, Sangha, and the Dhamma
phra upatcha	พระอุปัชฌาย์	*upajjhāya* (P.), ordination instructor, spiritual teacher
Phra Wet	พระเวส	see Vessantara
Phracao Luang Sethikhamfan	พระเจ้าหลวง เศรษฐีคำฝั้น	ruler of Chiang Mai, 1821 A.D.
Phræ	แพร่	name of city and province in Northern Thailand
phrom	พรหม	Brahma, brahmin
phrommalok	พรหมโลก	one of three Buddhist worlds
plongabat	ปลงอาบัติ	monks' confession of transgressions
po	ป้อ	father (Lanna Thai)
pret	เปรต	"hungry ghost" of an evil doer
Rahun	ราหุล	Rahula, son of the Buddha
rai	ไร่	2.5 rai = 1 acre
ramwong	รำวง	Thai "circle" dance
rao	เรา	we
rukkhamun	รุกขมูน	older name for a cemetery ceremony, now called *khao kam*
rupalok	รูปโลก	the world of forms; a subdivision of the Brahma world
rupaphrom	รูปพรหม	the bodily state; one of three evil states of mankind
sai ao	ใส่เอา	to accept a woman after sexual activity
sai sia	ใส่เสีย	to refuse a girl after sexual activity
sala	ศาลา	a roofed, open-sided structure for repose
salak	สลาก	lots, label
salak kinbæng	สลากกินแบ่ง	lottery
salak phat	สลากภัต	Thai for *kin salak*
Salak Phaya In	สลากพญาอินทร์	festival for Indra
sangsarawat	สังสารวัฏ	*saṁsāra* (P.), wheel of life, round of existence
Sanpasak	สันป่าสัก	smallest village in commune Nong Fæk

Santonkok	สันต้นกอก	name of a temple about three miles from Ku Dæng
satang	สตางค์	100 satang = 1 baht
sattha	ศรัทธา	devotion, faith
sawan	สวรรค์	heaven
sin	ศีล	*sīla* (P.) moral rule(s), precept(s)
sintham	ศีลธรรม	morality, moral codes
Songkran	สงกรานต์	Thai New Year in April
Sophonnathera	พระโสภณเถระ	one of two monks who introduced Buddhism into Chiang Mai in 1331 A.D.
suat	สวด	religious chant/chanting or verse
Suwannaphum	สุวรรณภูมิ	the old name for Nakon Pathom
süksathikan	ศึกษาธิการ	education commissioner
süp chata	สืบชะตา	*süp cata* (Lanna Thai), long-life ceremony
takro	ตะกร้อ	kickball game played with a small rattan ball
tambon	ตำบล	commune
tan	ต้าน	you (sing., Lanna Thai)
tang	ต๋าง	Northern Thai measure of volume, equals approx. 1.2 *thang* or 24 liters of paddy
taphon	ตะโพน	large drum in Northern Thai orchestra
Tathakhato	ตถาคะโต	*Tathagata* (P.), lit., "the thus gone one," the Lord Buddha
thæp	แถบ	an old Thai coin = 80 satang
Thakwang	ท่ากวาง	commune in Saraphi district
than	ทาน	*dāna* (P.), gifts, alms
than khao roi ho	ทานข้าวร้อยห่อ	offering of rice to beggars at Kin Salak festival
thang	ถัง	measure of volume = 20 liters
thambun	ทำบุญ	make merit
thamchua	ทำชั่ว	to do evil deeds
thamma	ธรรมะ	Dhamma, see *phra tham*
thammat	ธรรมาสน์	preaching pulpit usually found in a *wihan*
thepcao	เทพเจ้า	god(s)

thewada	เทวคา	*devatā* (P.), god(s); those in a higher realm than human beings
thewadalok	เทวคาโลก	one of the three Buddhist worlds
thewanakhari	เทวนาครี	"rounded-figure" Lanna Thai writing introduced in 788 A.D.
thong sam hang	ธงสามหาง	three-tailed flag representing the *phra trirat* or Three Jewels of Buddhism
thotkathin	ทอคกฐิน	the offering of robes to monks following the *phansa* retreat
thotphapa	ทอคผ้าป่า	"jungle cloth" ceremony
thungkhao	ถุงข้าว	sack of food placed on coffin before funeral
triam	เครียม	to prepare
truat nam	ครวคน้ำ	transferring merit by pouring water
tua liam	ตัวเหลี่ยม	see *khün*
tua pom	ตัวป้อม	see *thewanakhari*
tukkæ	ตุ๊กแก	a lizard *(Gekko verticilliatus)*
tunglek-tungtong	ถุงเหล็กถุงทอง	small gold and iron flags used at funerals
udom	ถคม	highest
ui	อุ๊ย	grandparent (Lanna Thai)
Uttarathera	พระอุคระเถระ	one of two monks who introduced Buddhism to Chiang Mai, 1131 A.D.
Vajiravudh or Wachirawut	วชิราวุธ	name of Rama VI (1910-1925 A.D.)
Vessantara	เวสสันคร	main character in the *Maha Vessantara Jataka,* the most popular jataka tale
wai	ไหว้	to put palms together as a greeting or sign of respect
wan	วัน	day
wan düan yi peng	วันเคือนยี่เป็ง	second-month full moon festival
wan pawarana	วันปวารณา	"forgiveness day" for monks
wan phra	วันพระ	Buddhist holy day, see *wan sin*
wan sin	วันศิล	(Lanna Thai) Buddhist holy day (lit., "precept day")
wat	วัค	temple

Wat Dapphai	วัดดับภัย	name of a temple in Chiang Mai
Wat Ku Süa	วัดกู่เสือ	a large temple in Saraphi district
Wat Loikhro	วัดลอยเคราะห์	name of a temple in Chiang Mai
Wat Pakæyong	วัดป่าแกยง	one of the larger temples in Saraphi
Wat Phra Nonpakethi	วัดพระนอนป่าเกธิ	temple of the reclining Buddha in Saraphi district
Wat Phra Sing	วัดพระสิงห์	one of the largest temples in Chiang Mai
wihan	วิหาร	main assembly hall in a Buddhist temple compound
winyan	วิญญาน	spirit
Wisakha Bucha	วิสาขบูชา	*Visakha pūjā* (P.), annual celebration of the Lord Buddha's birth, enlightenment, and death
ya	ยา	medicine
yai chi	ยายชี	Buddhist order of female devotees; "nuns"
yak	ยักษ์	giant
yam	ยาม	astrological tables
Yamuna	เยมุนา	Jumna River in India
yat nam	หยาดน้ำ	Lanna Thai for *truat nam*

296

Bibliography

Alabaster, Henry
1871   *The Wheel of the Law.* London: Trubner.

Anuman Rajadhon, *Phya*
1954   *"*The Phi.*" Journal of the Siam Society* 41, pp. 153-178.

1954   "The Water Throwing Festival." *Journal of the Siam Society* 42, pp. 23-30.

1955a   *A Brief Survey of Cultural Thailand,* Thailand Culture Series no. 2, third printing. Bangkok: National Culture Institute.

1955b   *Loy Krathong and Songkran Festival,* Thailand Culture Series no. 5, third printing. Bangkok: National Culture Institute.

1955c   *Chao Thi and Some Traditions of Thai,* Thailand Culture Series, no. 6, third printing. Bangkok: National Culture Institute.

Bau, David H.
1951   "Agricultural Economic Survey of Sarapee District." Food and Agricultural Organization of the United Nations. Mimeographed report.

Boon Chuey Srisavasdi
1950   *Samsip khati nai Chiang Rai* [Thirty tribes of Chiengrai]. Bangkok: Prachachon.

1963   *The Hill Tribes of Siam.* Bangkok: Khun Aroon.

1953-54 *Chaophut* [The Buddhist Citizen] (A monthly magazine issued by the Buddhist Association of Chiang Mai), vols. 1 and 2.

Coomaraswamy, Ananda K.
1914   *Buddha and the Gospel of Buddhism.* London: G. P. Putnam.

Davis, Richard B.
1984   *Muang Metaphysics.* Bangkok: Pandora Press.

deYoung, John E.
1955   *Village Life in Modern Thailand.* Berkeley: University of California Press.

Division of Central Services, Siam
1944   *Statistical Yearbook, 1939/40-1944,* no. 21. Bangkok: Thai Watana Panich.

Division of Central Services, Thailand
   Statistical Yearbook, Thailand 1945-55, no. 30. Bangkok: Central Statistical Office [and] Office of the National Economic Development Board.

Eliot, *Sir* Charles
1954   *Hinduism and Buddhism.* New York: Barnes and Noble (reissue).

Embree, John F.
1950   "Thailand—A Loosely Structured Social System." *American Anthropologist* 52, pp. 181-193.

Food and Agriculture Organization (FAO)
1951   *Agricultural Economic Survey of Sarapee District, Chiangmai Province, Thailand.* New York: United Nations Food and Agricultural Organization.

Haas, Mary R.
1945   *Spoken Thai.* New York: Holt.

Joint Thai-U.S. Task Force on Human Resource Development in Thailand
1963   *Preliminary Assessment of Education and Human Resources in Thailand.* Bangkok: Agency for International Development, USOM.

Kaufman, Howard K.
1960   *Bangkhuad: A Community Study in Thailand.* New York: Locust Valley.

1953-54 *Khon Müang* [The countryman] (A news magazine published five times monthly in Chiang Mai by Khon Müang Press), vols. 1 and 2.

Khemo, *Bhikkhu*
1935   *Phutthasatsana kü arai: kham-tham kham-top 300 prakan* [What is Buddhism?: 300 questions and answers]. Bangkok: Buddhist Association.

Kingshill, Konrad
1952   "Some Notes on Theravada Buddhism in Southeast Asia." Unpublished typescript.

1960   *Ku Dæng—The Red Tomb, A Village Study in Northern Thailand.* Chiang Mai: The Prince Royal's College.

1965   *Ku Dæng—The Red Tomb, A Village Study in Northern Thailand, A.D. 1954-1964.* 2nd edition. Bangkok: Bangkok Christian College.

1967 "The Seven Themes of Ku Dæng." In *Tribesmen and Peasants in North Thailand,* edited by Suthep Soontarapesach, pp. 29-34. Chiang Mai: The Tribal Research Center.

1976 *Ku Dæng—The Red Tomb, A Village Study in Northern Thailand, A.D. 1954-1974.* 3rd edition. Bangkok: Suriyaban Publishers.

Kittisobhanathera, *Somdet Phra* Wannarat (editor)
1951 *Suatmon chabap kromkansatsana* [Department of Religious Affairs' version of chants]. Bangkok: Religious Affairs Department.

Krai Krainiran
1953 "*Rüang thong lek læ thong thong*" [The story of the iron flag and the golden flag] *Khon Müang,* 1:50 (November 12).

Landon, Kenneth P.
1949 *Southeast Asia: Crossroads of Religion.* Chicago: The University of Chicago Press.

Lewis, Paul and Elaine Lewis
1984 *Peoples of the Golden Triangle.* London and New York: Thames & Hudson, Inc.

Ministry of Education
1962 *Teacher Survey A.D. 1962.* Bangkok: Educational Planning Office, Ministry of Education.

1966 *Current and Projected Secondary Education Programs for Thailand.* Bangkok: Educational Planning Office, Ministry of Education.

1977 *Thailand National Educational Scheme 1977.* Bangkok: Ministry of Education.

National Culture Institute
1953 *Thailand Culture Series,* vols. 1-17. Bangkok: The National Culture Institute.

Opler, Morris E.
1945 "Themes as Dynamic Forces in Culture." *American Journal of Sociology* 51:3, pp. 198-206.

Panyanantha, *Bhikkhu*
1953 *Khamtham-khamtop* [Questions and answers (regarding the Lord Buddha)]. Chiang Mai: Buddhist Association.

Penth, Hans
1983   *Prawat khwampenma khong Lan Na Thai.* Chiang Mai: Social
        Science Research Center, Chiang Mai University.

Phon Rattanasuwan
1952   *Kanson phutthasatsana to dek prathom 1-4* [Teaching Buddhism
        to elementary school children, prathom 1-4]. Chiang Mai:
        Buddhist Association.

Photcananukrom   chabap   ratchabandit-sathan [Royal Institute
Dictionary]. Bangkok: Aksorn Charœnthasana, 1950 and 1982.

Phutthasatsana kap tuathan [Buddhism and you]. Thonburi: Buddhist
Association, 1953.

Phillips, Herbert P.
1965   *Thai Peasant Personality.* Berkeley: University of California
        Press.

Plang Phloyphrom and Robert T. Golden
1955   *Pru's Standard Dictionary* (Thai-English Dictionary). Bangkok:
        Thai Watana Panich.

Potter, Jack M.
1976   *Thai Peasant Social Structure.* Chicago: The University of
        Chicago Press.

Potter, Sulamith Heins
1977   *Family Life in a Northern Thai Village.* Berkeley: University of
        California Press.

Prachakit Koracak, *Phya* (translator)
1907   *Rüang Yanok* [The story of the Yanok] (a translation from Lanna
        Thai into Thai). Bangkok: Buddhist Association.

Royal College of King Chulalongkorn
1954   *Bæp thamwat chao-yen* [A guide to morning and evening devo-
        tions]. Bangkok: Wat Mahathat.

Santhat Sermsri
1986   *Impacts of Rapid Urbanization on Health Status in Thailand.*
        Technical Paper no. 1. Tokyo: Second Asian Conference on
        Health and Medical Sociology.

Sharp, Lauriston, H. Hauck, K. Janlekha, and R. Textor
1953   *Siamese Rice Village, A Preliminary Study of Bang Chan, 1948-
        1949.* Bangkok: Cornell Research Center.

Sharp, Lauriston and Lucien M. Hanks
1978   *Bang Chan: Social History of a Rural Community in Thailand.*
        Ithaca: Cornell University Press.

Sommai Premchit
1975   *A List of Old Temples and Religious Sects in Chiengmai.* Chiang
        Mai: Chiang Mai University.

Thammanantha Bhikkhu
1953   *Krai kha khrai næ* [Who really kills whom?]. Chiang Mai:
        Buddhist Association.

Thammathat Phanit (editor)
1952   *Phutthasatsana* [Buddhism (twenty-year anniversary volume)].
        Chaiya, Suratthani: Buddhist Association.

Thawit Plengwitthaya, *Major*
1972   *Khop-tham* (An ecclesiastical encyclopedia). Bangkok: Buddhist
        Association.

Thomas, E. J.
1952   *The Life of Buddha* (reissue). New York: Knopf.

Thompson, W. J. S.
1951   "Integration of a Mission School System in Thailand," typescript.

Terwiel, B. J.
1975   *Monks and Magic: An Analysis of Religious Ceremonies in
        Central Thailand,* Scandinavian Institute of Asian Studies
        Monograph Series no. 24. London and Bangkok: Scandinavian
        Institute of Asian Studies.

Tylor, Edward B.
1871   *Primitive Culture.* New York: Brentano.

UNESCO (United Nations Educational, Scientific, and Cultural
        Organization)
1950   *Report of the Mission to Thailand.* Paris: United Nations.

Viriya, Malee
1985   *Kanplian-plæng khong kanlalen khong dek Thai phak nüa* [A
        case study of recreational activities of children in Northern
        Thailand (Ku Dæng)]. Bangkok: Sri Nakharinwirot University
        Press.

Wells, Kenneth E.
1939   *Thai Buddhism: Its Rites and Activities.* Bangkok: Church of
        Christ in Thailand.

Werasit Sittitrai
1985   "Rural Transformation in Two Northern Thai Villages." Ph.D. dissertation, University of Hawaii.

Wijeyewardene, Gehan
1967   "Some Aspects of Rural Life in Thailand." In *Thailand: Social and Economic Studies in Development,* edited by T. H. Silcock. Durham: University of North Carolina Press.

Wyatt, David
1984   *Thailand: A Short History.* New Haven: Yale University Press.

Index

administration
  educational 65
  northern states, of the 14
  village 92, 107
afterbirth 198
agnostic 178
akuson 126, 131
alcohol 56
alms 133
American Mutual Security Administration (MSA) 10, 16, 95, 247
amphœ 13, 93, 94, 108, 237
  schools 64, 69
ancestors 216
  spirits of 189
angel 163, 166
anger 166, 173
animism 188-189
anisong 182 (also see "merit-making")
antagonism 247
arahan 153
architecture
  temple 109, 118
astrology 148, 251
Ayutthaya 85, 244

baby 20, 59, 86, 197, 198-199, 207
  "fever" 154
  girls 86
ballot 102
banana 32, 37, 138, 170, 204
  leaves *(bai tong)* 29, 156, 204, 226
  stalks 45
beggar 134, 167, 197, 226
bell
  temple 210, 217
betel 56, 57, 117, 156, 165, 167, 170, 178, 196, 200, 201, 206, 223
bhikkhuni 84
bicycle 4, 13, 24, 47, 48, 70, 75, 139, 151, 239, 241, 248
birth 126, 150, 151, 153, 154, 158, 198, 200, 208
  Lord Buddha's 209
  registration 94
  tenth life of the Buddha 228
birth-father 159
birth-mother 159
birthmarks 86

birthrate 19
blacksmith 118, 163
bot 86, 111, 112, 115, 142, 220, 223
bowl
    monk's 165, 167
    rice 213
    silver 161, 202, 205, 217
Brahma 195, 211, 220
Brahmanism 158, 180, 181, 183, 188, 200, 233, 251
Brahmin 229
bride 51, 53, 54, 102, 202
    bride's family 201, 203
    bride's home 201, 202
    brideprice 53
bridegroom 53, 201
bronze 103, 110
Buddha 9, 46, 68, 110, 112-113, 114, 116, 117, 118, 119, 123, 127, 128, 133, 135,
        138, 140, 145, 146, 153, 162, 163, 165, 167, 173, 174, 181, 182, 193, 194,
        195, 196, 201, 211, 212, 214, 220, 222, 227, 232
    97 proverbs of 126
    birth stories 119
    birth, death and enlightenment 219
    birth, death, and enlightenment 209
    establishing order of nuns 84
    fifth life of 178
    footprints 240
    image 77, 87, 101, 103, 109, 110, 118, 121, 124, 127, 140, 144, 145, 172, 179,
        180, 195, 197, 205, 210, 213, 214, 216, 217, 219, 221, 223, 225
    reason for veneration 128
    relics 112
    shelf 196, 204
    son of 140
    tenth life of 228-230
    tomb of 110
buffalo 7, 8, 21, 25, 27, 30, 33, 40, 41, 44, 94, 100, 108, 139, 154, 185, 224, 251
    dung 37
bullock 25, 30, 40, 44, 251
Burmese 12
    border 12
    Buddhism 86, 112, 115
    dress and custom 138, 236
    medicine 198
    precious stones 110
    suzerainty 86, 115
butchery 45, 100, 116

cabbage 5, 16, 41
calendar
    Gregorian 215

lunar 215, 222
    religious 196, 209-233
    solar 215, 219
canal 10, 15, 16, 24, 26, 27, 29, 33, 35, 82, 84, 89, 97, 98, 99, 228
cangwat 12
carpenter 49, 111, 144, 162
cat 55, 117, 163
    dead cat 46, 163
cedi 14, 110-112, 216, 220, 221
cemetery 165, 166, 167, 169, 174, 176
    ceremony 209, 232-233
census 17, 18, 20, 21, 24, 26, 29, 51, 74, 93, 130, 203
charity 166, 167
chicken 194
childbirth 198-199
childhood 10, 58, 108, 126
Chinese 32, 49, 110, 116, 247
    lanterns 231
    lychee fruit 32
    medicine 148, 184
    noodles 139
    soldiers 242
Christianity 3, 108, 134, 195
cigarette 138, 164, 170, 172, 178, 180, 196
    lighter 5, 104, 105, 175
clinic 157
coconut 32, 49, 108, 141, 142, 165, 170, 171, 174, 175, 181, 200, 201, 204, 225
coffin 162, 163, 164, 165, 166, 167, 168, 169, 170, 172, 174, 175, 177
coming-of-age 199
commune 13, 14, 15, 17, 20, 23, 27, 36, 78, 90, 91, 92, 93, 100, 102, 155, 156, 157,
    218, 219, 237 (also see *"tambon"*)
    council 105, 107
    division into 89
    law and order 96
    leader 101, 102
    taxation 93, 151
communism 245, 246, 247
conch shell 216
cooperation 3, 10, 22, 31, 38, 74, 82, 104, 155, 250
    lack of 39, 243
cooperative 25, 106
corpse 101, 162, 163, 165, 171, 174, 175, 176, 177
    customs dealing with 164-170
courtship 21, 42, 53-54
creator 112
cremation 148, 162, 165, 167, 168, 169, 170, 171, 174, 175, 176, 177

dance 171
    spirit 191-192

death 101, 134, 136, 184, 190, 194, 199, 208, 237, 238
    Buddhist views towards 153-182
    Lord Buddha's 209, 219
    of an animal 45
democracy 246
dengue fever 20
devil 166, 211
diarrhea 20
dike 97, 100
discipline 101
    at Ku Dæng Temple 144
dog 46, 208
    magic 231
drugs 157, 158
    proper use of 106
drum 49, 111, 151, 152, 162, 195, 219, 221, 223, 224, 225, 232

earthenware 46, 49, 103, 138, 176
ecclesiastical
    Ecclesiastical Organization 14, 122
    Ministry of Ecclesiastical Affairs 60
    office 147
    organization 188
education 8, 60-79, 88, 101, 121, 143, 147, 157, 188, 235, 243, 245, 248, 250-251
    compulsory 59
    founder of modern education 102
    of novices 130, 150
    temple as center for 108
elders 78, 80, 172, 180, 190, 197, 205, 210, 213, 214, 216, 222
    temple 22
    village 3
election 109, 251
    village officials 90-93
electricity 28, 48, 57
elephant 14, 139, 158, 187, 195, 224, 229
emigration 18, 21, 22, 23, 24, 249, 250
employment 3, 23, 241
endogamy 52
environment 84, 104
    of research setting 12-28
epidemic 3, 18-20
ethics 119
    Buddhist 136
etiquette 80
evil 10, 11, 14, 117, 121, 124, 126, 131, 132, 135, 136, 153, 158, 160, 166, 168, 181,
        182, 185, 186, 190, 191, 195, 196, 205, 213, 214, 217, 236
ex-monk 125, 133, 143, 149, 150, 154, 171, 172, 177, 180, 184, 204, 210, 213, 239
ex-novice 125, 135, 172, 210, 213
exogamous marriages 52

exorcism 190

family
    bride's 201
    consumption 35
    destitute 134
    duty 68
    extended 80
    festivities 178, 190
    husband's 198
    kinship terminology 82
    labor 38
    merit 8
    Mr. Khieo's 154, 161, 174, 176
    nuclear 250
    planning 17, 20, 74, 82, 250
    royal 112, 176
    sickness in 21
    size 17
    spirits 189
    structure 6, 51-59, 250
    wife's 198
FAO 16, 17, 21, 25
fertilizer 8, 16, 23, 39, 44, 46, 174, 251
fish 5, 16, 29, 33, 34, 35, 37, 58, 59, 78, 94, 97, 104, 105, 116, 117, 216, 225
    catfish 35
    dried 55, 199
    fisherwomen 34
    releasing 186
    tilapia 95, 247
flag 47
    black 186
    golden and iron 163, 164
    one thousand 186
    raising ceremony 76
    small 216
    three-cornered 30
    three-tailed 162, 165, 167, 174, 186
    white 184, 186, 200
    yellow 186
flood 3, 29, 33, 39, 97, 134
foreigner 1, 3, 39, 164, 171, 240, 244, 247

gambling 96, 97, 170, 172
garlic 5, 24, 41, 48, 57
generosity 25, 230
ghost 135, 155, 156, 162, 171, 176, 178, 179, 180, 194, 195, 233, 251
    land of 160
    monk's 189

giant 173, 195
god 160, 162, 180, 190, 194, 195, 196, 197, 198, 200, 204, 211, 220, 223, 229, 231, 233
   Buddhist affirmation of 195
   Indra, head of 229
gold 150, 164, 165, 166, 208
   gold leaf 110, 164
   Mr. Gold 207
Governor 65
   appointment of 88
   people's knowledge of 244

hamlet
   as subdivision of commune *(tambon)* 89
   leadership 88, 90
   two of Ku Dæng 14
   total taxable land 26
handbook, monk's 125, 160, 184, 204
handicraft 17, 111
harvest 7, 9, 16, 24, 25, 29, 31, 33, 36, 38, 39, 40, 41, 42, 43, 44, 46, 56, 93, 95, 100, 117, 133, 169, 182, 216, 217, 224, 228
head monk
   biography of Ku Dæng Temple leader 150-152
   prestige of 5, 92
headman
   definition 91-93
healer 5, 11, 147, 156, 158, 160, 184, 235
heaven 86, 153, 154, 167, 194, 195, 220, 231
hell 153, 154, 166, 178, 194
hierarchy
   Buddhist 219
   temple 223
Hindu
   Hindu-Buddhist tradition 216
   mythology 216
   practices 188
ho thamma 111, 116, 119, 151
hospital 20, 21, 54, 109, 155, 156, 157, 159, 184, 191, 199
hospitality 56, 57, 247
house-blessing 80, 87, 134, 185, 203-207
house-building 203, 218

immigration 247
   through marriage 21
incantation 5, 29
income 25, 29, 47, 49, 50, 69, 104, 105
   for a doctor 23
   for teachers 47
   from land taxes 93

from lychee 32
from produce 17
temple income from festivals 227
Indian 49, 84, 108, 116, 139, 247
    monks 238
Indra 195, 196, 197, 229, 230
industry 49, 105
    agriculturally-oriented 64
    as tourist attraction 5
    cottage 5
    home 48-50
influenza 19
injection 109
    doctor 11, 23, 156, 159, 160, 184
insecticide 188
intercourse
    between husband and wife 174
    premarital 54
Islam 108

Japanese
    occupation 45, 100
Jataka 113, 119, 228
    Vessantara 228-230

kathin 209, 227
khatha 158, 189, 192, 198, 230
King 68, 112, 122, 140, 173, 195, 220, 244, 245, 246, 247
    Cao Küna 238
    Chulalongkorn, Rama V 12, 14, 60, 78, 102
    Mengrai 13, 16
    Mongkut, Rama IV 12
    of Chiang Mai 12, 150
    of the gods 231
    Phra Cao Luang Setthi Khampan 230
    Ramkhamhæng 60
    Vajiravudh, Rama VI 78
kinship terms 57, 82, 83, see appendix D
Kukrit Pramoj 102
kuson 131, 179, 213
kuti 111, 144

labor 6, 7, 9, 10, 17, 22, 23, 24, 31, 36, 38, 39, 42, 44, 45, 46, 63, 79, 82, 87, 100, 155,
    224, 249
    animal 8, 23
    childbirth 198
    children as part of labor force 55
lakhon 139, 242
Lampang 12, 19, 49, 151, 241

Lamphun 2, 3, 13, 14, 16, 19, 24, 27, 40, 47, 86, 109, 112, 115, 130, 133, 151, 156,
    218, 239, 241, 243
lamyai 17, 29, 31, 32, 46, 105, 251
landowner 22, 27
leprosy 226
liquor 96, 97, 117, 139, 169, 170, 192, 202, 207
literacy 60, 78
livestock 28, 93, 100, 241
Loi Krathong 209
lottery 47, 50, 103, 240, 242
lustral water 98, 168, 205, 218

magic 231
Makha Bucha 209
Malaria 17, 18, 19, 20, 23, 55, 117, 184
marriage 6, 21, 51, 52, 53-54, 58, 199, 208, 218
    ceremonies 201-203
matriarchy 55
matrilineal 83
matrilocal 51
meat 17, 45, 46, 48, 50, 100, 116, 169, 170, 173
    crab 35
meditation 126, 142, 166, 224, 232-233
medicine 5, 11, 49, 55, 106, 109, 147, 156, 157, 158, 160, 161, 184, 193, 198, 199,
    207, 235
    "foreign" 156
    Chinese 148, 184
    Faculty of, Chiang Mai University 72
    for malaria 20
    traditional 156
mediums 85, 190, 191-192
Mengrai 13, 16
merit-making 9, 119, 131, 134, 137, 145, 148, 169, 177, 181-182, 202, 209, 228,
    230, 251
    festival 224-227
miang 138, 170, 172
Middle Way 166
midwife 24, 54, 198, 207
milk 225
monarchy 12, 246, 247
    constitutional 88
mortality 18, 55
mosquito 19, 117
    net 161
motorcycle 8, 28, 47, 48, 241, 251
movie 139, 238, 241
    from USIS 137, 141
    idols 236
muban 14

music 114, 120, 138, 206, 242
Mæ Rim 23, 24

nai amphœ 88, 90, 91, 92, 93, 95, 107, 150
    appointment of 88
nan 149
newspapers 47, 110, 120, 163, 242, 247
nipphan 127, 166, 167, 173, 196, 211, 213, 219, 229
    definition of 153-154
    pari- 211
noi 149
Nong Fæk 13, 14, 15, 36, 89, 92, 93, 97, 102, 134, 139, 140, 150, 152, 154, 155, 156, 157, 219, 221, 223
nun 84

ordination 86, 130
    of a novice 109, 122, 137-144, 150, 219
ownership
    land 27
    of land 24

Pali 60, 85, 114, 121, 127, 128, 129, 145, 150, 154, 156, 159, 180, 196, 211, 215, 220, 224, 230
palm-leaf 119
patriarchy 55
patrilineal 83
patrilocal 51
patriotism 122
Payap University 69
peanuts 16, 24, 33, 41, 42-43, 57, 95, 104, 170, 175
peppers 37, 41, 56
phansa 110, 111, 114, 222
phi 135, 153, 156, 160, 179, 180, 189, 196, 198
Phibun Songkram 244
plowing 7, 8, 17, 23, 30, 31, 40, 44, 118, 249
    ceremony 30
pneumonia 19
police 35, 89, 90, 97, 241
pork 116, 169, 170, 199
Precept Day 75, 110, 111, 114, 116, 118, 120, 122, 123, 124, 125, 127, 134, 145, 146, 169, 172, 177, 189, 196, 219, 222, 227, 228, 242
precepts 85, 86, 110, 113, 114, 125, 126, 130, 163, 217
    as perceived in Ku Dæng 116-118
    eight 114, 145, 223
    five 77, 113, 128, 134, 140, 144, 145, 172, 180, 197, 206, 213, 225
    monk's 84, 85, 126, 140, 143, 145, 149, 150, 223
    ten 114, 140, 141, 143
prejudice 166
prison 98

productivity 23, 44, 48
of land 16, 39
profit 7-10, 21, 23, 28, 31, 33, 35, 42, 45, 48, 49, 50, 54, 55, 62, 104, 105, 106, 136, 157, 208, 235
Propaganda 245, 246
property 6, 21, 25, 46, 47, 48, 55, 57-58, 140, 141, 146, 155, 157, 174, 179, 186, 187, 203
common 35
giving up 145
loss of 136
private 117
temple 129
propitiation 188, 190, 208
of spirits 5, 11, 85, 194
proverb 126, 135
punishment 11, 96, 97, 121, 136, 153, 178, 190
pyre 167, 175

quarreling 55, 96

radio 15, 28, 47, 145, 171, 242, 251
rebirth 119, 153, 154, 174, 179
relic 112
rice 5, 6, 7, 9, 13, 15, 16, 17, 23, 24, 25, 29, 33, 35, 36, 37, 38, 39, 40, 41, 42, 43, 46, 48, 50, 55, 56, 93, 97, 99, 100, 108, 117, 118, 123, 133, 134, 137, 142, 143, 154, 158, 163, 164, 165, 167, 169, 174, 177, 182, 183, 186, 187, 188, 199, 200, 204, 207, 210, 213, 214, 216, 222, 224, 225, 226, 228, 231, 248, 251
"black" 36, 38
baskets 49
bran 45
glutinous 35, 36, 37, 178, 207, 210
liquor 170
milling 23
mills 118, 152, 248
popped 163, 196, 200, 210, 218, 220
Rice Sprouting Ceremony 30
Rice-Sprouting Ceremony 31
mill 91
surplus 146
three-month rice 36

sala 80, 111, 115, 123, 140, 144, 196, 210, 222, 225, 231
shaman 5, 156, 160, 190
shopkeeper 48, 170
shrine
house 113, 160, 196
silver 53, 151, 164, 165, 166, 208
Mr. Silver 207
sin 117, 118, 143, 167, 212

Songkran 102, 191, 209, 215-219
soybeans 16, 24, 40, 41, 42, 104
spirit 30, 85, 113, 158, 168, 173, 178, 183, 189, 198, 205, 217, 227, 231
    belief 189-197
    communication with 11
    healer 235
    land 179
    of rice planting 30
    of the dead 153, 162, 163, 173, 174, 176, 179, 181
State Railway of Thailand 13, 19
sugarcane 225

taboo 113, 191
tambon
    as subdivision of district 89
tattoo 236-237
tax 26, 66, 93-94, 122, 151
    exemption 91
    inheritance 58
    rice 39
tea 37, 48, 161, 170, 237
teacher
    teachers' day 77
teachers 47, 60, 68, 69, 71, 72, 75, 76, 78, 89, 102, 127, 128, 157, 213, 239
    teachers' day 77
teak 6, 49, 102, 171, 175, 203
television 28, 47, 48, 251
thewada 109, 111, 160, 162, 180, 194, 195, 204, 211, 223, 229, 231
tiger 14
    year of the 215
tobacco 7, 16, 24, 33, 37, 40, 41, 42, 55, 92, 138, 156
toilet 22, 53, 249
tomb 176
    of Lord Buddha 110, 112
    red tomb, *ku dæng* 14
topknot cutting ceremony 199
tractor 7, 23, 40, 44, 46, 249, 251
trader 25, 108, 151, 247
transportation 48, 50, 72, 74, 78, 79, 84, 139, 151, 240, 241, 251
travel 31, 49, 111, 120, 129, 151, 152, 203, 222, 224, 237, 239-242, 248
    traveling salesmen 8, 48, 184, 207
truat nam 180, 186

ultimogeniture 58
UNESCO 63, 65, 68
UNICEF 17, 102, 198
USIS 137, 141, 248

vegetables 5, 16, 17, 24, 41, 42, 48, 199, 206, 241

vitamins 45

wai 127, 159, 179, 180, 210, 211
   wan wai khru 77
watershovel 16
WHO 17, 184
widow 20, 51, 54
   Mr. Khieo's 176, 178
widower 54
winyan 153, 158, 160, 162, 163, 173, 176, 181, 189, 195
Wisakha Bucha 209, 219-222

CENTER FOR SOUTHEAST ASIAN STUDIES PUBLICATIONS

MONOGRAPH SERIES

Occasional Paper Series

#15—Michael Aung-Thwin. *Irrigation in the Heartland of Burma: Foundations of the Pre-Colonial Burmese State.* 1990. 76pp. Maps and chart. $8.00

#14—Susan D. Russell, editor. *Ritual, Power, and Economy: Upland-Lowland Contrasts in Mainland Southeast Asia.* 1989. 143pp. $10.00

#13—E. Paul Durrenberger. *Lisu Religion.* 1989. 44pp. Figures. $7.00

#12—Raymond Lee, editor. *Ethnicity and Ethnic Relations in Malaysia.* 1986. 178pp. Bibliography. $15.00

#11—John A. Lent and Kent Mulliner, editors. *Malaysian Studies: Archaeology, Historiography, Geography, and Bibliography.* 1985. 235pp. Bibliographies. $14.00

#10—Lawrence F. Ashmun. *Resettlement of Indochinese Refugees in the United States: A Selective and Annotated Bibliography.* 1983. 207pp. Indices (DAI; ERIC; RMC; subject). $14.00

#9—Penny Van Esterik, editor. *Women of Southeast Asia.* 1982. 279pp. Tables, figures, appendix, bibliography, index. **(Out of Print)**

#8—Donn V. Hart, editor. *Philippine Studies: Political Science, Economics, and Linguistics.* 1981. 285pp. Bibliographies, index. $14.00

#7—John A. Lent, editor. *Malaysian Studies: Present Knowledge and Research Trends.* 1979. 466pp. Charts, tables, bibliographies. **(Out of Print)**

#6—Donn V. Hart, editor. *Philippine Studies: History, Sociology, Mass Media and Bibliography.* 1978. 402pp. Charts, graphs, bibliographies, index. **(Out of Print)**

#5—Donn V. Hart. *Thailand: An Annotated Bibliography of Bibliographies.* 1977. 96pp. Index. **(Out of Print)**

#4—Donn V. Hart. *An Annotated Bibliography of Philippine Bibliographies, 1965-1974.* 1974. 158pp. Index. $7.50

#3—Gerald S. Marynov. *The Condition of Southeast Asian Studies in the United States: 1972.* In cooperation with the Southeast Asian

Regional Council, The Association of Asian Studies. 1974. 68pp. Tables, bibliography. **(Out of Print)**

#2—Ronald L. Krannich, Herbert J. Rubin, Pratya Vesarach, and Chakrapand Wongburanavart. *Urbanization in Thailand.* Center for Governmental Studies, Northern Illinois University. 1974. 116pp. Bibliographies. **(Out of Print)**

#1—David W. Dellinger, editor. *Language, Literature, and Society: Working Papers from the 1973 Conference of American Council of Teachers of Uncommonly-Taught Asian Languages.* 1974. 85pp. Tables, charts. **(Out of Print)**

Special Report Series

#25—Robert J. Bickner, *An Introduction to the Thai Poem "Lilit Phra Law" (The Story of King Law).* 1991. 265pp. Charts. $14.00

#24—Robert Wessing. *The Soul of Ambiguity: The Tiger in Southeast Asia.* 1986. 148pp. Bibliography. $9.50

#23—Phil Scanlon, Jr. *Southeast Asia: A Cultural Study through Celebration.* 1985. 185pp. Photographs, index. $14.00

#22—David Hicks. *A Maternal Religion: The Role of Women in Tetum Myth and Ritual.* 1984. 146pp. Index, photographs. **(Out of Print)**

#21—Theodora Helene Bofman. *The Poetics of the Ramakian.* 1984. 258pp. Appendices, bibliography. $15.00

#20—Dwight Y. King. *Interest Groups and Political Linkage in Indonesia, 1800-1965.* 1982. 187pp. Bibliography, index. $12.50

#19—Robert J. Morais. *Social Relations in a Philippine Town.* 1981. 151pp. Tables, photographs, bibliography, index. $11.00

#18—Carol J. Compton. *Courting Poetry in Laos: A Textual and Linguistic Analysis.* 1979. 257pp. Photographs, charts, appendices, bibliography. **(Out of Print)**

#17—John B. Haseman. *The Thai Resistance Movement During the Second World War.* 1978. 192pp. Maps, charts, tables, bibliography, index. **(Out of Print)**

#16—George Vinal Smith. *The Dutch in Seventeenth Century Thailand.* 1977. 203pp. Maps, charts, tables, glossary, appendices, bibliography, index. **(Out of Print)**

#15—Michael M. Calavan. *Decisions Against Nature: An Anthropological Study of Agriculture in Northern Thailand.* 1977. 210pp. Maps, illustrations, charts, tables, bibliography, index. **(Out of Print)**

#14—John A. Lent, editor. *Cultural Pluralism in Malaysia: Polity, Military, Mass Media, Education, Religion and Social Class.* 1977. 114pp. Charts, tables, bibliography, index. **(Out of Print)**

#13—Douglas E. Foley. *Philippine Rural Education: An Anthropological Perspective.* 1976. 114pp. Table, bibliography, index. **(Out of Print)**

#12—G. N. Appell, editor. *Studies in Borneo Societies: Social Process and Anthropological Explanation.* 1976. 158pp. Maps, bibliography, index. **(Out of Print)**

#11—Howard M. Leichter. *Political Regime and Public Policy in the Philippines: A Comparison of Bacolod and Iloilo Cities.* 1975. 163pp. Bibliography, maps, charts, table, index. $4.00

#10—Fredrik Wernstedt, Wilhelm Solheim II, Lee Sechrest, George Guthrie, and Leonard Casper. *Philippine Studies: Geography, Archaeology, Psychology, and Literature: Present Knowledge and Research Trends.* 1974. 113pp. Annotated bibliography, index. **(Out of Print)**

#9—Harry Aveling. *A Thematic History of Indonesian Poetry: 1920-1974.* 1974. 90pp. Selected bibliography. **(Out of Print)**

#8—Herbert J. Rubin. *The Dynamics of Development in Rural Thailand.* 1974. 159pp. Maps, charts, tables. **(Out of Print)**

#7—Carl H. Landé with the assistance of Shirley Advincula, Augusto Ferreros, and James Frane. *Southern Tagalog Voting, 1946-1963: Political Behavior in a Philippine Region.* 1973. 159pp. Bibliography, index, maps. $4.00

#6—Richard L. Stone. *Philippine Urbanization: The Politics of Public and Private Property in Greater Manila.* 1973. 149pp. Bibliography, appendices. **(Out of Print)**

#5—David H. de Queljoe. *A Preliminary Study of Some Phonetic Features of Pentani, with Glossaries.* 1971. 114pp. Glossary. **(Out of Print)**

#4—Clark D. Neher. *Rural Thai Government: The Politics of the Budgetary Process.* 1970. 60pp. **(Out of Print)**

#3—Chan Ansuchote. *The 1969 General Elections in Thailand.* 1970. 44pp. **(Out of Print)**

#2—David H. de Queljoe. *A Preliminary Study of Malay/Indonesian Orthography.* 1969. 91pp. Bibliography. **(Out of Print)**

#1—J. A. Niels Mulder. *Monks, Merit, and Motivation: Buddhism and National Development in Thailand.* Second (revised and enlarged) edition. 1973. 58pp. (*Monks, Merit, and Motivation: An Exploratory Study of the Social Functions of Buddhism in Thailand in Processes of Guided Social Change.* 1961. 43pp.) **(Out of Print)**

Other Center Publications:

Donn V. Hart, compiler. *Theses and Dissertations on Southeast Asia Presented at Northern Illinois University, 1960-1980: An Annotated Bibliography.* Bibliographical Publication no. 6, 1980. 33pp. $4.00

Richard M. Cooler. *British Romantic Views of the First Anglo-Burmese War, 1824-1826.* 1977. 41pp. $4.00

The Twenty-fifth Anniversary of the Center for Southeast Asian Studies, Northern Illinois University, DeKalb, Illinois. 1988. 40pp. $2.00

For information and order forms, contact the

Publications Program
Center for Southeast Asian Studies
140 Carroll Ave.
Northern Illinois University
DeKalb, IL 60115 USA

Crossroads
An Interdisciplinary Journal of Southeast Asian Studies

Volume 1, #1	Philippine Studies—Topical Issue **(Out of Print)**
Volume 1, #2	General Issue **(Out of Print)**
Volume 1, #3	Southeast Asian Studies and International Business **(Out of Print)**
Volume 2, #1	General Issue **(Out of Print)**
Volume 2, #2	Two Hundred Years of the Chakri Dynasty **(Out of Print)**
Volume 2, #3	General Issue
Volume 3, #1	Seven Hundred Years of Thai Writing
Volume 3, #2-3	General Issue
Volume 4, #1	Special Burma Issue **(Out of Print))**
Volume 4, #2	Special Thai Issue (Part One) ($8 for non-subscribers)
Volume 5, #1	Special Thai Issue (Part Two) ($8 for non-subscribers)
Volume 5, #2	General Issue ($8 for non-subscribers)
Volume 6, #1	Modern Malaysian Music ($8 for non-subscribers)

Subscriptions are available at $12 per year for two issues delivered at book rate. All back issues are $8. For air mail delivery, add $8 per subscription year. Send subscription orders to: CROSSROADS, Center for Southeast Asian Studies, 140 Carroll Ave., Northern Illinois University, DeKalb, IL 60115. Checks should be made payable to the "Center for Southeast Asian Studies."